Masters and Servants on the
Eastern Frontier 1760–1803

M000047798

This important study sheds light on the history of the South African interior during the eighteenth century, virtually a lost century in South African historiography, and yet one in which South Africa's specific variant of social discrimination first evolved. Susan Newton-King describes the tense and volatile relationship between European settlers and the indigenous Khoisan peoples. She probes beneath the surface to examine the underlying causes of the pervasive violence that marked relations between masters and servants in the eastern Cape. Focusing on the fate of the many women and children captured by Boer commandos, she shows why they were assimilated to the condition of captive labour. She also provides the first detailed account of the 'Bushman War' on the north-east frontier. Her analysis links the frontier economy and the markets and merchants of Cape Town, and indicates the overriding importance of the commercial policies of the Dutch East India Company.

SUSAN NEWTON-KING is senior lecturer in history at the University of the Western Cape, South Africa. She has published a number of articles dealing with frontier history in South Africa, and is co-author, with V. C. Malherbe, of *The Khoikhoi rebellion in the eastern Cape, 1799–1803* (1981).

Masters and Servants on the Cape Eastern Frontier 1760–1803

Susan Newton-King

CAMBRIDGE
UNIVERSITY PRESS

CAMBRIDGE UNIVERSITY PRESS
Cambridge, New York, Melbourne, Madrid, Cape Town, Singapore,
São Paulo, Delhi, Dubai, Tokyo

Cambridge University Press
The Edinburgh Building, Cambridge CB2 8RU, UK

Published in the United States of America by Cambridge University Press, New York

www.cambridge.org
Information on this title: www.cambridge.org/9780521121248

First published 1999
This digitally printed version 2009

A catalogue record for this publication is available from the British Library

ISBN 978-0-521-48153-3 Hardback
ISBN 978-0-521-12124-8 Paperback

Contents

Figures

Maps

Tables

Acknowledgments

It has taken me a long time to complete this book. During these years I have received support, guidance and encouragement from friends, teachers, colleagues and family members and I would like to thank them all, especially those who were there when I first embarked on the project and who stood by me and continued to encourage me when common sense might have inclined them to impatience or worse. Among the latter I think particularly of my late mother, Noel Newton-King, and my teacher, Shula Marks. My mother had a playful and incisive way with words which came to my aid when I could not decide how to write what I meant (or, she might add, how to mean what I wrote). She had a nice sense of the ridiculous which many times restored my sense of proportion when I was in danger of taking a serious task too seriously. She also had the grace never to ask when the book would be finished; perhaps she came to see it as a modern version of Penelope's shroud. Shula Marks was obliged to remind me of the passage of time, but she too was endlessly patient and it is largely thanks to her continuing encouragement that this book has reached the shelves. It was she who first introduced me to the harsh and fascinating world of the eighteenth-century Cape and, though she has long since moved on to write of other subjects, she never lost interest in my work, following its progress and affording me the benefit of her prodigious skills as teacher, writer and critic. Her incisive comments, her fine judgment, her enthusiasm for the minutiae of archival research and her gracious handling of an undisciplined student have helped to make this book what it is; obviously she is not responsible for its shortcomings.

I would also like to acknowledge the help of my friend and colleague, Robert Ross of the Rijks Universiteit Leiden. One day in 1978 (in an Indian restaurant in Charlotte Street) he helped me work through copies of letters from the missionary Van der Kemp to his principals in London, until I had acquired at least a passive grasp of Dutch grammar, and since that day he has been an unfailing source of support, criticism and encouragement, sharing ideas and work in progress with unstinting generosity.

He read and commented upon an earlier draft of this book. I hope I have done justice to his comments.

Among friends and family in England, I would especially like to thank Tom and Anne Noyes and Kevin and Pippa Shillington, who provided me with all the comforts of home life when the anonymity of London became too much to bear. David Fig, Neville Hogan, Victor Machingaidze, Peter Monck and Peter Richardson were a source of encouragement, criticism and companionship. Patrick Harries has been supportive in more ways than I can count, both in London and in Cape Town.

Many people in South Africa have contributed to the production of this book. Sister Kathleen Boner supported my application for study leave during my time at the University of Bophuthatswana (now the University of the North West) and set a standard of disciplined professionalism from which I learnt much; Andy Manson, Botlhale Tema, Hermien Kotze and Francine de Clercq provided (mirthful) encouragement. My colleagues at the University of the Western Cape have been a source of support, companionship, practical help and informed criticism. Leslie Witz and Andrew Bank have responded to every call for help with unfailing patience and good humour; Martin Legassick kept a watchful eye over the revision of the manuscript. In 1996 the University gave me sabbatical leave, which enabled me to complete the process.

Andrew Bank, Henry Bredekamp, Patricia Davison, Janette Deacon, Amy Jacot Guillarmod, Margaret Kinsman, Martin Legassick and Garth Sampson have all read and commented on parts of the manuscript. Jeffrey Peires read all of it and made many helpful suggestions. Jean Blanckenberg, Margaret Cairns, Wayne Dooling, Bill Freund, Hans Heese, Timothy Keegan, Canby Malherbe, John Mason (not, strictly speaking, a South African), Lalou Meltzer, Nigel Penn, Robert Shell, Nigel Worden and John Wright have all shared their expertise with me and greatly enriched my understanding of Dutch South Africa. Tim Dunne of the Department of Mathematical Statistics at the University of Cape Town generated the stratified random sample upon which much of chapter 8 is based; Ken Behr drew the maps with expert skill and efficiency. Stephen Watson kindly gave me permission to reproduce two of his poems. Professors P. J. de Wet and H. J. Heydenrich of the Department of Animal Science at the University of Stellenbosch took the time to explain the elementary principles of stock-raising to a researcher who knew less of sheep and cattle than the least experienced of their first-year students. As for the staff at the Cape Archives, I cannot thank them adequately for the help they have given me over the years, first in the lovely building in Queen Victoria Street and later in their new premises in Roeland Street. In recent years, Rehana Hussein, Erica Le Roux and Jaco van der Merwe have provided cheerful support and fielded my many inquiries, and Peter Jephta has gone out of his way to supply me with requested illustrations.

In the district of Graaff Reinet itself (now much diminished in size), the Kingwill family and, more recently, John and Marie Biggs and Andrew and Jenny McNaughton have welcomed me into their homes and shared their knowledge of the region's history and ecology. I hope this book will serve as some recompense for their generosity.

Finally I would like to thank Temba Nolutshungu, without whose unwavering support none of this would have been possible.

Glossary of Dutch terms used in the text

bijwoner/bijwoonder	tenant farmer
buijtenpost	outpost; outstation
d'oude	the elder
De Kaap	Cape Town
dominee	minister; clergyman
droster	deserter; runaway
erfportie	share of inheritance
in maatschappij	in partnership
kleinbaas	young master
knecht	servant; contracted wage labourer (usually white)
krijgsgevangenen	prisoners of war
krijgsraad	council of war
ledikant	four-poster bed; curtained bedstead
op de helft van aanteel	[farming] on the half; in return for half the increase
opgaaf	enumeration for the purposes of taxation
opstal	farm buildings
schuldboek	debt-book; debt register
sjambok	whip made of animal hide
smous	itinerant trader; pedlar
strooijhuis	mat house, probably circular
trekos	draught ox
veeboer	stock-farmer; grazier
veeplaats	grazing farm; stock-farm
velschoen	raw-hide shoe; roughly made leather shoe
vendurol	auction roll
volk	servants and slaves; people
volkstem	voice of the people; popular vote
weduwee	widow
werf	yard; enclosed space surrounding farm buildings
wildsvleisch	venison; meat of any game animal

Song of the broken string

Because
of a people,
because of others,
other people
who came
breaking
the string for me,
the earth
is not earth,
the place is
a place now
changed for me.

Because
the string is that which
has broken for me,
this earth
is no longer
a place to me.

Because
the string is broken,
the country feels
as if it lay
empty before me,
our country seems
as if it lay
both empty before me,
and dead before me.

Because
of this string,
because of a people
breaking the string,
this earth, my place
is the place
of something –
a thing broken –
that does not
stop sounding,
breaking within me.

Stephen Watson, *Return of the Moon: Versions from the /Xam,*
Cape Town: Carrefour Press, 1991

1   A note on the narration of colonial beginnings

This is the story of an unhappy relationship. Its subject is the encounter between immigrant European stock-farmers and native hunters and pastoralists in the arid hinterland of the Cape of Good Hope in the second half of the eighteenth century. Despite the particularities of the characters and the setting, it is not an altogether new story, neither is it unique. Its principal characters – Europeans and natives (who, together with the land to which both laid claim, comprise what the literary critic Peter Hulme has called 'the classic colonial triangle')[1] – have appeared in countless narratives of European colonisation from the sixteenth century onwards, in settings as diverse as Quebec and Surinam, Virginia and Australia.

However, the qualities with which they have been endowed and the roles in which they have been cast have varied greatly, not only with the vantage point of the narrator and the sources at his or her disposal, but also, as recent scholarship has demonstrated, with the 'discourse' which the narrator has employed to construct or 'configure' colonial relationships. The study of colonial discourse (or, more correctly, discourses) is still a relatively new field, and much of the work done thus far has focused upon representations of Europe's encounter with America, rather than its relations with Africa, but certain patterns are none the less beginning to emerge. It is clear, for example, that in the fifteenth and sixteenth centuries there was a fundamental difference between the language which Europeans used to describe their encounters with non-Christian regions of the Old World – the familiar world of Asia and North Africa – and that which they deployed in the understanding of the New World. In each case, it has been suggested, their discourse was structured around a central opposition – between Christians and non-Christians in the case of Asia and between civilisation and savagery in the case of America.[2] But these oppositions had different implications and were elaborated in very different ways. Thus while the Asian or 'oriental' discourse merely opposed one form of civilisation to another (antagonistic) form, the discourse of savagery opposed civilisation to its very antithesis: wildness – the condition of those living in

1

a state of nature, without law, religion, language or settled abode, that is, with none of the attributes of civilised man.

The discursive networks which grew up around these oppositions may have had some basis in an external reality, the first ('oriental discourse') being shaped by Europe's long history of commercial contact with the east and the second ('the discourse of savagery') by the early explorers' disappointment at finding (outside Mexico and Peru) no great states with crowded cities and overflowing treasuries. But each discourse contributed as much to the making of reality as to the description of it. For language is a way of seeing which structures perception, recasting the unfamiliar in the guise of the familiar; and perception in turn creates a framework for action.

In the case of the Cape, this was to have fateful consequences. Here the two discourses became intertwined, so that the indigenous inhabitants were perceived as simultaneously heathen and savage, their savagery denoted by the very names they were given: 'Bushmen' (men of the bush or the untamed wilderness) and 'Hottentots' (men so lacking in culture that their speech resembled the clucking of turkeys).[3] These ways of seeing were not peculiar to the Dutch; indeed they ante-dated the establishment of the Dutch settlement at the Cape of Good Hope in 1652. But in the course of the eighteenth century, as an increasing number of settlers began to spread through the arid interior, provoking the native population to a deadly battle for survival, they took on new life, helping to define the enemy in terms which permitted the use of savage force against him and legitimating the construction of a colonial order based upon informal slavery.

Twentieth-century historians have long abandoned the discourse of civilisation and savagery. However, as many eminent critics have been at pains to remind them, they cannot escape the structures of discourse itself. It is not simply a matter of plot construction and narrative form, but also, as Hayden White has demonstrated, of the very encoding of the data (the evidence) out of which the narrative is constructed.[4] The historian, as White observes, does not merely select and report his data as he finds them in the archives. In the very act of describing the data he subtly refashions them, encodes them, as it were, in such a way as to prepare the reader to receive his explanation of the relationship between them.[5] This process of encoding involves the use of figurative language and operates mainly at an unconscious level (its methods, as White has shown, are those of poetry rather than logic) and it functions as a subtext (of which the author himself may be unaware), subliminally nudging the reader towards acceptance of the author's viewpoint. In sum, to paraphrase White, *what* the historian says about his topic cannot be distinguished from *how* he says it.[6]

These points may seem abstruse or needlessly technical, but I raise them here in my introduction by way of a warning, or perhaps a disclaimer. For the historian of colonial beginnings bears a heavy responsibility. In choosing to investigate the origins of a colonial or post-colonial society, she enters a field which is fraught with anxiety. There is an analogy here (though one should not push it too far) between history and a therapeutic discipline like psychoanalysis. Just as the analysand obsessively replays the traumatic events of his past, so, in those societies born of European conquest, the heirs of both coloniser and colonised return again and again to the trauma which accompanied the birth of their nation. For the colonised this is the overwhelming trauma of usurpation, which has made them strangers in the land of their birth. For the colonisers it is more a question of nagging self-doubt; an awareness perhaps that their own sense of entitlement is sustained by the repression of other voices, other histories, whose claims may prove difficult to bear. For both, then, the investigation of colonial beginnings raises disturbing questions of identity.

However, whereas the analyst may be able to help her patient re-emplot the events of his life in such a way as to free him from their terrifying power, the historian and her reader can seldom achieve a similar catharsis. For, quite apart from the obvious differences in the nature of their craft, the historian, as I have suggested above, is as much the prisoner of unconscious forces as is her reader. This is not so much a matter of her individual psychology (a subject which is still all but taboo in the work of professional historians), as of the discursive repressions inherent in the very practice of her discipline. For the job of the historian, unlike that of the analyst, is not to create a space in which the reader can explore all the possible meanings of the events under consideration; it is rather to close that space (after having given due consideration to the alternative interpretations of other historians), to give her narrative a meaning and an ending which displaces all the others. And this process of closure begins, as White has demonstrated, in the very act of describing the data, prior to their final presentation in narrative form. The act of reading then becomes, as J. M. Coetzee has put it, not a reading, but a following.[7]

And yet it need not be entirely so. For the documentary record is alive with other voices besides those which the historian may choose to emphasise. They push through the thicket of words to challenge the preconceptions of both writer and reader. If the historian will only step back and listen, these voices may assert their autonomy and contest the script that she has written for them. Viewed in this manner, the historian's text becomes less a seamless web than, to quote another recent exponent of the literary approach to history, 'a network of resistances'.[8] It is in this spirit that I have written the narrative which follows. I have tried to strike a balance between my role as mediator of conflicting and contestatory sources and my role as interpreter. If in the latter capacity I have exercised an overweening dominance and robbed the historical actors of their autonomy and their 'otherness', this has not been my intention. If, on the other hand, I have managed to create a space in which the reader herself can listen and respond to voices other than mine, then the effort will not have been in vain.

It must be acknowledged, however, that in the case of the Cape, the many voices of the colonised can be heard only through the medium of the coloniser's language and, more often than not, through the agency of his courts and his officials. Thus, while slaves and Khoisan servants quite often gave evidence in court against their masters and voiced their needs and grievances to local officials, they did so within a context created and closely controlled by the colonial power (the Dutch East India Company) and its local representatives, many of whom had close links with the settler community. When they spoke in their native tongue, their statements were transcribed only in translation, and when they voiced their opinions to the educated travellers who ventured into the interior of the country, the latter put their own construction upon what they heard. Even more frustrating for the researcher is the fact that the depositions of witnesses were recorded in the third person ('there appeared before me X who, at the request of the Landdrost of this Colony . . . declared that it is true that . . .') rather than in direct speech. Only when the case went to trial was a witness directly examined. And even there, as I shall explain below, there was usually no counsel for the defence and nothing approaching a modern cross-examination. Nevertheless, in the court record, which has been preserved in full, we do have a remarkable body of testimony given from the point of view of those Khoisan who were drawn into colonial society. We are able, through this testimony, however muted and constricted in the presence of a hostile audience, to discern something of the manner in which the Khoisan themselves perceived the circumstances of their lives under settler domination and something of the construction which they placed upon the events in question. When the evidence of the courts is taken together with the mute testimony of action (as reflected, for example in the field reports compiled by militiamen who hunted down robbers and runaways) we can claim to have recovered some part of their identity, their many ways of being in a world in flux. Finally, one can draw on the work of colleagues in the disciplines of archaeology and ethnography in an attempt to compensate for the limited vision of eighteenth-century observers.

The settler population is – predictably – much better served by the documentary record. The sources are enormously rich and diverse. There may be little personal correspondence and even fewer diaries, apart from those kept by foreign visitors to the Cape, but the huge volume of official and semi-official documents partly compensates for this lack. These documents range from the elaborate and formal communications of the Dutch East India Company's senior employees at *De Kaap*,[9] to the plainer prose of its representatives in the back country and the often unpunctuated and sometimes impudent notes despatched by their recalcitrant subjects. There is also an extraordinary wealth of material in the archives of the Orphan Chamber, which served as executor of intestate and insolvent estates until its role was assumed by the Master of the Supreme Court at the beginning of the nineteenth century. There are inventories and auction rolls which list each possession of the deceased and the surviving spouse; there are records of moneys borrowed, lent and inherited and of goods bought and sold, and there are fragments of private correspondence relevant to the winding up of deceased estates. These documents form the basis of my argument in chapter 8.

Then there are the records of the district courts, comprising a *Landdrost* (magistrate) appointed by the Company and four or six *Heemraden* (chosen from among the freeburgher population), and of the Court of Justice in Cape Town, to which I referred above. The district courts were empowered to try all civil cases involving sums smaller than 1,000 guilders,[10] but their jurisdiction in criminal cases was limited to the holding of preparatory examinations and the conduct of inquests.[11] The papers were then sent up to the Cape, where the Independent Fiscal, in his capacity as public prosecutor, decided whether or not to try the case.[12]

A trial by the Cape Court of Justice, however, was not what the modern reader might suppose, for criminal procedure at the Cape in the eighteenth century was very different from the adversarial (or accusatorial) system with which we are familiar. There were, in effect, no written rules of court, apart from those laid down in two ordinances issued by Philip II of Spain in 1570.[13] These ordinances had recognised two forms of criminal procedure: the 'ordinary' and the 'extraordinary' process.[14] The majority of criminal cases at the Cape were tried under the extraordinary process which was inquisitorial rather than accusatorial in nature. The accused was not given the opportunity to challenge the evidence against him until he had undergone a preliminary examination, conducted in camera and based upon evidence collected in advance from unseen witnesses. He was normally under arrest when this examination was conducted and he had no right to remain silent. On the contrary, the court required him to 'co-operate' in the investigation since he could not be convicted without a confession, unless the evidence against him was conclusive.[15] If when the preliminary examination was complete he persisted in his denial, he would be confronted with the evidence and permitted to question the witnesses. However the extraordinary process did not permit the employment of counsel for the defence, and the questioning of the witnesses hardly amounted to cross-examination since the accused was not at any stage allowed access to their depositions. Moreover, if the judges were not satisfied with the responses of the accused, they could, provided there were sufficient grounds for believing him guilty, order that he be put to a 'sharper interrogation' – that is, tortured – so as to 'complete the proof'.[16] There are many cases where torture was used to extract a confession.[17] The judges were also not required to give reasons for their judgment; there was in fact no judgment, merely a sentence, which each member of the Council of Justice individually accepted or rejected.[18]

Given the secretive nature of these procedures, one must conclude that the evidence presented to the Court of Justice was not put to the test and evaluated in the modern sense. Consequently the record of a criminal trial often differs little from that compiled during the preparatory examination conducted by the Landdrost. The chief omission from the latter is the 'claim and demand' of the prosecutor, which usually took the form of a narrative account of the alleged crime, based upon the evidence collected from witnesses, interspersed with sententious utterances about the serious-ness of the accused's transgressions and appropriate citations from legal texts. The prosecutor's opening statement could be very revealing of the *Weltanschauung* of the Company elite. However if one takes the view that it is impossible, given the secretive nature of the inquisitorial process, to discover 'what really happened', then the prosecutor's 'claim and demand', however influential, becomes just another 'contestatory voice' in the grim proceedings of a criminal trial. His argument might intimidate the accused and would in most cases decide his fate, but it could not erase his voice from history.

In sum, then, the historian of early colonial encounters in the Cape interior has a rich documentary record on which to draw. I have used nearly everything which could serve as raw material for the narrative constructed here, except the archives of the Dutch Reformed Church, which, until 1780, was the only Christian denomination allowed in the colony. In one sense, this is not a serious omission, since there was no church or minister on the eastern frontier until 1792, and hence there were no records pertaining to the region before that date. Even after 1792 the documentary record is scant. But it should not be inferred that the church as a whole had no influence over the inhabitants of the eastern frontier. Many of the colonists had been raised in Reformed households closer to the Cape and baptised and married in Stellenbosch, Swellendam or the *Land van Waveren* before they set up house in the depths of the Karoo. A few, like the children of church elders Dawid and Isaak van der Merwe of the Bokkeveld, could claim a more intimate childhood connection with the

Reformed religion.[19] Certainly the Landdrost and Heemraden of the new district of Graaff Reinet wasted no time in sending a sick-comforter to assess the spiritual condition of the inhabitants and applying to the government for funds to build a church.[20] Thus, while church attendance must needs have been infrequent, confined primarily to baptisms and weddings,[21] and many colonists never became full members of the church,[22] there are, in my view, good grounds for believing that Reformed Christianity – or rather, a colonial variant thereof – had a considerable impact upon frontier relationships.

In particular, as Jonathan Gerstner has argued in an influential new study, the South African colonists seem to have evolved a heretical understanding of covenant theology according to which Christian status came to be seen as hereditary rather than acquired, so that children born to European parents (even to parents who were not themselves practising Christians) were either already saved, or else set apart for the receipt of grace in later life.[23] The children of the heathen, by contrast, were 'alienated from God from birth', and destined to remain that way, unless perchance they were offered access to church membership in later life, something which was strenuously opposed by most frontier colonists in the eighteenth century.[24] Although, as Gerstner observes, it is difficult to prove that individual colonists held these beliefs, there is adequate evidence that such beliefs formed part of the religious climate within which colonial relations unfolded. A full exploration of this religious climate lies beyond the scope of the present study, and indeed much of the work has already been done by Gerstner himself, but the reader should be aware that notions drawn from this context – a sense of ethnic calling, an identification with the Israel of old, and a theologically grounded contempt for people of 'heathen' origin – formed a sort of subtext to the discourse of frontiersmen and -women, especially in their dealings with the indigenous inhabitants of the Cape interior. This subtext will not be explicitly examined in the pages which follow, but the reader should be alert for its echo.

As for secondary sources, there are many which have helped to make this book. The scholarly study of Dutch South Africa has burgeoned in the last twenty years, adding to a number of pre-existing monographs concerned mainly with the expansion of the settlement and the functioning of colonial institutions and transforming our understanding of relations between slave and free, settler and indigene, in the first century and a half of colonial rule. Discussion of these sources is interspersed with the text which follows, but there are a handful which I would like to single out, because without them the present study would not have been possible.

Without Richard Elphick's skilful analysis of the disintegration of

Khoekhoe communities in the south-west Cape, I would not have been able to situate the beginning of my own story in the mid-eighteenth-century Karoo, secure in the knowledge that my readers would probably be familiar with the processes which had already undermined the integrity of the Khoekhoe chiefdoms nearer to Cape Town and which were even then working their way through the social fabric of those located further to the north and east.[25] Similarly, Nigel Penn's work on the interaction between the Khoisan and colonial stock-farmers on the north-west frontiers of the colony has allowed me to write with some confidence of the immediate antecedents of the settlers who established themselves in the eastern Karoo, for many were the progeny of families long established further west, in the Bokkeveld, the Hantam or the Roggeveld.[26] Indeed, the notion of a boundary between the northern and eastern frontier zones is largely arbitrary: in the eighteenth century people and animals moved freely between the two regions and the patterns of conflict were similar (but not identical) in both. I have thus derived great benefit from an exchange of views and information with Nigel Penn and I trust that the reader who has access to both his work and mine will gain an appreciation of the forces which shaped social relations right across the eighteenth-century South African frontier.

Again, however, both Penn's work and mine owes much to the stimulus provided by other scholars who, since the 1970s, have re-examined the processes which shaped the South African frontier. Shula Marks was the first to challenge the long-held belief that the pastoralist Khoekhoe were unable to mount effective resistance to the Dutch. Prefiguring Elphick's insistence upon the fluid and overlapping nature of the boundaries between hunters and herders at the Cape, she argued that there was little to distinguish cattleless Khoekhoe from the hunter-robbers (San, or Soaqua) traditionally cast in the role of resisters and that the former (dispossessed Khoekhoe) played as great a part as the latter in the persistent raiding which blocked the northward expansion of the colony.[27] Her arguments, together with those of Elphick, who formulated the idea of an 'ecological cycle' linking the lifeways of pastoralists and hunter-gatherers, have been largely responsible for the widespread acceptance of the portmanteau term Khoisan by subsequent students of indigenous responses to the Dutch.[28] While I do not disagree with their general thrust, I do believe that the permeability of the boundaries between hunting and herding communities has been exaggerated, to the detriment of the researcher wishing to gain a closer understanding of the motives and behaviour of raiding bands in specific instances. This issue will be raised below.[29]

Shula Marks' article appeared almost simultaneously with an equally influential paper by Martin Legassick.[30] This paper, together with a later article by Hermann Giliomee,[31] has substantially altered the way in which frontier relationships are viewed by students and scholars in South African universities. Whereas the frontier had previously been seen as a place of extremes, characterised by racial polarisation and rigid class divisions, Legassick suggested that this description better fits the slaveholding regions of the western Cape, and that the frontier was rather a place of blurred outlines and overlapping categories where enemies and friends were not (or not exclusively) defined by race. These ideas were skilfully elaborated by Giliomee, who incorporated them in his notion of an 'open' and a 'closing' frontier where class and racial categories initially displayed a degree of flexibility, but became more rigid as the settler population increased and Europeans began to achieve political and military hegemony. Both articles are distinguished by the subtlety with which their arguments are presented, and their central theses are inherently plausible, given the thin spread of white settlement and the relatively equal distribution of coercive power between Europeans and their Xhosa neighbours. Indeed, where the Xhosa are concerned, I have no quarrel with their interpretation and I have not engaged with it in the pages that follow. However, in so far as their conclusions apply to the Khoisan, I believe that they stand in need of modification. In particular, I believe that relations between master and servant were more fundamentally antagonistic than either author has allowed and that, amongst the colonists, this antagonism was both reflected in and mediated by an ideology of ethnic exclusivism. These issues will be explored in depth in the chapters which follow. Indeed the whole book can in a sense be read as an extended interrogation of the views of Giliomee and Legassick, and I do not wish to anticipate its argument here.

Finally, among published monographs on Cape history, I should mention a small book which, more than any other, awakened my interest in the turbulent affairs of the eastern frontier. Entitled *Maynier and the first Boer Republic* and written in the 1940s by the eminent liberal historian J. S. Marais, this book meticulously examines the charges levelled against Landdrost H. C. D. Maynier of Graaff Reinet by his rebellious freeburgher subjects.[32] Written at a time of rising political tension and openly supportive of Maynier's cause (which Marais interpreted broadly as the maintenance of the rule of law), the book is none the less a work of exemplary scholarship. It gave me my first glimpse of the treasures stored up in the Cape Archives and whetted my appetite for more. It also reminded me that 'committed scholarship' is not incompatible with the highest standards of archival research.

Among the many books on non-South African subjects which have influenced my thinking, I would like to mention only two. These are

Orlando Patterson's *Slavery and social death*,[33] which provided me with the analytical framework around which chapter 7 has been constructed, and Nathan Wachtel's *Vision of the vanquished*,[34] which inspired me with its commitment to represent the history of European conquest from the viewpoint of the conquered. Lacking the rich variety of native sources available to historians of early colonial Latin America, it is difficult, as I have already indicated, for the historian of Dutch South Africa to reconstruct the experience of the indigenous inhabitants with the same degree of authenticity, but Wachtel's book, among others, encouraged me to try.

Europeans

The European immigrants who laid the foundations of settlement in the rugged interior of the Cape Colony differed in one fundamental respect from their counterparts in other colonies: very few of them had left Europe with the deliberate intention of settling permanently in a faraway part of the world; even fewer had chosen the Cape as their ultimate destination. The majority had left Europe as sailors or soldiers on ships of the Dutch East India Company, bound for the Indies or Ceylon. A stop at the Cape was mandatory for both outward bound and return fleets,[1] but few crew-members, except those already assigned to the Cape Town garrison, had planned on an extended stay. Most of those who remained behind when their ships sailed did so by chance, because of illness or a last-minute posting to the garrison or the Company's shipyard. Many later returned to the sea. Those who stayed on did so in response to opportunities they had not foreseen on leaving Europe. They were, in other words, accidental colonists, whose absorption into the growing community of freeburghers[2] took place by degrees, often aided by a sudden twist of fate.

On the whole, the Dutch East India Company (*Verenigde Oostindische Compagnie*)[3] did not favour the establishment of settler communities in its overseas possessions. In the seventeenth century there had been a number of attempts to encourage emigration to the Company's overseas head-quarters at Batavia, but these had not been a success and the policy was discontinued in the early eighteenth century.[4] When the Company established a refreshment station at the southern tip of Africa in 1652, with a view to supplying its ships with water and fresh produce, colonisation was likewise not on its agenda. However, once it became apparent that the Company's own personnel would not be able to satisfy the growing demand for produce, it was deemed prudent to release a number of employees from their contracts so that they might farm on their own account, thereby saving the Company much trouble and expense. This settlement policy was not initially a great success, for the Cape com-mander, Jan van Riebeeck, had underestimated the cost of cultivating exotic crops in virgin soil,[5] and the Company was not willing to provide either labour or capital on the scale required for the intensive farming methods which Van Riebeeck had envisaged.[6] The settlement languished until 1679, when a new Governor, Simon van der Stel, was authorised to begin a second phase of expansion, this time on the basis of more realistic (i.e. much larger) land grants. In 1685 the Company offered free passages to Europeans wishing to settle at the Cape, but 'few availed themselves of the offer', apart from a handful of marriageable girls sent out from Dutch orphanages and workhouses to serve as brides for the immigrant bachelors.[7] Between 1685 and 1707, when the offer of free passages was terminated, by far the largest group of assisted immigrants comprised the 156 French Huguenots who were settled in Drakenstein, Paarl and Franschhoek by Van der Stel. Thereafter, the Company lost interest in assisted immigration, mainly because the supply of fresh produce was now more or less adequate to its own needs (though not necessarily to those of foreign ships) and because its experiments with free settlement in its eastern territories had not lived up to expectations.[8]

Nevertheless, as the historians S. D. Neumark and Robert Ross have emphasised, the local market for fresh produce, particularly meat, continued to expand during the eighteenth century and the Cape settlement was able to accommodate both the natural increase of the already settled population and a steady trickle of immigrants.[9] (How adequately they could be accommodated is a matter for debate – to which I will return in chapter 8.) Between 1701 and 1795 the freeburgher population (including women and children) grew at a rate of 2.6 per cent per annum, reaching 5,419 by 1753 and 14,929 by 1795.[10] In part this rapid growth was due to the low age at marriage and the high fertility of the settler women,[11] but it was also a function of continuing immigration. Scholars have yet to enumerate the total number of immigrants to the Cape during the eighteenth century, but J. A. Heese has calculated that between 1688 and 1807 some 1,920 male immigrants married into the 'white' freeburgher population, and there were many others who failed to find wives.[12] Among the 727 tax-payers listed on the first *opgaafrol* (tax roll) of the district of Graaff Reinet in 1787, there were twenty-two immigrants from German-speaking regions of western and central Europe and 169 men whose fathers or grandfathers had come from these areas.[13]

The large number of immigrants of German origin provides a clue to the social background of the new arrivals and their manner of entry into Cape society. Throughout the 200 years of its existence, the VOC was unable to man either its ships or its garrisons without recourse to the pool of migrant labour in the impoverished rural hinterland to the east and south-east of the Netherlands. A contract with the VOC was among the least desirable of all forms of employment open to workseekers along the North Sea coast. The wages – between fl. 7 and fl. 11 per month for an ordinary seaman and fl. 9 (3 rix dollars and 6 *schellingen*) per month for a soldier[14] – compared very unfavourably with the rates of pay for unskilled and semi-skilled work on shore. In the late eighteenth century, for example, a polder boy, a mower or a peat-cutter could earn approximately fl. 1.50 per day and a brick- or tile-maker even more.[15] Even the whaling fleets and the merchant navy paid more than the VOC.[16] It is true of course that the better-paying shore jobs were seasonal, providing employment only during the spring and summer months, whereas the VOC (like the army and the navy, which paid equally low wages) could offer long-term job security, since its contracts committed both parties to a five-year term of employment. However, against this protection from future destitution a prospective employee had to weigh the high risk of sickness and death while in the service of the VOC and the difficulty of escaping from his contract should conditions prove unbearable. Disease was rife on Company ships, especially on the long outward voyage, where overcrowding and the weakened constitutions of many new recruits encouraged the spread of respiratory infections, dysentery and diarrhoea. Typhus was a major killer too; it could flare up unexpectedly, rampaging through the orlop, where 300 men or more were packed together without adequate ventilation or sanitation.[17] And once arrived in Batavia, a new recruit was vulnerable to the tropical diseases which flourished in the hot and foetid atmosphere.[18] Finally, there was the risk of shipwreck or capture, though the VOC's record was relatively good in this respect – in two centuries of seafaring only 105 ships were wrecked and thirty-six captured by pirates or enemies of the Dutch Republic.[19]

Overall, personnel losses on the outward voyage averaged around 15 to 20 per cent per annum, those on the homeward voyage considerably less: between 2 and 4 per cent per annum until the 1770s, more than 6 per cent thereafter.[20] Given the many hazards attendant on a commerce which involved crossing two oceans and spending an average of eight months at sea on the outward voyage and seven and a half months on the return voyage,[21] it is in fact remarkable that these losses were not higher; the Danish and French Asiatic trading companies lost more men each year. However, for workseekers weighing the merits of enlistment in the VOC against those of an on-shore occupation, the Company's relative success in limiting mortality would not have counted for much. The death rate among adults ashore was in the region of 4 per cent per annum – some 13 to 20 per cent lower than that aboard Company ships.[22] Moreover, viewed from the perspective of relatives left behind in the Netherlands, the actual risk of loss was very much greater than the figures for mortality aboard ship and among new arrivals in Batavia can convey. For, throughout the two centuries of the VOC's existence, less than 40 per cent of those embarking in the Netherlands returned home again. In most decades, only one in three returned.[23] The remainder either died at sea or lived out the rest of their lives in Asia, where many died prematurely, or at the Cape, where, as we shall see, their prospects were rather more encouraging. The Company was therefore justly viewed by European contemporaries as 'a man-eating Moloch', and it was only its ability to attract a continuous stream of new recruits which allowed it to sustain its activities for nearly 200 years.

Where, then, did it find a continuous supply of men willing to risk their lives 15,000 nautical miles from home? The short answer is that it attracted those who had no other choice; those who, in the words of the historian Jan Lucassen, 'could think of no other solution to their problems'.[24] From the 1630s onwards, many of these men were foreign; by the mid-eighteenth century more than half the Company's sailors and nearly three quarters of its soldiers came from outside the boundaries of the Netherlands, and in both centuries the great majority of these foreigners were German.[25] They came from the rural hinterland of the North Sea coast, where the soil was less fertile and the infrastructure less developed than it was in the coastal strip. The majority probably came from areas where very small farms (less than 1.5 ha) predominated and where migrant labour had long been a component of the annual work cycle.[26] Indeed, in parts of Lower Saxony and Westphalia, *Hollands-* and *Frieslandsgängerei* had been a regular occurrence since the end of the Thirty Years War, when rapid population growth had led to a marked increase in the number of *heuerlinge* (tenant farmers with sub-economic landholdings).[27]

Unable to subsist on their tiny holdings, *heuerling* households supplemented their income from farming with the proceeds of domestic industry and, in some cases, with wages earned by the men of the household in the hay fields, peat bogs and brick ovens of Holland, Utrecht and Friesland, where wage levels were two or three times higher than they were in the German territories. As a rule, such labour was seasonal, the men leaving home in March or April, after their crops had been sown, and returning in time for the harvest in late July. However some migrants stayed on in the Netherlands, perhaps because they were offered winter employment, or merely because there was no longer anything to hold them at home. In truth, we know little as yet of the circumstances which led some men to loosen their ties with home, while others continued for years in a pattern of oscillating migration. But we can reasonably assume that it was the former – the footloose and deracinated – not the latter, who were most liable to fall prey to the wiles of the *volkhouders* who recruited for the VOC.

These *volkhouders*, as their name suggests, were in the business of housing and feeding newcomers to the port cities in which they lived. According to contemporary reports, they sent their servants and touts to the city gates, to watch for strangers who appeared to be friendless and down on their luck.[28] Those who agreed to accompany them would be taken to a lodging house (perhaps a *schaftkelder* below street level)[29] where they would be offered food and shelter and sometimes clothing too, all on credit. This could be a boon to the destitute, but there was a high price to pay. The 'guest' was required to sign a bond or *ceel*, committing him to the repayment of costs. As the days went by, the costs mounted, until the unwary visitor found himself well and truly snared. From there it was but a short step to the recruiting offices of the VOC, with which the *volkhouders* were in regular contact. In return for delivering new recruits, the *volkhouder* received a *transportbrief* (a sort of IOU), signed by the recruit and endorsed by the Company, which committed the former to the repayment of his debt, which by now might amount to as much as fl. 150, that is, nearly seventeen months' pay! A first instalment (usually fl. 18 less the fl. 1 deducted as fee for the *transportbrief*) was to be paid immediately, an act which the Company facilitated by the advance of two months' pay, the balance to be paid only upon completion of the contract. However, since the *volkhouders* were themselves often short of money and could not wait five years to receive the balance, they sold the bond to money-lenders, often at a considerable discount, thus acquiring the derogatory title of *zielverkopers* (soul-sellers), a pun on the word *ceel*.[30]

As one can imagine, this manner of acquiring recruits did not make for a healthy and contented crew. Allegations that the *volkhouders* forcibly detained their charges prior to embarkation may be untrue,[31] but even so the latter could seldom be described as willing recruits. Most were destined to become soldiers, since they lacked experience at sea and since sailors, being better paid, could more easily be recruited without the aid of crimps. This explains why the proportion of foreigners was higher among the Company's soldiers than among its sailors; by the 1740s, 63 per cent of all VOC soldiers were foreign and most of these were German.[32]

By all accounts, they were a miserable lot. Many were already ill when they came aboard. According to Carl Thunberg, a university educated doctor who sailed for the Cape in 1771, the soldiers on his ship were emaciated, inadequately clothed and 'dejected in mind'. Many fell victim to the 'putrid fevers' which thrived in the damp foggy air of the Texel roadstead, and their numbers had to be replenished before the fleet had left the harbour. 'Out of twenty patients at the beginning of the voyage', declared Thunberg, 'scarcely one is a sailor, but all of them soldiers from the kidnappers. Thus these dealers in human flesh undoubtedly cause great loss and injury to the Company with their wretched humans.'[33]

This, then, was the raw material from which the Cape's freeburgher population was moulded. For while sailors and even ship's officers did occasionally take their discharge at the Cape, sometimes after having been invalided off the ships, the great majority of the immigrants who augmented the free population of the colony were drawn from the ranks of the soldiers and craftsmen stationed at the Castle in Cape Town. Hence my reference to them at the beginning of this chapter as 'accidental colonists'. It was chance which had landed them on the shores of Table Bay, rather than at one of the Company's other stations in Indonesia, India or Ceylon. And it was largely through chance that they came to be absorbed into the community of freeburghers.

There were a number of ways in which soldiers stationed at the Castle or at one of the Company's *buijtenposten* (outposts) could come into regular contact with the free population. Probably the most common was through off-duty fraternisation in the taverns and gaming-rooms of Cape Town. But such intercourse is unlikely to have presented many opportunities for social advancement, since it generally involved the soldier with others as poor as himself – craftsmen, petty traders, slaves and prostitutes (both slave and free) and sailors from ships then in the roadstead. In truth, despite frequent references in the literature to the 'underclasses' of eighteenth-century Cape Town, we know little of them as yet, and it is therefore difficult to assess the role of such contacts in an individual's passage to burgher status.[34]

But we can say with some authority that a more reliable path to burgher status lay in taking advantage of unusually lenient regulations governing leave of absence from the garrison, regulations which allowed a proportion of Company soldiers (and occasionally sailors too) to work for long periods outside the Castle, at any trade they chose, provided they fulfilled certain conditions. Thus a soldier with special skills, such as a mason, a shoemaker, a carpenter or a baker, had the option of becoming a *pasganger*, plying his trade beyond the Castle walls on his own account, on condition that he paid 4 rix dollars monthly for the privilege, the money (known as *dienstgeld*) being handed to the chaplain of the garrison, who distributed it among the men doing duty in the *pasganger*'s stead. *Pasgangers* continued to draw their monthly pay and ration money and the time they served outside the Castle was counted towards the completion of their contracts.[35] In Mentzel's time (the 1730s) there were some twenty-four to thirty of them each year; when Thunberg arrived at the Cape in 1772 there were 150.[36]

Alternatively, a soldier seeking greener pastures might allow the Company to 'loan' his services on an annual basis to a farmer wanting a *knecht* (overseer) to supervise his farming operations, or a schoolmaster to educate his children.[37] These *lichten*, as they were called,[38] received no pay from the Company while they were absent from duty and no exemption from the terms of their contract, which they were required to fulfil before returning to Europe. Moreover they could, in theory, be recalled to the ranks at a moment's notice. However, as Mentzel observed, a return to the ranks could be indefinitely postponed by the intervention of 'influential friends', whom the soldier might have acquired during his leave of absence. And should the soldier marry during his time on loan he would be 'readily released from service'.[39]

Finally there were the so-called *vrijwerkers*, soldiers or sailors who were chosen to serve the Governor, the captain of the garrison and other high officials. Although they were effectively withdrawn from the garrison, they remained on the Company's payroll and their time spent in private employ was counted towards the completion of their five-year contract. Like the *pasgangers*, they were often possessed of special skills and were able to practise their trades on their own account once their masters' needs had been met.

Individuals in all three categories came into daily contact with the free population and were therefore well placed to investigate the opportunities which the Cape had to offer. Those among them who had craft skills would soon have learnt that artisans were in great demand in the colony, for, as will be explained below (in chapter 8), imported manufactures such as clothing and ironware were very expensive and there was consequently a high demand for local manufacture and repairs. A mason or a carpenter at the Cape could earn five times as much as a common soldier, a blacksmith or wheelwright even more.[40] It is not surprising then that many *pasgangers* and *vrijwerkers* stayed on in the colony after their contracts with the VOC had expired, some marrying and applying for burgher rights, others opting for the loan system and remaining on the Company's rolls for many years. In 1798, two years after the Company's withdrawal from the Cape, there were still eighty-five Company servants in the interior district of Graaff Reinet, twenty-six of whom were listed as artisans. One, a former sailor, a certain F. W. Zagner of Stockholm, had married a 47-year-old widow and was now joint owner of a loan-farm and six slaves. Two others, a tanner and a saddle-maker, had bought plots of ground in the growing village.[41]

However, while men who had acquired a trade before enlisting with the VOC could sometimes do well at the Cape, accumulating a tidy capital and consolidating their position by means of a judicious match (the career of the mason Martin Melck of Memel in Lithuania being the most frequently cited example of a successful transition from the status of hired help to man of substance[42]), it was the many obscure individuals placed as knech-

ten or schoolmasters with the stock-farmers of the interior who constituted the majority of new entrants to the settler community. By the second quarter of the eighteenth century, arable farming was no longer a viable option for those with little capital. Given the high cost of overland transport, the cultivation of grain or wine was not profitable at a distance of more than 110 km from Cape Town, and by 1717, when the system of freehold grants was terminated, most suitable land within this range was already in private hands.[43] The sons and daughters of the poorer arable farmers therefore increasingly turned to stock-farming as a means of survival, for here the entry requirements were lower (though, as we shall see, not insignificant) and the product could walk to market. Land in the interior was not free, but, at least until the last quarter of the eighteenth century, the loan-farm system adopted by the Company in 1703 enabled an individual to acquire a 6,000 acre farm on the peripheries of the expanding colony at a relatively low cost.[44] The older sons of wealthier wine and grain farmers were also attracted by the promise of cheap land in the interior. The acquisition of a loan-farm allowed them to marry and move away from home without waiting for the receipt of an inheritance.[45] By the 1770s then, stock-farming had become the majority occupation among the European colonists, some two thirds of all farmers being stockmen rather than cultivators.[46] Many of these farmers were too poor to employ a *knecht* (at an average wage of 5 rix dollars per month[47]), but there were always a number of absentee landowners (some being local residents and others arable farmers from the south-west Cape) who needed a man to supervise their slaves and livestock in the back country.[48] Moreover, the richer graziers considered it desirable to employ a teacher for their children. By these means, then, a steady trickle of Company employees found their way into the midst of the scattered *veeboer* communities of the Karoo and the coastal forelands[49] (see Map 2).

It should not be supposed, however, that a newcomer with no capital could set himself up as a *veeboer* in a matter of months, as some contemporary observers appear to have believed. John Barrow, for example, who came to the Cape in 1797 as private secretary to Lord Macartney, described the transition from Company servant to independent grazier as follows:

After quitting the ranks, or running away from his ship, he [the soldier or sailor] gets into a boor's family and marries. He begins the world with nothing, the usual practice being that of the wife's friends giving him a certain number of cattle and sheep to manage, half the yearly produce of which he is to restore to the owner, as interest for the capital placed in his hands. He has most of the necessaries of life, except clothing, within himself. His work is done by Hottentots, who cost him nothing but meat, tobacco, and skins for their clothing. His house and his furniture, such as they are, he makes himself; and he has no occasion for implements of husbandry. The first luxury he purchases is a waggon, which, indeed, the wandering life he usually leads at setting out in the world, makes as necessary as a hut, and frequently serves the purposes of one. A musquet and a small quantity of powder and lead will procure him as much game as his whole family can consume. The springboks are so plentiful on the borders of the colony, and so easily got at, that a farmer sends out his Hottentot to kill a couple of these deer with as much certainty as if he sent him among his flock of sheep. In a word, an African peasant of the lowest condition never knows want; and if he does not rise into affluence, the fault must be entirely his own.[50]

Barrow's description is compelling, partly because it incorporates certain well-documented features of frontier life, such as the abundance of game and the widespread use of home-made furniture, and also perhaps because it appeals to a certain prelapsarian sensibility among his readers. Its central images – of rustic simplicity and freedom from want ('in which the fruits of the earth are enjoyed as they drop into the hand'[51]) – can be found in the writings of other Europeans who visited the frontier in the eighteenth century and have frequently been invoked in the work of modern scholars. Even S. D. Neumark, who was until the 1980s the only scholar seriously to challenge the widely held belief in the isolated and autarchic nature of the frontier economy, has quoted Barrow with approval.[52]

However, despite its plausibility, Barrow's account contains a number of fundamental misconceptions. First, the entry requirements of stock-farming were much higher than his description implies. The idea that a man could set himself up as a stock-farmer with little more than a few head of cattle, fifty sheep, a waggon and a musket is deeply ingrained in the South African historical imagination, but it bears little relation to the complex realities of eighteenth-century frontier life. To understand why this was so one must address the two other misconceptions embedded in Barrow's account: the belief that white frontiersmen could meet most of their needs without recourse to the market and the equally firmly held belief that many of them led a wandering life without fixed abode.

I have engaged at length elsewhere with the proposition that frontier households were able to meet most of their needs without recourse to the market and can do no more than summarise my findings here.[53] In essence I have argued that, while it has now been generally accepted that the *veeboeren* were never entirely cut off from the exchange economy of the south-west Cape and that, in Leonard Guelke's words, 'their expansion could not have taken place without guns, gunpowder, wagons and other manufactured goods',[54] the range of such goods and the extent of the graziers' dependence upon them has been greatly underestimated. Thus, while there is no doubt that frontier households were able to meet *some* of their needs through domestic manufacture – making leather clothing and wooden furniture, for example, and performing a range of household repairs with simple tools – it is also quite clear from the contemporary record that every household required in addition a host of items which could only be procured by trade, sometimes from local suppliers but more often from the faraway port of Cape Town through which all imported goods were channelled.

The 'record' in this case refers to the liquidation accounts of intestate and insolvent estates which are housed in the archive of the Orphan Chamber in Cape Town. Since the *veeboeren* rarely chose to exercise their limited right to advantage one heir over another and thus seldom made a will except where it was necessary to ensure the integrity of a joint estate until the death of the longest-living spouse,[55] the papers lodged with the Orphan Chamber constitute a remarkably detailed record of the assets and liabilities of nearly every household on the frontier at at least one point in its life-cycle. Since all outstanding credits and debits were meticulously entered, and the invoices and IOUs serving as evidence thereof were preserved among the annexures to the accounts, we are able to gain a fairly comprehensive picture of the economic activity of the household just prior to the death of the person concerned. In some cases, for example, there are invoices made out to the deceased by Cape Town merchants and also by neighbours with whom he or she had traded land, livestock and local produce. There are records of sums owing to the rural artisans who serviced the local need for blacksmiths, coopers, tanners, carpenters and waggon-wrights and there are *schuldboeken* (debt-books) and promissory notes which indicate that the deceased had often been trading with his or her neighbours in a complementary capacity, perhaps as a purveyor of wine or pedlar of cloth and gewgaws.[56] In sum, then, the papers of the Orphan Chamber provide abundant evidence of the widespread commercialisation of frontier life. But perhaps most valuable for our present purpose is the evidence contained in the *vendurollen*, that is, the auction rolls compiled when the fixed and moveable assets of the estate were publicly auctioned in the presence of relatives, neighbours and other interested parties.[57] In theory, every single possession of the deceased was put up for auction, so as to ensure that all heirs benefited equally from the liquidation. In practice, certain items, such as clothing and bedding, were not always included in the auction rolls and in such cases we may assume that the family had divided these goods among themselves.[58] Nevertheless, the *vendurollen* are remarkably detailed. And they show quite clearly that, no matter how simple the lifestyle of the deceased, imported as well as locally purchased commodities comprised a very significant proportion of his or her moveable assets.

'Producer goods' were perhaps more amenable to domestic manufacture than consumer goods like cloth, porcelain, tobacco and tropical food-stuffs, but even here one finds a great variety of items which can only have been acquired through exchange and which more often than not were imported rather than locally made. Thus all but the poorest households owned an assortment of metal tools such as axes, spades, chisels, adzes, augers, bow-saws, hammers, planes, files and crowbars, and a range of other useful objects like buckets, bolts, hinges, padlocks, lanterns and scales.[59] In addition, items of recurrent expenditure such as nails, string, canvas, paint, turpentine, tar, flints, needles, clasp knives and paper, all of which were imported, feature again and again, in addition to the ubiquitous gunpowder and lead, in the invoices and promissory notes of the merchants and pedlars who supplied the back country with manufactured goods. Granted, expenditure on metal goods could be reduced if a farmer was able to do his own repairs, but for this he needed access to a supply of sheet metal or scrap iron, blacksmith's tongs, a 'cold chisel', a *voorslaghamer* (heavy hammer), bellows and an anvil, all involving further outlay. In practice, the record indicates that ironmongery was often performed by specialised smiths, whose workshops turned out hardware such as nails, axes, spades and barrel hoops for sale to neighbouring farmers.[60]

Livestock too was not as easily acquired as Barrow suggests, especially by men new to the colony. The system of 'farming on the half' (*op de helft van aanteel*) was indeed quite widely practised on the frontier, for it served the purposes of local graziers seeking a change of pasture or an outlet for surplus stock as well as the inhabitants of areas closer to *De Kaap* (Cape Town), who preferred to keep their stock in the interior where the grazing was better.[61] It was also favoured by the meat contractors of *De Kaap*, who sometimes provided the share-cropper with slaves and a firearm along with livestock.[62] However, while this system clearly did serve as a means of capital accumulation, one should not exaggerate its efficacy. In the first place, the rate at which the client or share-cropper was able to accumulate breeding stock was slower than one might imagine. In the most favourable case, a man might be given 300 ewes or thirty cows *op de helft van aanteel*.[63] Given a weaning percentage of 59.5, the ewes would yield 179 lambs in an average year.[64] Of these, approximately eighty-nine would be male and ninety female. Given a replacement rate of 20 per cent for ewes and 33 per cent for rams,[65] three male and sixty female lambs would be required to replace the existing breeding stock, leaving the share-cropper with just fifteen ewe-lambs with which to start his own flock. In the case of cattle, where the weaning percentage was, at best, only 52, and the replacement rate for cows 15 per cent,[66] the share-cropper would be left with just one female calf at the end of the first year and would have to wait another one and a half to two years before she reached breeding age. Where the initial breeding stock was smaller, as was usually the case, the client's share would be correspondingly lower. He would, of course, acquire a number of wethers or steers (forty-three and three respectively in our example) for sale or home consumption, which would allow him to buy in more breeding stock or satisfy some part of his need for imported commodities, but, as will be explained below, his options were limited by the very adverse terms of trade then prevailing at the Cape.

In the second place, contrary to the impression fostered by Barrow and other travellers, land was not really free on the frontier. As each new region was opened up, it was possible for the earliest arrivals to pick out the most favourable sites and occupy them free of charge for some months, or possibly even years. But once the number of new settlers increased, it became necessary to register one's farm, lest it be appropriated by someone else. For the system of land tenure introduced by the VOC was firmly based upon the principle of exclusive individual grazing rights and failure to register a place left one vulnerable to eviction. Moreover, given the extensive farming methods of the colonists and the shortage of usable surface water, especially in the Karoo,[67] suitable locations were rapidly taken up and then could only be acquired by purchase from the registered occupant. Thus as early as 1751 the authorities in Swellendam were obliged to report that 'although the district is very extensive . . . the families that live here are growing so fast that it is already difficult to find a place without causing injury to others'.[68] And in 1776, just a few years after the first settlers had entered the coastal forelands beyond the Gamtoos River, the Utrecht burgher Hendrik Swellengrebel, making a private tour of the eastern frontier, noted that 'unless they [the colonists] succeed through industry in reducing the amount of ground necessary for grazing on each farm' he did not think that many more inhabitants could be accommodated between the Gamtoos and the Great Fish Rivers.[69]

In these circumstances, it was difficult for a newcomer without capital or kin to find a secure and affordable site from which to launch his career as a grazier. His best option was perhaps to seek a position as a *bijwoner* (tenant farmer) in return for services rendered to the registered landholder, but even here he might find himself called upon to pay for the use of pasturage.[70] Alternatively he could move out to the very edges of the settled area, but here he would be exposed to the hostility of rival claimants from among the indigenous people. (Hence, presumably, the inclusion of an indemnity clause in some share-cropping contracts, stipulating that the share-cropper should not be held responsible for stock stolen by 'Bushmen' (Fig. 1).) Finally, he could join the ranks of the 'wandering men', the true nomads of the frontier, who moved with their stock from one temporary camp to another, making use of the interstitial spaces between registered farms and moving on when the water ran out or the pasture deterio-

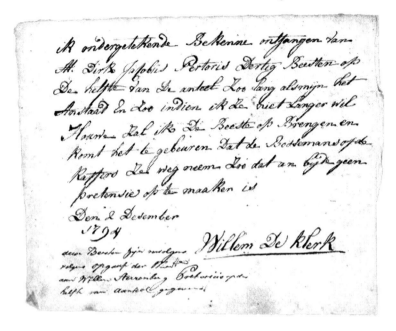

Figure 1   Document signed by Willem de Klerk, acknowledging receipt of thirty cattle 'op die helfte van de aanteel', 2 December 1794. *Source*: MOOC 14/96.

rated. This is the category in which Barrow would have us place him. However, contrary to popular belief, such men were in the minority in the eighteenth century. In Guelke's words, 'the majority of colonists were not trekkers, but settlers who, having acquired a desirable farm, often kept it for life'[71] (hence my preference for the contemporary term *veeboer* rather than the modern trekboer) and the wanderers were deeply resented by the 'respectable' burghers who disliked their encroachment upon private land and their misuse of the outspan places set aside for the use of *bona fide* travellers.[72] In the mid-eighteenth century such wanderers even ran the risk of deportation.[73] It is therefore unlikely that an established grazier would place his stock with such a man, unless perhaps he was bound to him by marriage, as Barrow suggests. A landed proprietor, or at least a *bijwoner*, would be a more reliable caretaker of one's surplus stock. But how was a former *knecht* to obtain land when he lacked the wherewithal to pay for it?

Once it is accepted, then, that even the poorest frontiersman could not escape the implications of an exchange economy, even where access to land

and the accumulation of livestock was concerned, the difficulties faced by a newcomer to the frontier can be more readily appreciated. At the heart of the matter lies the question of terms of trade. Since this question will be explored fully in chapter 8, it must suffice to state here that the terms of trade faced by an up-country *veeboer* were both adverse and erratic. In other words, the ratio at which he could exchange his produce (primarily sheep, cattle and butter) for the many imported and locally marketed commodities which he needed was both high and (in the case of imported commodities) subject to unpredictable fluctuations. In 1772, for example, 100 lb of iron cost 8 rix dollars new in Cape Town – the equivalent of sixteen sheep sold to a butcher's *knecht* in the back country – and a new waggon cost 140 rix dollars, the equivalent of 186 sheep. Ten years later, the ratio of sheep to iron had fallen by three quarters, while that of sheep to waggons had risen to 200: 1 (see Figures 16 and 17). As for guns, without which no *veeboer* could protect his stock, a new one 'of the best sort' could be acquired for 20 rix dollars (that is, ten wethers or two and a half steers) in 1791 and a second-hand one for approximately half that amount.[74] In respect of consumer goods like cloth, tobacco, sugar, coffee beans, tea, rice and spices, prices could be equally high and fluctuations sharper.[75] For example, a single piece of *voerchitz* (literally, lining chintz), a coarse red and black Indian cloth widely used by Boer women in the interior, was equal in value to three and a half sheep in 1781, and one ell (27 inches) of *laken* (broadcloth), from which the men's short blue jackets and the women's black mourning clothes were made, cost 14 *schellingen* – the price of two sheep[76] (see Figures 24 and 25). In the case of foodstuffs the pattern was more varied. Sugar, imported from Batavia, could be obtained for less than 10 *stuivers* per pound – that is, roughly the amount received by the farmers for a pound of butter throughout the last twenty-five years of the Company period – whereas tea (a staple drink in Boer households) cost anything from 3 to 12 *schellingen* per pound, depending on the state of the market. In 1793, for example, a bad year for the *veeboeren*,[77] a frontier household would have had to part with a whole sheep in order to acquire a little over one pound of tea!

Given terms of trade like these, a small stock-holder found it very difficult to make ends meet. A man with fifty sheep or thirty cattle would not have been in a position to support himself, even if virtually all his stock were ewes or cows, which was seldom if ever the case.[78] This conclusion is amply borne out by the analysis in chapter 8. The reader will see from appendix 2 that a capital of 333 rix dollars, which Guelke posits as a viable entry sum for a person contemplating a career as a grazier,[79] was (at least during the period covered by this study) nowhere near enough to ensure an independent lifestyle. Indeed, many individuals whose gross assets amounted to twice this sum were barely able to scrape a living; debt was widespread among them and creature comforts few.[80]

In conclusion then, while many former soldiers and sailors did successfully complete the transition from Company servant to *veeboer* and man of substance, eventually marrying and acquiring burgher rights,[81] others found it impossible to escape their near destitute condition and either returned to the ranks or ended their lives as *knechten* on remote and desolate grazing farms, dying penniless and without legal issue. It is these men whom Lichtenstein described as among the most wretched of all the 'white people' in the colony. 'Their pay is small', he wrote, 'and as old soldiers and people of low descent they may well be pardoned if they seek compensation for all other privations in the enjoyment of strong liquors. The propensity to this is so universal among them, that the whole class are known among the colonists by the general appellation of "the drunkards".'[82]

Men such as these were not infrequently implicated in crimes of violence against the slaves and Khoisan servants under their control.[83] This is perhaps to be expected, given their ambivalent position in the master's household and the harsh and brutal treatment to which they themselves had often been subjected while in the ranks. It is more remarkable, however, that similar acts of violence were perpetrated just as often by those more comfortably situated, including the children and grandchildren of established settlers. The reasons for the widespread resort to violence by the farmers of the interior will be explored in the chapters which follow; indeed, the search for an explanation is the chief focus of this book. But, without prejudging the matter, one may perhaps be permitted to wonder whether the Cape-born settlers had not absorbed something of their ancestors' drive to escape the poverty and humiliation of their origins, regardless of the cost in suffering to the native inhabitants of the colony.

Natives

For much of the eighteenth century the only permanent inhabitants of the vast region which in 1786 (Map 1) became the district of Graaff Reinet were pastoralists known to modern scholars as Khoekhoe (or Khoikhoi) and hunter-gatherers variously named San, Soaqua or Bushmen in scholarly publications. The term 'Khoekhoe' is best translated as 'men of men', or 'the real people', and is the modern Nama variant of a term once used by the pastoralists of the southern Cape in reference to themselves.[84] 'San', by contrast, is an adaptation of a word which the Khoekhoe used to refer to others – usually to people who were poorer than themselves and who lived by hunting, scavenging or robbery – and it almost certainly has a deroga-

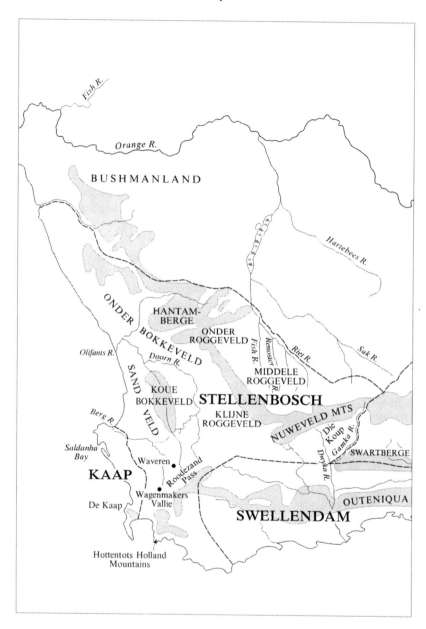

Map 1   The Cape of Good Hope in 1786

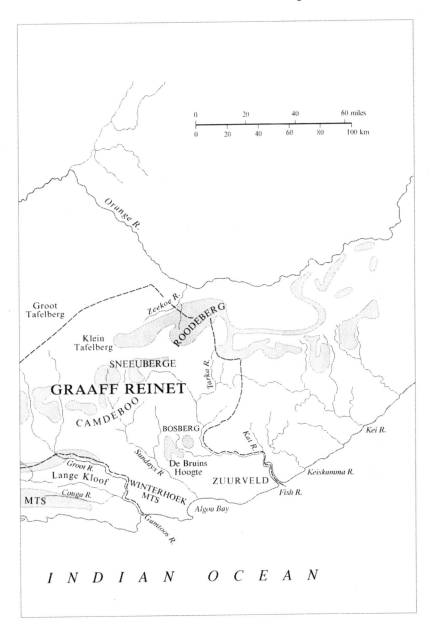

Groot
Tafelberg

Klein
Tafelberg

Orange R.

Zeekoe R.

ROODEBERG

SNEEUBERGE

Turka R.

GRAAFF REINET

CAMDEBOO

BOSBERG

Kei R.

Groot R.
Lange Kloof

Sundays R.

De Bruins
Hoogte

ZUURVELD

Keiskamma R.

Couga R.

WINTERHOEK
MTS

Fish R.

MTS

Gamtoos R.

Algoa Bay

I N D I A N   O C E A N

tory connotation.[85] However, in the absence of a generic term favoured by
hunter-gatherers themselves, and given our ignorance of the names assumed by individual hunter populations,[86] 'San' (or its western Cape
variants 'Soaqua' and 'Sonqua') is probably here to stay. It is at least
preferable to the colonial term 'Bushman', the eighteenth-century usage of
which is discussed in the next chapter.

The difficulty surrounding the choice of names is compounded by the
recognition that the ethnic boundaries suggested by the terms Khoekhoe
and San did not always coincide with differences in lifeways: there were
hunters who spoke Khoe languages and herders who considered themselves to be of 'Bushman' or San extraction.[87] This categorical confusion
has given rise to a vigorous and still continuing debate about the nature of
the historical relationship between hunters and herders in southern Africa
and the degree to which the two groups can be distinguished from each
other.[88] In the case which concerns us here, that of the southern and
south-eastern Cape, Richard Elphick has argued in favour of a view which
subsumes both hunters and herders within the notion of an 'ecological
cycle', involving a cyclical movement in and out of hunting and herding
lifestyles according to circumstance. This view, in my opinion, incorrectly
posits the superiority of pastoralism over hunting and gathering and
underestimates the tenacity of those hunter-gatherers who chose to preserve their mode of life in the face of pressures from immigrant pastoralists.[89] This is not to deny the abundant evidence of contact between
hunters and herders, nor the existence of common cultural traits which
facilitated transition from one lifeway to the other, but merely to insist that
the many forms which contact could take cannot, as Elphick implies, be
neatly integrated into a teleological model of interaction, progressing
inexorably (during the 'upward phase' of the ecological cycle) from conflict, through trade and clientage, to eventual incorporation. The outcome
of prolonged contact would, as Richard Lee has remarked in the context of
the Kalahari debate, depend on the circumstances;[90] and, in my view, it is
only with the benefit of hindsight that we can say for sure what a particular
set of circumstances dictated. But more on this in the next chapter.

In the area under consideration here, where the terrain varied from dry
karroid veld in the north to grassveld, thornveld and valley bushveld in the
south, along the better-watered coast, relations between hunters and herders ran the full gamut from open warfare to assimilation. On the plains of
Camdeboo, where the Inqua chiefdom reigned supreme in the late seventeenth century, some hunters served the chief as spies and messengers,
while others waged a continual battle against his presence at the foot of the
Sneeuberge.[91] Some sixty years later, the weakened Khoekhoe communities in the coastal forelands were barely able to hold their own against
'Bushman' robbers. Indeed, it was reported, they had been so impoverished

by stock-theft and internecine warfare that they 'presently lived like Bush-men' themselves, 'from robbery, hunting and whatever else they could find to eat in the veld and along the beaches'.[92] Further east, among the undulating hills of the Zuurveld, a motley band of 'Boshies-men', Gonaqua and 'bastard Caffers' had coalesced around the leadership of a talented and autocratic individual named Toena or Ruiter, an immigrant, or more properly a fugitive, from the Roggeveld. The story of their emergence as a distinctive people (the Hoengeyqua) and their recovery from poverty as a result of cattle raids carried out under Ruiter's direction, accords well with Elphick's model of recovery from the 'downward phase' of the ecological cycle. However, it should not be cited as an example of the potential destiny of 'Boshies-men' throughout the region, for, faraway to the north, on the rim of the Great Escarpment, there were others, perhaps numbering many thousands, who, it will be argued below, had maintained a hunting-and-gathering lifestyle for hundreds of years and continued to do so, under altered circumstances, right up to the moment when Euro-pean settlers first entered their territories.[93]

As for the Xhosa, it was only in the last third of the eighteenth century that subjects of the westernmost chiefdoms (imiDange, amaGwali, ama-Mbalu and amaGqunukhwebe) began to press in on the Khoisan in-habitants of the Zuurveld and Cape Midlands. The Xhosa kings appear to have exercised a loose suzerainty over Khoekhoe chiefdoms for a very long time[94] and it is possible that some of their people had made occasional use of pastures west of the Fish River in times of drought, but it was not until the 1760s that Xhosa villages were permanently established in the Zuur-veld. First came the Gqunukhwebe under Tshaka, who moved west to escape pressure from Rharhabe, head of the right-hand house of the Tshawe kingdom,[95] and after them the imiDange, who settled in the Fish River valley in the 1770s, hard by the Boers of De Bruins Hoogte.[96]

Until 1760, then, the Khoisan had near-exclusive occupation of the country immediately beyond the Gamtoos and Groot Rivers. However they did not live in peace: besides their contacts with the Xhosa (which could turn nasty at times), they were disturbed on several occasions by Europeans who travelled east to barter livestock and explore the still undiscovered country beyond the Outeniqua Mountains. The journals kept by these occasional visitors are virtually our only source of informa-tion about the condition of the eastern Cape Khoekhoe prior to 1760, for, as Elphick has confirmed, by the end of the seventeenth century the Company had all but lost interest in the affairs of its Khoekhoe neighbours and 'rarely bothered even to record their names'.[97] This growing indiffer-ence was brought on by the collapse of indigenous political structures in the western Cape and the Company's increasing reliance on freeburghers rather than Khoekhoe for the supply of livestock to its ships and its on-shore establishment. None the less, when reports of wealthy chiefs and fertile lands beyond the colony's borders filtered through to *De Kaap*, Company officials were occasionally moved to investigate. In addition, small parties of freemen sometimes defied the prohibition against barter with native peoples and made their way eastward in search of cheap livestock.

The first official expedition to the Inqua left Cape Town in January 1689. Van Riebeeck had learnt of the existence of the Inqua in 1657, though his informants had called them 'Hancumqua' rather than Inqua,[98] and in 1660 he received more information from the Chainouqua chief Soeswa, who described the Inqua chief as *khoebaha* or 'Lord of all the Hottentoo race'. He was rich in cattle and people, said Soeswa, and he lived 'far in the interior, about half way betwixt the two seas' and cultivated dagga which, as Van Riebeeck correctly observed, 'stupifies the brain like opium, ginger, strong tobacco, or brandy'.[99] It was not until 1686, however, that the authorities in Cape Town attempted to make contact with the Inqua, with a view to acquiring cattle for distribution to new settlers, and, after several failed attempts, they at last received word of them through an intermediary. Two years later the 'Inquahase' king sent an envoy to guide the Dutch to his country, to which, he said, 'no European or white man' had ever been before.[100]

The expedition was led by Ensign Isaq Schrijver of Leiden.[101] After travelling for a month through the territories of the Hessequa, Gouriqua and Attaqua, Schrijver's men reached the Kariega River (see Map 2) and followed its course northwards for several days across 'flat stony ground' until they reached a point which their Sonqua guides unanimously declared to fall within the territory of Hijkon (Gei!khub), the Inqua king. After a wait of some days, Hijkon himself arrived, accompanied by 150 men. He was taller than Schrijver had expected. 'This Captain is large in stature and stronger than any one of our people', the diarist recorded,[102] and his men were bigger than the Cape Hottentots, though they resembled them in other respects.[103] The Inqua chief also seems to have been able to command unusual respect from his subjects, for they obeyed him 'with running and jumping' and paid him tribute before consuming game killed within his territory.[104]

Chieftainship was a fragile institution among the Khoekhoe, as Elphick has explained, and Hijkon's hold over his people may well have been exceptional.[105] However we know little of the structure of his chiefdom; Schrijver did not visit his camp in the 'long and crooked' Elandskloof at the foot of the Camdeboo Mountain and we cannot tell whether it was composed of one clan or many. We do know that his territory was large, for besides the surrounding 'Sonquase Hottentots' his nearest neighbours

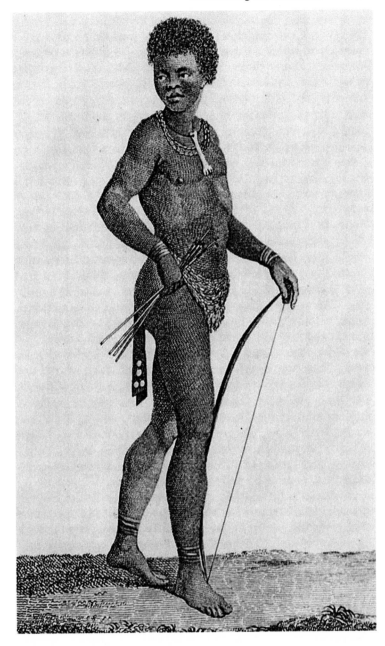

Figure 2   *Jeune Hottentot Gonaquoi*, François le Vaillant, Good Hope
Collection, Cape Town, GH 90/22.

lay several days' journey to the south, along the sea coast. Most probably, like other Khoekhoe chiefs, Hijkon had jurisdiction over several patrilineal clans, which ranged widely over the common territory, camping separately at some times and together at others, according to the dictates of social and ecological circumstance. His power would thus have been kept in check by the tendency of his subjects to disperse and he would have been obliged to govern in consultation with the heads of subordinate clans.[106] However that may be, his people were clearly prosperous, for Schrijver obtained 500 cattle and a few sheep in a week of barter.

Schrijver returned directly to *De Kaap* from Hijkon's country, without investigating the Inqua chief's information regarding cattle-keeping peoples to the south-east, along the coast. However, of the five coastal peoples named by Hijkon, at least three – the Kubuquaas, Damaquas and Gonaqua – have a definite historical identity. Harinck has convincingly identified the Kubuquaas with the 'Chobona', that is, in this context, the Xhosa, though the Khoekhoe appear to have used the term to refer to all dark-skinned people.[107] According to Hijkon, the Kubuquaas lived five days' journey from his camp, to the east-south-east, in houses made of clay. They possessed many cattle and sometimes came to barter with the Inqua; at other times, however, there was great enmity between the two peoples and they 'did one another much damage and harm'.[108] Bordering the Kubuquaas were the Damaquas, who 'also lived in clay houses and were rich in people and livestock'. They had beads of iron and copper, which they knew how to obtain from stranded ships, and there were Europeans living among them.[109] The Damaquas reappear in the narrative of another expedition sent out by the Company in 1752, though, as we shall see below, there was no mention then of clay houses, nor of riches.[110] Beyond them were three other peoples, the Ganumqua, Namkunqua and Gonaqua ('from whom the Inquahase Hottentots barter dagha'), all apparently well provided with cattle.[111]

Of the latter three, only the Gonaqua (Fig. 2) are named in other sources. In 1689, soon after Schrijver's return to the Cape, they received a passing mention in the testimony of three survivors from the wreck of the *Stavenisse*[112] and subsequently they featured many times in the diaries of European travellers, partly because they were numerous – by the mid-eighteenth century they were scattered throughout the territories of the cis-Keian Xhosa[113] – but also because their peculiar blend of Khoekhoe and Xhosa culture attracted the attention of the scholarly Europeans who visited the furthest reaches of the colony in search of curious and remarkable things. The first to record the affinities between Xhosa and Gonaqua was, however, not a botanist or an amateur ethnographer, but the Company's clerk Carel Albregt Haupt, official diarist of an expedition sent eastward in 1752 under the command of Ensign August Frederik Beutler.

In Haupt's opinion, 'their clothes and lifestyle [were] one and the same and they also intermarry without distinction . . .'.[114] To Anders Sparrman, a Swedish naturalist who visited the eastern borders of the colony in 1775–6, the Gonaqua appeared

certainly a mixture of Hottentots and Caffres, as their language had an affinity with that of both these nations; but in their utterance, which was more manly, in the natural blackness of their complexions, in the great strength and robustness of their limbs, and lastly in the height of their stature, they bore a greater resemblance to the Caffres, several of whom they likewise had at that time among them.[115]

François le Vaillant was likewise convinced that the Gonaqua 'must have been originally the produce of these two nations'.[116]

However, despite their physical resemblance to the Xhosa, most Gonaqua retained key elements of Khoekhoe culture. There is little evidence that they practised agriculture in any form (except perhaps the cultivation of dagga) and they also ignored the Xhosa taboo on female involvement with livestock. Indeed, as among other Khoekhoe, milking was largely women's work.[117] Moreover, most sources (except Sparrman) agree that they did not practise circumcision.[118] They were also adept in the use of the bow, a weapon which, according to Harinck, was 'never used by the Xhosa'.[119] And finally, despite Sparrman's observations concerning their language, they seem to have spoken a dialect of the Khoe language family, for their speech was intelligible (though not perfectly) to Khoekhoe who came from the western and south-central parts of the colony.[120]

The physical and cultural similarities between Xhosa and Gonaqua have led Harinck to speculate that the Gonaqua arose out of a process of assimilation which began around 1670, as a consequence of a bitter succession dispute between Tshiwo, the legitimate heir to the Great House of the Xhosa kingdom, and his uncle, Gandowentshaba.[121] However Jeff Peires, who is intimately acquainted with the recorded traditions of the Xhosa kingdom, believes that Harinck has incorrectly identified the Xhosa protagonists, who were in reality Phalo and his elder brother Gwali.[122] If Peires is correct, then the events described by Harinck took place not in 1670 but somewhere between 1700 and 1736, and the Khoekhoe chiefdom was Inqua, now led by a chief named Hinsati. According to Peires, Hinsati's chiefdom was entirely destroyed by the supporters of Phalo, and his people were subsequently incorporated into the Xhosa kingdom as the Sukwini, Gqwashu and Nqarwane clans.[123] Neither Peires' nor Harinck's account of the succession dispute and its consequences for the Khoekhoe can be fully substantiated, but Peires' version, besides being founded on a better knowledge of the traditions, has the merit of explaining the otherwise unaccountable disappearance of the Inqua from the historical stage

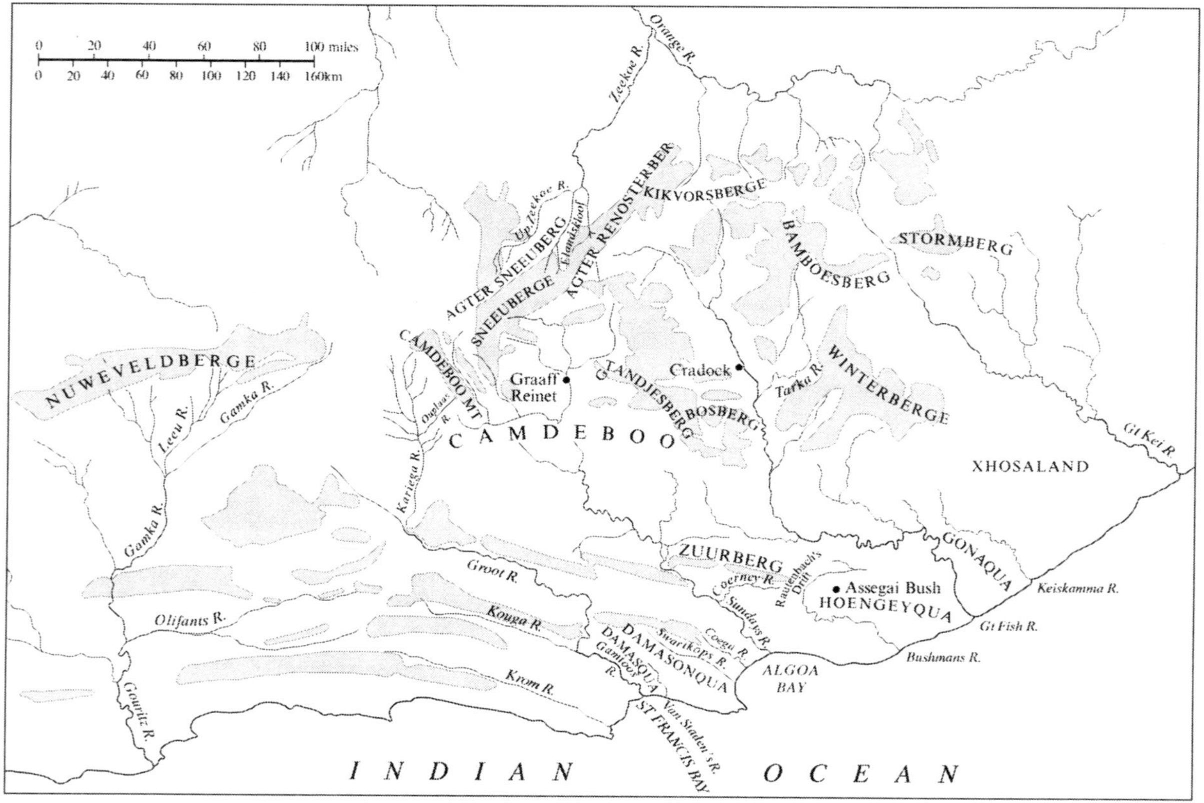

Map 2 The eastern frontier in 1752

after 1720.[124] As we have seen, the Inqua had once been a powerful people, yet Haupt makes no mention of them in his journal of the 1752 expedition, and when the *veeboeren* first began to settle the Camdeboo in the late 1760s, the Inqua were nowhere to be found. As to the Gonaqua, moreover, it is difficult to see how they could have acquired so extensive an admixture of Xhosa culture in so short a time.

Of more concern than the origins of the Gonaqua is the question as to the nature of their relations with the Xhosa. Hermann Giliomee has asserted that 'during the first phase of incorporation [into Xhosa society] Khoikhoi were usually simply menial servants'.[125] This statement is based on a sentence in Haupt's journal which refers to the Gonaqua as living among the Xhosa as servants and (in war time) as soldiers.[126] We should treat this sentence with some caution, however. Clearly, there had been a long and complex process of interaction between the Gonaqua and the Xhosa. In 1687 the three shipwrecked sailors alluded to above were introduced by their Xhosa hosts to a party of Gonaqua who visited Xhosaland each year for the purposes of trade, exchanging beads and copper rings for the dagga grown by the Xhosa.[127] Harinck has suggested that the Gonaqua obtained copper from the Inqua, who in turn bartered it from the Tswana, far to the north across the Orange River.[128] This suggestion is supported by an entry in Schrijver's journal; however it is also likely that by the 1680s the Gonaqua had become a vital link in a chain of exchange stretching from Xhosaland to the Dutch settlement at the Cape of Good Hope.

In June 1752 (see Map 2), after Beutler's party had crossed the Keiskamma into Xhosaland, they found many Gonaqua living 'mixed up' among the Xhosa and apparently serving Xhosa chiefs as cattle herds or spies.[129] However, as we have seen, Beutler's diarist also noted that the two peoples 'intermarried without distinction'. Even chiefs sometimes took Gonaqua women to wife.[130] Moreover, while it is clear that the Gonaqua generally occupied subordinate positions within Xhosa society, there is some evidence that they were allowed a measure of autonomy, at least at the level of the individual lineage or clan.[131] And on the western fringes of Xhosaland, many small Gonaqua groups retained a distinct identity until the end of the eighteenth century, while others were absorbed by the Gqunukhwebe, who were themselves partly of Gonaqua origin.[132]

If in 1689 Schrijver had been correct in representing the eastern Khoekhoe chiefdoms as stable and prosperous, albeit harassed by the San, by the time of Beutler's journey in 1752 this image was no longer appropriate. Not only do the Inqua seem to have vanished into thin air, but coastal peoples once rich in livestock had been reduced to scavenging along the sea-shore and plundering one another in a desperate attempt to survive;

territorial boundaries were no longer respected, centralised political structures had collapsed and, according to Haupt, with the exception of the 'Damasquas, Damasonquas and Hoengeyqhas . . . they [the Khoekhoe of the coastal forelands] no longer knew to which nation they belonged'.[133] What had caused this rapid degeneration? Haupt himself ascribed it to 'war among themselves and against the Caffers'. And Peires has suggested that Xhosa attacks had so weakened the political cohesion of Khoekhoe chiefdoms that their members were no longer able to withstand San raids.[134] Given the fissiparous tendencies inherent in Khoekhoe society, this explanation is entirely plausible. However we should be aware that the Xhosa were not the only source of external attack. On at least two occasions after 1700, and probably more, the eastern Khoekhoe were attacked by white freebooters who plundered their stock and killed their people indiscriminately. In 1702, an Inqua camp was ambushed by a mixed party of freemen, Company servants and Chainouqua Khoekhoe which, having failed in an attempt to barter cattle from the Xhosa, spread murder and mayhem on its journey home. The Inqua lost 2,000 cattle and 2,400 sheep and suffered an unknown number of fatalities.[135] Thereafter, in an attempt to protect the Khoekhoe of the borderlands, the cattle trade was temporarily closed to freemen. However, as Elphick has observed, the official trade could be equally damaging. In 1719 the Inqua were robbed again, this time by a bartering party under the command of a Company official.[136]

The disruption caused by direct attacks on Khoekhoe chiefdoms may have been compounded by the eastward migration of Khoisan refugees from the colony. There is no direct evidence of this, but it is perhaps no accident that the only group to prosper in these troubled times was one composed of individuals of diverse origin and led by a newcomer with no apparent claims to seniority in the region. At the time of Beutler's journey, Ruiter's Hoengeyqua chiefdom controlled a large teritory, extending from the Bushmans River on the edge of Damasonqua country to the lands of the Ntinde beyond the Keiskamma. However in the 1760s the Hoengeyqua too came under pressure from the Xhosa. Under Ruiter's leadership, they battled for more than a decade to retain their hold over the Zuurveld in the face of Gqunukhwebe encroachment, but in the end they failed and Ruiter retreated to the Bushmans River, where the first European settlers found him in the 1770s, 'old and infirm' and ruling over a ragged encampment of just thirty huts – 'a less considerable and less free society'.[137] As for his erstwhile followers, some were absorbed by the Gqunukhwebe, while others were left scattered in small groups throughout the Zuurveld: leaderless, unprotected and ill-equipped to meet the challenge posed by an altogether different kind of enemy.

3   Initial encounters of an uncertain kind

The differences between the Xhosa and the incoming *veeboeren* may not have been immediately apparent to the Khoekhoe of the eastern borderlands; or rather, these differences may not have had the sinister implications which they were to acquire with hindsight. Both the Xhosa and the European *veeboeren* were pastoral peoples, as several historians have been at pains to emphasise[1] (though the two peoples had very different approaches to land tenure and kin relations) and both could offer patronage and protection against the many perils of an increasingly turbulent frontier zone.[2] In such circumstances, it is conceivable that the hard-pressed Khoekhoe were not initially averse to co-operation with the intruders.

In any case, the historian wishing to penetrate the complex tangle of relationships on South Africa's early colonial frontiers has been well warned against the adoption of preconceived notions about the inherent incompatibility of the African and Afrikaner communities which met for the first time in the South African interior. It is all too easy, as Shula Marks and Anthony Atmore have observed, to project 'the bitter contemporary socio-political cleavages' of the twentieth century upon the less familiar contours of the pre-industrial past.[3] In fact, as they have shown, a historiography which 'starkly follows' these cleavages has tended to obscure rather than illuminate the earliest interactions between white settlers and indigenous peoples in the South African interior. Upon closer investigation, they contend, seen from the vantage point of the interior, 'it is the parallels between white and black societies, between African and Afrikaner, that are striking – at least superficially'.[4] Crucial differences did exist, especially in the sphere of property relations, but there were also important similarities. Both societies, for example, 'were based largely upon subsistence agriculture and pastoralism, with wealth accumulated in land and cattle, and the hunt supplying a useful source of animal protein and exchangeable commodities of high value in relation to transport costs'.[5] Both, moreover, could be construed as having similar socio-political institutions: thus it has been suggested that in both cases political power rested on control over land and cattle which gave rise to 'patriarchal' or chiefly forms of authority based as much upon clientship and patronage as upon coercion.[6] Afrikaner rule in the interior both before and after the Great Trek was, it is argued, personalised, dynastic, even 'quasi-feudal' in form.[7]

Further, recent research into the history of frontier relationships in southern Africa has emphasised the relative weakness of Afrikaner communities compared with their African neighbours.[8] Whereas earlier writers had often ascribed an inherent but largely unexamined superiority to the trekboers, recent monographs have revealed that these communities were often vulnerable, divided among themselves and dependent 'upon the acquiescence, and even collaboration, of African neighbours' for their survival.[9] In these circumstances, alliances were often constructed across ethnic lines – initially on the Cape eastern frontier prior to the intervention of British troops in 1812 and subsequently on the highveld, where African societies shattered by the impact of the Difaqane sought to enlist the newcomers in the struggles for reconstruction and hegemony which developed in the aftermath of the Ndebele withdrawal.[10] On the Cape frontier, according to Jeffrey Peires, the Xhosa at first 'saw no reason why Xhosa and European should not merge into a single society rather after the pattern of Xhosa and Khoi . . . Politically, Xhosa chiefs saw the Boers as potential allies or enemies, and they offered to help them in turn against the San and the English.'[11]

The most recent studies of relations between *veeboeren* and Khoisan in the eighteenth century must be assessed against this background of revision and reinterpretation of race relations on the South African frontier. Foremost among these studies is the work of Hermann Giliomee to which I have referred above. Writing of the Cape eastern frontier in *The shaping of South African society*,[12] a book which has become the standard text for students of Dutch South Africa, Giliomee has suggested that at least some of the indigenous Khoekhoe of the south-east Cape may have welcomed the advent of the 'trekboers', seeing in service with them a promising alternative to residence among the Xhosa or in the shadow of Xhosa hegemony.[13] Such individuals, he contends, or perhaps whole kin-groups, voluntarily transferred their allegiance from one set of cattle-keeping patrons to another. The racial, cultural and institutional differences between the new overlords and the old were, it is implied, less important than the economic similarities. These allowed for the development of mutually beneficial relationships, in terms of which the Khoekhoe received protection against the many predators of the region and opportunities for the conservation and expansion of their livestock holdings. Indeed, with respect to livestock, Giliomee contends that 'the Khoekhoe often obtained better economic terms from the colonists than from the Xhosa, who at times seized their stock'.[14] Richard Elphick, writing in the same collection of essays, has advanced a similarly 'consensual' explanation of the process by which Khoekhoe were first absorbed into colonial society on the frontier. Alluding to Haupt's description of the chaos which reigned beyond the eastern borders of the colony in 1752 and of the impoverished condition of Khoekhoe communities in these regions, he observed:

> In such conditions the few Khoikhoi with livestock may well have looked to the trekboer as the lesser of two evils. The trekboer was after all a defender of the pastoral way of life which Khoikhoi wished to preserve. He offered his Khoikhoi labourers security from hunger and robbery while allowing them to keep their own herds and flocks with them on the farm. Thus, instead of resisting the newcomers, many Khoikhoi took employment with them; for example, scarcely a decade after the opening up of the Camdebo, virtually all Khoikhoi there were in European service.[15]

An essential feature of these arguments is the view that for many Khoekhoe on the eastern frontier (especially, it is suggested, those with cattle), the passage from clientship or a precarious independence under the aegis of the Xhosa kingdom to residence and service with the Boers 'may not have been traumatic'. On the contrary, Giliomee suggests, during the first decade or so of white settlement in the area, Khoekhoe incorporation into Boer society was (as it had been among the Xhosa) a relatively smooth and peaceful process.[16] In many cases, he argues, there was no sudden break with the past, but rather a continuation of social practices and strategies for survival which had existed prior to contact.[17] Neither he nor Elphick would wish to deny the violence of the frontier – 'there were obviously trekboers', writes Giliomee, 'who from the beginning used violent methods against Khoikhoi, seizing their cattle and compelling them to stay in their service' [18] – but, they suggest, acts of violence and coercion were sporadic, rather than systematic. They contend, in other words, that the dislocation and violence normally associated with slavery or forced labour were a relatively minor theme in frontier relationships during the initial phase of interaction between *veeboer* and Khoekhoe.

This view, as many readers will recognise, is integral to Giliomee's conception of the history of the eastern frontier in terms of an 'open' and a 'closing' phase.[19] Giliomee's analysis, as he himself acknowledges, should be seen in the context of the growing tendency (alluded to above) to explore the 'non-conflictual' as well as the conflictual aspects of South African frontier history.[20] In the eighteenth century, he argues, conflict pervaded all aspects of social and political interaction on the frontier,[21] but it is possible to identify an initial 'open' phase, during which interethnic competition for resources and the antagonisms generated between white masters and black servants were muted by the formation of cross-cutting ties for the pursuit of mutual advantage across lines of colour and class. The long-term tendency, he agrees, was towards a growing polarisation between European settlers on the one hand and indigenous African groups on the other, as class conflicts came increasingly to coincide with differences in colour and culture, but there was an initial period of fluidity and flexibility in the social structure of the frontier, during which social and economic divisions did not always coincide with racial ones: during this phase, 'Europeans were not all masters, non-Europeans were not all servants.'[22]

The emphasis which Giliomee lays upon the relative freedom of Khoekhoe during the early years of trekboer penetration should be seen in this context. The open frontier was maintained, he argued, by the inability of any one ethnic community to impose its will upon the others.[23] As the colonists gradually gained the upper hand, first (during the 1780s and 1790s) over the Khoekhoe and subsequently, with the aid of a newly entrenched imperial government, over the Xhosa of the Zuurveld, the relative liberty and flexibility of the open frontier gave way to the rigidities and stark antagonisms of the closing frontier. Finding themselves hemmed in by an expanding settler population (which by the end of the century was itself beginning to experience a scarcity of land), the status of the Khoekhoe declined gradually from that of clients with the freedom to refuse their labour to that of unfree servants subject to the 'labour-repressive practices' of an increasingly powerful and self-confident master class.[24] Giliomee is concerned to emphasise that the shift from the open to the closing frontier involved a gradual, rather than a dramatic change in status.[25] Relations between *veeboer* and Khoekhoe towards the end of the eighteenth century ranged along a continuum from clientage to 'serfdom'. 'At the furthest extreme', he writes, 'some colonists abducted native children and sold them or kept them in bondage almost like slaves.'[26] With the return of the British in 1806, their unfree status was ratified and entrenched in the Hottentot Proclamation of 1809. By this time they had indeed become 'an undifferentiated servile class', whose status approached that of slaves.[27]

This view of the eighteenth-century frontier as a place of relative freedom and opportunity for people of colour has been echoed in several of the most important recent studies of Cape society. In fact, even before the publication of *The shaping of South African society*, it had been set forth in a seminal essay by Martin Legassick, in which he took issue with the long-accepted belief that the frontier was the primary source of the morbid white racism from which South Africa's subsequent racial polarities were said to have evolved.[28] 'The stereotype of the non-white as enemy', he contended, did not originate on the eighteenth-century frontier. Instead,

he intimated, its origins were to be sought primarily in the social trans-
formations of the industrial era. But in so far as they *could* be traced back
to the eighteenth century, then, he argued, 'if anything', it was the settled
slaveholding districts of the south-west which exhibited the most rigid
racial stratification:[29] 'If there was a trend in class relationships, indeed, it
was a trend away from master–slave towards chief–subject or patron–
client on the frontier.'[30]

Legassick's exploratory remarks have since been endorsed by Nigel
Worden in his excellent study of Cape slavery under the Dutch East India
Company.[31] Having shown (also contrary to a belief once widely held)
that slavery in the arable regions of the south-west Cape was harsh and
brutal in the extreme and that, by the end of the eighteenth century, it had
given rise to a rigidly stratified and deeply divided society in which distinctions of class and colour largely coincided,[32] Worden adds that, 'by
contrast, the urban and frontier environments did not produce such an
acute division within society before the end of the eighteenth century
. . .'.[33] On the frontier, he contends,

and especially in the eastern parts of the colony, slavery played a much less direct
role in the determination of social structure. Other forms of patron–client relationships emerged between stock farmers and labourers, although the use of slaves in
domestic work and on some pastoral farms for field labour did retain the structure
of master–slave subservience outside the western regions and indenture and the use
of the *inboek* system were ideologically based on this principle of absolute control
of labour.[34]

Perhaps the most distinguished exponent of an interpretation which
stresses the fluid and equivocal nature of social relations on the pastoral
frontier is Robert Ross, whose wide-ranging exploration and sophisticated
grasp of the major themes in eighteenth-century Cape history has made
him the foremost English-language historian of that era.[35] Like Giliomee,
Ross has argued that, in contrast to the increasingly rigid racial divisions
and harsh oppression of the nineteenth century, relations between trekboers and Khoisan on the eighteenth-century frontier were characterised
by relative freedom and mutual advantage. In particular, he points to the
fact that the *veeboeren* were heavily dependent on the pastoral and military
skills of the Khoekhoe; without their aid, he notes, the spread of white
settlement through unfamiliar country might well have been impossible.[36]
Yet he is more willing than Giliomee to acknowledge the pervasive and
systematic nature of the violence which the Boers inflicted upon their
Khoisan servants.[37] And he concedes that the evidence in this regard poses
a considerable problem for an analysis which highlights the 'non-conflictual' aspects of master–servant relations on the frontier. 'It seems incred-
ible', he writes, 'that men and women who at one moment were treated

with a certain measure of respect and trust and on whom the boers were dependent to a considerable degree for the daily functioning of their farms, could the next moment be flogged to death at the slightest provocation.'[38] Surely, he asks, such contradictory behaviour must have been counter-productive, serving only to alienate the loyalties of the very people on whom the Boers were most dependent and, it might be added, to provoke them to 'wicked revenge'.[39] The paradox might be resolved, he suggests, if we would admit a distinction between those Khoekhoe or Khoisan who entered the service of the Boers from a position of relative economic independence and those who were pressed into service by 'bitter poverty', or taken captive by commandos.[40] The former, he postulates, became trusted servants and were able to benefit from their position, while the latter were regarded as potential stock-thieves and possible allies of the 'Bushman-Hottentots'. They 'thus became the target of aggression and cruelty'.[41]

The question posed by Ross is profoundly important. It is quite clear that the expansion of Europeans into the interior depended upon the acquisition of skills and knowledge of the environment which only the Khoekhoe and the San could teach them. The very livestock on which their expansion depended had been acquired at one time or another from indigenous herders. And yet the evidence from contemporary records yields images of frequent and often savage assaults upon indigenes who did not respond with the requisite servility to the whims and demands of the settlers. This is indeed a paradox; and perhaps one which characterises the earliest encounters between European colonists and native peoples in many parts of the world. In this case, we will argue, it cannot be resolved merely by invoking the notion of frontier 'closure' or the demographic expansion of the trekboer community. Could the solution lie, as Ross suggests, in a distinction between different categories of servants, accord-ing to their origins? In particular, would closer scrutiny reveal that most cases of violence involved servants of 'Bushman' origin rather than the propertied and hence perhaps more tractable Khoekhoe? Similar distinc-tions have proved useful in explaining the many variations in the pattern of post-conquest relationships in Latin America, for example.[42]

To some extent, the evidence from the Cape interior does suggest that the initial responses of indigenous communities to the appearance of European settlers in their territories differed according to their economic status, with stock-keepers showing a greater tendency towards voluntary accommodation than cattleless 'hunter-robbers' (see below). However, differences in origin do not appear to have played a lasting role within the master–servant relationship. Certainly they afforded no protection against corporal punishment. For one thing, the boundaries between the two categories of indigenous people were by this time quite blurred and the majority of colonists were unable to tell one from another. As a result, the fear and suspicion generated by the savage border conflict between Europeans and hunter-robbers was visited upon all Khoisan, regardless of their origins. Even the most loyal and long-serving servants were liable to fall victim with little apparent provocation to brutal whippings or other punishments inflicted upon them by nervous masters. Ultimately none was exempt.

The paradox therefore remains. Why should a relatively weak and thinly spread European population, whose settlement in a strange and inhospitable land depended at least initially on the co-operation of the indigenous people, treat these people with what (as I hope to demonstrate below) can only be described as unrelenting and provocative harshness? Herein lies the riddle of this book. It may not be possible to 'solve' it, in the sense of eliminating all contradiction, but it should be possible to explain it, in the sense of laying bare the forces which fuelled antagonism between settler and native and propelled frontier relationships quite rapidly away from the accustomed tributary or client forms of African society towards the harsh and rigid forms of slavery practised in the western Cape. In the chapters which follow it will be argued that the stress laid on the mobility and fluidity of frontier processes and the preoccupation with clientage and other forms of mutual accommodation between European and African has diverted attention from the underlying polarities of the eighteenth-century frontier and led historians to underestimate their thrust in shaping social relationships. Specifically, there are three areas which require more careful examination.

First, there is the conflict to which we have just alluded, between white stock-farmers and the bands of hunter-robbers in the mountains of the south-east Cape and the Central Karoo Escarpment. While most writers acknowledge the impossibility of drawing clear boundaries between San (or Soaqua) and Khoekhoe in this context,[43] they have in practice tended to relegate this conflict to the status of a peripheral border war in which Europeans and stock-owning Khoekhoe jointly confronted the cattleless marauders of the north.[44] In so doing they may have underestimated the extent to which the animus of that conflict imbued *all* relations between Boer and Khoisan with an explosive tension, even those which took shape well away from the vortex of the 'Bushman War'.[45] The history of this struggle and its repercussions in frontier society will be explored in chapters 4, 5 and 6.

Second, while the pioneering work of P. J. van der Merwe and the subsequent studies of S. D. Neumark and Leonard Guelke have laid the foundations of our understanding of the frontier economy,[46] there is room for a closer investigation of the economic forces at work in the colonial interior. In particular, we need to pay closer attention both to the articulation of the local economy with the merchant-dominated settlement of *De Kaap* and to the internal dynamics of individual frontier households, if we are to understand the direction taken by social conflict in the outlying districts. These issues, which were raised briefly in chapter 2, will be fully addressed in chapter 8.

Finally, there is the vexed question of ideology and social attitudes, or, to use C. W. de Kiewiet's phrase, the 'habits of mind' of white frontiersmen, which were such a central concern of historians in the 1930s and 1940s. Legassick's warning against the idealism embedded in the approach of De Kiewiet and his contemporaries is well taken; the self-concept of the *veeboeren* and their attitudes towards their non-white neighbours and bondsmen cannot be divorced from the context in which they took shape, and Legassick is surely right to emphasise the wider dimensions of this context, which embraced the European inheritance of the colonists and their links with the parent society at the Cape, as well as the 'exigencies' they had to face on the frontier.[47] Nevertheless, it may be that the importance which his predecessors attached to the keen sense of group identity and cultural superiority felt by the trekboers was not entirely misplaced. Whether or not their attitudes amounted to racism is a moot point (the evidence in this regard is both scanty and contradictory), but the point to be noted here is that the emerging pattern of social relations on the frontier was buttressed by vehemently held attitudes and beliefs – about the rights of a master over his servants, for example, and the differences between Christians and 'heathens' – and that any study of the shaping of colonial society must take account of these beliefs and show how they functioned and were modified in the frontier environment.

Taken together, these three lines of inquiry should lead towards an explanation of the paradox to which Ross has drawn our attention. The integrative and assimilative tendencies emphasised by Elphick and Giliomee did not disappear and, in time, relations between master and servant may indeed have come to be characterised by mutual dependence and reciprocal obligation; but, it will be argued, these phenomena would be more clearly understood if they were viewed in the context of a coercive rather than a free labour system.[48] The struggle for mastery of the human and natural resources of the interior, of which the 'Bushman War' was but the most visible expression, holds the key to the rapid erosion of the voluntary principle on which clientage was based; but, viewed in isolation, it cannot adequately explain the harshness of the social order which resulted. Indeed, if territorial control had been the sole objective of the *veeboeren*, a gentler approach to the indigenous inhabitants might in the

the long run have been more effective. It is only when the broader dimensions of colonial expansion are taken into account – in particular its economic dimension – that we can begin to construct an adequate explanation for the emergence of slavery, or a form thereof, on the margins of the colony.

First, however, before attempting to impose a framework upon the interactions of Boer and Khoisan on the eastern frontier, one might do well to allow the evidence to speak for itself, for the historical record contains many references to the earliest encounters between the pioneers of European settlement in the eastern Cape and the fragmented but still autonomous Khoisan communities scattered throughout the region.

The general contours of the region which would later become the *Colonie* of Graaff Reinet had been familiar to white frontiersmen for many years before the first of them settled there. Apart from the officially sponsored expeditions sent out during the first half of the eighteenth century,[49] the area had been partially explored by hunters and by those engaged in the illicit cattle trade with the Xhosa and Khoekhoe.[50] However it was not until the 1760s that the loose chain of loan-places strung out along the Great Escarpment reached the banks of the Gamka River, which rose in the Nuweveld Mountains above present-day Beaufort West. From there, in the arid Karoo, it was but a short step to the enticing grasslands of the Sneeuberge and the Camdeboo. In the south, along the coast, a different group of settlers was playing out a similar process and by the end of the same decade members of this group were marking out farms across the boundaries of Swellendam district (see Map 1).

The first loan-farms in the Sneeuberge and the Camdeboo were officially registered in 1768,[51] whereas to the south, in the coastal forelands, registration of new farms was delayed by a prohibition issued in 1770 against the settlement of Europeans east of the Gamtoos River.[52] However, by November 1776, Hendrik Swellengrebel, travelling east along the coast during his journey to Xhosaland could remark:

The Colonie is now inhabited as far as the Great Fish River, which has been fixed as the boundary between us and the Kaffers. Unless they succeed through industry in reducing the amount of land necessary for grazing on each farm, I don't see that many more inhabitants could settle here, and if the population so continues to grow and the Bushmen continue with robbery there will quickly be a shortage of ground.[53]

Swellengrebel was perhaps exaggerating the shortage of land along the coast (though he was right about the extensive farming practices of the frontiersmen), for many new settlers were to find a home there during the

1780s. Nevertheless, the spread of settlement in the region as a whole was remarkably rapid, for by the end of 1774, scarcely six years after the arrival of the first settlers, some 256 loan-farms situated within the future district of Graaff Reinet had been formally registered in the Company's *Wildschutte Boeken*.[54] Most of these farms were concentrated in the north – in the Nuweveld, the Sneeuberge and the Camdeboo – but the records reveal that several inhabitants of Swellendam had taken advantage of the geographical ignorance of Company officials to register farms along the coast, east of the Gamtoos River, in defiance of the prohibition of 1770.[55]

As the two 'streams' of settlers advanced eastward, one along the base of the Great Escarpment and the other through the Little Karoo and the Lange Kloof, they began to merge. By the early 1770s it was not uncommon to find the younger members of southern Cape families such as the Bothas, Prinsloos, Potgieters and Viljoens, living among people raised in the Bokkeveld or the Roggeveld, like the sons of Dawid and Isaak van der Merwe and Jacob and Joseph de Clercq, on the terraces of the Sneeuberge or in the grasslands behind De Bruins Hoogte.[56] On the other hand, the presence of Karoo-bred pioneers among the first settlers in the coastal forelands is less well attested: apart from a single representative of the Pretorius family, few residents of Stellenbosch district appear to have moved down to the coast in order to take advantage of the eastward extension of Swellendam district in 1775.[57] Why was this?

The coastal forelands, a dissected plain which extends inland for some 35 km, rising gradually to a height of 300–400 m above sea level, are separated from the Karoo and Cape Midlands by a chain of mountains running parallel to the coast in an east-south-easterly direction. These mountains form the easternmost extension of the Cape Fold Belt and they mark a major ecological boundary. Not only do they have a rain-shadow effect on the regions immediately to the north, confining maritime influences within their bounds and greatly contributing to the aridity of the Karoo, but they also mark a geological boundary between the rocks of the Karoo System to the north and those of the Cape System to the south. The result is a semi-arid and predominantly summer-rainfall zone to the north of the mountains,[58] with relatively infertile desert soil, and a wetter, all-season rainfall zone to the south, with deeper and more fertile loamy soils[59] (see Figs. 3 and 4). Variations in temperature are also more extreme to the north of the Fold Belt, especially along the edges of the Great Escarpment, where nightly frosts may occur for four months or longer (from mid-May to late September in the Sneeuberge) and heavy snow falls are an annual event. Along the coast, by contrast, winters are moderate and frosts confined to June and July.[60]

These climatic and geological contrasts are associated with marked

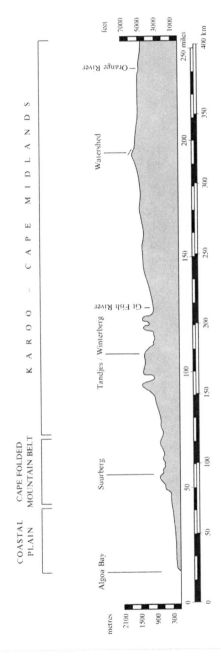

Figure 3 Transect across the eastern Cape. *Source:* Hilary Deacon, *Where hunters gathered* (1976).

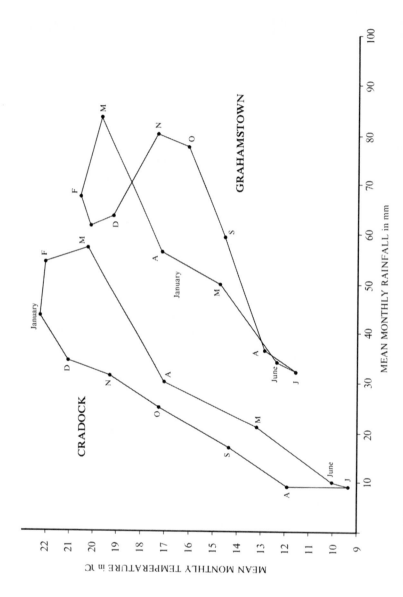

Figure 4   Climograms contrasting the general climate of the Cape Fold Mountain area (Grahamstown) and the Karoo–Cape Midlands area (Craddock). *Source:* Hilary Deacon, *Where hunters gathered* (1976).

differences in the fauna and flora of the eastern Cape. The region as a whole is today regarded as transitional, being the meeting-point between the winter-rainfall vegetation of the western Cape and the tropical bush, savannah and grassveld of the South African interior. On the arid plains between the Fold Belt and the Escarpment, the combination of these very different vegetation types has produced the distinctive mixture known as Karoo or Karroid veld – a blend of succulents, geophytes, grasses and thorny shrubs,[61] while in the Fold Belt it has given rise to a complex 'mozaic of bushveld, fynbos,[62] scree forest and grassveld'.[63] On the coastal plain, before the advent of large-scale agriculture, grassveld, thornveld and dense valley bushveld intermingled with the eastern borders of the temperate Knysna forest and the western margins of the dry tropical forest which once extended all along the coast east of the Drakensberg. This was good cattle country, with abundant sweetveld grazing on the low plains near the sea-shore and sourveld on the wetter mountain slopes.[64] Seasonal movement between the two types of veld would ensure the health of the animals,[65] while the succulents and sweet grasses in the tangled thickets of the river valleys offered a rich supply of palatable nutrients at all times of the year. Europeans who travelled through the coastal forelands towards the end of the eighteenth century were impressed by their fertility. 'The country between the Gamtoos river and this bay [Algoa Bay]', wrote John Barrow, who traversed it in 1799 in his capacity as private secretary and chief fact-gatherer of the Governor, Lord Macartney, 'is extremely rich and beautiful. Like a gentleman's park, or pleasure grounds, in England, the surface is diversified with thickets and knots of stately trees, planted, however, by the spontaneous and free hand of nature. The knolls are covered with thick grass, which, for want of cattle to eat it off, is suffered to rot upon the ground . . .'[66] Hendrik Swellengrebel was equally impressed by the quality of the grazing further east beyond the Sundays River mouth; the grass was exceptionally beautiful, he noted, 'standing knee high and without weeds'.[67] Indeed by the time of Barrow's visit the country between the Sundays and Fish Rivers (known then as the Zuurveld) had become a bitterly contested zone, coveted by Europeans and Xhosa alike. Why then did it not attract an initial influx of settlers to the same extent as the inland regions of Camdeboo and De Bruins Hoogte?

The answer lies primarily in an appreciation of the enormous changes which human occupation has wrought upon the landscape, especially since the coming of Europeans to the region.[68] Other factors, such as the limits imposed upon eastward expansion along the coast by the Resolutions of 1770 and 1775[69] and the growing presence of the Xhosa east of the Sundays River no doubt played some part, but ecological realities were paramount. The grazing potential of the coastal forelands was not lost upon the *veeboeren* – indeed, the low-lying sweetveld plains were rapidly occupied – but, during much of the eighteenth century, these plains were seldom more than ragged patches of open territory in a deeply dissected and wooded country. The largest expanses of low-lying open ground lay at either end of St Francis Bay (in the vicinity of present-day Humansdorp and Port Elizabeth) and on the hot dry plains between the Swartkops and Sundays Rivers (see Map 2).[70] East of the Sundays River, the coastal plain is 'seamed by transverse and deeply carved river valleys' which, even today, are clad in dense and impenetrable bush and forest.[71] Two hundred years ago this rough and bushy country covered a far greater area than it does today, and it was the habitat of lion and leopard as well as elephant and buffalo. On the raised platforms between the valleys there were stretches of excellent grazing,[72] but to reach them man and beast were obliged to find a way through the steep kloofs, or take a more circuitous route across the grassy hilltops of the Suurberge.[73] It was perhaps with this in mind that the Heemraden of Swellendam (exaggerating somewhat) informed the Governor in 1775 that '[the country] along the sea, even to Bosmans river, would be of little or no advantage, as, however extensive, from the drought and numerous useless tracts of wooded country, it is for the greater part useless, and would, at the utmost, not form more than twenty farms'.[74]

The country north of the Fold Belt, on the other hand, held many attractions in the eighteenth century which it can no longer offer today. West of the Kariega River the veld was even then Karoo, though no doubt richer in grasses than it is now.[75] Crossing the great plain north of the Swartberge, from De Queekvallij[76] to Beervlei, Swellengrebel described the terrain as 'a continuous Caroveld, with little water, which is why the few farms which were established here and there at a fountain have been again abandoned'.[77] Along the route north-east from Beervlei to the Kraai River in the vicinity of present-day Aberdeen (see Map 3), his party again suffered from the great scarcity of water, and were compelled to cross this country as fast as possible.[78] But once they reached De Doordrift (*vee-plaats* of the Oud Heemraad Hendrik Cloete) on the Swart River, the landscape changed. Here, to Swellengrebel's delight, on the north-west margins of the Camdeboo, they found good grass for the first time since quitting De Queekvallij.[79] He observed:

Camdeboo, which in the language of the Hottentots means Green Hollow, is a stretch of territory a good 3 hours in breadth that extends 6 or 7 hours in longitude beneath the Sneeuwbergen. It lies much lower than the Karooveld to the south and is, however, beautifully covered with grass, whereas the Karooveld is meagre and dry. . . The best grass is found in the thornbushes where it receives shade. On the banks of the river grows the so-called kweek or broadgrass which is here considered the best . . .[80]

Colonel Gordon, who stayed the following year at De Vreede,[81] further up the Swart River, was equally impressed: 'the land hereabouts is the prettiest and best that one can see', he wrote, 'full of luxuriant grass and full of trees, mostly mimosa thorns'.[82] And the plains abounded with game, not only springbok and impala, but also the large grazers typical of the African grassveld: hartebeest, wildebeest, buffalo and quagga.[83]

Grass was plentiful too on the plateaux of the Sneeuberge, but here it was composed of mixed sweet- and sourveld (the latter being unpalatable to sheep and cattle for all but three weeks of the year, when it was palatable to cattle only); moreover the snow which fell in winter ('sometimes to the depths of a man') drove all but the hardiest settlers from the higher reaches of the mountains.[84] Nevertheless the grazing was excellent in summer and the mountains were described by Barrow some years later as the colony's 'grand nursery of sheep and cattle', though even in Gordon's time they were recognised as better suited to the former.[85]

To the south-east, beneath the southern slopes of De Bruins Hoogte and the Bosberg, Swellengrebel found a country which pleased him still more. Here, in his opinion, the 'Caroveld' truly ended: 'the pastures along the Boschberg and Little Fish River are picturesque. The veld with short green grass; here and there in the hollows and among the rocks thorn trees which, from the frequent burning of the grass, are naked below and above have small crowns which look from afar much like palm trees.'[86]

Tall and sturdy trees grew in the kloofs, among them yellowwoods,[87] which were much in demand for the construction of houses and furniture. Behind the Bosberg, in Zwagershoek (along the banks of the Little Fish River) and Agter Bruins Hoogte, there was fertile irrigable land which could be used for the cultivation of corn.[88] And on the heights there was excellent grazing which even in Barrow's time, when the mountain tops were already showing signs of denudation, supported 'the finest oxen, without exception, in the whole Colony, and sheep equal to those of the snowy mountains'.[89]

Further north, in the basin of the Upper Fish River (around present-day Cradock) and on the plains behind the Sneeuberge, in the Zeekoe River valley, Gordon found the vegetation to be mostly pure sweet grassveld,[90] except along the upper reaches of the Zeekoe River, in the rain-shadow of the Sneeuberge mountains, where it was 'broken-veld' – a mixture of grasses and Karoo shrubs and succulents.[91]

One should bear in mind, however, that both Gordon and Swellengrebel may have visited the region north of the Cape Fold Mountains during a period of exceptionally heavy rains. It is possible that, as the archaeologist Garth Sampson believes, the vegetation of the whole region was merely episodic grassveld, reverting to Karoo in normal years.[92]

However that may be, with the exception of the mountain tops of the Sneeuberge and the Second Escarpment, the whole region is today mapped as Karoo or false Karoo.[93] Two centuries of overstocking and improvident veld management have reduced the grassy shrub savannah of the lowland plains and the dry cymbopogon grassveld behind the mountains to a semi-desert, still capable of producing excellent mutton, but no longer able to support cattle in any numbers.[94] Even in Swellengrebel's time, just seven or eight years after the first settlers had established themselves in the Camdeboo, the delicate balance between edible grasses and Karoo shrubs and succulents was showing signs of disruption: 'it is to be feared', he remarked, 'that the luxuriance of the grass that has already started to deteriorate markedly . . . will not last long, and this veld will become wholly deteriorated just like that which lies nearer the Cape'. Already Jacobus Botha had had to remove from the Camdeboo to the Great Fish River, on account (so he said) of the shortage of pasture, and Abraham van den Berg was planning to quit the Swart River for the same reason.[95] By the end of the century the Camdeboo appeared to Barrow as 'chiefly composed of Karroo plains'[96] and to others who came after him as a country 'covered with heath, mixed with grass'.[97] But even then it remained excellent sheep country and its oxen were 'large and strong'. And well into the nineteenth century it was able to offer an attractive alternative to the fertile but bushy cattle country along the coast.

None the less, despite the attractions of the country north of the Fold Mountains, it was in the coastal forelands, not the interior, that most of the earliest encounters between settlers and Khoekhoe were recorded. The frequency with which travellers remarked on the presence of small groups of Khoekhoe south of the Fold Belt, when contrasted with the relative scarcity of such observations in the Karoo or on the Escarpment, creates the distinct impression that by the last quarter of the eighteenth century these communities were predominantly concentrated along the coast. This had not always been so, as we know from Ensign Isaq Schrijver's reference to the presence of the Inqua at the foot of the Camdeboo Mountain in 1689,[98] but by the late eighteenth century there was little indication of a substantial pastoralist presence inland. It is of course conceivable that some communities had followed a pattern of transhumance between the low-lying coastal plains and the upland basin and Escarpment, moving north to the transitional grazing of the Escarpment in spring and early summer and south to the mixed veld of the coastal lowlands in winter, but while this may have occurred on the Coastal Plateau, between the Winterberge and the valleys of the Fish and Koonap Rivers,[99] the distances involved further west are enormous: the Camdeboo lies nearly 200 km from the sea and the Sneeuberge still further. Moreover, the dates on which European travellers recorded their encounters with Khoekhoe along the coast and in the interior do not conform to the notion of a winter presence along the coast and a summer migration inland, beyond the Fold Belt. Archaeological research, at present mainly concerned with the transhumance patterns of hunter-gatherers, may yet throw further light on this problem.[100] In the meantime, it seems reasonable to assume that the rich and varied pastures of the Fold Belt and the coastal forelands were adequate to support Khoekhoe communities all year round, in the context of a more localised pattern of transhumance.

The circumstances of the Khoekhoe groups encountered by travellers who went east in the 1770s tend on the whole to match Giliomee's portrait of client communities. At the mouth of the Gamtoos River, for example, right on the colonial boundary, there lived a small body of people who were in charge of cattle owned by the merchant and contracted butcher Jacobus van Reenen.[101] Van Reenen had been granted three farms in the vicinity – Kabeljouwsrivier, Loerierivier and Gamtoosriviermond, the last of which he had reserved for the use of his Khoekhoe herdsmen.[102] The arrangement seems to have suited both parties and the Khoekhoe grew rich in cattle; according to Van Reenen's son Dirk Gysbert, himself a contracted butcher, they sold some 300 head each year to the Company's *postholder* at the Riviersonderend.[103]

A little further inland, at the waggon drift on the Gamtoos River, the Swedish naturalist Anders Sparrman met an elderly chief or 'Hottentot Captain' known to the Dutch as Kees. When Sparrman met him in the midsummer of 1774 he was living in what appeared to be a temporary camp, 'his palace consisting only of a few poles set up slanting in the earth with a ragged mat thrown over them'. With respect to the number of his cattle and his subjects ('about half a hundred people') he was better off than Captain Rundganger whom Sparrman later met further west, in the heart of Swellendam district.[104] But like Rundganger, Kees was inseparable from his staff of office, sensing perhaps that it was his sole defence against the predatory intentions of his white neighbours and the envy and resentment of his less fortunate compatriots.[105] In return for the official recognition accorded him, he was required to lend his services to the burgher commandos sent out against delinquent Khoisan. Two years before Sparrman's visit, he and a certain Captain Boekebaas had been summoned to the Roggeveld to assist in the capture of the fugitive servants of Adriaan Louw, who had murdered a Roggeveld farmer and taken refuge in a cavern in the rocks. The successful capture of the fugitives, a bloody business involving the use of guns and hand grenades, was largely due to the two captains and their people.[106] Later in his life, however, as the tentacles of colonial settlement tightened around him, Kees became less co-operative. Asked by the Landdrost of Swellendam in 1788 to identify the 'Hottentot' agitators allegedly responsible for an attempted uprising in the district, he demurred: 'Christian people put us up to it', he said, 'and that is the truth, as I told your Honour.'[107]

On his way back to the Cape in February 1776, Sparrman found a small community of 'Gunjemans Hottentots' camped a little further east, across the Kraggakamma on the banks of the Swartkops River. They appear to have been a remnant of a once powerful branch of the Cochoqua nation, whose chief, Gonnema, had been humbled by the Dutch during the Second Khoekhoe–Dutch War one hundred years before. Despite their exile (the Cochoqua had lived in the south-west Cape) they still clung to his name and to a vague recollection of their former state. Though they had no chief, they were an orderly society, in Sparrman's estimation, and prosperous, one woman among them owning sixty milk-cows.[108] They now lived, he wrote, 'on friendly terms' with the burgher Gerrit Scheepers, who had settled on the Swartkops River, where Uitenhage stands today.[109] In November the same year Swellengrebel, also returning to Cape Town, found them about 12 km further east, on the Coega River, still in charge of Scheepers' stock.[110] Hard by was a group of Gonaqua, led by a captain named Tadi, who were tending the stock of Stephanus Ferreira.[111] They spoke a peculiar language, noted Swellengrebel, which his 'Hottentot' servants could not understand, and there were many 'bastard kaffers' among them. There was also a girl who spoke good Dutch, which she had learnt in the service of a certain Meyer.[112]

The previous day, while crossing the Sundays River just below its confluence with the Coerney (see Map 2),[113] Swellengrebel had been approached by a group of Khoekhoe belonging to Ruiter's kraal, who were likewise tending the stock of Stephanus Ferreira and his brother Petrus Hendrik.[114] Further east, at Rautenbach's Drift on the Bushmans River, he had found a small community of Gonaqua to whom he gave some tobacco and copper jewellery. They were amazed by his generosity – 'it seemed', he noted, 'that these people were not much used to friendly encounters' – and offered him milk in return. Some days later at his outspan on the banks of the Coerney, the emissaries of two nearby Gonaqua encampments had come to greet him, one party complaining bitterly of the annoyance caused them by a certain P. Louw, 'who had come to lie next to them with his stock and was trying to force them to give way to him, though they had lain here long before him'.[115]

Ruiter himself (whom Swellengrebel incorrectly identified as Gonaqua) lived at that time (November 1776) on a west-bank tributary of the Bushmans River, some 16 km south-east of the crossing at Rautenbach's Drift.[116] His village, which lay in a kloof among thickly wooded hills, comprised '20 to 30 rough huts' grouped in clusters of seven or eight, each accommodating a separate family with its own livestock and cattle kraal (Fig. 5).[117] Ruiter extended a warm welcome to Swellengrebel, offering him a fat ox as a gift, ensuring the safe-keeping of the oxen and baggage and sending his only son and heir to guide Swellengrebel through the buffalo-infested Sundays River bush.[118] He did the same for Colonel Robert Gordon two years later.[119] According to Sparrman's Christian informants, many of whom claimed to have met him, Ruiter had always been anxious to remain on good terms with the colony, 'and in return for the tobacco and other articles they presented him with, used to help them to make slaves of such straggling Boshies-men as did not live under his jurisdiction. By keeping the Caffres at a proper distance, he not only served his own turn, but was likewise extremely useful to the colonists.'[120] However, by January 1778 Ruiter's role as a bulwark against the Xhosa was clearly over – he was entirely surrounded by the villages of the Gqunukhwebe and Mbalu and, according to Gordon, his people and those of his 'Gounaqua' neighbour, Trompeter, were 'almost completely fused and mixed with the Caffers'.[121]

Perhaps the most interesting case of a mutually advantageous and voluntary form of clientage dating from this period concerns an elderly German named Heinrich Janse Nieuwenhuys.[122] In November 1777 Colonel Gordon and his young companion William Paterson[123] had found Nieuwenhuys living on the borders of Beervlei (see Map 3), in the company of a group of Khoekhoe to whom he had 'attached himself' some twenty years before. Paterson described him thus: 'His garment was composed of sheepskins, similar to those worn by the natives, and his method of living was the same . . . every three or four years he went to the Cape with a few cattle for sale and with the produce of his goods purchased powder, lead and trinkets for his Hottentots. . .'[124] To Gordon, Nieuwenhuys 'was like an old Jewish Patriarch in many ways'. Gordon gave a short and rather dour account of a dance performed at nightfall by the Khoekhoe with whom the old man lived:

The women sang, clapping their hands and one struck upon a pot which had a wet skin stretched across it. Their songs were: the song of the lion, of the wolf, of the eland and so on with other animals; singing the characteristics of each. Each song had a somewhat different melody. I noticed that they all took a turn in it together, but it was all very wild and disorderly.[125]

Client relations, for all that they are based upon a process of bargaining and accommodation, presuppose an inequality of power between the parties involved.[126] But the precise terms of the relationship will vary with the relative strength of the protagonists. Thus clientage can range along a continuum from an almost equal partnership to a position not far short of slavery. If this brief glimpse of the leather-clad German living alone with

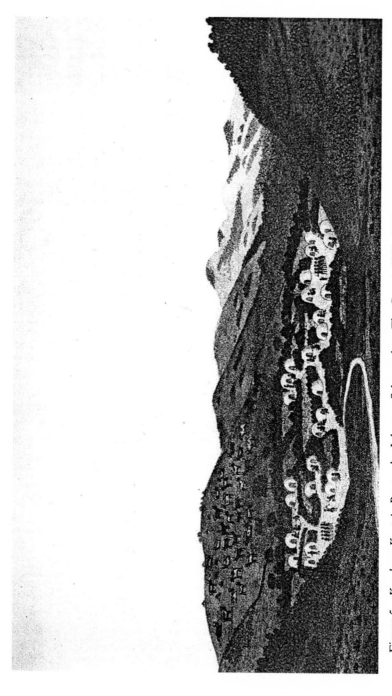

Figure 5   *Kraal van Kaptein Ruyter*, by Johannes Schumacher, *The Cape in 1776–1777: aquarelles by Johannes Schumacher from the Swellengrebel collection at Breda*, The Hague: A. A. M. Stols, 1951.

his cattle and his disorderly companions in the red wastes of the Karoo can serve as an example of a relatively equal partnership, perhaps even one in which the usual roles of European and indigene had been reversed, there were, alas, already many signs that in districts better suited to stock-raising, the bias was swinging rapidly in favour of the former. Even Ruiter had been forced to bend to pressure from his European neighbours. In former times, when he was 'in the meridian of life, and at the zenith of his power', they had treated him as befits an ally, stifling their discomfort at the 'pride and arrogance' of this 'sheep-skin prince'.[127] But now that his power was waning and his role as an intermediary between Christian and Xhosa was no longer necessary, they had begun to encroach upon his territory: 'This Captain Ruiter complains bitterly', Swellengrebel noted, 'that he has already had to vacate his former place for one of our people, and now he is being pestered to move again by a certain Lucas Meyer, who lies hereabouts with his stock.'[128] Now, when he met his 'old Christian acquaintances', he no longer expected tribute, but rather begged for to-bacco 'with tears in his eyes'.[129]

Other Khoekhoe communities in the coastal forelands were experien-cing similar pressures. The complaints of the Gonaqua on the Coerney River have already been noted. For a while they appear to have held the upper hand: Paterson recorded in January 1779 that 'an old German that lives on the banks of this river . . . had often been in danger with these people; they had hardly left anything in his hut in which he lived'.[130] But those who lived further west, like Captain Kees, were less able to resist. Thus when, in 1770, the colonial boundary commission had expelled a visiting Khoe captain from Kees' kraal because he had 'too many cattle, and thus injured the pasture of the inhabitants', Kees had made no obvious protest.[131]

In 1778, following Governor van Plettenberg's tour of the eastern boundaries, the Khoekhoe clients of Jacobus van Reenen were likewise displaced. Van Plettenberg had granted the loan-place Gamtoosrivier-mond to Hilgert Muller, who turned its valuable pastures to his own purpose and compelled its former occupants to find other grazing for their livestock.[132] Among those evicted was a youth who would later become known to the Dutch as Klaas Stuurman. Twenty-five years later, in the aftermath of the rebellion which he had helped to lead, Stuurman recalled bitterly how the Governor's action 'had caused poverty among the Hot-tentots, who no longer had grazing for their cattle and found themselves compelled to enter service with the inhabitants'. Since that time, he added, 'nearly all the kraals owned by the Hottentots had been occupied on ordonnance by the colonists'.[133]

Klaas Stuurman may have remembered the process of land loss as more abrupt and dramatic than it really was. European settlement in the 1770s was not on a scale sufficient to displace the Khoekhoe entirely and render them homeless. But the loss of favourite pastures and camp sites did them injury none the less, for it disrupted patterns of transhumance which had been refined over many centuries. It is true that the westward expansion of the Xhosa (who were more numerous than the Europeans) and the east-ward migration of Khoisan refugees from the colony had already disrup-ted long-established patterns, but the white colonists' exclusivist attitude to land and the speed with which they appeared to consume it introduced a new element into an already troubled situation. It was not that the coming of the *veeboeren* brought with it instant dispossession, as Stuurman's experience might lead one to believe, but rather that their seizure of the choicest sites prevented indigenous pastoralists from making optimum use of seasonal resources, and thus further undermined their prosperity and reduced their ability to choose the terms on which they would enter into relationships with the newcomers. Whether or not this slide into a position of dependence was experienced as 'traumatic' is difficult to ascertain in the absence of adequate testimony (though for Stuurman it clearly was), but given the intimate connection between land, people and animals in the world-view of the Khoisan,[134] it seems likely that changes which adversely affected any one of these elements and threw them into imbalance would be experienced as stressful.

Moreover, here and there in the newly settled territories, there were signs that alongside the gradual process of encirclement and displacement a more sinister and immediately disruptive pattern was taking shape. On the farm of Petrus Hendrik Ferreira in the Lange Kloof, for example, Sparr-man had seen 'an old Boshies-man Hottentot with his wife' who had been captured by Ferreira a few months before: the old man had formerly 'reigned over above a hundred Boshies-men', wrote Sparrman, but he and his wife 'were now translated by the farmer from that princely, or rather patriarchal dignity, to that of being shepherds to a few hundreds of sheep'.[135] As Sparrman followed the waggon-road eastward through the kloof, he passed several 'fugitive Hottentots' wandering in a pitiable state, feeding themselves as best they could on roots and bulbs and termites which they dug with their weighted sticks. Whether they were truly run-away servants, as he believed, who were now no longer pursued 'on account of their age and infirmities',[136] or remnants of Soaqua bands who had been flushed from the surrounding mountains by Boer commandos, is difficult to tell. Little is known about relations between settlers and Soaqua in what was then the Swellendam district, though court records reveal that 'Bushman' bands in the Swartberge had been the target of commando attacks in the 1750s.[137]

Be that as it may, it is clear that commandos were active in the Lange Kloof and surrounding areas in the 1770s. Upon his arrival at Jacob Kok's home farm on the Seekoei River (St Francis Bay), Sparrman (a doctor of medicine as well as a botanist) was asked to treat Kok's servants, who had contracted 'a bilious fever'. Several of the sick, he discovered, 'had been very lately caught' and had 'made too sudden a transition from their savage manner of living'. Finding them resistant to the emetic which he had prepared 'according to the Dispensary of the London College of 1762', Sparrman made them drink astonishing quantities of a tobacco decoction ('several large basons full') and swallow whole pieces of shag tobacco, which treatment, while it seems to have cured their fever, can have done little to reconcile them to captivity.[138]

During his journey eastward to Assegai Bush, Sparrman found further evidence of slave-raiding. He was sceptical of the claims of three old 'Boshies-men' who had come to him at the Sundays River Drift to complain that 'the farmers [had] been with them, and . . . carried off all their young people, so that they were now left alone in their old age to look after themselves and their cattle'. They were, he noted, able to rustle up support very quickly once the prospect of a hunt was put to them.[139] However among the Gonaqua on the Coerney River he had come face to face with a Khoekhoe servant who had in his custody 'three old Boshies-women with their children', whom he had captured with the help of the Gonaqua, 'with the intention of taking them home to his master for slaves'. The women had threatened to bewitch the man, but he purported to feel only contempt for 'their menaces and their savage manners'.[140]

Attempts to enslave the Xhosa fared less well. Swellengrebel had been witness to a failed attempt during his visit to the village of Chief Jalamba of the imiDange in October 1776.[141] Swellengrebel's Boer companions, frustrated perhaps by his refusal to allow them to barter cattle from Jalamba's people, had hunted down a group of Xhosa and seized a small boy, whom they 'gave to their Hottentot as an attendant'. But no sooner had they reached Jalamba's village than the boy's irate guardian came to claim him back. Small wonder, Swellengrebel reflected, that King Phalo was reluctant to allow the travellers deeper into his country, for given the rough manner in which the colonists treated the Xhosa and Hottentots (the former they designated 'rascally black heathens') the king could expect little good from them.[142]

In fact, as the references above suggest, the majority of captives came from groups identified as '*Bosjesmans*' or '*Bosjesmans-Hottentotten*' by the Boers. As indicated in chapter 2, there has been much debate concerning the identity of these people and the extent to which, at the time of first contact with Europeans, they constituted a category distinct from the pastoralist Khoekhoe. Richard Elphick has argued that the Khoekhoe mode of subsistence 'was merely an extension of the aboriginal [hunting and gathering] economy', and hence that the boundaries between the two lifeways were easily crossed.[143] And Carmel Schrire has castigated her fellow archaeologists for presenting what she considers a static view of the divisions between the two categories.[144] However a more cautious and discriminating approach is now gaining ground, supported by extensive archaeological research in the south-west Cape. Thus John Parkington of the University of Cape Town has argued that there is clear evidence in the archaeological record for the persistence of hunting and gathering as a separate and distinct lifeway in the two thousand years since the arrival of pastoralists at the Cape.[145] Clientship and trade undoubtedly drew some hunters into the embrace of pastoralism, but many others clung to their traditional lifestyle, which they pursued 'in the interstices of pastoralist society'. Parkington's approach is not static, however, for he shows how the spread of pastoralism promoted far-reaching changes in the subsistence strategies of indigenous hunters, as they were pushed into marginal mountainous areas, where they could no longer hunt large animals on a regular basis.[146] Parkington uses the Khoekhoe term 'soaqua' to refer to these 'residual hunter-gatherers who had survived the appearance of pastoralism'.[147] Andrew Smith has endorsed his findings, adding that both Schrire and Elphick have underestimated the differences in economy and social organisation between herders and hunters, thereby creating a false impression of an easy transition from one mode of subsistence to the other.[148] All parties would agree, however, that as the disruptive effects of European expansion made themselves felt among the Khoekhoe, causing widespread dislocation and impoverishment, dispossessed herders were likewise forced into mountain refugia, where they 'took up a lifestyle superficially similar to that implied by the term soaqua'.[149] The term 'Bushman', Parkington argues, is best reserved for this post-conquest context. It is, as he puts it, 'a wastepaper basket term for all those who lived by hunting, gathering, and stealing'.[150]

When the term 'Bushmen' occurs in the colonial record, it is often impossible to tell from the context whether its referents were of Soaqua or herder origin, or both. The dominant colonial image of the Bushman was that of an inveterate and irredeemable stock-thief. It was this alleged bent for robbery, rather than any ethnic characteristic, or the presence or absence of livestock among them, that distinguished Bushmen from 'good aborigines or Hottentots' who 'used the grassveld in a tolerable or industrious way' and, it was sometimes noted, liked the Bushmen as little as the colonists.[151] Thus to Landdrost Horak of Swellendam, the problem of identity was easily solved: the Bushmen were 'the scum of the Hottentots and even exiles who had been expelled from their society, and wandered as wild robbers in the mountains and rocks'.[152]

The record shows that individuals could and did cross over from one category to the other, and it was not uncommon to find persons with a foot in both camps, as it were. Thus among the Gooijemans Hottentots who had assisted a burgher commando against a 'Bushman' band in the Swartberge in 1750, there was one 'whose father and father's brother were also Bushman Captains', but who himself had refused to participate in stocktheft.[153] To be identified as a Bushman was to become the target of the merciless search-and-destroy tactics of the burgher commandos; thus it is hardly surprising that cattle-keeping communities tried to distance themselves from the mountain bands. 'I am no Bushman!' protested a wounded man captured during an attack on the Swartberge camp, 'I am a Hottentot of the Gooijemans nation and I do not belong to this kraal.'[154] On the other hand, it would be quite incorrect to attribute all such expressions of a sense of difference merely to expediency. Aside from the obvious conflict between those who stole stock and those who bred it, whatever their ethnic origins, there were, as Parkington has shown, real differences and historic enmities between Soaqua and Khoekhoe and, while the turbulence of the colonial period might blur them, it would not eradicate them entirely. This sense of separate identity was exploited by the colonists, who enlisted Khoekhoe in their commandos and slave-raiding parties and rewarded them with captured livestock, and in some cases, it seems, with the services of human captives.[155]

Despite the difficulties involved in distinguishing Soaqua from cattleless Khoekhoe in any particular case (and the haphazard way in which the terms 'Bushman' and 'Hottentot' are used in the records can often lay a false trail) the historian is obliged to acknowledge that the categories do have heuristic value and should not be abandoned or conflated. How, for example, would an approach which refuses to recognise difference account for the divergent responses to white settlement of indigenous commmunities in the northern mountains and the coastal forelands respectively? Why was it that along the interior Escarpment the expansion of the colony was greeted almost immediately with widespread and implacable resistance, whereas further south, apart from sporadic raiding in the Lange Kloof and a number of attacks by 'robber-bushmen' in the mountains just west of Swartkops Bay, there appears to have been little concerted resistance until the 1790s?[156]

Shula Marks has rightly rejected the essentialist explanations of earlier historians, who drew sharp distinctions between 'Hottentots' and 'Bushmen' and viewed the bitter resistance of the latter as 'almost a racial characteristic', a product of their 'more primitive' social organisation.[157]

But should we not allow for the possibility that the divergence in response has something to do with the apparent preponderance of hunters along the rim of the Escarpment?[158] Did the herders of the coastal forelands react more cautiously to Boer incursions because their livestock restricted their mobility? Or did they perhaps (as Giliomee suggests) initially view the arrival of the *veeboeren* as an opportunity to build up herds depleted by half a century of conflict in the coastal forelands? In time, of course, as the colonists closed in upon them and they found themselves stripped of their livestock and trapped in the same coercive relations as captive Soaqua, the distinctions *would* begin to lose their meaning. By the 1790s stock-theft had become common in the coastal forelands, often carried out by mixed parties of Xhosa and Khoekhoe, and the spiralling cycle of fear and violence initially fuelled by the 'Bushman War' on the northern frontier had drawn all indigenous Khoisan into its eddying vortex, regardless of their previous origins.

We turn now to a closer examination of the conflict on the northern frontier.

4 'A multitude of lawless banditti'

Following the defeat of the major Khoekhoe chiefdoms of the south-west Cape during the second half of the seventeenth century, the locus of resistance to the Dutch advance shifted to the Cape Fold Belt – the great chain of mountains which divides the coastal forelands from the arid basin of the Great Karoo. The Cape Fold Belt had long been the refuge of Soaqua hunter-gatherers;[1] from the 1690s they were joined in increasing numbers by Khoekhoe who had lost livestock and grazing lands and now sought to regroup and, if possible, drive the Dutch from the conquered territories. The nature of the interaction between these newly dispossessed Khoekhoe and the much longer-established Soaqua, is, as indicated in the previous chapter, one of the major puzzles in the history of resistance at the Cape in the eighteenth century. The Dutch habit of referring to all mountain raiders indiscriminately as 'Bushmen' or 'Bushman-Hottentots' tends to discourage attempts to achieve a more discriminating understanding of their identity and interrelationships. However here and there the records do afford a glimpse of a more definite identity, albeit not necessarily one which fits neatly into the scholarly categories 'Khoekhoe' or 'Soaqua'.

As the colony grew and European settlement spread inland beyond the mountains of the Cape Fold Belt, the resister communities found themselves encircled. Following a crushing defeat inflicted on the Khoisan of the Sandveld and Onder Bokkeveld in 1739 (see below) there was a temporary lull in the incidence of stock-theft and raids on freeburgher cattle-posts. However, soon after Europeans began to settle along the Great Escarpment, the southern boundary of South Africa's inland plateau, the border conflict erupted with renewed ferocity. By the late 1760s, when the first Europeans established themselves in the Camdeboo, at the foot of the Sneeuberge, there had been nearly seven decades of intermittent conflict between white frontiersmen and the '*Bosjesmans-Hottentotten*', ample time for the crystallisation of mutual antagonisms and the development of effective strategies of combat on both sides. The 'Bushman' conflict on the north-eastern frontier, then, should be understood in the context of the decades of struggle which had gone before.

Shula Marks was the first to characterise the *modus operandi* of Khoisan resistance to the Dutch as 'guerilla warfare'.[2] Elphick has shown that this 'hit-and-run' mode of combat, involving 'a series of sudden and massive attacks on the herds of the enemy', after which the attackers would 'melt away into the bush', had long been a strategy favoured by the Khoekhoe in conflicts among themselves, under circumstances where more formal and open confrontation was inappropriate.[3] It was also 'par excellence the tactic adopted by robber groups' (i.e. Soaqua) before the advent of the Dutch, whether as a means of procuring food from their pastoralist neighbours, or as a more conscious act of resistance against encroachment on their hunting grounds. The Khoekhoe had, moreover, often used Soaqua as spies, messengers and auxiliaries in warfare of this type.[4] The familiarity of both groups with this form of conflict and their history of occasional collaboration may well have facilitated co-operation under the special circumstances of the colonial frontier.

The first 'guerilla' attacks had come in 1701, immediately after the opening of the cattle trade to freemen and the settlement of European stock-farmers in the *Land van Waveren* (later to be known as Tulbagh) across the Roodezand Pass. In March of that year, the northern border-lands erupted in violence as robber-bands, sometimes several hundred strong, launched a 'barrage of rapid assaults' against the herds of free-burghers, the Dutch East India Company and its Khoekhoe allies.[5] The Company was never too sure who was responsible for these raids, but its Peninsular and Cochoqua informants unanimously identified the attackers as 'Bushmen or highwaymen, consisting mainly of the Grigriquas [Guriqua] and Namaquas'.[6] In the view of the new Governor, Willem Adriaan van der Stel, the border raids were a direct result of the opening of the livestock trade, an action he had been forced to take against his better judgment. In his opinion, the lifting of the ban on freeman involvement in the trade had created mayhem on the frontiers of the colony, for trade had degenerated into robbery and the Khoekhoe had been provoked into retaliation.[7] A report compiled four years later by the Landdrost of Stellenbosch, Johannes Starrenburgh, lent support to the Governor's view. Starrenburgh found that Gonnema's Cochoqua and the Guriqua who inhabited the Sandveld to the north of them had been devastated by the activities of predatory freemen.[8] During a 'journey of 12 days along a miserable and difficult road' between the Berg and Olifants Rivers, he had found only two Khoekhoe 'kraals', 'which, though consisting of ten cap-tains, were so ill-provided with cattle', he remarked:

With sorrow I had to experience it, how, in consequence of the last permission for free barter, and the irregularities committed by those vagrants, the whole country had been spoilt; for when one kraal is deprived of its cattle by the Dutch, it went in its turn to rob other kraals and so on, taking refuge in the mountains, and living on the spoils as long as they lasted. They then again went in search of more; and thus from a contented people divided into kraals under chiefs, and peacefully supporting themselves with their cattle, they have mostly all been changed into Bushmen, hunters and robbers, scattered everywhere, and among the mountains.[9]

However official opinion on this subject was not entirely reliable. As several writers have noted, the Governor may well have had his own reasons for wanting to preserve the Company's monopolistic control of the livestock trade with indigenous peoples.[10] Certainly, as Elphick has so fully demonstrated, the breakdown of Khoekhoe chiefdoms on the borders of the colony cannot be ascribed solely to the rapacity of freeburgher stock-traders. There were many other factors at work, such as the effects of the 'legal' trade, military defeat and colonial intervention in intra-Khoekhoe politics and warfare. The northern borderlands, moreover, had long been plagued by hunter-robbers[11] and, in their weakened state, the Cochoqua and Guriqua were less able to defend themselves. However in retrospect it is clear that the depredations of freemen and the inexorable territorial expansion of the colony pushed the Khoekhoe beyond the point of recovery.[12] Soaqua robber groups may initially have derived profit from the 'confused and deteriorating situation in the region', but they too faced unprecedented pressures as the *veeboeren* invaded their hunting grounds, while cattle and sheep devastated pastures and trampled water-holes.

Resistance does indeed appear at first mainly to have taken the form of retaliation against the predatory practices of white stock-traders,[13] but by 1715, in the wake of the devastating smallpox epidemic,[14] there were clear signs that the Khoisan were making an effort to recover land as well as livestock. In June 1715 a group of Soaqua resident somewhere (the records do not say precisely where) in the mountains surrounding the *Land van Waveren* launched the first of a series of devastating attacks on the property of settlers newly established in the valley. Over the next year the raiders made off with more than 200 cattle and several thousand sheep, but this was not all: in September 1715 the 'Bushmen' who stole the livestock of Pieter Willem van Heerden murdered two shepherds who had been in charge of the animals and killed 200 sheep during their retreat. In November another group of robbers abducted two slaves belonging to Joost Bevernagie and burnt the house of Pieter Roussouw to the ground.[15]

These tactics were to become increasingly familiar in later years, but in 1715 they came as a surprise and so alarmed the burghers of Waveren that 'nearly all slept with their guns in their hands'.[16] The attacks also provoked the Council of Policy into a re-examination of its attitude towards the defence of the colony's borderlands. In 1701 the Company had relied primarily on its own soldiers and its officers had gone so far as to order the arrest of a burgher who had raised his own force to pursue a band of thieves.[17] In 1715, by contrast, it authorised the first punitive expedition made up entirely of burgher volunteers, led by Jan Harmense Potgieter and Schalk Willem van der Merwe.[18]

Thereafter, the Company entrusted the defence of the colony's inland frontiers almost exclusively to its citizen militia, organised on a district basis with the Landdrost as commanding officer. During the 'Bushman War' of 1739 the Landdrost of Stellenbosch appointed the first *veldcorporaals* in outlying areas, granting them authority to conscript all able-bodied men in their divisions into 'commandos', the fighting units of frontier defence.[19] This authority subsequently became entrenched and was the source of many a dispute and falling-out between neighbours and not a few slights to the dignity of the Company's appointed servants. Nevertheless, despite the refractory behaviour of some conscripts, the commando was an institution well suited to the guerilla warfare favoured by the Khoisan. Its loose command structure rendered it highly flexible and capable of almost immediate response to surprise attack or robbery. The *veldcorporaals* were not required to obtain the Landdrost's permission before ordering their men into the field – they had merely to submit a report upon their return.[20] And individual burghers were likewise permitted to ride in hot pursuit of stock-thieves without prior permission, provided the local *veldcorporaal* was informed after the event.

This devolution of responsibility greatly increased the colonists' chances of recovering stolen livestock, for it ensured that the trail of a robber band could be followed while still fresh and before the thieves had had time to dispose of their booty. On the other hand, as many have observed with hindsight, the latitude granted to frontiersmen within the commando system involved an effective surrender of VOC control over the relations between freemen and indigenous communities in the far interior and exposed the latter to the summary vengeance of a cruel enemy.[21] The system was cheap, however, and this was perhaps its greatest recommendation. The Company was required only to meet the cost of powder and lead (and, in later years, shackles with which to secure the captives); horses, transport, weapons and provisions were supplied by the local citizenry. In the name of efficiency and economy, therefore, the VOC granted its inland subjects 'more or less complete freedom to act against the Bushmen as they saw fit'.[22] They would use this freedom, alas, to embark upon an orgy of destruction which, though on a smaller scale, rivalled the experience of the Spanish Caribbean in savagery and gratuitous violence.

By the 1730s European pastoralists had settled many of the habitable places south of the Olifants River and had begun to spread eastwards into the Bokkeveld. Khoekhoe south of the Berg River had mostly been compelled to enter the service of the settlers,[23] but there were still pockets of resistance in the Sandveld. In 1728 and again in 1731, bands of 'Bushman-Hottentots' raided the livestock of Europeans in the Sandveld. On the first occasion, a band three hundred strong put up spirited resistance against the commando which followed them, declaring that far from being willing to surrender their booty, 'they first wished to fight the Dutch [*duijtsen*] for it'.[24] In 1731 a group known only as 'the ten sons of Giebenaar' made off with thirty cattle belonging to Hans Jurgen Potgieter. After six days they were tracked down and, finding themselves cornered, they began to destroy the captured animals.[25] They fought bravely, with bow and arrow, but were soon overcome, with six dead and several wounded.[26] The commando recovered ten cattle and captured a woman and three children – this being the second occasion on which captives were taken by a commando.[27] But the band was not entirely cowed, for as the horsemen rode away, a lone survivor shouted from the safety of a rocky outcrop: 'We Bushmen have still more people; we shall give the Dutch no rest!'[28]

The same resolve was shown by a party of one hundred 'Bushmen' from the country of the Little Namaqua, who, in September 1738, stole the cattle of Augustus Louwerensz behind the Piketberg. Pursued, the robbers ran into a ditch in the midst of a thorny thicket, whence they let fly a shower of arrows upon the commando. Asked by a 'Hottentot' interpreter 'what reasons moved them to steal the cattle of the Dutch, while the latter had done them no harm?' they replied:

to chase them out of their country, since they were living in their country: and that this was only a beginning, but that they would do the same to all the people living thereabouts and if that didn't help, and they did not leave, they would burn all the corn presently standing in the fields, once it was ripe; that then the Dutch would be compelled to leave their country.[29]

The stolen animals which the raiders could not conceal were killed or so severely wounded that they were useless to Louwerensz. The destruction of livestock (already seen in 1715 and 1731) was to become an increasingly common practice and was clearly intended as an act of war.[30] Given the superior weaponry of the *veeboeren* (a colonial marksman was sure of his aim at 150 paces, whereas an arrow fired over the same distance was much less certain to hit its target)[31] and the mobility afforded them by their horses, the slaughter of captured stock was an economical way of striking at the enemy, with devastating effect.

The raid on Louwerensz's place in September 1738 heralded a wave of interconnected attacks on the persons and property of colonists in the Sandveld and Bokkeveld during the following year. Collectively, these raids and the commando reprisals which followed them have come to be known as the 'Bushman War' of 1739. This grandiose title was not undeserved: the destruction of property and loss of life was far greater in 1739 than during the Second Khoekhoe-Dutch War of the 1670s[32] and the consequences for the defeated Khoekhoe and 'Bushmen' were even more serious – by the end of 1739 there was no longer any possibility of an independent Khoisan existence in the Sandveld or the Bokkeveld.[33]

Nigel Penn has undertaken a detailed reconstruction of the events which led to this war. It appears that the immediate catalyst was yet another illegal bartering expedition.[34] In 1738, 'before the ploughing season', a number of freemen and *knechten* from the Langevlei and Jakkals Rivers in the Sandveld had journeyed to Namaqualand in the company of their Khoisan servants and clients.[35] They had bartered cattle from both the Little and the Great Namaqua and had apparently remained one month with a certain Captain Gal of the Great Namaqua. However, on the eve of their departure, the traders betrayed the Captain's trust, ordering their servants to attack his kraal and carry off his cattle. They repeated this perfidy during their return journey through the country of the Little Namaqua, where, again with the assistance of their Khoisan servants, they attacked a captain named Arisie and killed his wife.[36] It should not surprise us, then, that the injured Namaqua retaliated. The unusual feature of this war is that they allegedly did so at the instigation of the very servants who had participated in the original robberies.

These latter were apparently outraged by the failure of the European members of the expedition to surrender the share of the booty that they had promised them.[37] They therefore journeyed to the Castle at *De Kaap* to inform upon their masters and were followed soon after by the injured Namaqua chiefs. The Governor undertook to have the captured cattle returned to the chiefs, but reneged on his promise when he saw that confiscation of the cattle from members of the illegal expedition might provoke rebellion among the burghers of the north-west.[38] Animals already returned to the Namaqua chiefs were hurriedly repossessed.[39] Twice deceived, the Namaqua and their Khoisan allies attacked the freemen of the Sandveld in the autumn of 1739. The disturbances spread to the Onder Bokkeveld and there was soon 'a general panic . . . throughout the north-west'.[40] The prominent role played by renegade servants, most of whom were familiar with the methods of the commandos and some of whom were armed with captured muskets, was a particular cause of alarm.

By August ten farms had been burnt and a further forty-eight abandoned.[41] Commandos raised by the newly appointed *veldcorporaals* were unequal to the task of subduing the raiders. A bigger force was needed and, in an act of 'extreme cynicism', the authorities decided to raise it from among the original malefactors: in return for a free pardon, the men who had illegally journeyed to Namaqualand, together with those who had lent support to the stirrings of rebellion in the Roodezand, were required to join a commando under the leadership of the eminent Cape merchant, Johannes Cruywagen.[42] Cruywagen's commando, which took the field in May, was moderately successful. It tracked down two 'Bushman' bands in the Bokkeveld, and recovered a number of cattle. However, Cruywagen and three other members of his party were wounded during the attacks, and the commando did not stay long in the field.[43] It was left to a second force, mobilised in August 1739, to complete the job of pacification. This commando, led by Theunis Botha, adopted a method of 'search and destroy', scouring the Bokkeveld for signs of human habitation and attacking every group it found, whether or not there was evidence of participation in raids on colonial farms. By the end of September 101 Khoisan had been killed, many more injured and a number of women and children taken captive. While Botha's commando was still in the field, three of the surviving 'Bushman' captains accompanied the burgher Hendrik Kruger to Stellenbosch, where each formally received the gift of a copper-headed cane bearing the Company's insignia – in this context, a symbol of ignominious submission. The leaders of the Sandveld Khoisan held out for longer: it was not until October that a patrol on its way up the west coast accidentally came upon Captain Swartbooij and his son Titus, allegedly the 'wiliest instigators' of the unrest. The patrol fired upon them, killing 'thirty or forty', including Swartbooij, but Titus escaped and continued to plot revenge, until in December he was caught in an ambush at the Langevlei.

On the colonial side, since the outbreak of war in April, two men had been killed by poisoned arrows and four (one of whom was a 'Hottentot' auxiliary) by musket fire. Three horses, 541 cattle and 487 sheep (not all of which were identified as stolen stock) had been captured from the Khoisan and were sold to defray the expenses of the commandos.[44] The prolonged conflict had exacted a heavy price from farmers on the peripheries of the colony. Many places were left undefended while the menfolk were on commando and some of those most vulnerable to attack had lain abandoned for months at a time. However, by the end of 1739 the inhabitants of the Sandveld and Bokkeveld were able to return, secure in the knowledge that resistance to their presence had been crushed. The Khoisan of the north-west borderlands 'were now a cowed and broken people, living in isolated kraals'.[45] Their attempts to seek justice from the Company had initiated a chain of events whose savage repercussions they could not have foreseen. There was little they could do now to prevent the intruding colonists from consolidating their hold on the region and moving further into the interior, northward and eastward into the Hantam and the Roggeveld.

The defeat of 1739 was so severe that fifteen years passed before there were any further attempts at concerted resistance to the spread of the colony. By the 1750s settlers were scattered at intervals throughout the Karoo plains of the Onder Bokkeveld, the Hantam and the Roggeveld, yet, as far as we know, neither they nor their flocks and herds were molested.[46] Nigel Penn has suggested that an additional reason for the relative quiet of these years was the very low density of European settlement in the Karoo prior to the 1770s.[47] According to Leonard Guelke, densities might be 'anything from one free person to five square miles (12.9 km^2), to one free person to ten or more square miles (25.9 km^2)'.[48] Consequently, Penn argues, there was less immediate pressure on the hunting grounds and pasturage of the Soaqua and Khoekhoe than there had been west of the Fold Belt: ecological pressures built up gradually, until they exploded in the crisis of the 1770s.[49]

Penn is surely correct to stress the vastness of the area which opened up to the trekboers once they had passed beyond the mountains of the Bokkeveld, but his argument downplays the crucial importance of surface water in the harsh environment of the western Karoo. Rainfall in the Roggeveld Mountains rarely exceeds 250mm per annum; to the south and west, in the Tanqua Karoo and the Onder Bokkeveld, it is less than 150mm per annum.[50] Under such conditions access to sources of permanent or semi-permanent water, such as pans and fountains, took on immense value; without such access neither pastoralists nor foragers could make use of the veld. Yet one suspects that it was precisely these sites which were first appropriated by the *veeboeren*.[51] The experience of Oude Jantje, otherwise known as Jantje Links, who related how,

after having served out his time on a *veeplaats* in the Roggeveld he built a kraal for himself far from there and lived in it; then the Dutch came and through the taking of *veeplaatsen*, forced him to move from there and still further, as far as the dry mountain, where he then lived with his livestock and his sons Klijne Jantje and Klijne Dirk,[52]

may have been more common than the record suggests.

Nevertheless, it does appear that this process of expropriation by degrees was not initially contested, and it may also be true, as Penn suggests, that during the middle years of the century relations between Boer and Khoisan were characterised as much by co-operation and 'compliance' on the part of the Khoisan as by conflict.[53] Certainly in the 1750s there were still a number of independent Khoekhoe communities in the Roggeveld, living within reach of the *veeboeren*, but not under their direct control. However, such evidence as there is suggests that these communities were vulnerable and frequently exposed to the impromptu depredations of their new neighbours.

Some time in 1749, for example (no one was quite sure when), the Khoekhoe Captains Jurgen and Hermanus, who lived in the Klijne Roggeveld, were approached by the burgher Johannes de Beer and a person whom De Beer introduced as a Corporal of the Honourable Company, come to barter stock on its behalf. The Corporal had a hat with silver braid and a pistol at his hip; the captains should refuse him nothing, said De Beer. Accordingly they bartered some twenty head of cattle and seventy-two sheep in exchange for 'some glass beads, copper buckles and two rolls of tobacco', only to discover later that the Corporal was none other than De Beer's *knecht*, Jan Martens.[54]

The first signs of a reawakening of conflict on the northern frontier came in November 1754. The Governor was informed that the '*Bosjesmans Hottentotten*' were 'collecting together' in the Voorste and Agterste Roggevelden and in the Onder Bokkeveld and carrying off whole herds of cattle. 'So much so, that some of the inhabitants of the most remote farms have already fled with their livestock.' Commandos were called out and four Khoisan bands were tracked down and attacked. One band was found to be firmly entrenched behind stone fortifications, whence they shouted to the commando 'that there was nowhere they could hide their cattle where they would not be able to find it'.[55] But their bravado availed them little: sixty-four Khoisan were killed, while on the other side there were but three wounded, one 'a man' and the other two 'Hottentot' auxiliaries.

The captives taken by this commando allegedly informed their captors that the raids had been instigated by a man named Duijkerpens and that there would be no peace until he was defeated.[56] The commandos duly sought him out and found him (not surprisingly) willing to make peace. Together with three other captains, he accepted a copper-headed cane and a gift of breeding sheep from the colonists, and solemnly promised 'that in future he would steal no livestock from the Dutch, nor do them any other damage, but on the contrary would always live in rest and peace'.[57]

Following the submission of Duijkerpens, quiet returned to the northern frontiers of the colony and remained for a further fifteen years. There were one or two reports of terrible punishments inflicted on 'Hottentot' servants, and several complaints that livestock had been misappropriated,[58] but in general it appears that the 'several little kraals' of 'tame Hottentots' in the Roggeveld and Onder Bokkeveld lived interspersed among the Dutch in relative tranquillity.[59] By the time that open conflict broke out again in the 1770s the colony had spread eastward along the

Escarpment to the Nuweveld and the Camdeboo[60] and northward into the arid Karoo, following the course of the Fish and the Sak Rivers.[61]

If the oral tradition is to be believed, an incident which took place in the Hantam, involving a man named Andries Jacobs (a *knecht* in the service of meat contractor Jacobus van Reenen) and a 'Bushman' captain named Hacqua ('meaning "Horse" from his swiftness in running') was the immediate cause of the 'disasters' which befell the frontier in the 1770s. The two men had quarrelled (allegedly because Jacobs had abducted the captain's wife) and the captain had killed Jacobs and stolen his cattle. The commando sent out to avenge Jacobs' death had attacked Hacqua's kraal 'and put several persons to death'.[62] This event (according to tradition) was the spark which lit the fires of robbery and riot right across the frontier, causing a conflagration which would not be extinguished for a further thirty years:

The Commando had scarcely left their country [reported an Englishman who visited the Hantam in 1824], when the whole race of Bushmen along the frontier simultaneously commenced a system of predatory and murderous incursions against the colonists, from the Kamiesberg to the Stormberg . . . These depredations were retaliated by fresh commandos, who slew the old without pity, and carried off the young into bondage. The commandos were then avenged by new robberies and murders; and thus mutual injuries have been accumulated, and mutual rancour kept up to the present day.[63]

The traditional account, with its focus on a single catalytic incident, does not address the deeper causes of the unrest which swept the frontier in the 1770s, but it does make the point that the renewed outbreak of hostilities was remembered as a sudden phenomenon, rather than as the culmination of years of strife. The contemporary record lends support to this view: 'It occurs to me', wrote Swellengrebel in October 1776, 'that our inhabitants owe this discomfort to their unfriendliness towards the Hottentots, because formerly they ["the Hottentots"] lived among our people and then all at once they gathered together and began to attack the farms.'[64] The tradition's emphasis upon conspiracy and co-ordinated action, by contrast, may be more difficult to substantiate. There is no doubt, as we shall see below, that the socio-political structures of Khoisan communities of the northern frontier underwent drastic change under the impact of European expansion, but there is little if any evidence of co-operation on the scale suggested here. It should be noted, moreover, that, contrary to tradition, the first reports of unrest emanated from the north-east frontier and not from the Hantam, where the dispute between Jacobs and Captain Hacqua had allegedly occurred.

The alarm was first sounded in April 1770 by the *veldcorporaal* Adriaan van Jaarsveld who was then living in the Sneeuberge 'beyond the Salt

River, behind the Coup'. 'The Hottentots residing thereabouts', he reported, 'had robbed the farmer Casper Schols of thirty-four cattle.' The commando sent after them had shot six and recovered the carcasses of the stolen cattle. 'The remaining Hottentots being found lying near the cattle of another farmer, David van Heerden, they were there taken prisoners, excepting two, who, as they would not surrender, were then shot.'[65] In April the following year Van Jaarsveld sent word that 'the Hottentots living thereabouts had become so wicked that on several farms they had surrounded the houses at night and tried to break into them'.[66] They had stolen 900 sheep from Jacob Joubert, murdered three of his servants and 'shot his house full of arrows from the outside'. The inhabitants had fled with their livestock and it was left to the *veldcorporaal* and a handful of men to give chase; in the ensuing battle 'ninety two of that tribe ["Hottentots"] were killed'.[67]

In 1772 the first reports of disturbances in the Nuweveld and Roggeveld reached the authorities in Stellenbosch. On 10 April the Landdrost of Stellenbosch wrote that Jacob de Klerk, *veldcorporaal* in the Nuweveld, had informed him that the Bushmen had carried off 102 cattle and 519 sheep from farmers in the area; he had raised a commando to go after them 'and shot fifty-one of them, without, however, having recovered any of the stolen cattle'.[68] Then came the news that in two separate incidents runaway servants had collected together and attacked the dwellings of Europeans: in the Agter Roggeveld, the burgher Jan Hendrik Tuytman and his wife and daughter had been shot by the servants of Adriaan Louw, and in the Hantam, Christiaan Bock had been surprised in his bed by 'a gang of Hottentots' led by his former servant Claas.[69] In October 1772 Gerrit van Wijk, *veldcorporaal* in the Agter Roggeveld, reported that the Bushmen had stolen eighty-eight cattle from him, 'of which he retook thirty-nine and . . . with a commando which went out thereupon, shot thirty-one Bosjesmans'.[70] By December 1773 appeals for assistance were reaching Stellenbosch from all quarters of the Roggeveld and the Hantam. The inhabitants of those parts, it was noted, had made known that

they were not only constantly plundered of their livestock by the congregated gangs of Bosjesmans Hottentots, who maintained themselves in the mountains, but that those villains had proceeded to such extreme violence, that they had murdered their cattle herds in the fields, without their being enabled, in consequence of the great distance between their respective habitations, to assist each other in opposing the said robbers . . .[71]

Van Jaarsveld, meanwhile, continued to warn of 'the mischief and molestation of the Hottentots' in the Sneeuberge. 'They push in so', he wrote in April 1773, 'that the innermost suffer as much injury as the outermost.' The worst time was in spring and summer, from September to

April. This was the rainy season along the Escarpment and 'not a suitable time to attack them', because (though Van Jaarsveld does not mention it) the horses were afflicted by sickness after the rains[72] and during the warm summer nights the Bushmen could make do without fire and hence were not easily discovered in the trackless veld.[73] In winter, by contrast, commandos could operate with more success, 'because they [the robbers] cannot possibly do without fire then on account of the cold, by day as well as by night, which will enable us to discover them and get at them'.[74] Van Jaarsveld therefore requested permission 'to attack, at the proper time, the nearest of the kraals by which we are so plagued, and to shoot them, for we cannot wait until they steal again, because so many people are thus ruined, for we can never recapture anything, because they leave none of the stolen cattle alive'.[75] His winter commando must have availed little, however, for the following year, in June, he reported that 'the stealing daily becomes worse and the people on the Sneeuwberg are of one mind to abandon their farms'. He again requested permission to lead an expeditionary force, this time to the Zeekoe River, 'which is a place of concealment for all the thieves that escape from the fight'.[76]

By then, however, the authorities in Stellenbosch had decided that something more substantial should be done to halt the descent into chaos on the colony's borders. The beleaguered frontiersmen should be 're-established by the strong hand, and thereafter also maintained in the peaceful possession of their places'.[77] To this end, the combined Boards of Heemraden and Militia Officers resolved to send a 'general expedition', consisting of three commandos under the overall leadership of the Veld-corporaal Godlieb Rudolph Opperman,[78] 'to attack the robbers from all sides, in their dens and lurking places, and to reduce them either to a permanent state of peace and quiet, or otherwise, in case of necessity, entirely to destroy them'.[79] The combined force would be drawn from every ward on the frontier and would consist of 100 Europeans and 150 'faithful Bastard and other Hottentots'.[80] The officials set great store by the inclusion of the Hottentots, for without them it was deemed 'quite impossible' to trace the robbers and attack them in their mountain fast-nesses.[81] Their presence was all the more valued since no help could be expected from the arable districts, where the inhabitants lived in fear of 'murder and robbery by the slaves'.[82]

The three commandos took the field in the spring of 1774.[83] The first commando, led by Nicolaas van der Merwe, assembled in the Ceres Karoo and described a broad circle in an anti-clockwise direction, moving east-ward through the Moordenaars Karoo and the Koup, travelling along the foot of the Escarpment to the Dwyka River and thence northward through the Nuweveldberge to the lower reaches of the Sak River, returning south-westward through the Roggeveld and the Tanqua Karoo. The spies sent out at each stage of the journey tracked down seventeen 'Bushman' bands, four in the Koup, two in the Nuweveldberge and the remainder in the vicinity of the upper Sak River; one band surrendered and the others were attacked, mostly without prior warning. In all, Van der Merwe's commando killed 129 'Bushmen' and took seventy-one captives. His men suffered one casualty: Okkert van Schalkwyk died of a leg wound from a poisoned arrow.[84]

The second commando, under Gerrit van Wyk, ranged the dry Driedoringveld north-east of the Hantam, following the course of the Fish and lower Sak Rivers. Here the spies discovered nine camps, though in two cases the occupants had fled. The seven bands which were cornered by the commando offered fierce resistance, rolling stones down upon their assailants and showering them with arrows. The commando found evidence of stolen livestock on only one occasion, in a camp on the Honingbergs Vlakte. The occupants refused to surrender but, 'having ensconced themselves behind the fence of the kraal, shot Gerrit Bastert Minie through the hat'.[85] 'Therefore', the diarist records, with inscrutable logic, 'shot eight.' In all, 105 Khoisan were shot dead (among them two who had allegedly been implicated in the murder of Andries Jacobs) and thirty-one taken prisoner.[86]

The losses inflicted by Opperman's commando, charged with attacking the Khoisan behind the Sneeuberge, were even greater; his original report has been lost, but it seems that he met with fierce resistance and, as he saw it, was 'compelled to resort to force'. His men killed 265 Khoisan and captured 129.[87]

In sum then, the operations of the 'general expedition' had removed more than 700 people – men, women and children – by death or capture, from the Khoisan communities behind the Escarpment. This was a loss seven times greater than that suffered by the Khoisan of the Sandveld and Bokkeveld in 1739, yet it elicited an entirely different response. On only three occasions could anyone be found to assume the title of 'captain' under the auspices of the VOC;[88] most of those to whom overtures were made failed to appear at the appointed place,[89] while one 'Hottentot prisoner' refused Opperman's approaches on the grounds that 'his tribe would kill him' if he accepted the proffered staff of office.[90] And within months of the departure of the General Commando, the raids began again with renewed intensity.

In February 1775, for example, Opperman (who now held the permanent title of Field-Commandant) reported that on the Sneeuberge, in the division of Veldwagtmeester Adriaan van Jaarsveld, 'the Bushmen were stealing and robbing in a fearful manner'; Andries van der Walt had made a commando against them and captured eighty-two, but they had escaped during the night and attacked the waggon in which their bows and arrows were held.[91] By March, Van der Walt was asking for another 'great commando', as it had become 'almost impossible for the people to dwell in the Sneeuwberg'.[92]

In the Onder Roggeveld, the operations of the General Commando appear to have secured a brief respite for the colony, but by the autumn of 1776 Veldwagtmeester Willem Steenkamp was obliged to report that the troubles had begun again: at J. Louw's a slave had been murdered, three horses killed, and eighty-two oxen and 200 sheep stolen. At the place of C. Mouton, 'when [the family was] sitting at supper with the door open, they shot arrows into the house, and wounded a slave girl and a Hottentot'.[93] The house of J. Mouton had been broken into and its contents destroyed, and if help did not come soon the Veldwagtmeester and all his neighbours would be forced to flee.[94]

Neither was the Nuweveld free of depredations: in January 1776, fifty-two cattle were taken from Pieter Ernst Kruger *d'oude* and driven north across the Sak River, where rain effaced their tracks.[95] And things were no better in the Hantam. In mid-May Gerrit van Wyk (the same that had led the western section of the General Commando in 1774) sent word of his distress to Veldwagtmeester Adriaan van Zyl:

the Bushmen attacked my farm last night, they surrounded and shot upon all the straw huts, they cruelly murdered three Hottentot children in the huts, and severely wounded my Wittebooy; the very dogs and the whole premises are full of arrows; we have had to keep them off the whole night by firing on them. My goats stood in the cow kraal, from which they have taken them, and they are off with them, 249 goats . . . Whether they have taken any sheep I do not yet know, I had enough to do to save our lives.[96]

Evidently Sparrman was not exaggerating when he noted in January 1776 that 'the Boshies-men grew bolder every day, and seemed to increase in numbers, since people had with greater earnestness set about extirpating them'.[97]

The intensity and sustained character of this resistance raises many questions. Why did these people fight so long and so hard where others before them had given way within a matter of months? Why did they wait until the 1770s before opposing the spread of the colony (when, as we have seen, there had been a settler presence along the Escarpment since the 1750s)? What was the extent of co-operation among them? And what was the secret of their resilience in the face of such terrible losses? It seems to me that these questions lead back to the larger one raised at the end of the last chapter: who were these mountain raiders? Can we, in any given case, arrive at a more precise understanding of their identity than that already suggested by their designation as 'Bushmen'?

It should be noted that the problem of identity has not always been a central issue for historians concerned with the 'Bushman Wars' of the 1770s. Even Nigel Penn, who has always resisted an over-hasty blurring of distinctions between hunters and herders, has largely avoided it, preferring to explain the escalating violence of that period in terms of a generalised 'environmental crisis' affecting all Khoisan across the length and breadth of the frontier. 'Competition for resources', he writes, 'reached a climax towards the end of the 1760s and co-incided with an increasing demand for livestock by the VOC.'[98] The major factors at work, he suggests, were increases in the settler population and in the size of its flocks and herds. These demographic pressures induced the trekboers to strike deeper into the summer-rainfall areas behind the Escarpment than they had done heretofore, thereby encroaching on the territories of Khoisan communities north of the Sak River and (it is implied) depriving them of much-needed access to the better-watered 'all-season rainfall corridor' along the Escarpment.[99] Penn identifies these communities as mostly San, though their 'ranks . . . were indeed augmented with Khoikhoi resisters',[100] but he says little about the identity or location of specific groups. Thus, despite his stress on the ecological importance of the Escarpment, he leaves his readers uncertain as to why the expansion of white settlement met with such fierce resistance exactly when and where it did, and not further north for example.

Penn's reticence on the subject of group identity and settlement patterns is, as he himself acknowledges, largely dictated by the scarcity of information about the country immediately north of the Escarpment in the eighteenth century: travellers' accounts are few and archaeological research in the Hantam and Roggeveld almost non-existent.[101]

For an earlier generation of historians, by contrast, the question of the raiders' identity was not seen as a problem at all, despite the absence of detailed information. Thus Professor P. J. van der Merwe attributed the rise in the tempo of conflict in the 1770s to the proximity of the newly settled districts to 'the real Bushmanland', which lay north of the Sneeuberge, along the valley of the Zeekoe River.[102] The Bushmen were hungry, he added, and hence they responded to the temptation newly arrived on their doorstep, as it were.

In a paper written more than ten years ago, I took issue with Van der Merwe's explanation, on the grounds that 'Bushmen' (in the sense intended by Van der Merwe) and 'Hottentots' could not be distinguished. I also (somewhat contradictorily) presented evidence which suggested the presence of Khoekhoe along the Escarpment during the last quarter of the eighteenth century.[103] Since then, however, I have had access to the work of Professor Garth Sampson of the Zeekoe Valley Archaeological Project (ZVAP) and Van der Merwe's conclusions now appear in a new light.

Sampson has shown that the valley of the Zeekoe River has been periodically inhabited by modern humans and their archaic ancestors for more than a quarter of a million years.[104] During cold dry periods (some of which endured for tens of thousands of years) the valley was abandoned and during warm wet phases it was reoccupied.[105] Sampson now believes that the final occupation episode commenced some 4,000 years ago, following a mid-Holocene abandonment which, it seems, lasted for some millennia.[106] Throughout this period the valley supported a much larger population than during any preceding episode, but the greatest increase seems to have taken place about 1,000 years ago, at the time when the archaeological residue designated 'Interior Wilton' was replaced by the Smithfield industry.[107] The latter is generally assumed to be the archaeological trace left by the San of the central South African plateau, the immediate forebears of the San or Soaqua of historic times.[108] They apparently thrived and prospered in the environment of the Zeekoe valley, for the ZVAP has mapped 1,198 Smithfield camps and more than 4,000 smaller sites (lookouts, hunting blinds and chipping stations) in the central and upper valley.[109] Sampson notes that this was 'a massive increase' over earlier site numbers, and suggests that it may best be accounted for in terms of 'a population incursion into the valley' around 1,000 AD.[110]

Smithfield camps were positioned on the more accessible dolerite hills and ridges within easy reach of a permanent spring or, in the case of the central valley, within 1 km of the river bed.[111] Sampson suggests that an extended family of hunter-foragers would have ranged over a sizeable sub-territory, containing from four to seven springs or waterholes.[112] Sub-territories in turn formed part of much larger band territories. In the upper valley, the ZVAP has provisionally identified at least seven band territories with the aid of a detailed analysis of the decorative motifs on thousands of Smithfield pottery sherds collected from 972 camp sites. These territories appear to have been occupied over a period of some 400 years, c. 1300–1700 AD.[113] The identification of band territories in the central valley has not yet been attempted, but it seems likely that it supported almost as large a population of hunter-foragers as the upper valley during this period.

The secret of the valley's ability to sustain human occupation on this scale lay primarily in its underground water supplies. The Karoo flats behind the Sneeuberge are criss-crossed by dolerite hills and ridges which act as subterranean dams and dykes, trapping underground water and forcing it to the surface in many places. Thus were formed the numerous spring eyes which acted as magnets for human settlement.[114] In other respects the valley was fairly typical of the Central Upper Karoo: with a rainfall of less than 400mm per annum, the major rivers flowed only in summer and autumn, although the action of the underground springs created perennial meres and hippo pools (*zeekoegate*) up and down the Zeekoe River.[115] These were home not only to hippopotami, but also to water birds, fish, freshwater mussels and crabs.[116] The vegetation, even then, was an arid mix of seasonal grasses and Karoo scrub, with precious few trees on the flat plains; however, as in other parts of the Central Karoo, it was highly nutritious and could support enormous herds of game.[117] Plant foods were less abundant than in warmer climes, but a number of edible roots and tubers could be found on the hills and ridges where the hunters made their camps and edible grass seeds could be gathered on the plains.[118] In sum, then, the country behind the Sneeuberge was once a favourable habitat for man: 'its modern bleak appearance', writes Sampson, 'is highly misleading'.[119]

Strictly speaking, the findings of the ZVAP cannot be made to apply to areas beyond the immediate reach of the project, except in a very general sense. Since no comparable archaeological survey has been made of the country further west, behind the mountains of the Nuweveld and Rogge- veld, the historian is advised to tread very carefully. However it is tempting to consider the possibility that there were similar areas, equally favoured by hunter-foragers, behind the western rim of the Escarpment. In par- ticular, a number of clues in the historical record point to the valley of the Sak River and its tributaries as a region which may have held similar attractions for the San in pre-colonial times. The reader will already have noted that in 1774 the Sak River was a focus for the operations of commandos from the Roggeveld and Hantam.[120] And in 1776 Comman- dant Opperman again received reports that 'the Bushmen' had gathered at the Sak River, where they had so fortified themselves that he could do 'nothing against them'.[121] In addition, there is the information gathered in 1808 by Colonel Richard Collins, sent by the British authorities to report on the 'Bosjesman nation'. Collins wrote from the Hantam:

in the course of my journey I have seen several persons who remember the events of more than half a century. They relate that the colonists began to settle in this part of the country about sixty years ago, when they found it inhabited by the Hotten- tots, who readily entered their service. The Bosjesmen resided at that time beyond the Zak River, with the exception of a few kraals that lived a little on this side of it, for the convenience of exchanging skins for the tobacco of the Hottentots, who procured that article from the colonists in the Bokkeveld, south of the Karoo . . .[122]

It is true that Collins had an ulterior motive: he wished to justify the northward extension of the colony's boundary, which had just been moved from the Riet to the Sak River, and he was therefore concerned to show that 'the majority of that people ["the Bosjesmen"] had always resided north of the latter river'.[123] But in the course of his argument, he makes an observation which, when read in the context of Sampson's work, is illuminating. Were the colonists to be denied access to the Sak River, he comments, they 'would be deprived of the advantage they derive from the water and pasturage they procure at the former, in seasons where they cannot find them elsewhere'.[124] The Sak River, it seems, may have been a source of water during the dry summer months. In the driest part of the Karoo, this was precious indeed![125] It is true that the region was less well endowed with underground water than the Zeekoe valley; only in the Karreeberge (near present-day Carnarvon), home of the nineteenth-century 'Berg Bushmen', could one find an abundance of springs and fountains. Moreover rainfall seldom exceeded 200mm per annum, and was 'extremely erratic'.[126] However, the undulating plains supported several desert grasses and, west of the river and along its lower course, there were silty pans and flats, which even in the late nineteenth century supported several communities of foragers.[127] Thus while the area may not have rivalled the Zeekoe valley in its ability to support human settlement, it was apparently worth defending.

In addition to documenting the extent of pre-colonial San or Soaqua settlement in the Zeekoe valley, the ZVAP has also confirmed the presence of indigenous pastoralists behind the Escarpment. Again, its findings apply only to the Zeekoe valley, but they are very significant, for they suggest that the inland Khoekhoe presence attested in seventeenth-century colonial narratives and in Xhosa oral tradition had deep roots in the past.[128] They also confirm that the close interaction between Khoekhoe and Soaqua observed by Ensign Schrijver in 1689 had a long history. Sampson believes that herders first entered the upper Zeekoe valley (termed Agter Sneeuberg by the Boers) between 850 and 900 AD, that is, at roughly the same time that the Interior Wilton industry was replaced by the Smithfield.[129] The herders appear to have come from the south, through the mountain passes forged by the drainage basins of the Zeekoe's major tributaries. Certainly their major settlements were concentrated in the south-west corner of the valley, where the forage was particularly rich.[130] The ZVAP has mapped more than 299 stone kraals in this area, arranged in clusters of varying size. The two largest clusters are located on the banks of the upper Zeekoe River, and between them are 'secondary clusters of about 7–15 kraals'. 'Tertiary clusters of 3–5 kraals surround some of these', Sampson observes, 'but they also form the only clusters present in the Elandskloof [River] pattern.'[131] 'Lowest in the hierarchy', he concludes, 'are the isolated kraals scattered throughout each drainage basin.'[132] As Sampson notes, this hierarchical settlement pattern has parallels in the ethnographic record, and it seems not unreasonable to suggest that in this case it reflects the occupation of the area by a single chiefdom (though its identity and internal political structure may have changed over time), with the largest kraal clusters being the remains of semi-permanent base camps, occupied on a seasonal basis by the entire tribe, while the secondary and tertiary clusters served as the focus of dispersed camps and the isolated kraals as outlying stock posts.

Analysis of ceramic remains and lithic scatters found in association with some of the kraals points to close interaction between hunters and herders in the upper valley. 'Khoi sherds'[133] tend to predominate within the larger clusters, whereas the outlying stock posts are most commonly associated with Smithfield sherds and tool kits.[134] This suggests the presence of 'client-herders, hunters who periodically grazed livestock on their own territories and returned them to their herder owners at regular intervals', or perhaps a servant class of shepherds in the employ of Khoekhoe.[135] In addition, Smithfield sites containing a proportion of Khoe sherds and other items derived from herder material culture have been found far down the valley, well away from the main concentration of stock kraals, suggesting that contacts between hunters and herders extended over a very wide area.[136] These findings would seem to support the views of Elphick and Schrire with respect to the unstable boundaries and 'dynamic interaction' between hunting and herding lifeways,[137] and indeed they do, though Sampson's preliminary findings suggest that the influence of herders did not extend to the northern reaches of the valley and that even within the herder-dominated upper valley some hunters preferred to withdraw to the mountainous fringes rather than adopt a pastoralist lifestyle.[138] However Sampson believes that the herders disappeared from the valley (or 'lost all their stock') some time between 1500 and 1700 AD, that is, well before the coming of Europeans.[139] Following the departure of the herders, the valley seems to have been reclaimed by hunter-foragers, who remained in occupation until they were displaced by the colonists.[140]

The work of the ZVAP brings us closer than ever before to an understanding of the identity of the people 'on the other side' of the bitterly contested north-eastern frontier. It is important to stress, in light of the criticisms voiced by Elphick and Schrire, that the picture which emerges is not one of 'uninterrupted continuity between aboriginal . . . hunter communities' and those of the eighteenth-century historical record.[141] On the contrary, the impression created is of a long and complex process of change, involving adaptation, assimilation and restructuring of hunter-forager societies in response to changing social and environmental circumstances. The San who inhabited the valley in the wake of the herder withdrawal were not necessarily the direct descendants of the first Smithfield settlers, in either a cultural or a biological sense. Their settlement patterns had altered in response to the presence of the herders and they had adopted new techniques and subsistence strategies, among them, possibly, the keeping of livestock on a small scale.[142]

Furthermore, we may surmise that during the century immediately preceding European settlement on the Escarpment, their territories had been penetrated by a growing tide of refugees, among whom were both Soaqua and Khoekhoe who had been dislodged by the northward advance of the colonial frontier. The refugee influx apparently produced unprecedented ecological stresses and provoked far-reaching changes in social structure. Former territorial boundaries collapsed as the resource base diminished and bands began to be reorganised along entirely new lines.[143] The direct incursions of Europeans hastened this process of breakdown and reorganisation, which was to end with the eventual disappearance (or rather, cultural extinction) of the aboriginal inhabitants of the Escarpment.

European accounts of the 'Bushmen' of the Sneeuberge and De Bruins Hoogte date mainly from the mid-eighteenth century and thus may be expected to reflect this growing confusion. Nevertheless the majority of these accounts do tend to support the belief that this part of the Escarpment was predominantly occupied by hunter-foragers at the time of colonial contact.

By 1752, when Ensign Beutler made his journey beyond the eastern borders of the colony, the mountain people had already become known among the colonists as the 'Little Chinese' or 'Chinese Hottentots', though the Khoekhoe whom Beutler met called them 'd'Gauas'.[144] According to Beutler's diarist Haupt, their country began west of 'the country of the Bosjesmans', in the mountains surrounding the Cradock basin.[145] In their lifestyle they resembled the 'Bosjesmans', who 'lived more poorly than the Hottentots, since they had no livestock whatsoever', but the 'Chinese' were more adept with bow and arrow.[146] They were 'also a sort of Hottentot', Haupt explained, but smaller of stature and more fearful. They would flee at the very sight of a European or even of a Hottentot wearing a hat, and were so fleet of foot that horses could not overtake them.[147] Their language, too, was different from that of the Khoekhoe who had accompanied the expedition from Swellendam.[148] They were great lovers of painting, Beutler noted, and they 'painted all over on suitable rocks . . .', 'portraits of wild horses, baboons and people in varied postures, in red, white and black, some were very well executed and others again not . . .'.[149]

Sparrman, who did not see their paintings, gave a less favourable account of them[150] and Gordon, who did, pronounced them 'fair, but as a whole poor and exaggerated'. 'I can easily understand', he wrote, 'why it is said they had drawn unknown animals, because one had to make many guesses as to what they were.'[151] However both men confirmed Beutler's identification of the artists as 'Chinese', though Gordon questioned his use of the alternative term 'd'Gauas' (Figs. 6 and 7):

The farmers call them the Oeswana Hottentot People or Chinese. For this reason I do not know what to believe of the Dgaawas People mentioned in Beutler's journey. They ['Chinese'] speak Hottentot but their dialect as well as many of their words, though pronounced with clicks, differs from the others, so that they do not understand each other much.[152]

According to Sparrman, some colonists had told him that a distant branch of 'this yellow-skinned nation', situated eleven days' journey north-east of De Bruins Hoogte, on the Tsomo River, was 'occupied in the grazing and rearing of cattle'; but Gordon, who travelled some distance down the valley of the Zeekoe River and reached the banks of the Orange via the Bamboesberge to the east, found no evidence of cattle-rearing among the 'Chinese' of those parts.[153] Certainly it was widely believed among the colonists that the mountain people kept no livestock: 'with respect to the so-called Camdeboo Mountains', reported the Landdrosts and Heemraden of Swellendam and Stellenbosch in 1770, 'in those countries, there are no other inhabitants than wild Bushmen and Hottentots who possess no cattle, and who must subsist solely by the game in the fields . . .'.[154]

However at the foot of the Suurberg, half an hour's journey north of Johannes Jurgen de Beer's farm, De Vreede, on the Swart River, Gordon had observed a 'round hill of stones', 6 m in diameter, which he identified as 'the grave of one of the chiefs of the Camdeboo Hottentots (called the Korana People)', who had been 'killed here by an elephant'. 'There are none of these people here any more', he observed, 'except a few with the farmers.'[155] Sampson has demonstrated that small piles of stones could as reasonably be associated with hunter-foragers as with pastoralists, for the San used them to anchor windbreaks.[156] Nevertheless a cairn of this size was almost certainly the creation of Khoekhoe and the sketch made by Gordon (showing cattle-horns atop the pile of stones) clearly associates this one with a cattle-keeping community. The picture is further complicated by an enigmatic reference further on in Gordon's journal in which he notes that

the Hottentots who are on the Sneeuw Bergen and Fish River with the farmers call themselves there nothing but Cora (thus Coranas in the plural). All these Hotten-

Figure 6   *Head of Housouana man*, by François le Vaillant, in Library of Parliament, *François le Vaillant, traveller in South Africa, 1781–1784*, 2 vols., Cape Town: Library of Parliament, 1973.

tots are called "Hei 'Hei Tini' which means 'People who go without a covering in front of their genitals'. Saw some of them with the Caffers and with our farmers but they were all true, so called Bushman-Hottentots.[157]

Six years later, the French ornithologist François le Vaillant came upon two groups of Khoekhoe in the Camdeboo. At the foot of the Tandjesberg

Figure 7   *Head of Housouana woman*, by François le Vaillant, in Library of Parliament, *François le Vaillant, traveller in South Africa, 1781–1784*, 2 vols., Cape Town: Library of Parliament, 1973.

he found a community of some hundred people with a hundred cattle 'and perhaps twice that number of sheep'. They had been six months in the area, having removed there from a more westerly part of the Camdeboo, seeking to escape the 'persecutions' of the Boers, for whom they harboured 'the most inveterate and sanguinary hatred'.[158] Further west, on the banks of the Swart River, near where Gordon had found the 'Hottentot Captain's grave', Le Vaillant met 'sixteen Hottentots with their arms and baggage', who were going to join the group at the Tandjesberg. 'They had been compelled to this emigration', he noted, 'by formidable troops of Bushmen, who were carrying fire and sword through the Camdeboo, and burning the plantations in order to carry away the ammunition, arms and whole riches of the inhabitants.'[159]

One might infer from the above that when Europeans first penetrated the area, pastoralist settlements were confined to the valleys and plains at the foot of the Escarpment, while the mountains themselves and the Zeekoe valley behind (the Agter Sneeuberg) were the preserve of hunter-foragers. Given the inability of the mountain pastures to sustain stock throughout the year,[160] and the findings of Sampson with respect to the recent archaeology of the Zeekoe valley, this seems a reasonable supposition.

However it should be noted that freeburgher *veldwagtmeesters* sometimes referred in their reports to the presence of livestock in 'Bushman' encampments *behind* the Escarpment. As a rule, 'Bushman' raiders destroyed those beasts which could not keep pace with them in their flight[161] and, it was believed, consumed the remaining booty as soon as they returned to camp,[162] yet living animals were found among them: 'On 26th May', reported the leader of an expedition to Zeekoegat in the Renosterberg, 'we attacked the kraal, shot 27 dead and caught an ox . . .'.[163] 'On the 29th', wrote another militiaman, 'the spies came upon a kraal and shot 11 of them and captured 9 and found 5 cattle and 13 goats . . . on the 5th we trekked to the Dreunfontein with the horses and there a big kraal which still had much livestock fled before us and we followed them as far as the horses could go . . .'[164] And in the winter of 1786, during a sanguinary expedition through the Zeekoe valley, the Oud-Commandant Dawid de Villiers reported that near De Vlakfonteijn his spies had discovered a kraal containing 'a great many Hottentots, who had slaughtered many cattle, heifers and also mature cows, and had taken six oxen with them in their flight'. Further north, on the Bosjesmansberg near De Mijnfonteijn, De Villiers' men attacked a kraal in which they found twelve cattle alive and seventeen dead.[165]

References such as these cannot be taken as proof of a herder presence in the Agter Sneeuberg – they may merely indicate temporary 'storage' of the surplus booty of hunter- robbers (and in any case the frequent raids of the commandos made it impossible for would-be herders to keep stock for long in these regions) – but they do confirm that the robbers were adept at driving domestic stock over great distances, for animals were found both dead and alive as far afield as the Agter Renosterberg and Bamboesberg.[166]

Furthermore, while the records kept by militiamen may not provide evidence of a herder presence, they do testify to the profound social changes taking place behind the Escarpment. They show, for example, that 'Bushman' bands might be several hundred strong. Thus in March 1776 Veldcorporaal Jacob de Clercq of the Sneeuberge was obliged to call for reinforcements against a 'multitude of Bushmen' ensconced in caves in the mountains. They had tried to overrun the Dutch, he reported, 'but they [the Dutch] were brave and shot 111 of these robbers'.[167] In May Veldcommandant Opperman warned that 'the robbers have collected together by thousands' in the Sneeuberge,[168] and in December Carel van der Merwe wrote from his farm on the headwaters of the Buffels [Kariega] River that the Bushmen were round him 'day and night'. 'Oh Heavenly King', he implored, 'look down upon us to our comfort and to the terror of our haughty enemies, for murder and riot are daily getting more and more the upper hand . . . we are much too weak to oppose the numbers that have collected together in hundreds and thousands and advanced against us.'[169] The raiders were traced to a 'great kraal', encamped in the Duivelsberg beyond the Waaij Hoek.[170] They were attacked at the New Year and sixty-two were shot or captured, 'but the greatest part escaped, having seen us from a distance'.[171]

Three months later Veldwagtmeester Hendrik Meintjies van den Berg reported finding a kraal in the Agter Sneeuberg 'in which there were 300 Hottentots, but having too few men, they only shot 20'.[172] And in November, during his visit to the rock shelter at De Schanse Kraal, Gordon was informed that '400 sometimes gathered' there.[173] These large congregations of people were apparently not a phenomenon of the 1770s only, for nine years later, near the Verjaarsfonteijn, Dawid de Villiers' commando discovered 'a Great kraal which had divided into three parts, the largest of which alone comprised of 56 huts'.[174]

Aggregations of people on the scale suggested here would appear to have been without precedent in pre-colonial times. Archaeologists tend to be cautious with regard to estimates of group size among prehistoric foragers, but most would agree that a band or camp seldom if ever comprised more than sixty people. Tim Maggs, for example, who has compared the sizes of bands depicted in prehistoric rock paintings with 'kraal' sizes recorded by the commandos of 1774 and band sizes recorded

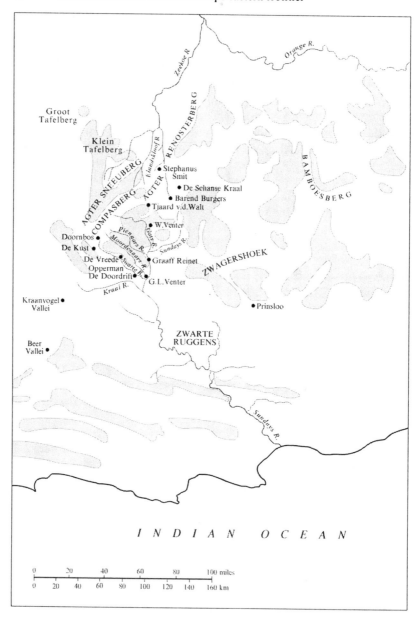

Map 3   The north-east frontier, *c.* 1779

by anthropologists among the present-day !Kung of the Kalahari, has concluded that, in all but a few cases, band sizes fell within a range of either eight to twelve members or twenty to twenty-five members;[175] while David Lewis-Williams, drawing on ethnographic material compiled by the Bleek family, has reached the same conclusions with respect to the /Xam of the arid Karoo.[176] 'Larger groups of seventy or even a hundred were reported', Lewis-Williams adds, 'but these were exceptional and might have resulted from several groups being forced to unite in opposition to the white farmers' advance.'[177]

It is known that camp sizes fluctuated in response to seasonal changes in the environment. Thus, for example, forager camps in the southern Drakensberg appear to have amalgamated in spring and early summer, when hunters moved to higher altitudes in pursuit of migratory antelope, and dispersed during the cold winter months, when they returned to the lower regions;[178] the San of the Zeekoe valley apparently followed an opposite pattern, gathering in larger camps during winter and spring (when water was scarce) and separating into smaller groups in summer.[179]

It seems unlikely, however, that environmental factors alone could account for gatherings of the size reported by the Boer commandos. A more likely explanation is that suggested by Lewis-Williams and by the commandos themselves – that the Bushmen had gathered together express-ly to attack them. Lewis-Williams has laid great stress on the role of inter-camp co-operation in the pre-colonial context; no camp, he observes, could exist in isolation from its neighbours, 'wider social relationships were necessary to afford members of the camp access to more distant resources'.[180] These relationships were based primarily on kinship (both consanguinal and affinal) and upon formalised exchange patterns such as the *hxaro* gift-giving system among the present-day !Kung of the Kalahari. They allowed an easy coming and going between camps, as kin visited one another, sometimes changing residence for long periods.[181] There thus existed an extensive inter-camp network or 'band nexus', based on recipro-cal obligation, which could be activated in a time of crisis. When the people of the Escarpment were faced with the common peril of trekboer expan-sion, this network may have served as the basis for the emergence of new forms of inter-camp co-operation.

There were signs, too, that new or modified forms of leadership were emerging on the Escarpment. It is generally agreed that the southern San had no chiefs or headmen.[182] Yet several references in the journals of travellers and commandos suggest that leaders of some sort did exist among the mountain people in the eighteenth century. In 1752 Beutler's diarist had referred to a 'general chief' of the d'Gauas, named Goechoe Moua.[183] This chief may have been a mythical figure, for the expedition

never found him, but the 'captains' named by later diarists were undoubtedly mortal. In September 1774, for example, Adriaan van Jaarsveld
was told by the children he captured during an attack on a fugitive band in
the Rodeberg that 'a captain' was among the forty-four people shot by his
men, 'but not the chief captain who governed over the whole Seacow
River'.[184] And in 1777, during his passage through the Sneeuberge, Gordon learnt from Veldwagtmeester Dawid Schalk van der Merwe Dawid-
zoon that 'these so-called Bushmen or Chinese have a famous chief called
Koerikei, or "bullet-escaper"'.[185] This Koerikei had not minced his words
with Van der Merwe: 'What are you doing in my land?' he asked, standing
out of range upon a krans: 'You have taken all the places where the eland
and other game live. Why did you not stay where the sun goes down, where
you first came from?'[186] Van der Merwe asked him, Gordon continued,
'why he did not live in peace as before, and why he did not go hunting with
them and live with them (he had been living with the farmers) and whether
he did not have enough country as it was?' But Koerikei replied 'that he did
not want to lose the country of his birth and that he would kill their
herdsmen, and that he would chase them all away'. And 'as he went off he
further said that it would be seen who would win'.[187]

In sum, then, it seems that we can identify the anonymous raiders of the
Escarpment with greater precision than one might have hoped. They were,
I have suggested, predominantly San or Soaqua. However, it is important
to stress that, while it may indeed be possible to trace their cultural origins
all the way back to the eleventh-century 'Smithfield' inhabitants of the
Central Karoo, they had undergone many changes since that time. They
had had several centuries of contact with immigrant herder communities,
which almost certainly involved biological as well as cultural interchange.
And since the beginning of the eighteenth century they had been obliged to
play host to a growing number of refugees (some of whom must have been
dispossessed Khoekhoe) from the expanding European colony. By the late
1760s they were feeling the direct pressure of European expansion as the
colonists appropriated new grazing farms on the plains behind the Escarpment. The resultant ecological stress and the need for defence of life and
limb produced major changes in social organisation: former territorial
boundaries collapsed, band sizes increased and new forms of leadership
emerged.

One could perhaps argue that so changed a people deserve a new name –
that they should no longer be known by historians and archaeologists as
San or Soaqua, but rather, as Shula Marks suggested in 1972, as Khoisan,
so as to indicate the mutability of their status.[188] It is my contention,
however, that this term is unnecessarily ambiguous. If they must be
renamed, it is perhaps best that we call them simply mountain people, for,

whatever their ethnic origins, the mountains of the Central Karoo had become their fortress and their refuge as they battled to defend their way of life against an unprecedented threat.

5   Strong things

If it is true, as I have suggested above, that the country into which white stock-breeders had moved since the 1760s was the age-old territory of hunting peoples, then the exchange between Koerikei and Dawid Schalk van der Merwe takes on a more particular meaning than might otherwise be the case. Koerikei himself disappears from the historical stage as suddenly as he had entered it. We shall never know more of him than the brief glimpse afforded us by Robert Jacob Gordon. However, if we allow ourselves to venture once more across disciplinary boundaries, this time following a group of pioneering archaeologists into the realms of contemporary ethnography, we can perhaps gain a deeper insight into the beliefs which underlay Koerikei's brief but impassioned speech in defence of his birthright. Such an exercise comes no more easily to the historian than it did to the archaeologists in whose footsteps she must follow. The use of ethnographic data from other times and places violates one's sense of historical specificity; one must tread carefully lest one's desire to compensate for the lack of data about the beliefs and values of the southern San in the eighteenth century lead one to grasp at generalisations which cannot be sustained in a given context. However, despite these necessary caveats, the historian of frontier conflict in Dutch South Africa should not eschew new insights achieved in sister disciplines: recent discoveries in ethnography and archaeology have revolutionised our understanding of the mental world of the southern San and any history which ignored them would be the poorer for it.

Specifically, it is in the field of rock art research that the breakthroughs have been made. The linguist Wilhelm Bleek had concluded in the 1870s that Bushman rock paintings 'were an attempt, however imperfect', to give expression to 'the ideas which most deeply moved the Bushman mind',[1] but his insights were largely forgotten by subsequent students, who preferred to see the paintings as literal representations of everyday activities or as 'sympathetic magic' designed to aid the hunter.[2] It was not until a hundred years after Bleek's death that archaeologists began a serious study of the symbolic content of the paintings.

Patricia Vinnicombe was among the first to abandon a literal interpretation. In the course of her study of rock paintings in the southern Drakensberg, she discovered that the artists had chosen to paint certain animals, especially the eland, over and over again, while other equally common animals, such as the zebra and wildebeest, did not appear in the paintings at all.[3] The reason, she suggested, was that the paintings were not intended as a 'realistic reflection of the daily pursuits or environment of the Bushmen', as her predecessors had thought, but rather 'reflected a set of values', of which the eland was in some sense the focal point.[4] The eland, she argued, was the Bushman's 'most potent symbol', 'the focus of [his] deepest aesthetic feelings and of his highest moral and intellectual speculations'.[5] It symbolised the 'regulated unity of the Bushman band' and the cohesion of the wider society and, she suggested, the act of painting it over and over again allowed the San to resolve 'the mental conflict' involved in hunting so valued a creature.[6]

Vinnicombe was correct in identifying the eland as a 'central symbol' in the thought of the southern San. But it was another archaeologist, David Lewis-Williams, who found the key to its meaning in the context of the paintings. For it was he who rediscovered the essential similarities, first perceived by Bleek, between the beliefs of historical San communities and the conceptions which informed the work of the prehistoric artists. And in the ethnographic record gathered from Bleek's /Xam informants,[7] together with research conducted over the past four decades among the modern Kalahari San, he found the tools he needed to explain the paintings. His arguments were set out in detail in his first book, *Believing and seeing*, and elaborated in later works.[8] For our purposes, it is his conclusions which are significant: there was, he contended, a common theme in South African rock art which transcended temporal and spatial divisions.[9] Paintings from different regions and different epochs might exhibit variations in style and to some extent in the choice of symbol and metaphor, but nearly all, he argued, were related to the 'central religious experience' of the southern San, the trance or healing dance.[10] This insight was taken up by other scholars and 'shamanistic elements' were indeed found to be common to the rock art of many regions in southern Africa, including areas as widely separated as the south-west Cape and Zimbabwe.[11] It seemed therefore that one could make a convincing case for the existence of a 'pan-San' cosmology or 'cognitive system', the main elements of which were common to all the hunting peoples of southern Africa, both modern and prehistoric.[12]

In recent years the notion of a 'pan-San cognitive system' has been modified somewhat to accommodate a greater awareness of regional and temporal variation. For example, scholars are now more alert to the variable effects on San religious life of interaction with non-San groups, such as Khoekhoe herders in the south-west Cape and Nguni and Sotho farmers in the vicinity of the Drakensberg and Maluti mountains. Thus John Parkington and his colleagues at the University of Cape Town have concluded that the tradition of finely detailed rock painting, so closely associated with shamanistic practices, probably came to an end in the Sandveld region of the south-west Cape more than a thousand years ago, as pastoralism became an established way of life on the coastal plains.[13] The tradition persisted for longer in the mountains east of the Sandveld, but there too it was eventually replaced by a much cruder art consisting of handprints and finger dots. One can only guess at the religious changes associated with these changes in the art. With respect to the Drakensberg and Maluti mountains, the archaeologist Pieter Jolly has recently suggested that a kind of religious syncretism emerged among some San communities as they absorbed the beliefs of their Nguni and Sotho neighbours (to whom they were sometimes related by marriage).[14] Other scholars have pointed to the mutable and 'pervasively ambiguous' nature of San religious traditions and the scope allowed for individual creativity.[15] Criticisms such as these have led Lewis-Williams to modify his original confident description of the commonalities in San religious life as a 'pan-San cognitive system'. He now writes more cautiously that: 'While some beliefs and rituals were clearly intrinsically Bushman and, moreover, shared by numerous Bushman groups, others seem to have a much wider currency; these constitute a subcontinental cognitive set (rather than a system) that was variously expressed in different regions at different times by different ethnic groups.'[16] None the less, despite these recent qualifications, both Lewis-Williams and his critics agree that certain concepts and beliefs were common to hunter-gatherer populations throughout southern Africa, though these beliefs were perhaps not as fixed and standardised as the original formulation may have implied. Chief among these beliefs was the notion of a 'supernatural potency' or spirit power, which could be harnessed by certain individuals (usually not full-time shamans) so as to enter an altered state of consciousness in which healing could be accomplished and external threats averted. In general, this power was activated in the context of the trance or healing dance, which involved every member of the community.

While the belief in spirit power and its activation during trance were the most prominent features of San cosmology, these elements were underpinned, I would suggest, by something even more fundamental: an attitude to reality (an attitude shared with other practitioners of 'shamanistic' religions) in which no clear distinction was made between the religious and the secular, the physical and the metaphysical, the sacred and the profane.

In the words of Harvard psychologist Richard Katz, who spent some time among the !Kung of the Kalahari (also known as the Ju/'hoansi), studying their healing practices:

The life of the spirit is an inextricable aspect of everyday life among the Kung. To say that what in the west are called the 'profane' and 'sacred', or the 'ordinary' and 'extraordinary', are merged in Kung life would obscure the fact that the Kung do not even categorize their experience in such a dualistic fashion in the first place. Such things as the sacred and profane are constantly and playfully mingled in Kung life. 'Religion' as a separate enterprise does not exist for the Kung; it is simply their way of living.[17]

This sense of unity between the material and the spiritual, the sacred and the profane, was inherent in the healing dance, with which prehistoric rock paintings are concerned. Not only were the dancers often the subject of ribald jesting, even as they entered the dangerous state of 'kia', or trance, in which they could establish direct contact with the supernatural,[18] but the potency or 'supernatural energy' activated in the healing trance was channelled through ordinary and familiar objects: animals and (from our point of view) inanimate substances which, while 'sacred' in their capacity as 'strong things' endowed with peculiar potency, were also very much a part of everyday life.[19] Thus the eland antelope, favourite of the trickster god /Kaggen[20] and principal among the 'maieutic creatures' of /Xam trance performance, was also a valued source of food. The southern San believed, according to Lewis-Williams, that the being of a medicine man who achieved trance through the medium of eland potency became in some sense fused with that of the eland, assuming certain of its characteristics. (Hence, Lewis-Williams argues, the prevalence of therianthropic figures with antelope heads and hooves in so many of the Drakensberg rock paintings.[21]) Yet they also took pleasure in hunting and eating the eland.

Other 'strong things', such as bees, locusts, honey, rain, falling stars and the rising sun, were likewise at once natural and supernatural, a source of invisible potency and a means of sustenance in everyday life. The rain might be conceived as masculine or feminine, or as a giant 'rain-animal' whose blood watered the land, yet it was also real, a phenomenon of nature.[22] As Katz has observed with respect to the !Kung, 'symbols are not merely symbolic; they are also real'.[23] And conversely, 'real' things are not merely material objects – they are also symbols and have a spiritual or metaphysical dimension. Put another way, one might say that for the San, man and nature were part of a single moral order.[24] Man was not set apart from the rest of creation; he was a participant in its drama. (Here Sparrman's description of the 'Boshies-men' who 'used in stormy weather to abuse the thunder' and wave their shoes at the lightning comes vividly to mind.[25]) Vinnicombe has written of 'the integration between land and culture' common to hunter-gatherer communities the world over.[26] Like the Australian Aborigines, she suggests, the San held 'a view of the land as inseparable from the process of living and as identical with communal human life'.[27]

Like the Aborigines, the San acknowledged a kinship with the animals they hunted. The /Xam, like the present-day Nharo of the Kalahari, believed in a 'myth of double creation, which states that the people of today were the animals of the past and the animals of today were the dawn-time people'.[28] The first order of creation had been reversed because it was flawed, but the people of today still carried within themselves aspects of their 'dawn-time' animal identity and the animals retained certain human characteristics. The distinction, as the anthropologist Mathias Guenther has observed of the Nharo, 'is by no means clearcut . . . Animals carry within themselves humanness, men animalness – a cogent doctrine of communion between man and beast.'[29] It should not surprise us, then, that the eland could be a source of trance potency for the /Xam, or that medicine men could assume the form of birds or lions during out-of-body travel.[30] For humans and animals were closely linked in a single 'moral community'.[31]

Features of the landscape such as fountains, pans and ridges seem also to have had a metaphorical or symbolic meaning for the southern San. Lewis-Williams has stated that 'the notion of sacred areas is foreign to the San',[32] and indeed it appears that their gods and ancestor spirits were not as closely linked to specific locations as were those of the Australian Aborigines.[33] The /Xam god /Kaggen was omnipresent, like the sky god of the Maluti San, 'not seen with the eyes, but . . . known with the heart'.[34] He was said to be wherever the eland gathered, wherever the powers of man as hunter were in the balance.[35] The spirits of the dead were likewise not attached to a specific site. Bleek's informants spoke of apparitions which appeared without warning, while the present-day !Kung believe that, like the gods, the spirits of the dead live in the sky.[36] There thus appears to have been no equivalent of the Khoekhoe belief that the spirits of the dead hovered about the places where their mortal remains were buried.[37] Nevertheless, many places were associated with other aspects of myth and ritual. For example, Janette Deacon's careful investigation of the testimony of Bleek's informants has revealed a close association between certain hilltops and springs in Bushmanland and nineteenth-century /Xam beliefs related to rainmaking.[38] More recently, Deacon has suggested that the positioning of rock engravings on hilltops and mountains in the Upper Karoo was used to mark places of ritual significance 'and thereby give added meaning to the landscape'.[39] And the Nharo creation myths retold by Mathias Guenther (some of them deliciously bawdy) suggest a similar 'congruence of natural features and mythical structure'.[40]

These examples are drawn from the recent past, and from regions to the north of the Central Karoo Escarpment, and they cannot throw direct light on the meanings which the people of the Camdeboo and the Zeekoe valley attached to their landscape, but they do add weight to the general point which I wish to make: that in the world-view of the southern San, land and culture, matter and spirit, nature and community, were aspects of a whole and could not be separated. For these people, the loss of territory and the violation of hunting grounds entailed more than the loss of livelihood and exile from the places to which memory attached; it was an attack on the symbolic system through which they understood their world. As such, it was an attack on their very being. In the words of an Aboriginal Land Council cited by Patricia Vinnicombe: 'The land is our "bone", not the flesh, because it goes deeper than that. Cultural spirits control our land and if you take away the power to control this land you are taking away our spirit.'[41] Could this be what Koerikei meant?

In 1777, at the time of Gordon's journey, white frontiersmen had not penetrated very deeply into the country behind the Sneeuberge. Several loan-places had been staked out in the Camdeboo, and quite a few more in the mountains themselves, mostly on the tributaries of the Sundays River.[42] But during his descent into the Zeekoe valley, Gordon had noted only three dwellings – those of Tjaard van der Walt, Willem Burgers (actually Barend Burgers) and Stephanus Smit, the latter occupying 'the last farm' on Gordon's route (see Map 3).[43] Moreover, although the Sneeuberge and the 'broken veld' behind were already known as excellent sheep country,[44] the flocks of the first settlers had not yet attained the great size they would reach at the end of the century.[45] In the tax rolls of Stellenbosch in 1777 Tjaard van der Walt was listed as the owner of forty cattle and 300 sheep, while Stephanus Smit declared himself the owner of twenty-four cattle and 150 sheep.[46] The actual size of their stock-holdings may have been three or four times as large,[47] but they were still modest in comparison with the vast flocks of the next generation.

Nevertheless, a small group of settlers with modest livestock holdings could dramatically disturb the ecology of forager communities. Although domestic stock and large game (especially bovids) were attracted by the same kind of pasturage,[48] the introduction of domestic stock was not in itself damaging to the environment – there is little evidence for example that the advent of the Khoekhoe was accompanied by veld damage or a decline in the game population[49] – but in the hands of European colonists, the introduction of cattle and sheep could spell disaster for the fragile

Karoo ecosystem, leading to the disappearance of edible grasses and shrubs, and the growth of unpalatable plants like the renosterbos, which Sparrman found to be widespread in the settled parts of Swellendam district.[50] The colonists, indeed, expected their pastures to deteriorate. They referred to the process revealingly as the 'aging' of the veld and attributed the cause of it to their sins.[51] 'A *veeboer* can scarcely survive', lamented the inhabitants of Swellendam in 1757, 'as much because of the great change in the veld, which is becoming unhealthier for our livestock, as because of the low prices at which we must presently sell our stock.'[52] 'Our inhabitants are from time to time obliged', explained the Landdrost and Heemraden of Stellenbosch some twenty years later, 'on account of the progressive deterioration of the places and pastures in the nearby districts . . . to seek better places in the faraway districts.' They proposed, he continued, to settle in the 'luxuriant pastures' whence the 'good natives or Hottentots' had been driven by the Bushmen, since the latter did not use the veld in a 'tolerable or industrious manner', as the Hottentots had done.[53]

It should not surprise us that the colonists had little regard for the lifeways of hunter-gatherers – their attitudes were mirrored by their European counterparts in other colonies.[54] But had they looked more closely at the farming practices of the pastoralist Khoekhoe whom they professed to commend, they might have discovered that sinfulness was not the only cause of their own destructive impact on the land. Sparrman, always a perceptive observer, came close to the heart of the matter:

> In direct contradiction to the custom and example of the original inhabitants the Hottentots, the colonists turn their cattle out constantly into the same fields, and that too in a much greater quantity than used to graze there in the time of the Hottentots; as they keep not only a number sufficient for their own use, but likewise enough to supply the more plentiful tables of the numerous inhabitants of Cape Town, as well as for the victualling of the ships in their passage to and from the East Indies.

The result, he continued, was the impoverishment of the veld and the encroachment of the renosterbos 'together with several other dry barren shrubs and bushes'. However, 'notwithstanding these inconveniences, the colonists remain immoveable in their stone houses; while, on the contrary, the Hottentots (and this was the case in former times) on the least panic remove their huts and their cattle to another place, so that the grass is nowhere eaten off too close'.[55]

What Sparrman omitted to say, perhaps because he took it so much for granted, was that these contrasting ways of using the land rested on fundamentally different conceptions of landed property. It was not, as

William Cronon has so succinctly observed with respect to the differences between Europeans and Indians in seventeenth-century New England, 'that one had property and the other had none; rather, it was that they loved property differently'.[56] The Khoekhoe, like the San, held land in common; ownership was vested in the chief, but every member of the tribe had unrestricted access to waterholes and pastures within the common territory, except to those which the chief might declare out of bounds during drought.[57] The colonists, by contrast, as explained in chapter 2, were wedded to a system of private land tenure which gave individuals exclusive rights over the territory they had leased from the Company. These rights were not absolute – Cronon's observations concerning the distinction between sovereignty and ownership in New England property systems ('between possession by communities and possession by individuals') are equally applicable to the frontier districts of the Cape, where the Company retained a number of rights over the land it granted on loan – but, in practice, lessees of the Company enjoyed security of tenure and could buy, sell and inherit their loan-farms much as if they were freehold property.[58] The colonial system of land tenure was therefore not only private, but integrally linked to a market in commodities. Land was both commodity and capital and its value was related to the value of its products, which, as Sparrman had noted, were produced for sale as well as for home consumption.[59] Sharing of pastures did occur, but it usually involved the payment of some form of rent, in cash, kind or services.[60] The image of the wandering trekboer, as Guelke has observed, is something of a myth. Such people did exist, as we have seen, often living on the wrong side of the law, taking advantage of abandoned loan-places and the *uijtspanplaatsen* set aside for travellers.[61] In Bushmanland, where there were no perennial springs and rainfall was irregular and unpredictable, a transhumant lifestyle may even have been the norm.[62] But in general, the inhabitants of the pastoral districts kept their loan-farms for many years, and the most desirable sites, with plenty of water and irrigable land, were often occupied for life.[63] Certainly white frontiersmen were obsessed with boundaries – and many a hapless shepherd or cowherd was caught in the crossfire as neighbours battled over access to forage and water.[64]

Given this system of land tenure, a small number of settlers could have a devastating impact on the ecology of indigenous life. The adverse terms of trade which dominated the frontier economy encouraged the *veeboeren* to expand their herds and flocks to a maximum,[65] while the abundance of land (albeit not vacant land) in relation to labour and capital encouraged them to add to their existing landholdings rather than to conserve or improve them.[66]

One might thus say, adapting a phrase used by Martin Legassick, that it was the 'logic of commodities' which drove the *veeboeren* into ever-increasing conflict with the forager communities of the Central Karoo, in so far as it compelled them to consume ever-larger tracts of land. Not only did their way of using the land deplete and damage the veld, but their newly demarcated domains cut across long-established foraging ranges and denied the original owners access to essential resources; resources which, I have argued, were not merely a means to physical survival, but also landmarks on a mental map, essential components of the community's identity. At issue, in Patricia Vinnicombe's illuminating phrase, was 'whether the earth should be considered economic real estate or spiritual reality'.[67]

In the short term, however, the hunting activities of the colonists probably posed more of a threat to forager communities than did the expansion of their landholdings. With the notable exception of elephant hunting, the colonists hunted for the pot rather than pecuniary gain. The 'logic of commodities' was therefore less evident in the hunt than it was with respect to stock-raising. However, even where products of the chase were destined for domestic consumption, the influence of the market could still be felt, for by relying heavily on a diet of fresh and dried venison, hippopotamus 'bacon' and buffalo biltong, the grazier could conserve his precious slaughter stock for the Cape market.

There is ample evidence in the contemporary record of the role played by *wildsvleisch* in the diet of frontier families – Gordon, for example, observed that in the Camdeboo dried venison was used 'like bread'.[68] But the best description of its role in relation to the market is in Thunberg's account of his visit in 1772 to the *veeplaats* of the Oud Heemraad Jacobus Botha *d'oude*, located near the sea-shore at Plettenberg Bay. Botha's place, he wrote, was inhabited by a 'a whole community, consisting of more than fifty Hottentots in the service of this farmer'. The veld round about was 'full of wild buffaloes' and the rafters of the crude farmhouse were 'hung with thick slices of buffalo's flesh, which, being dried and smoked, they ate as hung-beef'.[69] He explained:

Buffaloes were shot here by a Hottentot who had been trained to this business by the farmer, and in this manner found the whole family in meat, without having recourse to the herd. The balls were counted out to him every time he went a shooting, and he was obliged to furnish the same number of dead buffaloes as he received of balls. Thus the many Hottentots that lived here were supported without expense, and without the decrease of the same cattle, which constitute the whole of the farmer's wealth.[70]

Besides being a valuable source of food, wild animals provided the *veeboeren* with a wide range of other articles necessary to the domestic economy. Buffalo skins made excellent halters, harnesses, thongs and *velschoenen;*[71] eland fat ('among the most potent of substances' for the southern San[72]) could be used in the manufacture of candles;[73] hippo and rhinoceros hides provided the materials for whips, and the hides of springbok and other antelope were made up into saddle cloths, sacks, blankets (karosses), thongs and men's clothing.[74] But here too the pressures exerted by the market made themselves felt, for clothing, sacking and cordage had otherwise to be purchased at great expense from the Company or from private merchants in Cape Town.[75]

In either case, whether the purpose of the hunt was domestic manufacture or commercial profit, European hunters were distinguished from their indigenous counterparts by the sheer scale of the destruction they wrought. This was particularly evident among the semi-professional elephant hunters, who ranged far into the interior in their search for ivory.

Elephant hunting had long been a favoured occupation among the younger colonists, for it was lucrative, despite the price controls imposed by the Company.[76] There seems to have been a thriving clandestine trade with the officers of passing ships (both foreign and Dutch) and many a freeburgher risked deportation and a heavy fine to bring undeclared ivory into *De Kaap,*[77] for the ivory trade could lay the foundations of a young man's fortune.[78] Long after his return to Europe, Otto Mentzel recalled the drunken talk of the 'young Africans' who gathered in the taverns of *De Kaap* after handing over their ivory. He had been irritated by their bravado and his credulity had been stretched to the limit by their tales of heroic exploits.[79] But in truth, as he acknowledged, an *elephantstogt* was a dangerous affair. A hunting party could be in the field for three months or more, far beyond the boundaries of the settled districts.[80] By the 1750s the elephant hunters of Swellendam were already ranging beyond Outeniqualand, as far as the banks of the Swartkops and Sundays Rivers,[81] and by the 1770s, as the elephants retreated eastward, experienced hunters like Willem Prinsloo and Petrus Hendrik Ferreira had begun to venture across the Orange River and thence south-east into Thembuland.[82]

These expeditions were not cheap – each participant had to contribute a considerable sum towards the shared cost of transport and supplies, including waggons, oxen, ammunition and goods for barter – and the toll in elephants was correspondingly high. Jacobus Botha, a veteran elephant hunter whose experience was probably not atypical, boasted of having 'often shot four or five in a day, and sometimes twelve or thirteen'.[83] Small wonder, then, that by the 1770s these animals had all but vanished from the south-eastern parts of the colony, though some were still to be found in the Tsitsikamma forest. Along the west coast, according to Thunberg, the elephants were 'quite extirpated'.[84]

The disruption caused by the *elephantstogten* was not confined to this unfortunate beast, however, for during the long months in the veld elephant hunters derived their food almost entirely from the game they shot.[85] However, since they had no wish to waste valuable waggon space on biltong and carcasses, they were less destructive in this regard than their comrades who shot solely for the pot and the pantry. The latter could create havoc on an astonishing scale. 'Wild beasts are destroyed without mercy, consideration or oeconomy', Thunberg observed, 'so much so that some are killed for amusement, and others are destroyed on account of the damage they do, and for their skins or hides.'[86]

Even the most responsible colonists hunted on a scale far in excess of their immediate needs. Like the San, they greatly loved the flesh of the eland, but unlike the San, they killed far more eland than they could eat at one time and butchered the carcasses without ceremony. Lichtenstein describes a hunt in Bushman country north of the Roggeveldberge:

The company had gone five days northwards, beyond the boundaries of the Colony, and besides all the smaller game they had killed, which served as their daily food, they brought home seventeen elands. These animals weighed from seven to eight hundred pounds apiece, so that the portion of each of the hunters was about four thousand pounds of pure, excellent flesh. This was cut to pieces upon the spot, salted and packed in the skins, and thus brought home in a waggon they had taken with them. Here it was to be smoked, and would then be a plentiful supply of cheap and wholesome food.[87]

Gordon's journey through the valley of the Zeekoe River, in the company of a similar expedition, was accompanied by even greater slaughter: he and his eleven Boer companions shot eighteen eland, ten hippopotami and a wildebeest, besides an unspecified amount of smaller game, all in a mere thirteen days[88] (Fig. 8).

The San, by contrast, like the Amerindian hunters of pre-colonial New England, had been accustomed to kill animals 'only in proportion as they had need of them'.[89] This was partly a function of their simple technology – neither San nor Khoekhoe could take on a whole herd of elephants and therefore hunted only those which they could separate from the herd or lure into carefully disguised pit-traps[90] – but also of their mobile lifestyle. Nature was their storehouse; they had no need of large quantities of preserved meat; it would merely have hindered their mobility. To the colonists, bound as they were by their own notions of property, such behaviour was instead a sign of indolence, or worse, of irresponsibility; if the owners of the land chose to waste its resources, they reasoned, they would do better. And the Bushmen would benefit from their exertions, since they could consume the plentiful supplies of offal left behind at the site of a kill.[91]

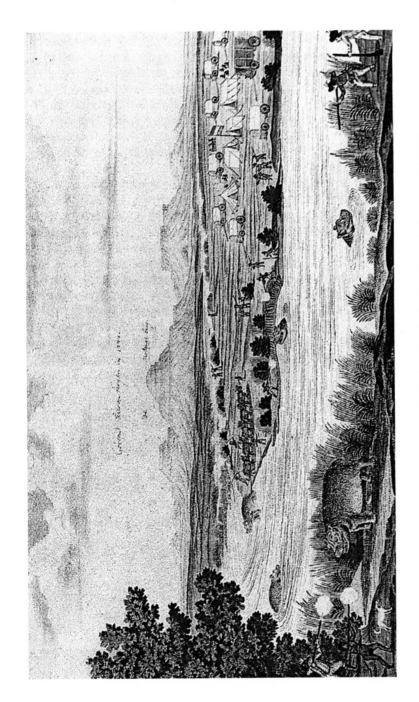

Figure 8 *Hippopotamus hunt at the Zeekoe River*, by Robert Jacob Gordon, Cape Archives, AG 7146.77.

There was truth in this last argument. Besides the heads, feet and entrails discarded by European hunters, whole carcasses were sometimes left at the site of a kill. Elephant flesh, for example, was never eaten by the colonists.[92] The Khoisan could therefore derive some benefit from association with colonial hunting parties; this indeed may have been the basis for Koerikei's initial co-operation with Dawid Schalk van der Merwe.[93] But this early phase of co-operation did not last. Within two or three years of the first settlers' arrival in the Camdeboo it gave way, as we have seen, to a fairly constant state of warfare.

It is difficult, despite all that has been said above, to determine with exactitude the cause of the mountain people's change of heart. Incidents such as the notorious massacre at the Blaauwbank on the Zeekoe River, where 122 'Bushmen' were lured to their death by a Boer commando posing as hippopotamus hunters, can have done little to improve relations between the two groups,[94] but hostilities had commenced before this. Presumably the breaking point came at different times and for different reasons for different groups of 'Bushmen', but if there was a common theme in their quickening hatred, it was, I suggest, their growing perception that their very being was under threat. The trespass of Europeans on their hunting grounds and the decimation of their game was more than a threat to their livelihood; it was an attack upon their spirit, a desecration of their world.

6 'The frenzy of the heathen'

When in 1774 Marthinus Adriaan Bergh, Landdrost of Stellenbosch, had instructed Commandant Opperman either to reduce the *Bosjesmans Hottentotten* 'to a permanent state of peace and quiet, or otherwise, in case of necessity, entirely to destroy them', he could not have imagined that twenty years later the commandos would not yet have achieved this objective. Yet so it was. As early as 1776 Adriaan van Jaarsveld had been moved to declare that 'the commandos, according to the times, are now in vain'; while Veldcorporaal Andries Petrus Burgers had warned that 'the frenzy of the heathen is striving to get the upperhand more every day . . . Whoever looks upon the present state of Christendom with an attentive eye, and with judgment', he lamented, 'must perceive that it is in a dead and unfruitful state, and that all is plunged into a confused and lifeless mass.'[1]

Fifteen years later, the situation had changed but little. Commandos still took the field on a more or less monthly basis, and well over 3,000 'Bushman' lives had been lost since the onset of hostilities in 1771, yet in 1791 the Heemraden of the newly proclaimed district of Graaff Reinet were obliged to inform the Governor that 'the raids of the robbers become ever worse' and that as a result of the losses the inhabitants had suffered for so long, they were not in a position to pay their loan-rents, 'without risking total ruin'. 'It may be possible', the Heemraden added, 'to weaken the Bushman Hottentots by means of commandos, and to restrain their morale, but never to destroy them.'[2] In the opinion of the Company's butcher J. G. van Reenen, whose business required him to keep abreast of events on the eastern frontier, the mountain people had already gained the upper hand:

It may be . . . [illegible] by way of illustration that 100 Bushmen previously all fled at the sight of a single Christian, while they are now so bold that they stopped on the public road a servant with eight well-armed slaves and the flock of sheep which they were driving for two days, at the Gamka; that while one or two waggons might safely . . . [illegible] formerly, six or seven are now forced to join on a journey to the Cape for fear of the Bushmen.[3]

The methods which the raiders employed were not new. Stock-theft and the deliberate destruction of captured animals remained their principal means of injuring the colonists.[4] As stock-thieves, the mountain people had early acquired a reputation for cunning and stealth. They were 'the most injurious enemy one could imagine', complained the burghers of Camdeboo in 1788, 'for they were treacherous and secretive'.[5] They would strike while the householder was away, the shepherd unarmed, or a part of the flock out of sight behind a corner of the mountain. Then they would pounce upon the animals and make off as quickly as possible to their hiding-places, moving so fast that if they were not pursued within the day, even mounted men could not overtake them.[6]

Increasingly, however, the 'Bushmen' made bold to attack the houses of the colonists, most often at night, but sometimes in broad daylight. 'It has never been before as now, from January to the present time', wrote Veldwagtmeester C. Kruger of the Middel Roggeveld in March 1778, 'with stealing and surrounding the houses at night, and discharging arrows at them, so that the people dare not venture out to protect the cattle.'[7]

Occasionally, Europeans were killed or wounded in such attacks. In the autumn of 1777, for example, one Klaas Smit was 'severely wounded' by robbers in the Sneeuberge,[8] and in 1791 the home of Willem Jacobus van der Merwe, Petruszoon, was attacked 'in broad daylight'.[9] His house was 'shot through with arrows, inside and out', and his wife, Geertruy Viljoen, was 'tragically murdered ninety paces from the front door'.[10] More often, however, it was the colonists' Khoisan servants who bore the brunt of the mountain people's fury. 'On the seventh of January', wrote Alewijn Jacobus Forster in 1787, 'the Bushmen came rushing among the servants and livestock of Daniel Liebenberg – 3 maids [meiden] were murdered and 108 sheep taken.'[11] And, the year before, A. C. Grijling had reported that the 'Bushmen' had been molesting the servant girls in his very house. He was sick, he added, and could do little, and his two old Hottentots were not fit to bear arms.[12]

The highest casualties were sustained by the servants and slaves who accompanied their masters' sheep and cattle into the veld. According to Baron van Plettenberg, who toured the north-east frontier in October 1778, the robbers generally murdered the herdsmen so as to prevent them raising the alarm.[13] An additional motive, however, was the capture of firearms. Most shepherds carried guns so as to protect themselves and their flocks against wild beasts, as much as human predators. Ironically, the very weapons intended for their defence were more often, one suspects, the cause of their premature death. The records show that the 'Bushmen' nearly always killed the shepherds whose guns they stole. In the eighteen months following the establishment of the new Drostdy in the Camdeboo (in July 1786), 107 herdsmen were murdered (seven of whom were slaves) and twenty-four guns stolen.[14] The death toll in the years before the establishment of the Drostdy was, if anything, higher. A few examples taken from the letters of *veldwagtmeesters* in the year 1783 must suffice. Thus, on an unknown date: 'two Hottentots of Carel Erasmus murdered and the guns taken'; two days later, 'a shepherd of Dirk Coetzee murdered and the gun with bandolier taken and 300 sheep taken too'. On 19 February, at the place of Pieter Fourie *d'oude*, 'the robbers killed two shepherds and took both guns with their bandoliers, and stabbed over 400 sheep to death'. On 15 June, at Barend Jacobus Burgers' place, 'a cattle herd murdered and the gun with appurtenances stolen'.[15] And a similar catalogue of destruction could be compiled for all the other years since the onset of hostilities in 1771.

The presence of so many guns among the mountain people was a source of great consternation to the colonists, more especially since the commandos reported that they 'knew how to use them'.[16] The authorities had long been mindful of this danger and had tried to forestall it by prohibiting Khoekhoe 'in the kraals' and on the farms from owning either guns or horses, lest these fall into the hands of robber bands.[17] In practice, the robbers probably acquired far more guns by murdering herdsmen than by collaborating with the 'tame Hottentots' in the kraals. Nevertheless the fear of such collaboration was ever present among the *veeboeren*. In 1772 the Bastaard Hottentot Thijs, resident on a farm belonging to Adriaan Louw in the Groote Roggeveld, had informed his fellow servants that a commando coming up from the Bokkeveld was planning to shoot dead all the tame *kraals Hottentotten* thereabouts because of their involvement in stock robberies. He had been told this, he said, by the burgher Pieter van Heerden, who was to lead the commando.[18] Thijs was subsequently flogged and sentenced to ten years' hard labour for spreading false rumours.[19] However his allegations were perhaps not as preposterous as the court believed, for fifteen years later the Veldwagtmeester Gerrit Maritz and thirty of his neighbours in the Middel Roggeveld asked the Landdrost's permission to remove or destroy all the Hottentot kraals in the area between the Middel and Klijn Roggevelden because the occupants were in possession of guns and 'might make common cause with the Bushmen who already have many guns'.[20]

Even more frightening to the colonists than the prospect of collaboration between robber bands and the few surviving independent Khoekhoe communities was the prospect of co-operation between farm servants and robber bands. These servants, as will become clear below, were often closely connected to the robbers, since many were captives seized during commando attacks on Bushman camps. Should they choose to assist the robbers they could do great damage, for, as Adriaan van Jaarsveld observed of his 'captain' who had betrayed him to his 'mates' whilst he (Van Jaarsveld) was away from home, they 'knew all the circumstances' on their masters' farms.[21] They were usually adept in the handling of horses and firearms and spoke at least a smattering of Dutch. Many a 'faithful Hottentot' had been known to warn the Bushmen of the approach of a commando; some indeed were believed to be the chief instigators of stock-theft: 'such fellows induce the robbers to plunder', explained Commandant Opperman, 'and when they expect to be discovered, they join them, and are then the principal robbers and murderers'.[22] This explains, then, why desertion was the most savagely punished of all a servant's 'crimes'.

Whereas the mountain raiders went to great lengths to acquire guns, they very rarely stole horses. They did however kill horses whenever they got the opportunity, even in the thick of battle.[23] According to Colonel Collins, the 'Bushmen' were afraid of horses: 'their dread of horses is so great', he wrote, 'that a few horsemen will defeat almost any number in a plain . . . They never drive away horses, but frequently kill them on mountains, where they are sent to avoid the sickness that afflicts them periodically on the plains.'[24]

Horses were highly valued on the frontier. They were always in short supply, since the horse sickness caused many deaths and the frequent commandos exhausted their strength. 'One cannot get horses here for less than 50 to 60 rix dollars', complained Landdrost Woeke in 1789. 'It is well known that we have a high annual mortality among the horses here, and most inhabitants have to buy horses every year in order to do the commandos.'[25] Thus when robbers shot poison arrows at horses, or burnt down the stables in which they were sheltered, they inflicted very severe damage on the colonists. Woeke recorded the destruction of ninety-nine horses during the first eighteen months of his tenure as magistrate, and many more had been shot or burnt to death before his time.[26]

The raiders presumably hoped that the destruction of horses would hinder pursuit and weaken the commandos. Runaway servants used the same tactics. 'My Hottentots have run away', lamented an unknown frontiersman. 'Yes, they have not merely run away. They ran away but first they burnt my stables with all my horses and then they ran away. The father and the mother with three children.'[27] Yet until the servants' rebellion of 1799 there is very little evidence to suggest that robber bands incorporated horses into their own strategies of attack and defence. The evidence which does exist for the use of horses by resisters in the period before 1800 refers only to Khoisan (here the term seems appropriate because of the confused situation on the farms) who had lived in close contact with the Dutch. In the 1790s, for example, an anonymous *veld-wagtmeester* reported that 'the Bushmen who lived with Fredrik Botha and looked after his sheep rounded up 164 of his cattle and made off with them, and also took the horses which helped their getaway'.[28]

Horses played a major role in the rebellion of 1799–1802, but again those who made use of them were runaway servants, rather than Khoisan from beyond the frontiers.[29] It was not until 1808 that commandos began to report the presence of horses in 'Bushman' encampments behind the Escarpment.[30] One cannot say for certain why the mountain raiders did not make better use of horses before this time. Perhaps, as Andrew Smith suggests, the transition from hunting and foraging to herding is more difficult than many have supposed.[31] Or was it merely that horses could not be kept hidden from the commandos long enough for the Soaqua to become accustomed to their use? Whatever the reason, it is fairly certain that the hunter-robbers of the Escarpment were largely foot-soldiers until the end of the eighteenth century.

Fire was a favourite weapon of the mountain people. It could be used with dramatic effect against the thatched timber-frame structures of the frontiersmen and they soon came to dread this form of attack. 'Jacob de Klerk has written to me', Opperman informed the Governor in 1776, 'and made me acquainted with the whole conspiracy of the robbers – that a multitude has collected together to overrun the Germans' farms at night and set the houses on fire.'[32] 'Those who have already fled have had their houses burnt afterwards', he added. Horses, grain stores, farm implements – all could be lost in such attacks,[33] and there was reason to fear that the colonists themselves might be roasted alive; 'the furious heathen' have said 'that they intend to set fire to the houses over the people's heads', wrote Andries Petrus Burgers from the Sneeuberge in 1785, 'and I am obliged to do a commando for they are gaining the upper hand'.[34]

The continual commandos placed an immense strain on the resources of the colonists and this in turn gave rise to mounting friction between the burgher militia and the men who commanded them – the *veldwagtmeesters* and *veldcorporaals* whose responsibility it was to ensure that a commando was properly equipped. A commando generally spent four to five weeks in the field, though a small force (comprising perhaps twelve freeburghers and an equal number of 'Hottentot' auxiliaries) might be away for less than two weeks, and a large one, such as the General Commando of 1774, might remain in the field for more than two months. During this time the men were entirely dependent on labour and supplies requisitioned from the tax-payers of their respective wards: servants, draft oxen, waggons, guns, blankets, food, tobacco, not to mention horses and saddles – all were supplied by the local citizenry.

The high cost of horses has already been mentioned (and two or three were needed for each member of a commando);[35] but the requisitioning of draft oxen and waggons was equally burdensome to the *veeboeren*. A good *trekos* might fetch 15 rix dollars in the mid-1780s,[36] and the *veeboeren* were understandably reluctant to have them used by the commandos: 'What say you to this?', asked an indignant Corporal Albertus van Jaarsveld of the Veldwagtmeester Carel van der Merwe in August 1779. 'The provision waggon has come to a stand at Gerrit Koekemoer's, in Camdeboo, with [only] four oxen, I shall go back in spite of you and report accordingly, else it will never do.'[37] 'Abraham Grijling told me that he bought his oxen for himself and not for the commando', wrote Dawid Schalk van der Merwe to the Landdrost in 1786, 'and he won't supply a single one to the commando unless you support his request.'[38]

The commandeering of waggons met with even greater resistance, for they were among the most expensive items in a grazier's budget[39] and the rough uncharted terrain covered by the commandos could leave them badly damaged. 'Waggons cost too much to have them driven around in the veld for nothing', protested an inhabitant of De Bruins Hoogte in 1786,[40] echoing the refractory sentiment so memorably expressed by Cornelius de Clerk some years earlier. 'Monsieur D. S. van der Merwe', began De Clerk, in response to a request to send his waggon 'with all its appurtances' for the use of a commando, 'you write me to send my waggon tilt tomorrow, which it is impossible that I can do, as it is the bolster of my bed. I am not unwilling, if I had enough bed clothes, to give the tilt, but I am deficient in these. I remain therefore, your friend, Cornelius de Clerk.' 'Turning over [the paper]', added Van der Merwe, 'I found the following words written': 'the tilt of which I write you, is the bolster for my head, and my wife is my *matras*; so if you claim the tilt by force, order the *matras* with it, as cook'.[41]

The commandos also posed a threat to the health of the fencible men, since they were required to spend weeks on end in the open air, exposed to searing heat in summer and 'penetrating cold' in winter, sheltering themselves in the mountains, without, so they said, so much as the comfort of an open fire, lest the Bushmen discover their whereabouts.[42] 'Not only are we wasting the prime of our lives', complained the inhabitants of Graaff Reinet in 1788, 'but we are made miserable by hills and dales, cold, rain, wind or heat, according to the time of year; waggons, oxen, horses, saddles, guns, clothes, yes, even life and health are lost thereby.'[43]

On many occasions the militia officers had difficulty finding enough men to make up a viable force; some pleaded ill-health, others that they were needed to guard their own farms; many sent their Khoisan servants in place of themselves. 'I am a Corporal of the burgers', protested Albertus van Jaarsveld, 'but not of the Hottentots; are there no men in Camdeboo?'[44] '. . . when I order men I get more excuses than men', echoed D. S. van der Merwe just six months later, 'and according to present appearances, I cannot continue as Veldwagtmeester, for without men, we can make no expedition'.[45]

Worse still, it was rumoured on at least one occasion that the inhabitants of Agter Sneeuberg had made a pact with the Bushmen; in 1779 the sons of Barend Burgers and Geele Andries van der Walt had moved again behind the mountains to 'the middle of the Bushman country' where, it was alleged, in exchange for being left in peace themselves, they had agreed to allow the robbers to pass by with stock stolen from the people of Camdeboo. Not so, protested Tjaart van der Walt – it was simply that he and his neighbours had been unable to hold out any longer in the mountains and had deemed it best to move to a more open country where there was pasture for their cattle. Besides, he added, 'I think it . . . much better, if we must move, to move up towards the Bushmen than to fly from them.'[46]

In 1774, on the eve of the General Commando, Adriaan van Jaarsveld had warned that the people were planning to fly from the Sneeuberge;[47] by April 1776 he himself had moved away and by the time of the allegations against the Van der Walts, flight from the mountains had become general. 'The inhabitants do nothing but fly from the Sneeuwberg', reported Joshua Joubert, 'first one, then another, without knowing where to go.'[48] The Nuweveld was also becoming depopulated, so that the inhabitants of the Swartberge and the Camdeboo were increasingly exposed to the depredations of the mountain people.[49] By 1791, according to J. G. van Reenen, 'the whole Nieuweveld, the Coup, part of the Sneeuwberg and the Tarka' had been abandoned.[50]

Had the commandos had more success in their attempts to recover stolen stock, the inhabitants of the outermost areas might have been less inclined to abandon their farms; however, despite the considerable effort spent in pursuit of stock-thieves, the proportion of stolen animals actually recovered by the commandos was depressingly small. In part this was due to the robbers' determination to destroy their booty rather than surrender it to their pursuers ('they saw me coming from afar', reported Johannes Ludovicus Pretorius, 'and then they stabbed all the sheep';[51] 'we never recapture anything', lamented Adriaan van Jaarsveld, 'because they leave none of the stolen cattle alive'[52]). And in part it was due to their skill in eluding the commandos. 'The Hottentots hide in the mountains like baboons', observed Swellengrebel, 'and fortify themselves by piling up stones, behind which they are shot-proof.'[53] A robber band seldom remained long in one place, but moved 'from the one mountain to the other . . . as soon as they have made their fires, so as not to be caught'.[54] Fire served as a means of communication among them, the smoke alerting neighbouring bands to the approach of a commando.[55] Time and again a commando would set off in the direction of a fire, only to find a deserted camp containing nothing but the remains of slaughtered cattle. And on more than one occasion, the men returned home to find that the robbers had been following their movements and had taken advantage of their absence to 'make an irruption in the rear'.[56]

When the commandos did succeed in taking an encampment by surprise, they exacted a savage revenge; with few exceptions the adult men were killed and the surviving women and children taken captive. According to calculations based on the reports of the militia officers of Graaff Reinet district, a total of 2,504 'Bushmen' were killed and 669 taken captive during the first decade of the district's existence (1786–95).[57] The number killed and captured during the preceding decade, when the north-eastern frontier was still within the jurisdiction of Stellenbosch, was, if anything, even greater. No-one has yet attempted to estimate the size of the aboriginal population of the eastern Karoo, but if it was in the region of one person per square kilometre, as Hilary Deacon has suggested was the case in the coastal forelands, then the carnage wrought by the commandos was truly genocidal.[58]

Yet despite these staggering losses, the indigenous communities were somehow able to sustain their will to resist – possibly because their world was by now so disrupted that robbery had become the only way they could survive – and their attacks on colonial property continued unabated well into the 1790s.[59]

By 1795 the European inhabitants of the north-eastern frontier were on the verge of despair. In the nine years since the establishment of the Drostdy of Graaff Reinet they had lost an estimated 19,161 cattle and 84,094 sheep, in addition to guns captured and slaves and horses murdered. Many had allegedly been 'completely ruined' and were dependent on the charity of their neighbours.

From the point of view of the authorities in Cape Town, the most alarming aspect of this situation was its effect upon the Company's coffers. Land-rents were by far the most important source of local revenue,[60] yet there was little the Company's agents could do to enforce payment of the annual loan-rent in the face of the colonists' repeated appeals for relief.[61] The sum of rent arrears mounted year by year until by 1795 the inhabitants of Graaff Reinet owed 69,221 rix dollars in unpaid rental.[62]

Equally worrisome to Company officials was the effect of the unsettled frontier conditions upon their carefully laid plans for control of the colony's meat market. The provision of fresh meat to the Company's ships, hospital, garrison and slaves remained one of the major functions of the Cape settlement and the authorities were determined that it should be accomplished at the lowest possible cost.[63] To this end the freeburghers of Cape Town were invited to tender for the exclusive right to supply the Company with fresh meat and live sheep, the contract going to the person or persons who proposed to deliver the goods at the lowest price.[64] The contract could be awarded for one, three or five years, depending on market conditions, so that the Company could protect itself against a sudden rise in the purchase price of livestock, or take advantage of a temporary fall. The prices agreed upon were invariably well below market levels, so that the contractors were obliged to carry substantial losses; in return, however, they were granted the exclusive right to sell meat to foreign ships, and this trade, being without price restrictions, amply compensated them for the losses they incurred in their trade with the Company.[65] In addition, they were permitted to participate in the supply of meat to the inhabitants of Cape Town, alongside a handful of licensed 'private' butchers.[66] This 'private' trade was much less profitable than the trade with foreign ships, for, in an attempt to forestall demands for wage increases from those of its employees who bought meat on the open market, the Company had placed a ceiling on the prices at which meat (a commodity 'as indispensable . . . as bread, even to townsmen') could be sold to the inhabitants of Cape Town.[67] Nevertheless, as the population of Cape Town grew, reaching a total of 11,341 (including freeburghers and slaves) by 1793, the contracted butchers took an increasing interest in the sale of meat to private citizens.

In a market this closely regulated, the opportunities for profit were few, even for the enterprising Van Reenen family, which dominated the meat trade for much of the eighteenth century.[68] Even the smallest rise in the price of slaughter stock could bring ruin to the contracted butchers and render them unable to fulfil their promises to the authorities. Such, according to J. G. van Reenen, was the situation they faced in 1791, as a result of the spreading chaos on the frontier. Not only had more than one hundred farms been abandoned, he wrote, but the fury of the Bushmen obliged the *veeboeren* to keep their livestock at the farms on which they resided, so that the animals' condition deteriorated and their weight fell.[69] In addition, the butchers' flocks increasingly fell prey to the robberies of 'these destructive people' – towards the end of 1790 he himself had lost 1,200 wethers in such an attack – and they were obliged to double the number of slaves and *knechten* sent inland to buy up livestock from the farmers.[70] The result, Van Reenen concluded, was an inevitable rise in the price of cattle and sheep, such that his company was quite unable to fulfil its promise (made prior to the award of the meat contract in 1789) to lower the price at which meat was sold to the inhabitants of Cape Town.[71] The solution, he argued, lay not in sanctions against himself and his brothers, but rather in a concerted effort to expel the predatory Bushmen from the district of Graaff Reinet. This district, he noted, was 'for nine months of the year' the sole source of the 75,000 sheep required annually by the Company and the inhabitants of Cape Town. 'Let any one say', he concluded, 'whence this number is to be procured, should the district of Graaff Reinet be destroyed by the Bushmen.'[72]

The following year (1792) the Van Reenen brothers suffered further losses at the hands of the Bushmen. On 11 June two captains named Vlamink and Couragie waylaid the brothers' servants at the Gamka River and carried off 6,000 sheep and 253 cattle valued at between 10,000 and 11,000 rix dollars.[73] A commando was at length assembled to pursue them and (allegedly) 300 of Vlamink's people were killed (an astonishingly large number, given the low density of Khoisan populations in the Karoo).[74] Couragie was traced to the Sak River some two months later and his 'kraal' too was annihilated.[75] In all, 478 Bushmen were killed and sixty-six captured. On the colonial side, one 'Hottentot' was wounded by a bullet and one by an arrow. But for all the bloodshed, only 1,585 sheep, forty-five cattle, four horses, a pocket watch and a handful of silver buttons were recovered.[76]

Following this incident, J. G. van Reenen was obliged to ask the Company for an advance. He had made such requests before, and been turned down, but this time his request was granted, for he had found favour with the two Commissioners-General newly arrived from Holland, S. C. Nederburgh and S. H. Frijkenius, who believed Van Reenen could assist them in their mission to find ways to reduce the Company's expenditure at the Cape.[77]

However, while the Commissioners valued the Van Reenen family's experience in the meat trade, they barely acknowledged detailed proposals submitted by J. G. van Reenen for the restoration of order in the district of Graaff Reinet. It was not that they were unaware of the mounting chaos on the frontier, nor that they were entirely opposed to the use of force, though they had initially recoiled from the bloodshed associated with the commandos.[78] It was rather that Van Reenen's plans for the establishment of a permanent border guard, partly comprised of Company soldiers,[79] were simply too expensive. By the 1790s the Dutch East India Company's financial position was catastrophic: corruption, conspicuous consumption and the competition of rival trading companies had brought it to its knees.[80] It had neither the means nor the will to undertake new initiatives in its far-flung empire, even one as modest as that proposed by J. G. van Reenen. The Commissioners had in any case been sent to curb local expenditure, not to expand it.[81] The best they could do within these constraints was to authorise the despatch of a small contingent of soldiers under Captain van Baalen, to aid the commandos against Vlamink and Couragie.[82]

For Nederburgh and Frijkenius the authorisation of Van Baalen's expedition was a sad admission of failure. Nederburgh had thundered his disapproval of the bloody exploits of the burgher commandos: 'Who does not tremble,' he asked, 'when he sees innocent people mercilessly robbed of their goods and livestock, yes, even their women and children, by violence and cupidity? Yes, whose heart is not filled with fear and horror when he sees not only civil institutions but even the laws of nature . . . openly trodden underfoot . . . ?'[83] Yet, as should be clear from the figures cited above, the commandos against Vlamink and Couragie were more than usually murderous. The only mitigating measure the Commissioners had been able to devise – the introduction of a premium for every Bushman taken alive – had merely served to encourage the despatch of further sanguinary expeditions.[84]

It was, as J. G. van Reenen may well have reflected, a case of too little, too late. Despite its desire to see order restored, the Company lacked the means to impose its will upon the frontier. The colonists and the Bushmen would, as before, be left to fight it out alone. This, as the reader will recognise, was exactly the situation of uncertain control and contested sovereignty which Hermann Giliomee has defined as characteristic of the open frontier.[85] However, the consequences for people of colour were not as he supposed. The inter-ethnic relationships which emerged from this maelstrom of raid and counter-raid were neither fluid nor flexible, nor did they accord with our notions of clientship. They were founded on violence, shot through with fear and characterised by a degree of unfreedom more consistent with slavery than clientship.

7   The enemy within

The story of Ruyter

Ruyter, brought up by white men – Ruyter died
amidst white men at a place called Springkaan's Kolk.
He was bound to a wagon with straps from the oxen;
they tied him face-down because of herding the sheep.
Then the Boer who was master, the Boer began beating
him with the riem that they use for tying a beast.
He said Ruyter, the herder, had not herded well.

This happened, this beating that led to his death.
The Boer hit him and hit him; the other Boers too.
When at last they unloosed him, Ruyter, he fainted.
Those who were there – they all must have known,
they must have known then, when picking him up,
that Ruyter, the herder, was near beaten to death.

This happened. He, Ruyter, said to those people,
he said white people did not believe he felt pain;
they would not believe he felt half-beaten to death.
But to him, to himself, it did not seem he could live.
He kept whispering, repeating, 'I looked after the sheep.
I, Ruyter, looked after the sheep.' He kept saying
the pain was such, so bad, he could not last long.

It was he, Ruyter, who told the white people there
that his body's middle, here, ached badly, very bad.
It was he who tried still to walk without help.
But the Boer, his master, the one whom he served,
had trampled his body while beating his body.
And Ruyter, before dying, the white men around him,
Ruyter said: 'the Boer has broken my body's middle.'

Stephen Watson, *Return of the moon: versions from the /Xam,*
Cape Town: Carrefour Press, 1991

I have asserted several times in the course of the preceding chapters that
the war against the 'Bushmen' on the north-eastern borders of the colony
played a major role in shaping labour relations in frontier districts,

undermining the voluntary ties of clientage, and propelling relations between masters and servants in the direction of a violent, comprehensive and permanent domination more consistent with our concept of slavery then of patron–client relations. It remains to show how and why this was so. In keeping with the limited geographical scope of this study, I will confine my observations as far as possible to the area which in 1786 became the *Colonie* of Graaff Reinet,[1] though I believe that the patterns uncovered there may well have existed right across the frontier.[2]

The most direct and visible link between the Bushman frontier and the structure of social relations in the Boer domain was embodied in the persons of the captives taken by the commandos and distributed among the men at the close of an expedition.[3] These war captives (sometimes explicitly called *krijgsgevangenen* in the records) made up a significant proportion of the total labour force in frontier districts. It is nearly impossible to make an exact assessment of their number, since the primary source of information – the reports of *veldwagtmeesters* – sometimes did not mention the taking of captives, listing only the number of 'Bushmen' killed. And the other major source of information – the registers of *inboekselingen*[4] compiled by the local authorities – did not always distinguish clearly between 'Bushman' captives, *huisboorlingen* (Khoisan children indentured to the European on whose farm they were born) and *Bastaard Hottentotten* (the offspring of slaves and 'Hottentots'), all of whom were indentured to their masters until the ages of 18 or 25.[5] Moreover, several entries in the registers refer simply to children 'without father or mother', who could be either captives or orphaned *huisboorlingen*.[6] Nevertheless, despite the less than satisfactory nature of the sources, one can establish with some certainty that between the years 1774 and 1786, at least 548 'Bushmen' were brought home as captives by commandos sent out from Stellenbosch district,[7] while 669 were captured by the militia of Graaff Reinet during the following decade (1786–95).[8] Of these latter, 332 were formally registered as *inboekselingen*.[9] Since a good number of the men involved in the Stellenbosch commandos were actually resident in wards (such as the Sneeuberge and the Camdeboo) which in 1786 became part of the new district of Graaff Reinet, one can reasonably assume that by 1795 there were upwards of 1,000 war captives among the labour force of this district. To these should be added the small number of captives taken by commandos operating from the district of Swellendam before 1786 and the unknown number of 'Bushmen' and Khoekhoe kidnapped by unauthorised raiding parties.[10] Unfortunately, it was not until 1798 that the authorities began to record the total number of 'Hottentots' in service with the Boers, but even if we make the unlikely assumption that their number in the 1780s had not been much lower than the 1798 figure of 8,635 men, women and children, it is apparent that war captives made up a very substantial segment of the total servant population.[11] It is also worth noting that by the last decade of the eighteenth century they probably outnumbered the officially acknowledged slave population of Graaff Reinet by nearly two to one.[12]

The majority of these captives were women and children, for men of fighting age did not often survive an engagement with a Boer commando. According to the lists of *inboekselingen*, the children's ages could range from just a few months to 16 or even 20 years.[13] Perhaps, like slave raiders in other parts of Africa, the Boers preferred not to have to deal with adult male captives.[14] However we would be deceived if we supposed that grown men were never taken captive. The rules governing the apprenticeship of 'Bushman' children were not formally codified under the Dutch East India Company[15] and they appear to have varied according to the whim of the local authorities (thus between 1786 and 1790 'Bushman' children were usually apprenticed *until* the age of 18 or 25, whereas after 1790 they might be apprenticed *for* twenty-five years), but it was always in a master's interest to give the lowest possible estimate of an apprentice's age. In the eighteenth century, such subterfuges went undetected, but we may assume that the gross irregularities exposed by members of the London Missionary Society early in the nineteenth century had a long history. As Dr John Philip observed in 1828:

I have frequently had my attention called to cases in which young people, who had arrived at the ages of fourteen and sixteen years, have been rated, at that period of life, as being eight years of age only, and then apprenticed for ten years. In one case of this nature, after being assured by the local authorities of the district that an apprenticed boy was not more than eight years of age, I proved, by the evidence of the farmer at whose place he was born, that he was fifteen years of age at the very time he was apprenticed by them as a child not exceeding eight years of age. This fact, however, would not have been so easily established, if it had not been that the magistrate had used his dispensing power in this case, in taking the boy from the farmer with whom the father lived . . .[16]

Moreover, every now and again, in documents appended to the reports of *veldwagtmeesters*, one finds incontrovertible evidence that adult men and women were included among the captives parcelled out to commando members. In the aftermath of the General Commando of 1774, for example, Nicolaas van der Merwe distributed seven male captives whose ages (according to his estimates) ranged from 20 to 50 years. Three of them were paired with women, aged respectively 30, 40 and 50 years, who may perhaps have been their wives.[17]

In general, however, the commandos preferred to avoid taking grown men captive. From the perspective of a harassed militiaman who had coaxed and bullied an under-manned expedition through four or five weeks in the open veld, adult captives were a burden he could do without. The means to restrain them were often lacking – even the General Commando had not received its full complement of handcuffs and leg-irons – and they had to be kept under constant guard.[18] Not every *veldwagtmeester* had the unfortunate experience of Andries van der Walt, whose eighty-two captives attempted to escape under cover of night, 'while some of the males attacked the wagon in which their bows and arrows had been placed'; but many, one suspects, shared Van der Walt's opinion that the taking of prisoners was altogether too much trouble and that it would be far better 'to destroy the robbers without giving quarter'.[19]

Sentiments such as these do not accord with a view of the burgher commando sometimes espoused by historians, namely that slave-raiding was one of its primary functions.[20] There is little doubt that some men banded together explicitly for the purpose of taking captives, while others made occasional kidnapping forays as a diversion from the hunt.[21] Indeed, Sparrman has left us a vivid account of the *modus operandi* on such occasions. Although not an eye-witness account, it is worth quoting in full because of the unusual detail with which it describes the process of enslavement. He explained:

The capture of slaves from among this race of men ['Boshies-men'] is by no means difficult, and is effected in the following manner. Several farmers, that are in want of servants, join together, and take a journey to that part of the country where the Boshies-men live. They themselves, as well as their Lego-Hottentots,[22] or else such Boshies-men as have been caught some time before, and have been trained up to fidelity in their service, endeavour to spy out where the wild Boshies-men have their haunts. This is best discovered by the smoke of their fires. They are found in societies from ten to fifty and a hundred, reckoning great and small together. Notwithstanding this, the farmers will venture on a dark night to set upon them with six or eight people, which they contrive to do, by previously stationing themselves at some distance round about the *craal*. Then they give the alarm by firing a gun or two. By this means there is such a consternation spread over the whole body of these savages, that it is only the most bold and intelligent among them, that have the courage to break through the circle and steal off. These the captors are glad enough to get rid of at so easy a rate, being better pleased with those that are stupid, timorous, and struck with amazement, and who consequently allow themselves to be taken and carried into bondage. They are, however, at first, treated by gentle methods; that is, the victors intermix the fairest promises with their threats, and endeavour, if possible, to shoot some of the larger kinds of game for their prisoners, such as buffaloes, sea-cows and the like. Such agreeable baits, together with a little tobacco, soon induce them, continually cockered and feasted as they are, to go with a tolerable degree of cheerfulness to the colonists's (*sic*) place of abode. There this luxurious junketing upon meat and fat is exchanged for more moderate portions, consisting for the most part of butter-milk, gruel and porridges . . .[23]

However, despite the great value of Sparrman's account, it would be a mistake to view the slaving activities of the generality of commandos in these terms. In most cases, slaving was a by-product of a commando's activities, not its primary goal. Were it otherwise, militia officers would have made some attempt to curb the random slaughter so as to maximise the supply of young and tractable prisoners. How, for example, if slaving were the prime concern of the commandos, would one account for behaviour such as that of Veldcorporaal Dirk Marx, who, after overcoming a 'Bushman' band in the Little Karoo, had all but six of the survivors shot in cold blood?[24] And how would one explain the massacre orchestrated by Adriaan van Jaarsveld at the Blaauwbank in August 1775?[25] The only reasonable conclusion is that the taking of captives was not the first concern of the commandos; their primary objective was to incapacitate their enemies, but captives were a valuable perquisite of this endeavour.

The authorities in Cape Town held an ambivalent position with regard to the taking of Bushman captives. The Council of Policy had long abandoned hopes of a negotiated settlement with the mountain people and therefore lent support to the commandos, yet its members recoiled from the immoderate and 'vindictive' conduct of the militiamen and constantly exhorted them to avoid unnecessary bloodshed.[26] The taking of captives was seen as an alternative to wanton bloodshed and was therefore encouraged.[27] On the other hand, the Company had always been mindful of the consequences which might follow from the enslavement of the native population. The instructions issued to Jan van Riebeeck in 1651 had enjoined him to avoid injury to the persons and property of the natives, lest 'they be rendered averse to our people', and this had remained Company policy from that time onwards.[28] Van Riebeeck's proposal to enslave the Peninsular Khoekhoe had not been rejected out of hand, but neither was it approved.[29] One hundred and forty years later, the *veldwagtmeester* Petrus Pienaar was sharply rebuked for his over-zealous response to the Company's offer of a premium, payable in rix dollars, for every Bushman taken alive by the commandos.[30] The intention of the Council of Policy, its members insisted, had been solely to 'prevent the unnecessary shedding of human blood', not to encourage a trade in human beings. Pienaar was informed that his proposal to raise commandos at his own expense, specifically for the purpose of taking captives, was entirely contrary to Company policy; such actions would merely 'incite the natives to further hostilities' and bring 'the greatest disorders and confusion' upon the colony.[31] Again, in 1795, O. G. de Wet, President of the Council of Justice and special commissioner to the troubled district of Graaff Reinet, firmly vetoed a request from the Krijgsraad of that district to the effect that those who did commando duty should be allowed to sell their captives 'by legal transfer even as slaves', upon payment of a sum of money into the Company's chest. De Wet was no less concerned than were local officials to find a means of rekindling the 'departed military ardour' of frontiersmen, but he could not countenance so radical a departure from Company policy.[32]

However, while the authorities may have shrunk from giving sanction to the deliberate enslavement of Bushmen, they knew only too well that war captives made up a steadily increasing component of the labour force on farms in the interior. (De Wet, indeed, had gone out of his way to find means to secure the farmers' hold over their captives, short of granting them the rights of slaveholders.[33]) They found refuge, perhaps, from the disturbing implications of their paradoxical stance, in the comforting fact that Bushman captives remained free persons in the eyes of the law. Unlike slaves, their status as involuntary servants was neither permanent nor heritable; they would be freed at the expiry of 'a fixed and equitable [but unspecified] term of years'; and whilst in service they would (according to the instructions issued to Veldcommandant Opperman in 1774) be well treated and properly maintained.[34] Moreover, as we have seen, they were not to be bought or sold. Good treatment was particularly emphasised by the authorities: they noted that war captives had 'more than once' been maltreated in the past and 'thus excited to wicked revenge'.

Alas, these provisions were for the most part a dead letter and the authorities must have known it. Certainly the visiting Commissioners, Nederburgh and Frijkenius, knew it.[35] It is true that the local registers of captives and other *inboekselingen* specified a fixed term of indenture, but only a small proportion of captives were actually entered in these registers, and of those that were, many were apprenticed *for* twenty-five years rather than until the age of 25.[36] In the case of adult captives, twenty-five years would entail a lifetime of servitude. Moreover, there is little positive evidence that Bushman captives were ever released at the expiry of their term of indenture. Indeed, if truth be told, it is peculiarly difficult to follow the lives of captive Bushmen for any distance in the historical record; all too often they disappear without trace after the moment of capture. The reason, I believe, is not that there was a conspiracy of silence, nor that the majority escaped, but rather that as they were absorbed into the servant body on the farms, they lost their distinctive identity, at least in the eyes of their masters, and were subsumed within the general category of 'Hottentots', along with the other servants of indigenous origin. 'The Hottentots at Graaff Reinet . . . [were] mostly generated from the Bosjesmen', explained the elder Andries Stockenstrom in 1807, 'and only trained to be herdsmen.'[37] And Stockenstrom's son, who knew the frontier even better than his father, echoed the latter's opinion: the Bushmen 'that had lived for a length of time among the farmers', he explained, '[and become] accustomed to a more civilized mode of life . . . were in general accounted as Hottentots' and should not be confused with 'the wild Bushmen without the limits of the Colony'.[38] As a rule, then, adult captives cannot be distinguished in the historical record, for they have become one with other 'Hottentots'. Their fate, one supposes, was similar to that of many *huisboorlingen*, who, though nominally free at the age of 18 or 25, were *de facto* tied to their masters for life.

Occasionally one catches a brief glimpse of their condition. In the summer of 1798, for example, Jacobus Jooste had laid a complaint against his stepfather, Johannes Schalk Hugo, regarding a slave girl whom Hugo was allegedly withholding from him. Hugo admitted the charge, but explained that 'his Hottentot' was 'coupled' with the girl and that if he were to give her up he would surely lose his Hottentot too, something he could not afford. 'It is a Bushman Hottentot', he explained, 'whom my wife's late husband brought as a child from the Zeekoe River . . . I am not unwilling to give up the girl, if I could but be sure that my Hottentot would not abscond . . . but that will be the upshot of it and I cannot do without him as I have few *volk*.'[39]

As to the heritability of slave status, the children of Bushman captives were *de jure* exempt from this fate, but in practice such children would have been indentured to their masters or their masters' descendants as *huisboorlingen*, along with the children of other 'tame Hottentots'. As Orlando Patterson has so convincingly argued, the heritability of slavery was a function of the 'natal alienation' or radical deracination of the victims of enslavement. The slave was 'a socially dead person. Alienated from all rights or claims of birth, he ceased to belong in his own right to any legitimate social order.'[40] It followed that:

having no natal claims of his own, he had none to pass on to his children. And because no one else had any [recognised] claim or interest in such children, the master could claim them as his own essentially on the grounds that whatever the parents of such children expended in their upbringing incurred a debt to him.[41]

As we shall see in a moment, the extent to which Bushman captives were really 'natally alienated' was precisely the issue around which the ferocious struggle between master and servant revolved. But the very existence of the *inboekseling* system presupposed an assumption on the part of the masters that their 'Hottentot' servants had lost their independent social existence and with it their capacity to assert their claims upon their kin.

Of the several measures instituted to protect the Bushmen against enslavement, only the prohibition on the sale of captives appears to have been adhered to. Company officials, as we have seen, had consistently stood firm on this point, perhaps because they considered chattel status to be the determining characteristic of slavery.[42] Thus while O. G. de Wet had been willing to support whatever measures were necessary to secure a captor's hold over his *inboekseling* for the full twenty-five-year term, he had stopped short at purchase and sale.[43]

There is no doubt, however, that the Company's stance was deeply resented by the *veeboeren*. On De Wet's arrival in Graaff Reinet in April 1795 the rebellious citizenry had presented him with a *klachtschrift*, or written statement of their grievances. A rambling and irreverent document, written in a tone of high indignation, it gave vent to the freeburghers' great anger against the officials who had been placed over them, in particular Landdrost Maynier, whom they had recently evicted from the Drostdy.[44] Maynier, they alleged, was an upstart and a rogue, an oppressor of widows and orphans, a thief and a 'destroyer of the land and people' who had put the interests of the heathen above those of his Christian subjects.[45] His Hottentot policy, as we shall have occasion to observe in more detail below, was a particular source of grievance. Not only had he opened his court to the complaints of 'deserters' from service; he had also, so they alleged, allowed the district gaoler, a certain Bodenstrom, to sell arrested runaways 'by way of prison expenses'. 'Is this right?' they demanded to know:

As these men [their former masters] had brought them up from childhood? It may be answered they are a free people – then why may one sell them, and not another? If a burgher may not do that, still less may a gaoler – Granted, there is a show of right about the expenses – but what have we for our trouble? Almost all of them were deserving of death – we have risked our lives; and must see them taken away, after all our trouble and risk.[46]

No sooner had De Wet in his turn been expelled from the district, than the rebel leaders declared their intention to remedy this defect in the law: henceforth, they declared, 'Bushman Hottentots, male or female, taken on commando, or by individuals, [were] to remain the property from generation to generation, of those with whom they reside.'[47] This innovation presumably survived no longer than the short-lived 'republic' which had spawned it; however, lest we place too much trust in the power of the newly installed British authorities to suppress an illegal trade, we should recall that in 1817 Landdrost Stockenstrom himself felt obliged to inform government of the existence of a widespread traffic in Bushman children. Referring to the 'ancient custom', by which the farmers procured Bushman children from their parents in exchange for 'trifles', he confessed to a strong suspicion that this custom:

was beginning to be seriously abused; that these children . . . are transferred from one hand to another, and that payment is secretly taken; that many, by these means, are gradually taken from the frontier, brought into the inner districts, and passed off as orphans; that itinerant merchants are beginning to be supplied with them, through some channel or other . . .[48]

As to the question of proper maintenance and 'good treatment', it was a non-starter in the context of violent domination established by the forcible seizure and subsequent detention of Bushman captives. The problem, at root, was precisely that which (as we have noted) the authorities had foreseen but failed to confront: it was imprudent to enslave the local population; it was unwise to take their children; it was dangerous to hold them captive in their native land. No amount of legal cant could disguise the fact that the Dutch had ignored a cardinal maxim in the annals of slavery: that 'neighbours made difficult slaves'.[49] Throughout the history of enslavement, Orlando Patterson reminds us, there has been 'a strong tendency on the part of a conquering group not to enslave a conquered population en masse and in situ'. There have been exceptions to this tendency, but, he observes, 'the exceptions bring us to a second generalization, which can be stated in much stronger terms: attempts by a conquering group to enslave a conquered population en masse and in situ are almost always disastrous failures'.[50]

For Patterson, the primary reason for the failure of such attempts lies in the inversion of the critical outsider or alien status of slaves in the slaveholding society.

When a people was conquered [he explains], it was by definition the conquerors who were the outsiders to the local community and the conquered who were the natives. In this situation one of the most fundamental elements of slavery – natal alienation – was almost impossible to achieve . . .[51]

In such a situation it was the master, not the slave, who was the intruder, the one without ancestral claims to belonging. Or at least, this is how it would appear to the slave, and, though they might not care to admit it, to many members of the master class as well. The 'moral community', from which in the normal course of events the slave would be excluded, was in this case defined by the conquered as much as by the conqueror. Who, in such circumstances, was 'the enemy within'? The very phrase – which describes the position of the slave in those societies where slaves were externally recruited, often as prisoners of war – took on a new meaning in cases where the slave was himself a native. It was not simply in a negative sense, by virtue of his alienation from the community of the conqueror, that he was the enemy within, it was also in a positive sense, by virtue of his kinship with the still existent (albeit damaged) community of the conquered.

In such circumstances, the very basis of the slave relation was under threat. The power of the slaveholder, as Patterson has emphasised, rests not only on brute force, but also, crucially, on authority, by which force was transformed into right and obedience into duty; and authority in turn derived from the master's control of symbolic and ritual processes. It was this control which allowed him to define the slave as a non-person, alien, dishonoured and degraded. And the slave, cut off from his own cultural heritage, and lacking the social support which could reinforce an alternative definition of himself, came to obey the master, 'not only out of fear, but out of the basic need to exist as a quasi-person, however marginal and vicarious that existence might be'.[52] However, where the slave was held captive on his native terrain, he had access from the outset to an alternative symbolic universe and to a living cultural heritage, on which he could draw in his struggle to combat and contradict the master's conception of himself. He was not obliged to create a new community on foreign soil, as was the case with slaves uprooted and transported far from home.[53]

How true was this of captive Soaqua! Every krans, every fountain, every pool of water carried the imprint of a cosmic order whose foundations had been laid long before the coming of the Europeans. The *veeboeren* had blundered into this world, ignorant of its principles, unaware of its secrets, recklessly careless of its prohibitions. They had desecrated its landscape and destroyed its most precious treasures, killing eland like cattle, piling the carcasses high on their waggons, without regard to the meaning of their actions. In time perhaps, like the Nharo of Botswana, the San would come to accept and rationalise the superiority of the intruders, integrating their explanations into the old cosmology;[54] or worse, like the Inca of Peru and the Aztecs of Mexico, they might conclude that their gods had failed them and their world was lost:

> Let us die then,
> Let us perish then,
> For our gods are already dead![55]

But, to the best of our knowledge, no such sense of moral collapse had taken root among the /Xam of the Escarpment before the end of the eighteenth century. On the contrary, as we have seen, the hegemony of Europeans was resisted tooth and nail; nowhere, until the nineteenth century, did the mountain people concede defeat. (And even then, as the very existence of the Bleek collection demonstrates, indigenous culture and cosmology displayed an extraordinary durability.) 'Of all those people whom the avarice of the Europeans has treated with cruelty', declared Le Vaillant, 'there are none who preserve a stronger remembrance of the injuries they have sustained, or who hold the name of the whites in greater detestation . . . Their resentment is so violent that they have always the dreaded word '"vengeance" in their mouth . . .'[56] Indeed, so resilient was the 'moral community' of the conquered in this case, that, in 1799, more than thirty years after the first occupation of their territories by Europeans, the rebel leader Klaas Stuurman could rally hundreds of 'Hottentot' servants to his cause with his powerful restorationist vision:

Restore [he said] the country of which our forefathers were despoiled by the Dutch and we have nothing more to ask . . . We have lived very contentedly . . . before these Dutch plunderers molested us, and why should we not do so again if left to ourselves? Has not the Groot Baas given plenty of grass roots, and berries and grasshoppers for our use; and, till the Dutch destroyed them, abundance of wild animals to hunt? And will they not return and multiply when these destroyers are gone?[57]

Clearly, in such a context, 'good treatment' and 'proper maintenance' would not suffice to reconcile the captured to their condition, nor restrain them from 'wicked revenge'. And irreconcilable captives were unlikely to be well treated. Mayhem was the more likely result, as we shall see.

On a more practical level too, the enslavement of natives was a peculiarly 'arduous option'.[58] Members of a conquered population held captive on their own terrain could resist captivity in numerous ways which were not available to 'natally alienated' slaves. Here again, one should stress that the decisive factor is the existence of an alternative 'moral community'. In every slave society many slaves were native-born; in some societies even newly recruited slaves were natives – 'fallen' persons who had been excluded from normal participation in the community because they had breached its norms; but in such cases the ideological hegemony of the master class usually ensured that there were few free persons to whom a runaway could turn.[59] Only communities of former slaves, such as Free Blacks in the Americas, or outlawed maroon bands, might be expected to shelter the recalcitrant slave.[60] Where slaves were drawn from a conquered group, however, runaways would be welcomed as heroes by those who had as yet escaped enslavement. They would, moreover, bring skills and information which could be put to good use in the service of continuing resistance. And their intimate knowledge of the environment would enable them to survive the dangerous passage to freedom far better than those whose roots lay in another land and whose only experience of the local terrain had been gleaned in captivity.

Vis-à-vis the slaveowner, the natal community of the war captive played a role not unlike that of maroon communities in the Americas. Like the maroon community, but perhaps more starkly, it represented 'the antithesis of all that slavery stood for'; its presence on the fringes of the colonised domain rendered the master's hold over his slave critically insecure, and ensured that, as in Brazil or the Caribbean, 'the most brutal punishments were reserved for recaptured runaways'.[61]

All these factors were present on the Cape frontier, and they go a long way, I would argue, towards explaining the peculiar violence which punctuated relations between a master and his *volk*. Captive Bushmen could and did desert with relative ease. Some escaped repeatedly, despite the ordeal they faced on recapture.[62] And while most escapees may have chosen to steal silently into the night, there were some who made a more dramatic departure, or who, having gone, returned with reinforcements to wreak a noisy revenge.

I have already mentioned the 'captain' in the service of Adriaan van Jaarsveld, who on the eve of his departure gave seventy-eight of Van Jaarsveld's sheep to his 'mates' in the veld, and the 'Bushmen' who made off on horseback with 164 cattle belonging to their master, Fredrik Botha.[63] But there was also the 'Hottentot' Claas, who absconded from the service of Christiaan Bock in the Hantam, and returned with 'a gang of Hottentots' to shoot poisoned arrows at Bock and set fire to his house. Claas was apprehended some weeks later and sent up to *De Kaap*, where he was subjected to an exemplary punishment, being 'condemned to be bound to a post and severely flogged by the public executioner, with rods upon the bare back, and thereupon branded and riveted in chains, in order therein to labour for life at the Company's public works on Robben Island, without wages'.[64]

This public chastisement may have helped to allay the anxieties of those in authority, but it had little effect on the behaviour of others who may have been moved to act as Claas had done. In 1777, for example, on the very night that Stephanus Naude was robbed of fifteen oxen and his herdsman murdered, 'a Hottentot of Naude's ran off, hid himself about the farm for some days, and coming to the farm by night, killed Naude's principal Hottentot with a poisoned arrow'.[65] Again, in 1778, a 'Hottentot' named Carel deserted with a gun and joined a band of 'Bushman' robbers in the Roode Berg (Agter Renosterberg).[66] In October the following year he was rumoured to have been among the sheep of Johannes Jurgen de Beer in the Camdeboo, together with another runaway who spoke 'good Dutch and had lived with Barend Burger'. No effort was spared in the attempt to recapture the elusive Carel, but, with the aid of an unknown companion, who paid with his life for misleading the avenging commando, Carel escaped to rob again: on 25 October De Beer's entire flock was stolen and barely one third was recovered.[67]

Perhaps the most flamboyant of the runaways was a man known to the colonists as Dikkop, who in July 1781 'deserted from Lodewyk Pretorius with a gun'. Dikkop's wife stole the gun from him and returned it to Pretorius. Dikkop, undaunted by this betrayal, 'contrived to procure another gun from one of his master's Hottentots, named Vlaminck, and went on the hill behind Pretorius' house, at which he fired seven shots; the balls fell among the servants', reported Adriaan van Jaarsveld, in whose jurisdiction the incident occurred; 'and when Pretorius the same day went away to his other place, stationing another Hottentot to fire upon Dikkop, so as to keep him from the path, he [Dikkop] fired a bullet under the horse on which Pretorius' wife was mounted, and then went back and set fire to the house; but was at last caught while asleep'. 'I beg', concluded Van Jaarsveld, 'that this Hottentot may, at least, be placed on the island;[68] for if such things go on, it will not be possible to oppose the public enemy.'[69]

But alas, the enemy was already within, and Adriaan van Jaarsveld, among others, had played a major part in bringing this about. Moreover Robben Island, although a veritable chamber of horrors for those acquainted with it, was too far away to inspire fear among the servants of the interior. Without authority, then, and lacking even the primitive instruments of state repression available to slaveholders in the arable districts, the man who would be master of his Bushman servants was compelled to rely in large part on naked force – on what Machiavelli has called the 'beastly' aspect of power. There were other strategies available to him, notably the option which Patterson has termed 'divide and partially enslave',[70] which in this case would involve an attempt to differentiate between captive Bushmen and voluntarily contracted Khoekhoe servants; however, for reasons which I shall explore in the next chapter, such strategies were largely ignored by the *veeboeren*. Voluntary arrangements (such as labour tenancy and various forms of wage labour) did exist. Indeed, as we saw in chapter 3, such arrangements had probably predominated during the initial period of white settlement east of the Gamtoos, but they were soon swallowed up in the atmosphere of fear and tension which rapidly enveloped the whole sphere of relations between Europeans and native Khoisan. Very soon, as we shall see, the same forces which had created an inherent instability in the relation between Boer master and Bushman captive would engender a 'static electricity of violence' in nearly every household on the frontier.[71]

Runaway Bushmen were relentlessly pursued; 'as soon as they have eloped', noted Sparrman, 'men are set to lie in ambush for them at such places by the rivers sides, as it is supposed they must take in their way, and by this means they are often retaken'.[72] Those recaptured were summarily and often cruelly punished. Nevertheless, despite the risks attendant on recapture, many runaways, driven perhaps by their failure to find refuge at a safe distance from their former masters, would return to the farmstead to seek food or companionship from the other servants. Thus the 'Bushman Hottentot' Dwa, who in 1788 had absconded from Johannes van der Walt, returned frequently to the *werf* at night 'to visit his mates'. One evening, while he was begging tobacco at the *strooijhuis* of the Hottentots Legtvoet and Mannel, he was betrayed by the Hottentot Ruijter, whom Van der Walt had set to watch for him. Van der Walt then ordered his *knecht*, Jacob Nieman, to have the Bushman caught and beaten 'so that he could not leave again'. So faithfully did Nieman execute this order that Dwa quickly lost consciousness and died the very same night – the next morning his body was found in the veld 'by a pool of water' and 'the following night was devoured by the wolves and jackals'.[73]

Van der Walt had been overheard to say, explained the Hottentot Jan Bries, 'that, by order of the Veldwagtmeester, whenever a strange Hottentot came upon the werf, he should be driven away with a beating'.[74] Such an order had indeed been issued some years before by Veldwagtmeester Hendrik Schalk Burger.[75] The intention of the order was to deter Hottentots from 'wandering about'; but in this case it apparently failed, for soon after the incident involving Dwa another servant of Van der Walt's, a Hottentot named Bakker, who had testified during the preparatory examination into the death of the Bushman Dwa, ran off and himself joined the 'Bushman robbers', in whose company he stole and destroyed 'a considerable number' of sheep and cattle belonging to certain members of the Van der Merwe family, who lived, like Van der Walt, in the Agter Sneeuberg.[76]

If naked force was the primary means by which Bushman captives were prevented from escaping, it was scarcely less important in the everyday management of the relationship between master and bondsman. In the case of a captive child, the exercise of force might not amount to more than 'a few curses and blows', accompanied by the constant 'maundering and grumbling of his master and mistress', who might abuse him verbally, calling him *t'guzeri* or *t'gaunatsi* (which meant, according to Sparrman, 'young goblin' and 'evil spirit').[77] But in the case of adults, the imposition of a master's will frequently involved a tense physical confrontation, culminating all too often in explosive violence.

Thus the dramatic confrontation recalled so vividly in the Circuit Court at Graaff Reinet in 1817 had been played out many times before, though with minor variations. The occasion was an inquiry into the death of the Bushman Hottentot Klaas, who had been one of five 'Bushman' servants on the farm of Petrus Coenraad van der Westhuizen in the Agter Sneeuberg.[78] In December 1816 Petrus Coenraad had gone up to the Cape with his *bijwoonder* Leendert Louw, leaving his farm in the hands of his sons, Pieter Willem and Nicolaas Johannes van der Westhuizen. One hot summer evening, 'shortly before New Year', as the Bastard Hottentot Klaas later recalled, bad blood had erupted between the Bushman Klaas and his young master, Nicolaas Johannes. Needless to say, the witnesses could not agree on the cause of the confrontation, except that it involved an ewe which had recently lambed. According to the Veldcornet Michiel Adriaan Oberholster, who was called to inspect the body, Klaas had 'thrown away' the lamb, causing distress to its mother and arousing the wrath of Nicolaas van der Westhuizen, who threatened to 'klap' him. The next morning at daybreak, as Oberholster understood it, Nicolaas had 'given him [Klaas] a push' when the ewe came up to the kraal, and Klaas had at once sprung over the fence and fetched his bow and arrow from the *strooijhuis*.[79] According to Nicolaas, Klaas had twice refused to come when he was called to fetch the ewe and had instead approached him with a kierie in his hand. Nicolaas thereupon seized the kierie, while Klaas picked up a stone. Both then went to fetch their arms, Nicolaas to the house whence he returned with a *sjambok* and a gun, Klaas to the *strooijhuis* whence he fetched an assegai and his bow and poison arrows. Nicolaas seized the bow and arrow and called to the other Hottentots to grab hold of Klaas. 'While he stood thus captive', testified the *kleinbaas*, 'I gave him six or seven blows.'

The Bushman Hottentot Snel, who with three others had been forced to hold Klaas down while he was beaten, omitted to mention Klaas' alleged refusal to obey orders, saying instead that '*Kleinbaas* Nicolaas' had come up to them, shaken Klaas' kierie from his hand and hit him with it (Klaas 'had done nothing', testified the Bushman Booij), but agreed that Klaas had attempted to defend himself with poison arrows. He had spread his arrows out in front of himself, said Snel, and his bow was taut. All the witnesses agreed, however, that Klaas had received in excess of forty lashes with a *handsjambok*, one finger thick and $4\frac{1}{2}$ feet long. Snel had counted 230 lashes, he said, while Oberholster had found the marks of forty-four *sjambok* blows upon his body, all of which had cut through his skin and some of which had injured his genitals. By midday Klaas was dead. He was buried immediately after the Veldcornet's inspection, wrapped in his kaross. He was 'hit too high up', said Oberholster, and rode away in anger.[80]

Incidents like this were not unusual on the frontier. On the contrary, they were a common part of daily life. Each phase of the colony's expansion had brought its harvest of domestic violence.[81] Whippings might occur in response to what a master or mistress perceived as idleness or negligence, as well as outright defiance. Shepherds and shepherdesses unlucky enough to lose a sheep in the veld, albeit to a beast of prey, were particularly at risk, but so were kitchen maids who rose too late in the morning, or tarried too long in the garden.[82] However, it should not be assumed that the frequency of such punishments rendered them any the less shocking to the victims. On the contrary, it seems that the memory of these brutal incidents was sometimes burned so deeply into the psyche of the victims and their relatives that they could be recalled decades later, by persons who had never known the protagonists. Thus in 1878 /Han ǂKass'o, one of Wilhelm Bleek's informants, could still recall the story of his great-grandmother, +Gui-an, or Doortje, and her mistress, Trina de Klerk, the wife of Jacob de Klerk of Klerksfontein.[83] Doortje had been drying the dishes, said /Han ǂKass'o, so that her mistress could give food to the visitors, but 'she also did not see nicely', and she was afraid the dishes might break, so she dried them slowly and carefully, arousing impatience in the breast of Trina de Klerk. So Trina beat her, and 'stood upon her', and Doortje fainted. 'When the wind was cold', recalled /Han ǂKass'o, 'she became cool, she became insensible, insensible . . . and the place became dark, as she lay, while she could not breathe.'[84]

Granted then that direct physical coercion, which in practice often meant the infliction of life-threatening injuries, was integral to the everyday relationship between European masters and their 'Bushman' servants. But how did it come to play so large a role in the interaction between the *veeboeren* and the servant population as a whole, even those who were not originally war captives? We have already noted that the colonists in their own minds perceived a distinction, albeit muddled, between 'thieving Bushmen' on the one hand, and 'good natives or Hottentots' on the other. And they frequently reminded themselves that these 'good natives' despised and disliked the Bushmen as much as they themselves did.[85] Indeed, in 1777, the Council of Policy, issuing one of its many warnings against the abuse of Bushman captives, had seen fit to lay the blame for much of the cruelty already perpetrated at the door of the commandos' Hottentot attendants, 'as these last', opined the Councillors, 'being in general very much ill-used by the Bushman nations, may be naturally inclined to take revenge'.[86]

There is indeed a fair amount of evidence that servants of Khoekhoe origin could be willing participants in the capture and enslavement of San women and children. The reader will recall that the Khoekhoe Captain Ruiter used to help his European neighbours 'to make slaves of such straggling Boshies-men as did not live under his jurisdiction'.[87] But Ruiter was not alone in this. In 1751, for example, when Elias Campher was accused by his neighbour Jacobus Botha of involvement in slave-raiding in Outeniqualand, he replied: 'It wasn't I who did it, but my Hottentots.'[88]

And again, in an appendix to a list of captives distributed in the aftermath of Gerrit van Wyk's commando of 1774, it was noted that the commando had 'liberated (*sic*) 12 women, with six sucklings, and five girls besides, whom some of our Hottentots took to wife'.[89] Finally, we should recall Sparrman's encounter with an unnamed 'Hottentot' on the Coerney River in December 1777: 'this Hottentot', he noted, 'had caught, and then had in his custody, three old Boshies-women with their children, with an intention to take them home to his master for slaves'. The man 'had been brought up in a village near the Christians, in the service of whom he had always been', and professed to feel nothing but contempt for the 'savage manners' of his Bushman captives. He was unperturbed by their attempts to bewitch him, he said, for he 'had no faith in witchcraft'.[90]

Such sentiments could, one assumes, have been successfully exploited by a master class seeking to implement the strategy of 'divide and partially enslave' to which Patterson referred. And indeed, a careful scrutiny of the documentary record does suggest that Khoekhoe servants – or at least (since the record seldom allows so definite an attribution of identity) servants of non-captive origin – did feel their status to be different from that of Bushman captives. '*Baas, dat is niet bosjesmans of drosters kinderen dat baas die met de ketting om de hals moet vast maaken*' ('Master, those are not Bushman or *droster* children whom you should make fast with a chain around the neck'), protested the Hottentot Jacob to his master, Johannes Roos, the latter having chained Jacob's children to a tree with a brake chain.[91]

We can detect intimations of a similar attitude in a statement made by the Hottentot Truij, following the death of her sister Griet in 1791. Griet had run away from their common master, Jacobus Schalkwyk, in the company of her Bushman husband Jas. They were recaptured by Griet's brother, the Hottentot Wildeman, and handed over to their master and mistress, who beat and tormented Griet, hounding and dragging her from the house to the pack shed and back again and rubbing her wounds with gunpowder, until eventually she was overcome by convulsions and died. Testifying before the Landdrost, Truij averred that she had been eight years with her master and mistress and never once had they laid a hand on her, nor had they beaten her sister before the latter took up with the Bushman Hottentot Jas. The aforesaid Jas had been the ruin of her sister, she declared; he had many times merited a beating, for he had often run away 'without the least reason'. However, like the other servants, he had been indulgently treated and had only once been beaten, when he was cheeky to his mistress, who then hit him with a *jukscheede* (ox-yoke).[92]

One must also remember that 'Hottentot' servants were the chief victims of 'Bushman' attacks on colonial herds and flocks,[93] and that they often

Figure 9   *Bastaard Hotentot* (*sic*), watercolour by H. J. Klein (1802),
South African Library, INIL 8686.

bore the brunt of the fighting when commandos were in the field. One
might expect, then, that they would come increasingly to identify with their
masters' view of themselves as loyalists, willing defenders of the colonial
order against 'land-destroying' savages. As we have seen, most herdsmen
carried guns, though they were not allowed to own them[94] and many a
veeboer was saved from ruin by the timely action of his armed servants: 'On
31 March', reported G. R. Opperman in 1776, 'the robbers attacked the
place of Willem Jansen and tried to take the livestock by force from the
kraals, but they failed because the *volk* on the farm shot at them from
evening until morning . . .'[95]

However, before we accept too readily the notion of an emerging
dichotomy between loyal and freely contracted Hottentots on the one
hand and persecuted Bushmen on the other,[96] we should consider that
among the defending Hottentots there were many who were themselves of
Bushman origin.[97] And of those who were not, the great majority were, I
would argue, bound to their masters in almost as rigid a fashion.

In the first place, many Hottentots, although not of captive origin, had
been *ingeboekt* as *huisboorlingenen* or *Bastaard Hottentotten*, legally
obliged to serve the same master for anything up to twenty-five years.[98]
And even those who had voluntarily contracted themselves were liable to

find their children indentured under one or other of these two headings. Male slaves outnumbered females in the outlying districts of the colony (though the gender imbalance was less marked in the purely pastoral districts than in the mixed arable and pastoral districts),[99] so that liaisons between slave men and Khoisan women were fairly common. Consequently those children who escaped indenture as *huisboorlingenen* were quite likely to be *ingeboekt* as *Bastaarden* instead. The registers of Graaff Reinet district show that at least 581 children were indentured under one or the other heading between 1787 and 1800.[100]

This system of 'apprenticeship', as several contemporary observers, from Anders Sparrman to John Philip, had clearly perceived, served to bind whole families to the person who had apprenticed the children.[101] Should the parents abscond or obtain permission to leave, they were faced with enforced separation from their offspring. Philip's florid prose and his tone of righteous indignation have led many a modern researcher to doubt the authenticity of his evidence, but in truth his account of the desperate struggle of an unnamed Hottentot woman to recover her children from the farmer who had purchased their slave father is matched in the records by numerous documented cases.[102]

Few perhaps leave as lasting an impression on the reader as that of the *Bastaard Hottentot* Sara, who cut the throats of her two youngest children rather than return with them to the family of her mistress, the *Weduwee* Hans Jurgen de Beer. Sara had been twelve years in the service of Hans Jurgen de Beer, during which time she had, she said, been reasonably well treated.[103] She had stayed on after his death in 1785 because she had children by the Hottentot Flink, who was contracted to one of her master's sons, Andries Jacobus de Beer. However, soon after the old man's death, Andries Jacobus, unbeknown to his mother, had, Sara said, impregnated a Hottentot servant named Feitje, and the Widow de Beer, in her determination to discover the identity of the child's father, had beaten and maltreated Feitje until Sara could bear it no more and encouraged Feitje to name Andries Jacobus. For this, Sara declared, she had been persecuted by the widow and her sons, 'and forced to undergo the severest chastisements for trivial reasons'.[104] Following the break-up of her relationship with Flink (which he himself ascribed to the intervention of Andries Jacobus), she determined to leave 'and seek her fortune elsewhere'. The widow eventually gave her permission, but only on condition that Sara leave her eldest daughter, Leentje, behind. This Sara refused: 'My children are my cattle, after all, and everything that I possess.'[105] And shortly thereafter she left secretly, with all three of her children.

However Dawid de Beer caught up with them on the big waggon road and, ordering Sara to follow with the two smaller children, he drove

Leentje back to the house before his horse.[106] Some hours later Dawid
Schalk van der Merwe's son Willem arrived at the farmhouse with the
news that he had found two Hottentot children beside the road with their
throats cut. Sara was with them, badly wounded. When confronted by
Dawid de Beer and a party of burghers, Sara admitted to the murders and,
as though 'to prove that she herself had done it', she cut herself in the
throat and stomach.[107] Two years later the Court of Justice sentenced her
to death, though Commissioner-General Sluyksen was convinced that
'grief and desperation' had driven her to this 'unnatural deed'.[108]

The reader will be relieved to learn that very few parents were driven to
such extremes of desperation. Others caught in the same dilemma as Sara
opted either to stay, or to leave without their children. Either way, the
consequences could be severe: staying might entail the endurance of
further persecution, or the forfeit of improved conditions elsewhere; going
could mean a prolonged or even permanent separation from family
members. In 1834, during a meeting at Philipston in the Kat River valley,
the Hottentot Magerman recalled his experience of such a separation:

In Mr Fischer's time,[109] I was 'ingeboekd' for ten years, when I was so young
(here showing his height then), to my Baas Dawid van der Merwe in the Camdeboo
– my Baas promised then to bring me up and instruct me as his own children – but I
had to lie among the dogs in the ashes – I was many a time lifted out of the ashes by
the arm and flogged well so that when I ran from the hearth the ashes were strewed
and the coals after me, and the dogs, alarmed, would pursue me – I got no
instruction and no clothes – I know nothing – my Mother was obliged from the bad
treatment to run away and leave me – and my father soon after – and when he
would attempt to get a sight of me, the dogs were sent after him – O! my poor
father!. . .

Magerman eventually escaped, and was reunited with his mother in the
neighbourhood of Cape Town.[110] In this he was lucky, for the Boers
pursued their runaway *huisboorlingen* with quite as much fervour as they
did their 'Bushman' apprentices. Thus Christiaan Rudolph Opperman
waited two years for an opportunity to recapture his 'little Hottentot'
Hendrik who had absconded in the Hex River valley during a journey to
the Cape in 1789.[111] In 1791 Opperman travelled to the Cape again and,
while traversing *de straat*, a rock-walled defile at the top of the Hex River
pass, came to hear that Hendrik was with the Widow Daniel van der
Merwe in the Bokkeveld. He at once sent his son Godlieb Rudolph to
catch him, truss him and bring him home, without so much as a 'by your
leave' to the Widow van der Merwe.[112]

In the second place, even those Khoisan who had not been entrapped by
the *inboek* system could find their freedom of movement restricted by
masters whose attitudes had been shaped within the dominant slave mode

Figure 10   *Khoisan woman*, watercolour by H. J. Klein (1802), South African Library, INIL 8689.

of production and whose urgent need for labour in any case predisposed them to ignore the finer distinctions between Khoisan and slaves. Company officials reminded such men repeatedly that the Hottentots were a free people – 'fellow human beings', as the Landdrost of Stellenbosch boldly declared in 1800, 'having equal right with us to the protection of the law'[113] – but their pronouncements too often fell on deaf ears: '*Het is ons volk*', explained the brothers Johannes and Stephanus Schoeman as they captured and bound a Hottentot family who had deserted them six years before, '*wij kunnen daarmee leeven zo als wij willen*'[114] ('They are our people; we can do what we want with them').

The Landdrosts' attempts to intervene in disputes between a master and his '*volk*', or even between rival masters, were deeply resented, except where the *veeboeren* felt they could turn the ambiguous status of the Khoisan to their advantage. 'You can't frighten me with your Landdrost of Graaff Reinet', the Schoeman brothers had said to Johannes Nel, who had earlier caught their runaway servants in the veld and now wished to keep them: 'this Landdrost means nothing to me; I don't want to be bothered with this Landdrost'. And they added, 'who makes such orders that if a Hottentot has been six years away, the Baas must give him up? No! Even if this Hottentot had been seven years away, I must have him back, because he's done me too much damage.'[115]

Gabriel Stoltz had responded in similar vein when ordered by Landdrost Woeke to release the elderly Hottentot Willem Bruintjes, with his children and livestock. 'Even if the matter came before the Court of Justice', Stoltz was overheard to say, 'he would never let old Willem Bruintjes go, nor would he give up any livestock.' And when the younger Willem Bruintjes had found the courage to go to Stoltz's farm to fetch his father, with the foreknowledge of both the Landdrost and his own master, Andries Piek, Stoltz and his wife had chased him from the *werf* 'with sticks, dry bones and stones, so much so that Willem Bruintjes *d'oude* was bleeding at the nose and mouth'.[116]

The Landdrosts' position was made the more difficult by the absence of any codified regulations governing the relationship between masters and their 'Hottentot' servants. Written contracts appear to have been unknown before the reforms of 1799 (except in the case of apprentices)[117] and even verbal contracts were not made in the presence of witnesses. The Khoisan themselves clearly believed their relations with the *veeboeren* to be governed by contract. 'I asked the *oude nonje* for permission to leave', Sara had said to Dawid de Beer, 'why should I have asked you too? Do I then stand under you? (*Staan ik dan onder jou?*)'[118] But when the terms were in dispute, it was one person's word against another and, despite the stated intentions of government, the words of white men and Hottentots seldom carried equal weight in court.

The resultant vulnerability of Khoisan servants can be clearly discerned in the court records of the period. One could cite, for example, the case of the Landdrost of Swellendam versus Francina Vosloo, who in 1753 was 'graciously pardoned' for her part in the death of the Hottentot Pieter, who had been accidentally shot during a scuffle on the *werf* of her homestead, De Riet Vallij, early one October morning in 1752. Pieter and a fellow-servant, named Kieviet, had intended to leave the employ of Vosloo and her husband Hans Jurgen Gilbert and were in the process of leading their cattle from the kraal when Gilbert discovered them and disputed their right to leave. According to Kieviet, Gilbert hit Pieter with his stick and dagger and Pieter attempted to parry the blows with his kierie and his kaross.[119] Vosloo testified, however, that Pieter had overpowered her husband, who was old and weak, and that she believed his life was in danger. She had therefore taken a musket from the house 'so as to assist her husband with it'. The Hottentot Kieviet had, she said, immediately sprung forward to disarm her and during the ensuing struggle, the gun had gone off, fatally wounding Pieter.[120] The court concluded that there was no case against Vosloo – she had merely been doing her duty in going to the aid of her husband – and that even if her husband had initiated the brawl by raising his hand against Pieter, he was justified in doing so, for the two Hottentots were guilty of insolence and annoyance, having 'molested aforesaid Gilbert on his own farm, not only in that they had tried to leave secretly and without reason, *before the expiration of their contracted time'*, but also in that, through the 'stealthy opening' of the kraal, they had exposed Gilbert's cattle to risk.[121] No contract was submitted to the court in support of this judgment, nor was one requested by the bench. A master's word had been enough.

It should not be supposed, however, that the absence of written contracts left the Khoisan entirely unprotected. Like slaves, they had the right to lay complaints against their masters and (as is evident from the cases cited above) the right to testify against them in court. A Hottentot was generally not considered to be an 'irreproachable witness' – his evidence was frequently subject to 'objections to credit' raised by the accused[122] – but, as Robert Ross has argued, the evidence of 'heathens and slaves' was essential to the maintenance of the VOC's control over its extensive and thinly settled colony and the courts consequently continued to make use of such evidence.[123] 'Yes', insisted Landdrost Horak, prosecutor at the trial of the alleged disturber of the peace, Jacobus Botha, Jacobuszoon, 'if such witnesses were never acceptable, the most gruesome crimes would, at least in this country, go unpunished.' And in support of his position he cited the esteemed legal scholar Benedictus Carpzovicus, who had written that 'when it is a question of crimes committed in deserts, forests, mountains and other isolated places, even *inhabiele* [incapable?] witnesses are admissible, if one cannot get at the truth by other means'.[124]

Khoisan servants made enthusiastic use of this privilege, often braving hostile farmers and wild beasts in order to reach the Landdrost's seat. 'If you want to go there', Johannes Roos had warned his servant Jacob when the latter had threatened to report Roos' abusive treatment of his children, 'you'd better take your gun, because it's too dangerous to go from here to there without a gun, because of the Bushmen.'[125] In some cases, it seems, aggrieved Khoisan entertained exaggerated expectations of the benefits to be derived from access to the courts. 'Listen', the *Bastaard Hottentot* Jantje had said to his fellow-servant Draabok, as they travelled to the Cape with Jantje's master Okkert Goosen, 'now you must help me to nail Baas Okkert, now that he has beaten me – then we will be free people, then no Christian person can ever hire us again – we must just say that Baas Okkert shot Witbooij dead and cut him in pieces.'[126] Okkert Goosen had indeed shot the Hottentot Witbooij, but he had not cut him in pieces; he had merely left the corpse for the vultures.[127] And Draabok, finding himself, on his return to Graaff Reinet, haltered and led to the Drostdy, was soon to regret his testimony: he had, he confessed, 'to his utmost sorrow', been misled by the *Bastaard Hottentot* Jantje.[128]

Nevertheless, if access to the courts could not bring freedom, it could at least provide some protection against the worst excesses of arbitrary power. In the case of corporal punishment, for example, while there were no rules which referred specifically to the Khoisan, the Landdrosts of the country districts appear to have been guided by the regulations governing the punishment of slaves. These regulations, based partly on Roman Law and partly on the Statutes of India of 1642,[129] laid down that a master 'cannot at his pleasure dispose over the life or limbs of his slave, but is obliged when they behave well reciprocally to behave well to them'.[130] Admittedly, the limits of 'good behaviour' were narrowly circumscribed: a slave who got drunk, ran away, wilfully disobeyed a command (provided such command was not illegal or immoral), stole domestic property, occasioned loss to his master through neglect or carelessness, or was believed to be guilty of negligence or impudence, was deemed to have overstepped the limits and could be subjected to 'domestic punishment'.[131] Domestic punishment, however, was not to exceed thirty-nine lashes and, though it was not specified 'in what manner and with what instrument' such punishment was to be inflicted, it was 'recommended', according to Fiscal Denyssen, that a slave not be beaten on the naked body, 'or otherwise than on the back or buttocks', and that no other instruments but *sjamboks* (which, as we have seen, could be more than half an inch thick), leather thongs, or rattans be used for the purpose.[132] A master who transgressed these norms, or failed to provide his slaves with adequate food and clothing, could, at least in theory, be brought to book, though woe betide the slave whose complaints were found to be groundless![133] In practice, especially in the outlying districts, cases of maltreatment or deprivation were seldom reported unless death was the consequence thereof. And when a slave did die after being beaten by his master, his death was held to be an accident, unless it could be proved that his master had deliberately set out to kill him, and his master would therefore not be charged with murder, but with a lesser offence, for which the penalty might be corporal punishment or a fine, 'according to the circumstances of the case'.[134]

These rules were not explicitly invoked in cases involving the maltreatment of Khoisan servants. However an examination of such cases suggests that the slave code did indeed serve as a guide to magistrates investigating complaints of assault and brutalisation. It seems, for example, that only the most serious allegations attracted the attention of the authorities: a whipping which did no permanent physical damage was unlikely to invite inquiry and, as with slaves, a prosecution was rarely instituted unless at least one of the victims had died. The charge in such cases, moreover, was usually 'impermissible punishment' or 'mistreatment', rather than murder, and the punishment was normally a fine.[135]

In 1746, for example, the soldier Hendrik Tessenaar, *knecht* of the Burgerraad Jan Louwrens Bestbier, was fined 50 rix dollars for the 'impermissible punishment' of a Hottentot named Stuurman.[136] Stuurman had openly defied the *knecht*, disobeying an order and dismissing Tessenaar's promise of a reward for a job well done with the words 'You are a cheat, you give me nothing.' The two had become embroiled in a hand to hand struggle which ended when Stuurman pinned Tessenaar to the ground and sat on his chest.[137] The following morning, with the assistance of a visitor named Anthony Minie, Tessenaar caught Stuurman, carried him bodily into the house and suspended him by his hands from a roof-beam, with his right foot tied to a pillar of the chimney and his left foot on the ground. Then, according to a witness, 'first Hendrik Tessenaar and shortly thereafter Anthony Minie each hit the Hottentot with a sjambok on his naked back and rear body for about half an hour'.[138] They stopped when another person present warned them that the Hottentot might die. It was already too late, however, for he died three days later. Minie, who said in his defence that he 'hadn't known it was not permitted to tie up and hit someone like that', was fined 25 rix dollars.[139]

The judgment in this case was consistent with the attitude of the Court of Justice right up to the end of the period of Company rule. It was not until 1801, during the trial of Rudolph Brits, that a magistrate set out to prove 'murderous intent' in a case involving the whipping and subsequent death (from gangrene) of a Hottentot servant.[140] And it was not until well into the nineteenth century that such a charge was made to stick. Throughout the Company period, the heaviest punishment imposed on a European for the maltreatment of Khoisan servants was banishment from the colony. In 1744 Marthinus Spangenburg was banished for life for having molested and shot a servant of the Widow Mouton, near the Piketberg.[141] In 1765 Jan Otto Diederikse, employed as *knecht* on the farm of Jacobus van Reenen in the Hantam, was charged with 'far-reaching excesses and maltreatment of the Hottentots living with him' and condemned to be 'tied to a pole and severely scourged with rods on his bare back, then to be banished for 25 consecutive years to Robben Island'.[142] And finally, in 1776, Carel Hendrik Buijtendag of the Bokkeveld was banished from the district of Stellenbosch after being found guilty on a similar charge.[143]

Moreover in all these cases one could argue that, from the viewpoint of the authorities, there had been aggravating circumstances. In the first and last cases, for example, the accused had not merely maltreated their own servants, they had also molested the servants of their neighbours, and this, given the timocratic ethos of Cape society, was a more serious offence, since it was as much an affront to the dignity of the master as it was an injury to his servant.[144] In the case of Diederikse, the aggravating factors are less evident, but it appears that at least one of his victims had links with an independent Khoekhoe kraal in the area and the authorities perhaps feared that his behaviour would provoke reprisals.[145]

Now it could be argued that to receive the same protection from the law as slaves was no protection at all. It merely goes to show, one might say, that there really was no difference in status between 'Hottentots' and slaves, and that the Boers, and more to the point their merchant overlords, had entirely failed to implement the strategy of 'divide and partially enslave' which had been within their grasp. The second part of this statement is substantially correct, but to accept the first part uncritically would be to overlook not only the crucial ambiguities in the status of 'Hottentot' servants, which I have been at pains to document, but, more importantly, the determination with which they themselves exploited these ambiguities in their struggle against subjection.

We have already noted that they made energetic use of their right to complain. They complained not only of murder and assault, but also of wages unpaid, contracts dishonoured, parents and children detained and

Figure 11   *Captain Benedict Plaatjes (Ruiter Beesje)*, watercolour by
H. J. Klein (1802), Cape Town City Council, 89-247U.

livestock misappropriated. 'But Master, what damage did I ever do you?', the Hottentot Kieviet had said to Jan Schoeman.[146] 'What did I ever get from you but a mouthful of meat, and otherwise nothing? I'm not a slave, you know' ('*Ik ben immers tog ook geen slaaf*').[147]

In particular, 'Hottentot' servants used their access to the Landdrost and the courts to assert custodial claims in their parents and children. And to the extent that they succeeded, they were clearly set apart from slaves, who, according to the Roman Law, did 'not possess the right of disposing of their children, even if they be minors'.[148] They had, as we have seen in the cases of the Bastard Hottentot Sara and the younger Willem Bruintjes, to contend with the *inboek* system and with the dogged tenacity of slaveholding masters; but a plaintiff who persevered had a good chance of receiving support from the Drostdy.

The story of the Khoekhoe Captain Ruiter Platje's efforts to be reunited with his family is a case in point.[149] Ruiter (Fig. 11) first complained in November 1791 that his wife and child and two young relatives had been kidnapped by a party of Boers.[150] His wife had escaped soon afterwards, but had been obliged to leave her child and her livestock behind. Landdrost Woeke had summoned the offending burghers to the Drostdy, but to no avail, and by July 1792 Ruiter evidently felt it necessary to make a direct appeal to the government in Cape Town.[151] He was fortunate in that his visit coincided with the arrival of Commissioners Nederburgh and Frijkenius, who were immediately sympathetic to his cause,[152] and by the end of that year his case had received a preliminary hearing in Graaff Reinet, from which he may have received some satisfaction. In October 1793, however, he was arrested on suspicion of conspiracy and held for some time in Cape Town[153] and on his release he apparently found that another burgher, this time the infamous Coenraad Frederik Bezuiden-hout,[154] had hold of two of his wives, together with their children and livestock, so that the Landdrost was again obliged to take up his pen.[155]

The allegations against Ruiter were not necessarily unconnected with his untiring struggle for personal redress. For, despite their bravado in the face of authority, the Boers were acutely sensitive to the insecurity of their position. They were only too well aware that a 'faithful Hottentot', just like a captive Bushman, might at any moment be transformed, emerging as a rascal and an enemy. He might, like Van der Walt's servant Bakker, throw in his lot with the Bushmen, escaping alone, like Bakker,[156] or absconding in the company of others, like the Hottentots who set out from the Roggeveld in 1791, taking muskets, powder and shot to their Bushman allies.[157] Alternatively, like the 'Captain of the Bokkeveld', he might warn the Bushmen of a commando's approach.[158] If he had no connections with the mountain people, he might opt for the life of a 'vagabond', skulking in the interstices of colonial society, appearing unexpectedly to molest unwary travellers[159] or terrorise a former master.[160] Worse still, at least for settlers on the borders of Xhosa country, he might make common cause with the Zuurveld Xhosa.

The Boers believed that the Xhosa chiefs deliberately encouraged the desertion of slaves and Hottentots, so that they might thereby acquire guns. However when Veldwagtmeester Lucas Meyer had raised the issue with the Gqunukhwebe chief Chungwa, the latter had told him the Boers should 'remain quiet about the slaves and Hottentots, seeing that it was not he that took them away from the farms – he had not enticed them away, so he need not return them'.[161] Both during and after the Second Frontier War of 1793 it was reported that Hottentots were 'daily absconding from the Boers' and joining the Xhosa, and it seemed there was little their masters could do to stop them.[162]

In this context, the simple act of going to the Landdrost to complain could be construed as a dangerous threat to a master's authority – or even as a challenge to European dominion as a whole. And a complaint made in good faith could become a pretext for murder. For, having disregarded the restraining counsel of the authorities in Cape Town and aborted what chance they might have had to win the loyalty of the Khoekhoe, the *veeboeren* were obliged to live in a state of constant apprehension. Daily life on the farms became a continual battle of wills and suspicion lurked in every recess. So great was the Boers' fear of their Hottentot servants that they could never appreciate the wisdom of Company policy towards the Khoisan. The legal safeguards granted the latter and their resultant access to the courts of Landdrost and Heemraden were consistently perceived as an intolerable affront. 'How dare you accuse me?', Jacobus Scheepers had asked his servant Jan Blaauw. 'You are the first Hottentot who has dared to testify against me [*die mij durft verklagen*], and I'll get you Hottentotje, I'll get you.' Three weeks later, Jan Blaauw was found dead in the veld, but since his body had been destroyed by wolves, no satisfactory case could be brought against Scheepers.[163]

As for the Landdrosts who 'opened their courts to the heathen', they were at best resented, as we have seen, and at worst, as in the case of Honoratus Maynier of Graaff Reinet, painted in lurid colours as traducers of honest men and traitors to the Christian cause.[164] Maynier's willingness to hear the complaints of the Boers' Hottentot servants was seen as an outright betrayal of European interests, rather than as a politic attempt to forestall the servants' total disaffection from their masters.[165] He might profess, explained the rebellious colonists in their *tesamenstemming* of February 1795, to have the public good at heart, but his real intention was to bring ruin to the colony and subjugate the citizenry.[166] 'We ask', they continued in a later document, 'did we request this magistracy for us, or for the Hottentots? All know what schelms [rascals] they are – and we may ask if, since the first foundation of the Colony, so much Christian blood has ever been shed by the heathens as since the foundation of this district? . . . *Why are we to be placed under the heathen?*'[167]

This was fertile soil for the growth of rumour. In the fevered imaginations of frontiersmen, a few disparate shreds of information could be woven together to form a dense blanket of fear. Thus it was that in September 1793 Ruiter Platje found himself accused with the Hottentot Captain Kees and thirty-three others of having formed 'a conspiracy . . . with the Hottentots of Namaqualand to burn down the Drostdy of Swellendam and lay waste the whole land'.[168]

The sequence of events which preceded these allegations was as follows: in March 1793, two Swellendam burghers, one a woman, had been murdered by unknown assailants.[169] Towards the end of March, Captain Kees, like Ruiter before him, had journeyed to the Cape to lay a complaint before the Council of Policy.[170] In April, during his stay at the Cape, Kees was engaged by Philip Albertus Meyburg (Myburgh), Captain of the Stellenbosch militia, to lead an expedition against a band of maroons living in the Hangklip caves.[171] To this end, Kees and his party (amongst whom were several of Meyburg's employees, including one Klaas Kees) were provided with sixteen muskets and a large quantity of powder and shot. Kees returned three weeks later with one recaptured runaway and all but a handful of the ammunition. The remaining ammunition had, according to Meyburg, been used to shoot *klipspringers*.[172]

This incident appears to have been the immediate catalyst of the agitation against Kees. In August it was reported from the Hantam and Roggeveld that 'the Bushman Hottentots had stolen a great number of cattle and murdered several shepherds', and that the *veldwagtmeesters* of these districts deemed it necessary to send a commando against them as soon as possible.[173] By September, the inhabitants of the Bokkeveld were in the grip of a 'general panic', and those of the Roggeveld, where the men were absent on commando against the Bushmen, were tremulously awaiting the arrival from Namaqualand of '500 revolted Hottentots', led or instigated by Captain Kees.[174]

During the course of September some thirty-five Hottentots, including several of Philip Meyburg's servants, were detained by the burghers of Swellendam and Stellenbosch and handed over to the authorities: among them was one named Dirk, who told how he had accompanied Kees on his return from the Cape, and had learnt that Kees and another Hottentot named Jantje Hermanus had been instructed by Commissioners

Nederburgh and Frijkenius to make peace with the Bushmen, or, if that failed, to attack them. When they reached the interior, however, Jantje Hermanus had allegedly told Dirk that his real intention was 'to ravage the farms of the Inhabitants and to murder them, and that Captain Kees also had this intention'.[175]

The authorities in Cape Town quickly came to the conclusion that there was no substance to these allegations.[176] Commissioner Sluyksen decided, however, to keep Captain Kees in custody at the Castle, 'until the country people have recovered from their fright'.[177]

Alas, in the troubled atmosphere of the mid-1790s there was to be no recovery. If anything, the level of tension rose and the pressures faced by frontiersmen multiplied during the course of 1794. These pressures were both political and economic. On the political front, Bushman robberies, though occurring with decreasing frequency in the Camdeboo, continued unabated in the Sneeuberge and the Koup; in September 1794 Adriaan van Jaarsveld reported that the robbers from behind the 'Groote Tafelberg' were appearing *met hele complotten* on the Sneeuberge.[178] According to figures compiled by Donald Moodie from the records of Graaff Reinet district, a total of 1,546 cattle and 11,719 sheep were destroyed or driven off by the Bushmen between January and December 1794.[179] Moreover, the inconclusive battles between the Boers and the Zuurveld Xhosa in 1793 had left the latter firmly entrenched in the coastal forelands, and by 1795 Ndlambe's people, seeking refuge from the ire of their chief's rebellious nephew Ngqika, were pressing in on the inhabitants of De Bruins Hoogte.[180] The proximity of the Xhosa, in turn, further emboldened the Boers' unwilling servants and encouraged a spate of desertions.[181] Indeed, Maynier for one believed that much of the stock-theft reported from the Zuurveld in 1794 was the work of 'discontented Hottentots'.[182]

As though this were not enough, the economic difficulties of the *veeboeren* had also assumed critical proportions. By the mid-1790s the whole colony was caught in the grip of economic depression.[183] A falling-off in demand, combined with the unsettled state of the interior, had at last enabled the Company's butchers to bring down the price of slaughter-stock to a level which suited them: by mid-1793 the Boers were receiving 9 or 10 *schellingen* for sheep which in 1791 had fetched 16 *schellingen* a head and by the end of the following year the situation had not improved.[184]

At the same time, a shortage of specie in the colony's commodity markets was inducing the Company's butchers to suspend cash payments for livestock.[185] The *veeboeren* had a deep (and not ill-founded) distrust of the Company's paper money and they had always preferred to be paid in specie. They had, however, been prepared to accept the butchers' *briefjes,* or credit notes, provided the latter could be exchanged for cash in Cape Town. Now, however, the Van Reenen *Maatschappij* declared itself unable to provide cash in exchange for the notes; even those of their creditors who had been induced to part with stock at a price below the prevailing level, in return for a promise of prompt cash payment on presentation of the *slagters briefjes*, found themselves deceived. On arrival in Cape Town they were given the choice between waiting a further six months for payment, or exchanging the *briefjes* directly for trade goods, all too often at shops belonging to friends or business associates of the Van Reenen brothers.[186] Finally, to add insult to injury, the butchers were given the job of implementing the VOC's new hardline rent policy.[187] The vast majority of loan-farm holders were in arrears with their rent, some by as much as twenty years.[188] By 1792 the total arrears on loan-farms amounted to the enormous sum of 376,360 rix dollars and by 1795 arrears due from the district of Graaff Reinet alone amounted to 69,221 rix dollars.[189] Acting on the advice of Commissioners Nederburgh and Frijkenius, who, as we have seen, had been deputed to find ways of reducing the colony's deficit, the Council of Policy instructed the butchers to collect three years' back-rent annually from the *veeboeren* with whom they did business. To this end, the butchers' servants were to be provided with lists of debtors whom they would 'encourage' to part with slaughter stock in lieu of rent.[190] The *veeboeren* were scandalised by these arrangements and, by the end of 1793, many were refusing to sell any livestock at all to the Van Reenen brothers.[191] If Maynier had become the focus of their social and political insecurity, J. G. van Reenen, as his biographer observes, had become the personification of their economic grievances.[192]

It should come as no surprise, then, that the rumours surrounding Captain Kees could not be laid to rest, and further, that when these rumours were resurrected at the height of the burgher rebellion of 1795, J. G. van Reenen was named as one of Kees' co-conspirators, along with Colonel Robert Jacob Gordon (Commander of the Company's garrison) and the recently evicted Special Commissioner, O. G. de Wet.[193] Gordon apparently came under suspicion because of his role in the recruitment of Khoisan for the newly formed Hottentot Corps,[194] while De Wet, having been insulted and humiliated by the rebellious *volkstem* and its leaders,[195] had now sprung up from the collective unconscious, as it were, to wreak a fantastic revenge.[196] One observes, moreover, that the rumours surrounding Kees had grown in scope and fearfulness in proportion to the greater vulnerability of the citizenry: the district was now under the control of the rebel party and could expect no succour from Cape Town; even private shopkeepers had refused to extend credit to the 'people's representatives' (*volks representanten*) and their citizen Landdrost.[197]

The first 'signs' of a new conspiracy were detected in July of 1795. On Saturday, 11 July, the Bastard Hottentot Louis was brought into a meeting of Landdrost, Heemraden and *volks representanten*, so that he might testify to his connection with Captain Kees.[198] His testimony, as recorded in the minutes, was less than satisfactory, but it was sufficient to serve as a foundation for the belief that Kees had left the Castle,[199] and that his accomplices in the interior were experimenting with ammunition and possibly also with magic.[200] The meeting may also have detected evidence of a possible combination between Xhosa and Hottentot, inspired by Colonel Gordon.[201]

The Bastaard Louis having been dismissed, a certain Johannes Reichard entered the Council Chamber and told how he had heard from Jan van Zyl at the Cogmans Kloof that 'there were three hundred male Hottentots lying in a kraal in the Rodeberg, with two knapsacks of powder and many guns; and that they were just waiting for the citizenry here to revolt so as to revolt themselves and attack the Christians'.[202] Having heard these witnesses, the Board determined that henceforth 'no Hottentot should travel more than an hour's distance from his master's place without a pass', and the meeting was dissolved.[203]

By August it had become clear to the people's representatives that the entire colonial government was ranged against them in a diabolical conspiracy. Gerrit Rautenbach wrote:

Sworn brothers, we must no longer doubt our country is betrayed . . . the general presumption is that the greater number of the men in office are concerned: watch narrowly our appointed Landdrost [Carel David Gerotz], and as soon as treason is discovered, at once arrest him as a criminal, for he is suspected by many persons of judgment. Everything agrees, Captain Kees has left the Cape; we begin to collect together; be brave and honourable, and trust that God will not allow us to live under the heathen. One of Kees's men is taken in the Lange Kloof; he confesses that Ruiter Beestjes is gone to Outeniqualand. We have ordered as much powder and lead as can be fetched by three men, on account of the *volkstem*.[204]

In the event of these three men being arrested on arrival at *De Kaap*, Rautenbach added, the *volkstem* (people's voice) should be ready to proceed thither 'in a body', so as to arrest the chief conspirators.

As to the purported aims of the conspiracy, there were no doubt many variations, of which we unfortunately have no record. However Moodie has left us one account, which is as follows:

The Hottentots were to have destroyed all the males of the white inhabitants, excepting Messrs De Wet, Gordon and Van Reenen, who were to be spared to manage their political concerns, and to be further rewarded by permitting each to select for himself three of the handsomest females previous to their general distribution among the Hottentots.[205]

It would seem, then, that the dangers inherent in the enslavement of a native population *in situ* could rapidly transcend the bounds of the master–servant relationship, escalating, in the minds of a beleaguered master class, to the point where the very foundations of their identity were under threat! Maynier, who had borne the first brunt of the burghers' paranoia, was no longer in Graaff Reinet when the rumours surrounding Kees resurfaced. After his expulsion from the Drostdy in February 1795, he had retired to *De Kaap*, where he could reflect more calmly on the injudicious conduct of his erstwhile charges. Some years later he wrote:

I have continually endeavoured to convince the Peasantry of their error, but in vain; as long as they were with me they agreed with me, they were fully convinced; they promised to rely on Government, and to join hands with the Landdrosts and Commissaries to promote the public Good; but as soon as they meet with some or other ill-intentioned Person, with some or other Vagabond Schoolmaster, or with some Butcher's worthless servant, they suffer themselves to be immediately imposed on by such sort of People, and everything done or said on the side of Government is looked upon with distrust; and this is not only the case at present, but it has been the case for many years and will always remain so, as long as the people do not see with their own eyes and learn to know their own Interest.[206]

Their own interest, Maynier was certain, lay in the fair and conciliatory treatment of their Hottentot servants and the preservation of the peace recently concluded with the Zuurveld Xhosa. Decent treatment was the only way, as he patiently explained to a man whose servants had recently absconded, 'to render the Hottentots faithful and prevent them from going away . . . although they are your servants it is best to treat them as we would wish to be treated, if in their place'.[207]

This advice was excellent. Indeed, it has been the central argument of this chapter that the failure of the colonists to respect the free status of the Khoisan was bound to end in disaster, aggravating an already turbulent frontier conflict and rendering the master–servant relationship fundamentally unstable. In May 1799, as the burghers of Graaff Reinet fled in panic before a combined 'confederacy' of Xhosa and 'vagabond Hottentots', Maynier could feel himself fully vindicated.[208]

Why then, if Maynier's counsel was wise, could his subjects not follow it? What kept them from seeing what Maynier saw, and acting in their own best interest? Were they merely short-sighted, blinded by the arrogance of a slaveholding culture? Or were there other factors perhaps, other interests, which they could see, while Maynier could not?

8　'We do not live like beasts'

It may appear that the questions posed at the end of the previous chapter were merely rhetorical – that the 'other interests' which impelled the *veeboeren* to follow an apparently self-defeating course of action have in fact been known all along, but kept hidden merely for effect. In one sense, this is true: the reader may recall allusions in chapter 3 to 'hidden forces' and 'underlying polarities' which helped to shape the intense antagonisms of frontier life. The first of these – the explosive psychological tension generated by the border conflict between settlers and hunter-robbers – has already been discussed. I have demonstrated, I hope, that the repercussions of this conflict (specifically, the implications of the labour relations which emerged from it) ultimately threatened to destabilise the whole structure of Boer society on the frontier (though not necessarily in quite the ways imagined by the Boers themselves). I have also alluded, though only obliquely, to the timocratic ethos which led the Boers to view their own moral stature as inversely proportionate to the social power of their servants.[1] It remains, therefore, to examine the 'economic forces' mentioned in chapter 3. And it was indeed these forces that I had in mind when I referred to the 'other interests' which may have influenced the behaviour of Maynier's troublesome subjects.

In another sense, however, the questions posed at the end of chapter 7 were not rhetorical. The dynamics of the eighteenth-century frontier economy are not as well understood as one might wish. The work of Neumark, Guelke and Ross, which I will discuss below, has done much to illuminate the relationship between the pastoral sector and the merchant-dominated sea-port of Cape Town. However all three of these authors have been primarily concerned with macro-economic problems; they have paid little attention to the *internal* dynamics of the pastoral sector and the articulation between the individual household and the Cape Town market. Our knowledge of the pressures experienced by individual farmers has been correspondingly limited. Yet it is precisely these pressures which must be understood if we are to speak with authority of the stock-farmers' economic interests. I will try, in this chapter, to arrive at such an understanding;

150

however, to the extent that the subject matter is new and the method experimental, my conclusions will be tentative. I would therefore ask the reader to join me in a spirit of genuine inquiry.

The first step, I think, should be a review of current opinion regarding the nature of the pastoral economy. Essentially, as indicated in chapter 2, debate on this subject has centred around the extent to which production in this sector was oriented towards the market. The contending positions have been most clearly articulated by S. D. Neumark on the one hand and Leonard Guelke on the other, the former arguing that the frontier economy was 'to a considerable extent' an exchange economy dominated by commercial considerations, the latter stressing the self-sufficiency of frontiersmen and their relative isolation from the markets of the colony.[2] All subsequent studies of frontier life have (though sometimes only implicitly) paid homage to one or other of these positions, or tried to steer a middle path between them.[3] Most recently, Robert Ross, who with Pieter van Duin has completed a valuable study of the eighteenth-century Cape economy, has revised his earlier mediatory stance in favour of a more clearly Neumarkian position.[4]

In chapter 2 I too took issue with the view (so vividly expressed by John Barrow) that the frontier household was economically isolated and nearly autarchic. I argued, as the reader may recall, that all settler households on the frontier were bound tightly to the wheel of local commerce. From whatever perspective one might choose to approach the frontier household – whether as work group, kin group or consumption unit[5] – it can be demonstrated, I contended, that its reproduction was mediated by the exchange of commodities. The image of the self-sufficient pioneer household, able to meet most of its needs without recourse to exchange and therefore cushioned from the vagaries of the market, is, I insisted, inconsistent with the evidence, though the diligent researcher will be able discover one or two roving stockmen who embody this conception.

Now, it may seem that in taking this position I have entirely rejected Guelke's view of the frontier economy, and adopted that of Neumark and Ross. But this is not so, for, while I disagree fundamentally with Guelke's stress on the limited nature of the *veeboer*'s exchanges with the outside world, I find myself equally at variance with the corollary which his opponents have appended to their own position – Neumark explicitly, Ross implicitly – namely that once it has been demonstrated that a given sector of an economy is sensitive to the fluctuations of the market, it follows that the expansion or contraction of that sector is essentially a function of its profitability. If, therefore, it can be shown that the pastoral sector of the Cape economy expanded during the eighteenth century (and clearly it *did* expand), then, according to Neumark, this must be due to the sector's general profitability and its ability to promote the prosperity of the majority of its members.[6]

On the face of it, this reasoning appears unassailable. An enterprise subject to market forces must either make a profit or go under, at least in the long run. Moreover, as Ross observes, a 'rational entrepreneur' would not remain long in a market in which he continually operated at a loss.[7] Therefore, since it can be shown that the pastoral sector expanded rather than contracted during the course of the eighteenth century[8] and since it is clear that much of the increased output was destined for an expanding market, it surely follows that the sector was, as Ross tentatively puts it, 'relatively dynamic', and capable of providing the farmers 'as a body' with 'reason to expand and opportunity to flourish'.[9] Neumark was more explicit: whereas Ross attributes a modest but growing prosperity to the agrarian economy as a whole, Neumark singled out the stock-farming sector for special praise; his *veeboer* was *homo oeconomicus par excellence*, and the rapid expansion of the pastoral sector was taken as evidence that it was decisively more profitable than the 'deteriorating' arable sector.[10]

Despite its apparent logic, this argument has two fundamental weaknesses. First, it is anachronistic – it assumes that eighteenth-century producers were operating in the context of a modern market environment, in which debts were called in when they fell due, owners and managers kept detailed records of revenue and expenditure, and competitors stood poised to take advantage of weaker parties; above all, it assumes that rural entrepreneurs possessed a wide range of choices – or at least, *some* choices – with respect to the investment of their capital and the employment of their skills. (Even today, one should remember, the South African agrarian sector contains a high level of hidden unemployment.) Second, as indicated above, the argument is based on a macro- rather than a micro-analysis of the pastoral economy; both Ross and Neumark (as Ross explicitly acknowledges) have dealt in grand totals; they have not analysed the distribution of wealth *within* the pastoral sector.[11] The same, incidentally, could be said of Guelke's conclusion that most inhabitants of the Cape interior were 'rather poor, although they lived in rough comfort and were free of large debts'.[12] Neither party to the debate has analysed variation in levels of wealth or income *within* the broad group of stock-farmers: Ross' method has allowed him to demonstrate a considerable rise in *aggregate* wealth during the eighteenth century, while Guelke, using a different method, has been able to show that *average* wealth actually declined over the same period, but neither has approached the *veeboeren* as a differentiated group, with disparities in living standards, income levels, indebtedness and accumulated wealth.[13] This, however, is precisely the task which must be attempted if we are to arrive at a sufficient and satisfactory explanation of the motives which led so many of Maynier's charges to rise up in vehement defence of imprudent and provocative labour practices. Such an explanation will continue to elude us while we cling to the image of a simple and homogeneous trekboer community.

A home grown methodology

The analysis which follows is largely based on the study of the liquidation papers of deceased estates, to which I referred in chapter 2.[14] The reader may recall that the original statistical population, from which a stratified random sample was drawn, comprised 303 intestate deceased estates, arranged in ascending order according to the value of their net assets.[15] These 303 estates, drawn from the records of the Orphan Chamber, were those of deceased members of the 235 patrilineages (or patrilineal descent groups) represented on the first Graaff Reinet tax roll of 1787.[16] With few exceptions, all deceased persons who had been members of any one of the 235 patrilineages were included in the study, irrespective of their place of residence, provided only that they had died intestate between *c.* 1760 and 1812.[17]

I chose this method of data collection (according to lineage, rather than place of residence) because I believed it would assist me, at a later stage, to examine the economic relationships between households which were linked by ties of blood and marriage.[18] However, the method does have its drawbacks. Specifically, it has meant that the statistical population includes many decedents from the eastern parts of Swellendam district and the north-eastern parts of the Stellenbosch district, including several who died long after the formation of the new district of Graaff Reinet in 1786. The population also includes a handful of estates of deceased urban residents and arable farmers from the south-west Cape. It could be argued that the inclusion of these latter 'non-pastoralist' households will distort the results of the study, or at least detract from its use as a tool for understanding the frontier economy. This might well be so if one were dealing in large numbers, where the identity of individual households would be lost in aggregates and averages. However in this case the sample selected from the total population is relatively small; moreover, for much of the discussion which follows, individual estates will be examined in the context of the stratum to which they belong, and therefore the peculiarities of each estate will be the more readily identifiable.

The stratified random sample comprises seventy-four deceased estates (that is, 24 per cent of the statistical population, including insolvent estates, which will not be discussed below), selected at random from the stratified population of 303.[19] Taken together, the seventy-four liquidation accounts and the documents annexed to them (including *vendurollen*,[20] invoices, IOUs and fragments of account books) comprise a database of enormous richness, the more so since, owing to the random selection process, the information gathered, while neither complete nor perfect, can be expected to lead in the main to representative data sets.

For those interested in the demographic history of the Dutch colony, the possibilities are immense. If the liquidation accounts are used in conjunction with *opgaafrollen*, transfer documents[21] and loan-farm registers, it becomes possible to reconstruct the life-cycle of the frontier family, examining patterns of inheritance, wealth accumulation and family formation. Notions long cherished by students of Afrikaner history, such as that of the stem family[22] and the patriarchal household, can be re-examined in the light of a wealth of new data.

Unfortunately, such a project is well beyond the scope of the present chapter. Our concern here is only with those aspects of household reproduction which had a direct bearing on the labour market – if such it can be called – and our attention must therefore be confined to the economic functions of the household and to the associated categories of output, income, expenditure and profitability. The latter varied with the scale of the operation, hence my focus upon wealth differentials.

It will become clear, I hope, in the course of the discussion which follows, that during the second half of the eighteenth century there was indeed a very wide variation in wealth within the European frontier community. On the one hand, there was a tiny minority of really prosperous households, whose material position compared favourably with that of well-to-do arable farmers in the south-west Cape.[23] On the other hand, there was a much larger minority – some 40 per cent of all frontier households – which was barely able to make ends meet. In between the two extremes came a quite substantial group of households which, to a greater or lesser extent, fitted Guelke's image of a people living in 'rough comfort', unencumbered by heavy debt. However, even in this middle group there were many, as we shall see, who would not have considered themselves economically secure.

Before proceeding to a more detailed analysis of the domestic economy of households in each group, it would be as well to consider two further problems arising from the nature of the sources. The first concerns the distinction between estate and household. There is no necessary correlation between the two. A person (or persons, in the case of a couple married in community of property)[24] whose estate was administered by the Orphan Chamber was not necessarily the head of a household. If the household is defined as a co-resident domestic group whose members contribute to a common fund,[25] then it is clear that many persons whom the law regarded as independent for the purposes of estate settlement may in fact have been attached to households headed by others: thus unmarried adult offspring may have resided with their parents, and elderly parents with their sons or sons-in-law. Several estates in our sample belong in this category. They occur in all strata, but their incidence is disproportionate in the two lowest decimae,[26] since, as will become clear below, the gross value of estates in these decimae was normally too low to permit the maintenance of an independent household.

The second problem arising from the nature of the sources concerns the age profile of the sampled estates.[27] This was influenced by the testamentary practices of the *veeboeren* as well as the variation in mortality rates among different age groups. Thus, while wills were rarely used by frontiersmen to privilege one heir over another, it was quite common for a married couple to draw up a will designating the 'longest living' of the two as sole heir to the estate, provided that appropriate sums were set aside to be paid to the children when they came of age, married, or reached 'another approved status'.[28] If the surviving spouse intended to remarry, he or she was normally obliged by the terms of the will to appoint two 'irreproachable men' as trustees of these portions. Sometimes a remarrying spouse was also obliged to have the estate inventoried and valued, so that there should be no underestimation of the shares due to the children. However, in such a case, he or she was still allowed to retain usufruct of the full estate until the children reached the required age or status. Only on the death of the surviving spouse was the joint estate put into liquidation.

It could also happen that, upon remarriage, a widow or widower entered into a new testamentary agreement with his or her second spouse, in terms of which the longest living was again appointed as sole heir. In this case, if the party entering into a second marriage subsequently predeceased his or her second spouse, the property he or she brought into the second marriage would now become part of the second spouse's estate, with the proviso that the children's portions (called *kinderbewijsen* in the liquidation accounts) still due to the offspring of the deceased's first marriage be paid out or set aside until they came of age and that *kinderbewijsen* from the deceased's share of the second matrimonial estate be allotted to all the children of the deceased, including those born of the second marriage.[29] Such complicated arrangements were probably fairly rare[30] – perhaps they were made only when the remarrying spouse brought minor children into the new marriage – but where they did occur one imagines that they had the potential to generate considerable tension among the members of the reconstituted family![31]

Be that as it may, what concerns us here is that, in so far as married couples made use of these forms of testamentary agreement, the sample of deceased estates will be biased towards older members of the frontier population, since, where a will existed, a joint estate would not reach the desk (and thence the archive) of the Orphan Masters until after the death of the surviving spouse.[32] There would, by the same token, be a high proportion of widows and widowers among the deceased in the sample. If the liquidation accounts are to be used, as I intend here, to provide insight into the trading position and general economic viability of frontier households, then a bias in favour of the elderly might further complicate the task, since elderly persons were less likely than others to have been heading independent households at the time of their death. The extent to which elderly people continued to play an active role in the management of the household economy would have been determined, for the most part, by the retirement customs of the *veeboeren*. Little is known about these at present, but there is evidence, some of it in the liquidation papers themselves, which suggests that it was common for men and women to withdraw from active farming once they reached a certain age.[33] In this they were following a pattern common to peasant communities in many parts of north and central Europe.[34] However in Europe peasant retirement was usually associated with a system of anticipated inheritance, or inheritance *inter vivos*, in terms of which a retiring couple or widowed parent would transfer the farmstead and its equipment to one of their heirs, on the understanding that he or she would maintain them until they died.[35] Such transfers were not necessarily accompanied by formal change of ownership – formal transfer might be delayed until the death of the old people – but they always involved a change in the headship or management of the household.

At the Cape, by contrast, anticipated inheritance was probably far less common. In the first place, it was not easily reconciled with the strict egalitarianism of local inheritance customs; in the second place, the relative ease with which young men could acquire land of their own probably reduced the pressure on parents to relinquish control of their estate to their heirs. These factors may account for the apparent absence at the Cape of formal 'retirement contracts' such as those found among peasants in Scandinavia and many parts of central Europe.[36] None the less, we do know that farmsteads at the Cape were sometimes 'prelegated' to a single heir, on condition that he compensated the testators' estate upon their death,[37] and we know that, in at least one such case, the bequest was explicitly made in return for 'services rendered . . . to the testators over a number of years'.[38]

Without further research we cannot make generalisations about retirement practices at the Cape, but it must be acknowledged that, in so far as retirement was accompanied by a *de facto* (as opposed to *de jure*) transfer of assets *inter vivos*, we may find that the estate papers of retired people do not constitute a full and accurate statement of the actual wealth of the household, for the assets of the parents (or at least, their landed wealth and farming equipment) may in reality have been incorporated with those of the care-taking heir. Conversely, should the care-taking heir predecease his parents, the liquidation account of his estate would not truly reflect the wealth of his household. Unfortunately, there is no ready way of identifying such cases, except when entries in the *opgaafrollen* or fragments in the papers of the Orphan Chamber clearly indicate co-residence.

In Table 1 (below), the seventy sampled estates with a net value greater than zero (i.e. excluding insolvent estates) are ranked according to both the net wealth and the age of the deceased.[39] It can be seen that one third of the decedents whose estates were investigated were more than 65 years old at the time of their death. Of these, 65 per cent were in the five poorer categories and 35 per cent in the five richer categories.[40] Clearly then, elderly persons are well represented in the sample. Against this, however, one can set the twenty-four persons (34 per cent of all those whose estates were investigated) who died in the prime of life – between the ages of 35 and 55. And if to them are added the seven persons who died between the ages of 25 and 35, and the fourteen who died between the ages of 55 and 65, we have a total of forty-five estates (that is, 64 per cent of all those investigated) which are likely to reflect the condition of households at an early or middle stage of the developmental cycle.

The right-hand column of Table 1 contains the deciles of the variable net wealth, according to which the 292 solvent deceased estates were stratified. If the spread of wealth is illustrated in graphic form, as in Fig. 12, it can be seen that there were marked disparities in the distribution of wealth within the statistical population. For example, all estates in the fourth decima were worth at least 3.5 times as much as those in the first (i.e. lowest) decima. Again, those in the tenth (i.e. the highest) decima were between 5.8 and 57 times more valuable than the largest estate in the fifth decima, and between 23 and 221 times more valuable than all estates in the lowest two decimae. Moreover, just thirty-four of the 292 solvent estates accounted for 50 per cent of the aggregate net wealth of all 292 put together. These thirty-four estates, in other words, made up a 'minimal majority' of just 11.6 per cent.[41]

If one examines the variation in *average* net wealth from one decima to the next, the extent of socio-economic differentiation within frontier communities becomes even clearer (Table 2).

It can be seen that fully 50 per cent of the estates included in the study[42] had an average net value of less than 2,000 rix dollars. One notices too that, while average net wealth increases fairly steadily between the second and

Table 1. *Age profile of deceased estates*

Decima	Approximate age at death						Decile[a]	
	< 16	16–25	25–35	35–55	55–65	> 65	rds	sts
1st			xx	x[b]	xx	xx	245	28.5
2nd			xx			xxxx	520	42
3rd		x	x	xx	x		890	39.5
4th			x	xxxxx[c]		xxx	1,479	43.5
5th				x	x	xxxxx	2,011	10.5
6th			x	xxxxxx	xx		3,634	23.5
7th	x		x	x	x	x	5,065	14.5
8th			x	xx	xxxx	xx	6,813	6
9th				xxx	x	xx	11,722	7.5
10th				x	xxx	xxx	115,050	40
TOTAL	1	1	7	24	14	23		

[a]Deciles are numbers which separate an ordered array of values (in this case, positive values) into one-tenth parts. The first decile demarcates the lowest 10 per cent of observed values and the tenth decile demarcates the end of the highest 10 per cent (i.e. the maximal value).
[b]This estate belonged to the German Volkert Schoenmaker of Brewitzj, whose birth date is unknown. He arrived at the Cape in the Company's service some time before 1766. He achieved freeburgher status in 1789 and died in the district of Swellendam *c.* 1796. If one assumes that he was about 20 years old at the time of his arrival, then it follows that he was approximately 50 years old at the time of his death. However, if he came to the Cape as a man already entering middle age, he would have been an old man in 1796. See J. Hoge, 'Personalia of the Germans at the Cape, 1652–1806', *Archives Year Book for South African History* 9 (1946) and vc 45, General muster rolls, 1760–71.
[c]The last x in this cell represents a certain Pieter van Wyk *d'oude*, whose estate was liquidated in 1812. The liquidation account names neither his spouse nor his only surviving child. Thus there is no way of knowing which Pieter van Wyk he is. He could be one of two: one christened in 1738 and the other in 1758. (See De Villiers and Pama, *Geslagsregisters*, vol. III, pp. 1152–3.)

ninth decimae, there is a sharp jump or hiatus in the pattern between the first and second and the ninth and tenth decimae respectively. (Again, this irregular pattern is best illustrated in graphic form, as in Fig. 13.) There was, in other words, one category of households which were very much poorer than the rest and another category of households which were significantly richer than all the others. One was set apart by extreme poverty, the other by (in relative terms) extreme wealth.

So much for the figures. They are useful as an index of the distribution of wealth; they demonstrate that the frontier population was far from homogeneous with respect to the ownership of property.[43] Our concern here,

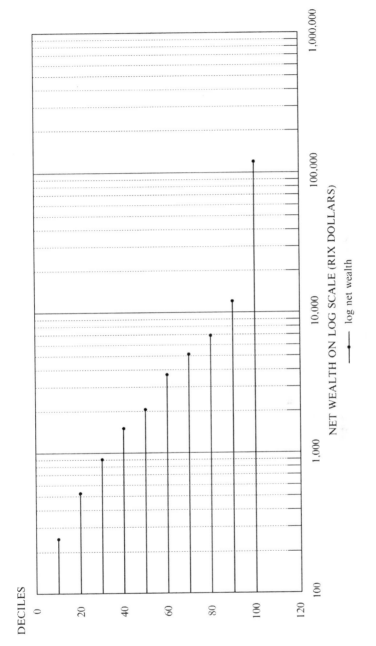

Figure 12 Distribution of net wealth. *Source:* MOOC 13/1/5-35.

Table 2. *Average net wealth of deceased estates,*
1764–1812, by decima

Decima	Average net wealth in rix dollars
1st	112
2nd	380
3rd	679
4th	1,145
5th	1,730
6th	2,683
7th	4,412
8th	5,881
9th	9,009
10th	22,501

however, is not with wealth *per se*, but with the income which it could generate. What did it mean to be among the poorest 20 per cent of the frontier community? What did it mean to belong to a household of average means? How much cash could one earn? How much food would one have? What could one wear? What luxuries could one afford? Where could one live? What debts could one incur without risking bankruptcy? And how much of one's income could one set aside to pay for labour?

The distinctions between wealth and poverty, superfluity and sufficiency, are, as Braudel reminds us, essentially relative, changing constantly across time and space.[44] Even destitution will have different features in different epochs. Our focus, then, should be on the *relative* distribution of assets – land, livestock, slaves, waggons, tools, furniture, etc. – between households. But since we are primarily concerned with income and profitability, and not with differences in living standards *per se*, we must do more than analyse variation in the composition of wealth: we must attempt to estimate its annual yield – the income which could be derived from it. If annual yield is then compared with an estimate of annual costs, including labour costs, the costs of replacement and depreciation, interest payments and land rentals, one should be left with an estimate of the amount available for consumption and investment; that is, with an overall picture of the viability of the enterprise.

Obviously, this exercise cannot be performed with anything approaching the precision of a modern audit; the documentation contained in estate papers provides a more or less full and accurate statement of the assets of

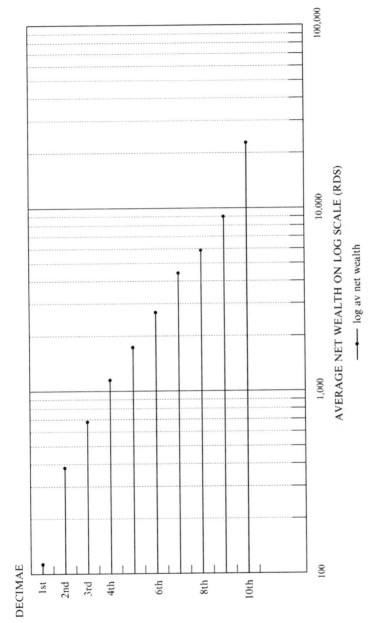

Figure 13   Distribution of average net wealth. *Source:* MOOC 13/1/5-35.

an individual at the time of his death, but his expenditure is not documented, except in so far as he had debts still outstanding. Eighteenth-century frontiersmen did not keep accurate accounts. They kept rudimentary *schuldboeken* in which they listed moneys owed to them, and occasionally they made lists of the sums they owed to others, but, unlike their merchant contemporaries, they made no attempt to balance their books and they made no distinction between operating costs and personal consumption. Furthermore, nearly all had access to resources which were not reflected in the liquidation accounts; one thinks particularly of wild foods such as game and *veldkos* (edible plants), as well as household necessities like salt, berry wax, thatching grass and soda ash,[45] but poultry and the resources of the kitchen garden were also often omitted from inventories. Any attempt to reconstruct a balance sheet will suffer from these omissions; yet it is impossible to estimate income from invisible sources, except in cases where an individual was clearly unable to subsist from his recorded means. Moreover, since it has been demonstrated that frontier households could not escape from the thrall of the market, it seems legitimate to focus first on *marketable* produce – livestock, butter, soap, candles, fruit, wheat, wine, brandy, domestic manufactures and, where possible (which is seldom), aloe gum, berry wax, ivory and skins – for it was this which determined the ability of a household to keep its head above water. The hidden sources of income were valuable, I would argue, precisely because they enabled a household to maximise its sales of marketable produce.

'The intolerable shackles laid on trade'

The critical role of marketable output in the determination of an individual's solvency was not merely a function of the extent and depths of the *veeboer*'s involvement with the market; it derived also from the peculiar nature of the market itself. It is common cause among historians that trade at the Cape was severely restricted by the mercantilist policies of the VOC. It may be true, as Ross contends, that the restrictions did not serve as a brake on the development of the colony to the extent that has been hitherto supposed.[46] Nevertheless I believe it can be demonstrated that, for the *veeboeren* at least, the VOC's policies spelt severe hardship, if not disaster. In essence, these policies meant that the *veeboeren* faced extremely adverse terms of trade: on the one hand, the monopsonistic organisation of the meat market ensured that the prices they received for their livestock, while not entirely static, were lower than those they would have received in a more open market;[47] on the other hand, the restrictions placed on manufacturing in the colony,[48] coupled with the uncertainties and ambiguities surrounding the import trade, ensured that the prices of the myriad consumer and producer goods that frontiersmen required were not only inflated but also subject to wild fluctuations.

Strictly speaking, all imports to the Cape were controlled by the VOC; neither freeburghers nor officials were permitted to import goods on their own account, unless they paid the exorbitant freight charges and import dues levied by the Company. The importation of goods carried in foreign ships was prohibited and, prior to November 1792, when new regulations concerning 'free navigation' were introduced by Nederburgh and Frijkenius, freeburghers were not permitted to purchase or charter ships for their own use.[49] Furthermore, private importation of East Indian products (spices, pepper, coffee, tea, tobacco, indigo, rice, sugar, porcelain, teak, arak, rattans and a huge variety of textiles being among the most important) was totally forbidden.

In practice, however, these regulations were honoured mainly in the breach. Despite the VOC's avowed concern for the preservation of its monopoly, it consistently failed to supply its growing colony with the wherewithal to meet its needs. In Mentzel's time only one ship per year was set aside for the transport of Asian products from Batavia to the Cape. She carried rice for the garrison and the Company's slaves; spices, sugar candy, tea and coffee for the population at large; and a consignment of textiles including chintzes, plain calicoes, linens and muslins, for sale to the colonists.[50] Company imports from the Netherlands were rather more substantial, since they were carried as ballast on outward bound ships. In the 1730s, according to Mentzel, their annual value was approximately 100,000 Dutch guilders (41,666 rix dollars).[51] However after 1750 the annual proceeds from official sales of Dutch goods at the Cape seldom exceeded 40,000 guilders: in 1772, for example, they amounted to only 16,745 guilders (6,977 rix dollars) and in 1776 to 31,612 guilders (13,171 rix dollars).[52]

The goods on offer were, as Mentzel observed, 'a miscellaneous assortment'. Among the most important were supplies for the ships – tar, rope, timber, canvas, masts and anchors – and hardware required by Company and colonists alike. Since the colony had neither mines nor metal processing industries, all metals were imported: iron, steel, copper, tin and lead being the most prominent. Manufactured metal goods were likewise imported; the colony's blacksmiths, it seems, concentrated mainly on repairs. Thus a typical shipload of European imports might include everything from agricultural implements, pots and pans, pins and needles, axes, cleavers, nails, carpenters' tools, firearms, razors and cutlery, to gewgaws like ear-rings, hairpins and brass buttons.[53] It would also include coal for the blacksmith's furnace and textiles for the use of colonists and officials: linen and broadcloth, kerseys and corduroys, silks, says and velvets, and the coarse woollen baize so popular in Karoo households. There might also be an assortment of less bulky goods – cotton-wool and thread, paper and ink, soap, string and handkerchiefs, mirrors, penknives, tinderboxes and flints, beer and brandy, brushes and brooms, paints and linseed oil, hats and stockings – everything, in short, except the extremely limited range of produce with which the Cape could supply itself. The goods imported were, as Mentzel commented, 'too numerous to detail',[54] but their very variety serves to underline the extent of the colony's dependence upon imports.

Despite the great diversity of the European manufactures imported under the auspices of the VOC, these too fell far short of actual demand – a large portion was in any case destined for the use of the Company's own establishment[55] – and, as in the case of Asian imports, it was left to private trade to fill the gap. Since this trade was technically illegal, its mechanisms remain somewhat obscure, but it is clear that they centred around the limited privileges granted to the officers and crew of Company ships. Each member of the crew (including soldiers) was allowed to bring a sea-chest aboard in which to store his belongings. As Thunberg explained, the size of the chest varied with the status of the crew-member:

A soldier is only allowed to have a little box about three feet square, to contain his scanty store. A sailor, who needs a greater change of clothes, is allowed one double as large; but the officers may bring one or more large chests (besides baskets, bottle cases and casks of beer) as well for stowing merchandise in as for provisions; though for the most part, besides these, they find means of conveying separate chests of clothes and provisions on board. [56]

Prior to embarkation, all authorised baggage was assembled at India House and branded with the Company's mark. However, as Thunberg indicates, the officers in particular found ways of carrying unauthorised containers aboard. In these they stowed all manner of merchandise for sale at the Cape and in Batavia: 'wines, beer, cured hams, cheese, clay pipes, tobacco and sometimes some haberdashery'.[57] Homeward bound ships were crammed with merchandise belonging to senior officers. Indeed, Company officials noted on several occasions that the practice of storing bulky trade goods, 'such as Arak, Rice, sugar and rattans' in the already confined space between decks was causing damage to the health of the crews. Nothing was done, however, for those charged with enforcing the regulations were often among the worst offenders.[58]

At the Cape itself purveyors of illicit merchandise were very rarely prosecuted. Indeed, it seems that the regulations were entirely ignored, except in the case of certain heavily protected goods like spices and tobacco. Here too, however, it was mainly the lowly crew-members who fell victim to the vigilance of officials:

Should a poor soldier or sailor have a single roll [of tobacco] with him, it is speedily pounced upon as contraband . . . yet the captains and other high officers who have received permission from the Independent Fiscal to bring some merchandise for private trading smuggle in enormous quantities of tobacco. The other officers, the helmsman, the bookkeeper and the chief surgeon, make common cause for this purpose and are equally successful . . . Ways and means have been found to smuggle a few thousand pounds of tobacco from every ship.[59]

The Independent Fiscal, as a matter of fact, was a pivotal figure in the operation of private trade. It was he who gave permission for the landing and sale of the officers' merchandise, receiving 5 per cent of the proceeds for his pains.[60] Fiscal van Lynden, among others, was said to have made a very good living by this means.[61] The only restriction imposed, apparently, was that sales of private imports should be held over until after the Company's own merchandise had been disposed of.[62] Since the Fiscal was also the official charged with the apprehension of smugglers, it is no wonder the sea captains believed that the regulations restricting private trade had fallen into disuse at the Cape, and indeed, that 'this contraband and illicit trade' was 'actually authorised by Government'.[63]

The ambiguities surrounding the prerogatives of the Company's seamen could also be exploited by Cape-based merchants who wished to import goods directly from Europe. In such cases the crew-member (or passenger) served merely as an intermediary, having made over his baggage allowance, in return for a fee, to the merchant's supplier or agent in the Netherlands. This procedure could be cumbersome, for a large shipment would have to be dispersed among several crew-members, and sometimes even among several ships, so as to disguise its true nature.[64] The goods might also be addressed to several different recipients in Cape Town, again for purposes of camouflage.[65] Nevertheless, despite its intricacies, the system appears to have functioned remarkably smoothly: there were printed contracts (Fig. 14) which defined the responsibilities of the intermediary and spelt out the limits of his role, and there were tried and tested mechanisms by which money could be transfered from the Cape to Europe for the payment of suppliers.[66] During the second half of the eighteenth century large consignments of goods were moved in this way, in both VOC and foreign vessels.[67]

One might conclude, then, from the above, that the restrictions on private trade were so loosely applied as to be meaningless, or rather that the obstacles in the way of the free movement of goods were so easily circumvented as to be of little consequence to the Cape consumer.[68] But this was not so. In the first place, since residents of the Cape were not permitted to import goods in their own ships, or to charter vessels for this purpose, the supply of imported products was entirely dependent on

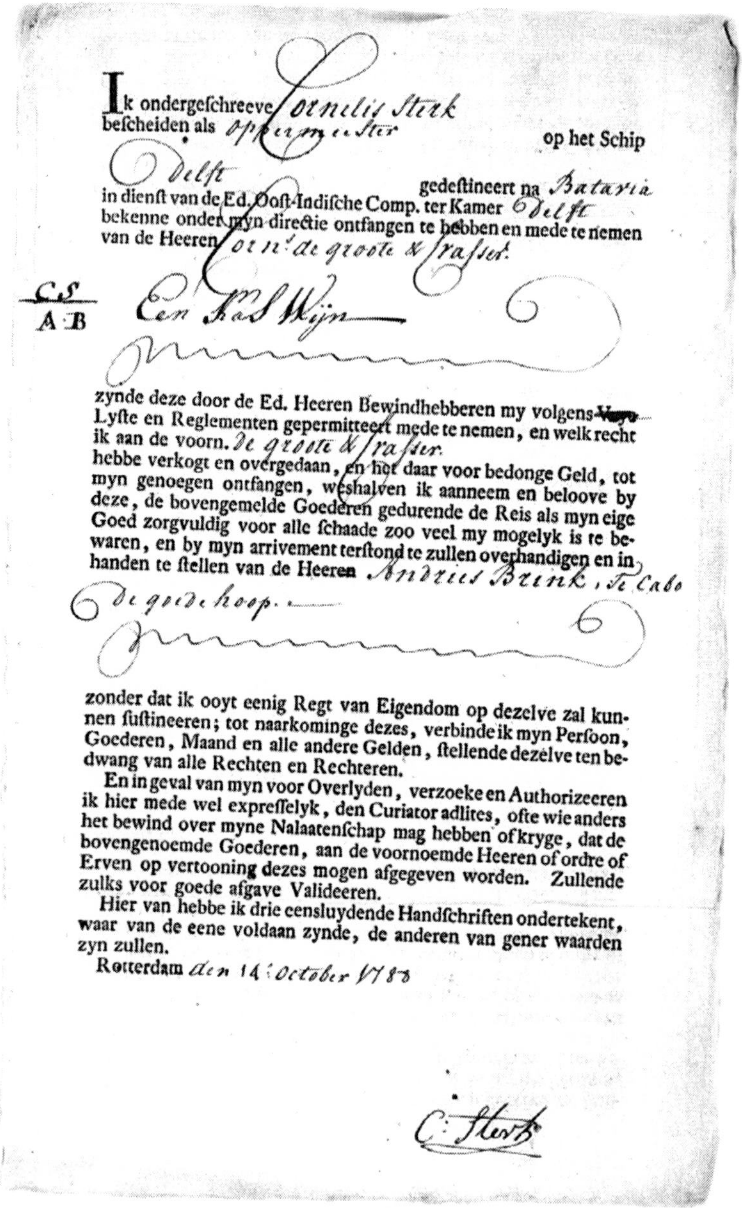

Ik ondergefchreeve *Cornelis Sterk*
befcheiden als *oppermeester*   op het Schip

Delft   gedeftineert na *Batavia*
in dienft van de Ed. Ooft-Indifche Comp. ter Kamer *Delft*
bekenne onder myn directie ontfangen te hebben en mede te nemen
van de Heeren *Corn: de groote & Crasser:*

C S
―――
A B   *Een fcas Wijn*

zynde deze door de Ed. Heeren Bewindhebberen my volgens
Lyfte en Reglementen gepermitteert mede te nemen, en welk recht
ik aan de voorn. *De groote & Crasfer.*
hebbe verkogt en overgedaan, en het daar voor bedonge Geld, tot
myn genoegen ontfangen, weshalven ik aanneem en beloove by
deze, de bovengemelde Goederen gedurende de Reis als myn eige
Goed zorgvuldig voor alle fchaade zoo veel my mogelyk is te be-
waren, en by myn arrivement terftond te zullen overhandigen en in
handen te ftellen van de Heeren *Andries Brink , Te Cabo*

de goede hoop. ―

zonder dat ik ooyt eenig Regt van Eigendom op dezelve zal kunnen fuftineeren; tot naarkominge dezes, verbinde ik myn Perfoon,
Goederen, Maand en alle andere Gelden, ftellende dezelve ten be-
dwang van alle Rechten en Rechteren.
En in geval van myn voor Overlyden, verzoeke en Authorizeeren
ik hier mede wel expreffelyk, den Curator adlites, ofte wie anders
het bewind over myne Nalaatenfchap mag hebben of kryge, dat de
bovengenoemde Goederen, aan de voornoemde Heeren of ordre of
Erven op vertooning dezes mogen afgegeven worden.   Zullende
zulks voor goede afgave Valideeren.
Hier van hebbe ik drie eensluydende Handfchriften ondertekent,
waar van de eene voldaan zynde, de anderen van gener waarden
zyn zullen.
Rotterdam *den 14: October 1788*

C: Sterk

Figure 14   Contract between Cornelis Sterk, first mate on the ship *Delft*,
and Messrs Cornelis de Groote and Crasser, agents of the Cape Town
merchant Andries Brink, for the transport of a case of wine to the Cape in
1788. *Source:* MOOC 14/73.

shipping time-tables drawn up in Europe or the Indies, largely without regard to the needs of the Cape market. Consequently, the supply of specific goods was erratic and unpredictable, with periods of shortage and glut alternating in giddy succession. The resulting fluctuation in prices presented the canny businessman with excellent opportunities for profit, provided only that he be 'wide-awake and well acquainted with shipping matters'.[69] As Mentzel explained:

prices at the Cape are never stable. An article may be very expensive one day and ridiculously cheap a few weeks later. Everything depends on the quantity of goods available and the prospect of speedy replacement. Should there be many Dutch ships in the Bay upon their outward voyage, there would be a glut in the supply of many articles. Everybody would lay in a stock of these commodities that were purchased at a low price and hold out for a rise. Supposing that, a few weeks later, other Dutch ships would put in the Bay with more goods of the same type, prices would tumble. On the other hand, should an unusually long interval elapse between the visits of outward bound vessels, prices would go up because, apart from local consumers, ready customers for Dutch wares are always to be found on homeward bound Indiamen. In a short time prices would soar to giddy heights and the goods would soon be unobtainable.[70]

In the case of tobacco, for example, for which there was 'enormous' local demand, since 'it is the custom here to give each slave, male or female, a span of tobacco weekly', prices might rise from 9 to 10 *stuivers* per pound to between 12 and 20 *stuivers* per pound in a matter of weeks, if a homeward bound fleet should 'put into Table Bay before the stock is replenished'.[71]

The instability of the market could enable foreign visitors to make a tidy profit. In November 1794 the Dutch Vice-Admiral Cornelis de Jong discovered that European products were 'unimaginably expensive' in Cape Town and that an article which cost 20 *stuivers* in the Netherlands could be sold for 44 at the Cape.[72] And during his stay at the Cape in 1772-3, Thunberg noted that 'all European merchandizes are sold here at thirty, fifty and one hundred percent profit'.[73] Asian goods could likewise fetch an excellent price.[74]

There were excellent pickings to be had by local people too, as Mentzel indicated. Here, however, the benefits of speculative buying and selling (which was said by some to be the chief preoccupation of the inhabitants of Cape Town) were largely confined to those who could attend and bid at the frequent auction sales of newly disembarked goods. Country people could seldom time their rare visits to the Cape to coincide with the arrival of a particular cargo. Nor could they tarry long enough to shop around.[75] Moreover, if they should be lucky enough to attend a sale of their choice they might well be prevented from bidding by the 'tight oligarchy of businessmen' who controlled the Vendue Department and decided upon the creditworthiness of patrons.[76] Creditworthiness was a status conferred on those who were personally known to the auctioneer, or who were able to find a man of substance to stand surety.[77] For those who were excluded from the auctions, whether by accident or design, there was nothing for it but to purchase one's necessities from retailers, often at inflated prices. The upcountry *veeboeren* were well aware of the disadvantages of this state of affairs, as can be seen in the following extract from a petition addressed to the British Governor, Lord Macartney, in 1798. The signatories expressed their joy at the arrival of a cargo of agricultural implements, but explained 'that selling these goods by auction, the merchants provide themselves first, and afterwards sell them for an exorbitant price to people that live in a remote part and that cannot embrace the moment the auctions are held'.[78]

In the second place, the on-shore retail trade was also set about with numerous restrictions. With the exception of the handful of licensed *pachters*, Capetonians were not permitted to establish warehouses and shops for the purposes of private trade. Private shops did exist, of course – indeed, many visitors observed that there was scarcely a household in Cape Town which did not have something to sell[79] – but they were located in private houses and their business was conducted in a semi-clandestine manner. Under these conditions, it was impossible to hold large volumes of stock for any length of time, and consequently the goods on offer tended to reflect the erratic patterns of the clandestine import trade. As Mentzel explained:

Much depends upon what is offered at auction or is obtainable indirectly. Sometimes a stock of soft goods is on hand – silk, linen, woollen and cotton goods; sometimes groceries and spices – coffee, tea, sugar, rice, English bloaters, Dutch herrings and Cape butter; or it might be crockery, cutlery and utensils – spoons, knives, scissors, glassware, mirrors, buttons, buckles, etc. In short, it is possible to purchase every conceivable article of merchandise, but never at the same place, or at the same time, or at the same price.[80]

It can be imagined that such conditions made shopping rather difficult for the out-of-town visitor! To be sure, there were bargains to be had, and the astute frontiersman might be able to acquire a stock of cheap goods which could be resold in the interior at a comfortable profit, but much depended upon the timing of his visit and the nature of his contacts. Indeed, it can be argued that, for the *veeboer*, one of the chief consequences of the restrictions on Cape Town's retail trade was the reinforcement of his dependence upon a small number of urban merchants – those who had cultivated the inland trade and, above all, those to whom he was already bound by a complicated network of credit and debt.

The primary causes of the *veeboer*'s dependence upon urban merchants – and hence his vulnerability to exploitation – were the difficulties he faced in travelling to and from the Cape and his perennial shortage of cash. Much has been written about the arduous nature and high cost of overland travel between the Cape and the interior. It could take from two to three months to make the return trip from Cape Town to Graaff Reinet and the cost in man-hours, oxen, and wear and tear on the waggons might well outweigh the benefits of the journey.[81] It is these circumstances which, in Guelke's view, led frontiersmen to keep their contacts with the market to a minimum. However, there were ways of circumventing the tyranny of distance – though always at a cost.

The most common method was to entrust one's commission to a relative or neighbour who was travelling to *De Kaap*. Occasionally, this individual might transact the business himself, but more often he would hand the commission to a professional middleman or agent, who would settle debts and make purchases on behalf of his absent client. These middlemen might be substantial merchants themselves, like the former butcher Jan Adam Rens, or the importer Andries Brink, both of whom did a thriving trade with the interior districts;[82] or they might merely be the keepers of lodging houses, who, as Barrow acidly opined, made a living from defrauding their upcountry guests.[83] Barrow may have exaggerated the vulnerability of the *veeboer* in an urban setting,[84] but there is little doubt that in the complex and secretive commercial environment of Cape Town, an agent who knew the ropes enjoyed a great deal of latitude.

This latitude could extend from the choice of merchandise ('I am sending Your Worship in addition two els of blue broadcloth', wrote the merchant J. Hoets to Dirk Jacobus Pretorius, 'which will prove cheaper to Your Worship than a half-worn jacket')[85] to the granting of unsolicited credit.[86] Liberality in the latter sphere may not have been taken amiss, since the graziers were in desperate need of credit. Many months might elapse between visits of the butcher's *knecht* and, as we have seen, it could be many months more before the farmer was paid in hard cash.[87] It was therefore necessary that Cape Town suppliers extend credit to their upcountry clients and that, when occasion arose, they be willing to accept the butchers' IOUs in exchange for merchandise. It is clear that the *veeboeren* much preferred to pay cash where they could,[88] but this was not always possible. Many owed substantial sums to Cape Town traders and, from time to time, were obliged to hand over the butchers' credit notes in partial settlement.[89]

However, as might be expected, there was a price to pay for credit. Most merchants charged interest on the larger advances and, though some exercised extraordinary forbearance with debtors, chiding them good-naturedly as the months ran into years,[90] others were not above suing for default. The real price of credit, however, lay not so much in the interest charged as in the ties of dependence forged between debtor and creditor. It was not easy to end one's connection with a supplier to whom one owed several hundred rix dollars and it was therefore not easy to query his prices.

One way to avoid indebtedness (apart from paying cash) was to barter directly with the *smousen* who wandered the country in defiance of Company regulations, exchanging merchandise for cattle and sheep. At least one could see what one was buying. The Company had from time to time issued stern warnings to those who 'made it their business to wander about everywhere . . . with goods and merchandise conveyed on wagons, cars, horses, or pack oxen . . . causing many irregularities'.[91] In 1774 Hermanus Lucas Crouse and Arnoldus Heering were stripped of their freeburgher status and returned to their former station as seamen in the Company's service as punishment for their part in the illicit trade.[92] But the *smousen* were not so easily deterred. In the early 1780s Andries Brink sent consignments of cloth and household wares to the pontoon on the Breede River, presumably for sale to passers-by,[93] and in 1789 a certain Veldbron, a dragoon in the Company's service, rode right through the village of Swellendam with three waggons of merchandise.[94] It was also possible to barter trade goods from one's neighbours, some of whom ordered a surplus from their Cape Town agents expressly for this purpose[95] (Fig. 15).

However barter too had its price. One had to weigh the advantages of direct exchange against the monopolistic premiums charged by the *smous*. Even in 1809, when many of the restrictions on peddling and hawking had been lifted and the country trade had greatly expanded, Landdrost Stockenstrom could report that the pedlars 'gain a much greater profit' by bartering their trade goods for cattle 'than they would if they were to sell them for ready money'.[96] The few documents in which reference is made to such transactions would seem to bear him out. In 1791, for example, when the going price for wethers was approximately 15.5 *schellingen* apiece, the cornet Philip Hendrik Morkel obtained fifty sheep from Johannes Hendrik Hattingh at a nominal rate of 12 *schellingen* apiece, in exchange for fourteen pieces of white linen.[97]

In sum, then, the restrictive commercial policies of the VOC, together with the remoteness of the graziers' habitations, combined to produce a very unfavourable trading environment for those living on the fringes of the colony. Geographical isolation did not prevent interaction with the market; it merely compounded the difficulties of survival within it. To suggest, as Ross has done, that the Company's restrictive legislation was so

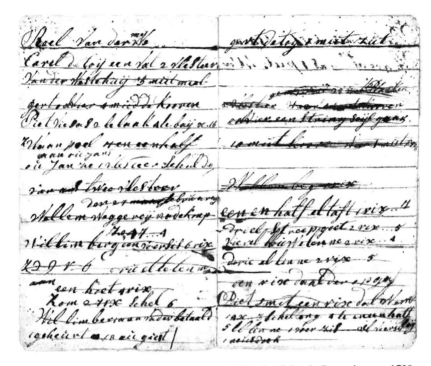

Figure 15   Extract from the *schuldboek* of D. J. Pretorius, *c.* 1790. *Source:* MOOC 14/96, no. 15.

loosely applied as to be of little consequence to the Cape economy, is to overlook its effects upon the people of the interior.[98] These effects were felt daily in the form of low producer prices and high – sometimes staggeringly high – consumer prices. The resulting battle for survival is reflected time and again in the letters and memorials of the *veeboeren*. For example in 1757 sixty inhabitants of Swellendam district wrote:

We earnestly wish that some equilibrium could be established between the wares we bring for sale at the Cape and those things that we upcountry people cannot do without, because, with everything so expensive in Cape Town, we shall soon have to go naked; and we shall no longer be able to provide ourselves either with waggons or with ironwork, on account of the big sums of money we must lay out at the waggon-makers' and the smiths'.[99]

A group of petitioners from De Bruins Hoogte echoed this in 1781:

We have hardly anything with which to clothe our families . . . in former times the stockkeepers lay more than half-way nearer to the Cape and lived very restfully.

And in those days the butchers gave at least 10 to 12 rix dollars for a slaughter beast, six guilders[100] for a wether. And so the *veeboeren* lying 15 or 16 shifts[101] nearer to the Cape could make a living, and they could get a waggon for 130 rix dollars, whereas these days we have to pay 180 rix dollars for a waggon. And then it doesn't last us nearly as long as it did people those days because they didn't have such a distance to travel . . .[102]

Surprisingly, the terms of trade showed little immediate improvement under the British, despite the greater volume of imports, the gradual relaxation of restrictions on internal trade and a rapid rise in demand for frontier produce. To be sure, the price of trek oxen and slaughter stock rose markedly, but, under pressure from a greatly expanded garrison, so did the price of imported goods, at least until 1810 or thereabouts, by which time the gradual stabilisation of the new trading patterns established under British rule may have brought some relief.[103] The price of iron more than doubled during the first British occupation[104] and the price of waggons increased by 60 per cent. 'A waggon . . . costs at this period 350 to 400 [rix dollars]', explained the inhabitants of the Hantam in 1798, 'and . . . the places for rearing cattle are dearer in proportion to the aforesaid . . . The cultivator of corn and wine sells his products at the same time at a high price, the wheelwright, smiths and every trading person equally exorbitant in their demands.' If the price of slaughter cattle were to be fixed at 8 rix dollars, they would be ruined, they said, 'whilst the remainder of the colonists flourish . . .'.[105]

It is possible, of course, that the *veeboeren* exaggerated the extent of their indigence – protestations of poverty often served as a preamble to a request for the reduction of rents, for example – but there is little doubt that there was a real basis for their abiding sense of grievance. A more exact appreciation of the difficulties they faced with respect to the terms of trade can be gained from an examination of the graphs (Figs. 16–27).

The price data on which these graphs are based are drawn mainly from the invoices and promissory notes filed among the annexures to the liquidation accounts of the 303 deceased estates comprising our statistical population,[106] including those estates selected for closer scrutiny by the generation of random numbers. In the case of livestock prices, however, additional data have been culled from other sources.[107]

It is perhaps worthy of note that the annexures to the liquidation accounts contain more information about the prices of consumer goods, especially groceries, clothing and textiles, than producer goods such as guns, iron, waggons and farm implements. One reason for this may be that country people preferred to purchase their guns and farm implements second-hand, at the *venduties* of family and neighbours, so as to avoid paying the high prices demanded by retailers. A comprehensive assessment

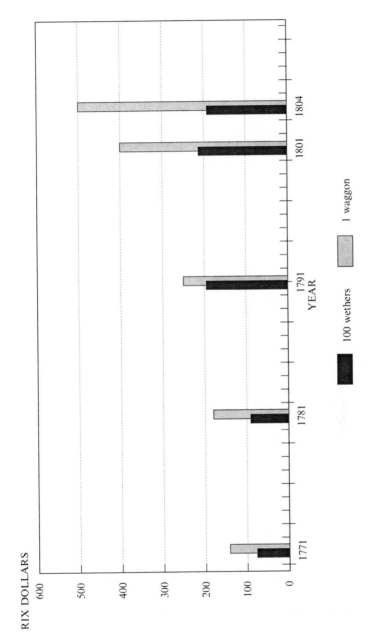

Figure 16 Terms of trade: waggons and sheep. *Source:* MOOC series.

Table 3. *Terms of trade: waggons and sheep*

Year	Price of 100 wethers	Price of one new waggon	Ratio
1771	75 rds	140 rds	1.86
1781	88 rds	180 rds	2
1791	194 rds	250 rds	1.29
1801	213 rds	400 rds	1.87
1804	191 rds	500 rds	2.61

of the terms of trade faced by frontiersmen should therefore take account of the prices of second-hand goods sold at auction. However the wide variation in the quality of goods on offer at the *venduties* makes it difficult to incorporate auction data in reliable price series. Exceptions should nevertheless be made in the case of horses, slaves and land, which did not exist anywhere in 'standard' form. All three commonly changed hands at public auctions, though they might also be traded privately. As with other goods sold at auction, prices varied enormously, depending on the quality of the item (and perhaps also the composition of the group of buyers); therefore the annual average prices reflected in Figs. 18–21 below necessarily conceal a high degree of variation. However, horses, slaves and land were of such key importance to the stock-farmer that even the blandest of averages can throw some light on the sort of market in which he was obliged to operate.

Fig. 16 illustrates the changing terms of trade between waggons and sheep over the period 1770–1804. Clearly there was some substance to the graziers' repeated allegations that the terms of trade were moving against them, though the pattern was more varied than they would care to admit. In 1771 a new waggon could be acquired in exchange for 186 wethers, whereas by 1781 an individual would have to dispose of 200 wethers in order to acquire a waggon. During the boom years of the late 1780s, however, the terms of trade moved in favour of the *veeboeren* – a waggon could now be traded against 129 sheep. By 1801 the rate of exchange was exactly where it had been thirty years before. But by 1804 it had moved decisively against the stock-farmer, who was now compelled to part with 261 sheep in order to purchase a new waggon. The changes are set out in tabular form in Table 3. Fig. 17 illustrates the changing ratio between the prices of sheep and iron over the period 1768–98. I could find no information about iron prices in the 1780s; nevertheless it is clear that in this case the terms of trade had moved in favour of the farmers – the ratio of sheep to 100 lbs of iron improved from 9 in 1778 to 3.7 in 1798.

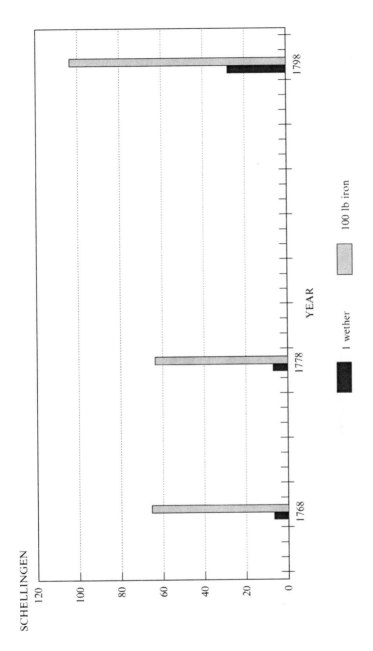

Figure 17   Terms of trade: iron and sheep. *Source:* MOOC series.

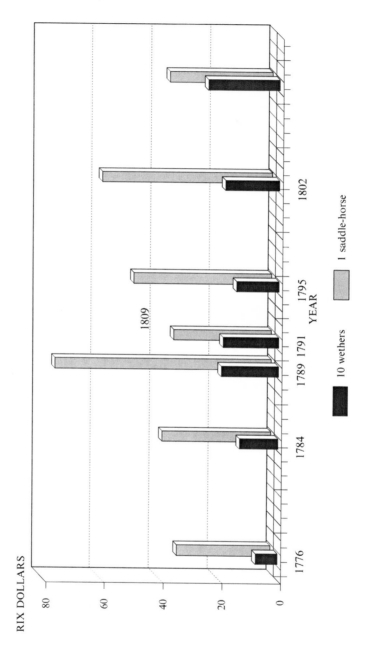

RIX DOLLARS

Figure 18   Terms of trade: saddle-horses and sheep. *Source:* MOOC 10/8–25.

RIX DOLLARS (THOUSANDS)

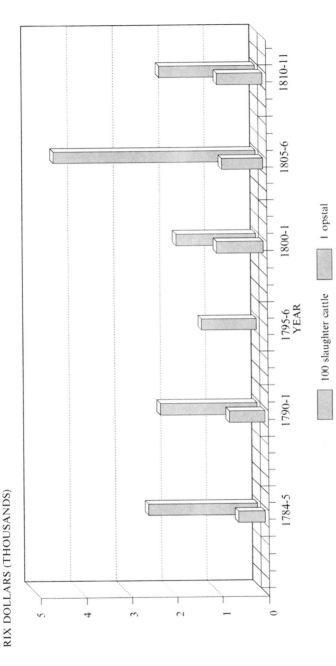

Figure 19 Terms of trade: land and cattle. *Source:* MOOC 10/8-25, 14/25–114.

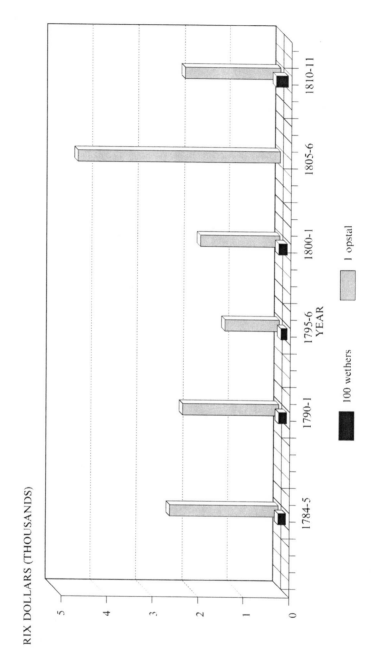

Figure 20 Terms of trade: land and sheep. *Source:* MOOC 10/8–25, 14/25–114.

Fig. 18 illustrates the rate of exchange between sheep and saddle-horses between 1776 and 1809. The wealthier farmers were often in a position to breed and train their own mounts; yet there was a thriving trade in saddle-broken horses, stimulated, no doubt, by the high death rate of horses in the eastern Karoo. Prices fluctuated, but average prices rarely fell below 35 rix dollars a head. Horses were essential to the operations of settled stock-farmers, who were obliged to pasture their flocks at some distance from the homestead; yet acquiring them made heavy demands on disposable income. In 1776 one would have had to earmark forty-four wethers for the purpose – the marketable increase (as we shall see) of 163 ewes.

Fig. 19 illustrates the changing relationship between the average prices of land and slaughter cattle during the last quarter of the eighteenth century.[108] The prices of individual farms could vary considerably. In 1785, for example, Johannes Jurgen de Beer's home farm De Vreede in the Camdeboo was sold for 3,333 rix dollars, whereas his grazing farm on the Verkeerde Vlei near the eastern exit of the Hex River valley fetched a mere 151 rix dollars.[109] There were many reasons for such sharp variations in price, among the most important being the nature of improvements made, the quality of the veld, the availability of water and the degree of proximity to the main waggon routes. Mixed grain and stock farms situated in the coastal forelands west of the Gamtoos River, such as Het Goetgeloof on the Krom River, or De Hartebeestekuijl on the Gourits River, were often sold for more than 2,000 rix dollars.[110] However, as one can see in the case of De Vreede, established grazing farms with irrigable land in the eastern Karoo were considered just as valuable.[111] It can be assumed, therefore, that the data presented in Figure 19 have not been unduly distorted by the inclusion of a number of land prices taken from the estate papers of Swellendam residents.[112]

Figure 19, then, represents the terms of trade confronting a stock-farmer wanting to acquire an average sort of farm in the eastern Karoo or the coastal forelands. The rate of exchange between cattle and land fluctuated considerably, falling from a high point of 400:1 in 1784–5 to a low of 170:1 in 1800–1 and rising again to 490 in 1805–6. The fluctuations appear random, and may be as much a function of the availability of data as of conditions in the property market. Nevertheless, Fig. 19 does reveal that the cost of acquiring a loan-farm at any time during the late eighteenth century was remarkably high – far higher than one would have expected.[113] Depending on the date of purchase and the arrangements made for repayment,[114] a prospective buyer would have had to sell between 170 and 490 cattle to the butchers – not an easy feat, as we shall see, even for the largest ranchers. If we substitute sheep for cattle, as in Fig. 20, we can see

that he would have had to sell between 700 and 1,950 wethers.[115] If he was
to do this in one year without eating into his capital, he would need a
breeding stock of between 2,593 and 7,222 ewes, giving a total flock size of
between 6,482 and 18,055 sheep, a capital way beyond the reach of all but
the wealthiest stockmen.[116] In practice, of course, as with all major
investments, an individual would accumulate the necessary cash over a
number of years, or take a loan, if possible. Nevertheless, it should not
surprise us that of the twenty-two deceased persons in the lowest three
strata of our sample, only six (27 per cent) owned registered loan-farms at
the time of their death.[117] And among the landowners in the higher
decimae, many were still owing large sums to the Orphan Chamber for the
purchase of their farms.

There were other ways of securing access to land, as the reader will
know. One could live as a *bijwoner* on someone else's land, one could lease
ground *op de helft van aanteel*,[118] or one could occupy unregistered land
on the fringes of the colony. The low level of registered landownership
reflected in the sample is therefore not a measure of landlessness, but the
figures do reveal that there was a high price to pay for security of tenure,
and that few of the smaller farmers were in a position to pay it.

If Figures 19 and 20 help us to understand why many frontiersmen
showed a preference for unregistered land occupancy, Fig. 21 may help us
to understand why so many sought informal solutions to their problems of
labour supply. If in 1784 one had to pay 582 rix dollars (the market value
of 415 wethers) to acquire one adult male slave of 'average' capabilities,[119]
there may well have been reason to look for a cheaper source of supply
from within the indigenous population. The choice was not a simple one: if
viewed from the perspective of modern business economics, it would
depend upon the difference between the purchase price of the slave and his
net present value,[120] but the *veeboeren* are unlikely to have made such a
sophisticated calculation. They must none the less have had an intuitive
sense of the relative profitability of different kinds of labour. Indeed, one
assumes it was just such an intuition which had prompted the rebel
authorities of Graaff Reinet to propose that commandos be permitted to
buy and sell Bushman prisoners, though they had couched their request in
the language of national interest. The legalisation of a trade in prisoners
would not only serve to rekindle 'military ardour', they explained; it would
also ensure that 'the inhabitants [would be] relieved from the payment to
foreign nations of the enormous sums now paid for slaves. The money
would remain in the country for the use of the inhabitants and the
maintenance of their families.'[121]

Yet the enslavement of natives, as I have argued in the preceding
chapter, was a dangerous strategy, bringing with it unexpected socio-

RIX DOLLARS

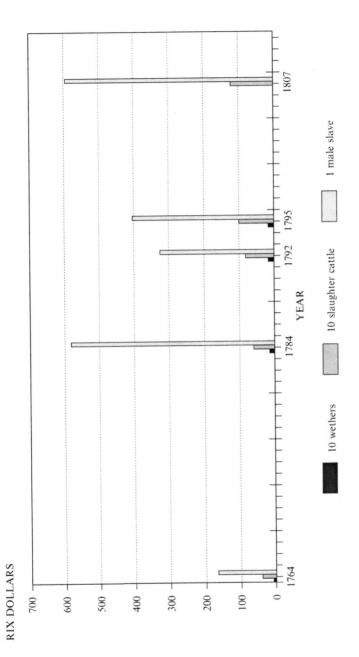

Figure 21 Terms of trade: slaves, cattle and sheep. *Source:* MOOC series.

political costs ('externalities', in the language of economists), which at times threatened to negate the economic savings it was intended to effect. Maynier, as we have seen, had been aware of the risk, and had repeatedly tried to warn the colonists, but they had wilfully ignored him. Yet Maynier had not proposed that they do without Khoisan labour; he had merely urged that they respect the principle of voluntary service – that they offer some remuneration for services rendered and that they allow servants to leave at the expiry of their term.[122] The question, then, is not why the farmers preferred the labour of the Khoisan to that of slaves – one may assume that they were searching for a cheaper and hence more profitable alternative – but rather, why they preferred *forced* Khoisan labour to free. Why was it that they baulked at paying the wages recommended by Maynier? Would not the cost of upholding the voluntary principle be repaid a hundredfold in terms of increased stability and security?

One way to approach this question is to try to establish what the level of wages might have been in a less coercive labour market, and then attempt to assess the impact of such wage levels upon the cost structure of rural producers. The notion of market-related wages is not entirely hypothetical, since there were pockets of freedom within a generally unfree market and these provide some indication of the level wages might have reached if restrictions were relaxed.

First, there are the contracts registered by Maynier himself between November 1799 and January 1801, during the lull in hostilities between the colonists and the rebels of the 'Hottentot Confederacy'.[123] In 1793 Land-drost Woeke had accused Maynier, then district secretary, of 'ruining' the Hottentots by paying them 12 rix dollars and more per year.[124] In 1800, however, the boot was on the other foot. 'I have learnt from the Hottentot Letta', Maynier wrote to Barend Grijling in February 1800, 'that she is in your service without wages. You must give her yearly 12 ewe lambs, since it is the express order of the Government that these people must be paid for their services; if she cannot earn that, you must let her go.'[125]

Analysis of the 402 contracts drawn up under Maynier's supervision reveals that sheep were indeed the preferred currency in such transactions (Fig. 22). In 236 cases (59 per cent) it was recorded that payment would be made wholly or partly in the form of sheep. The average number of sheep (presumably ewes) promised in return for one year of service was 9.3, the individual numbers varying between a maximum of twenty-four (there was only one such case) and a minimum of two. Sometimes sheep were supplemented by a flint and tinderbox, a pound of beads, a knife, a hat, a handkerchief or a suit of clothes.[126] Occasionally a servant was promised a heifer as well as a number of sheep, but more often it was one or the other. Fifty-four contracts (13 per cent of the total) stipulated that the servant

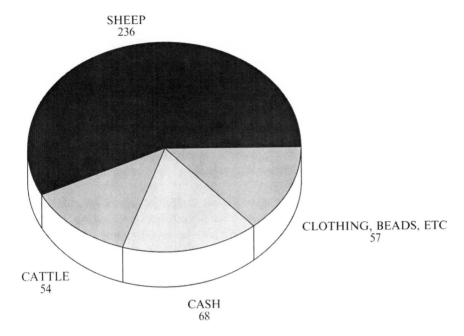

SHEEP
236

CLOTHING, BEADS, ETC
57

CATTLE
54

CASH
68

Figure 22 Labour contracts, 1799–1801: forms of remuneration.
Source: 1/GR 15/43, Contracts of service.

would receive a heifer or a cow in calf. And sixty-eight (17 per cent) promised payment in cash, sometimes augmented by a number of sheep, the average cash wage being exactly 12 rix dollars per annum. Finally, fifty-seven individuals – all but eleven of them female – were contracted to work for nothing apart from a package comprising one or more of the following goods: tobacco, beads, knives, clothing, kerchiefs, flints and tinderboxes. Of the 236 individuals paid in sheep, forty-five were women, but of the sixty-eight paid in cash, only four were women. It would appear, then, that even under conditions relatively favourable to voluntary contract, women consistently received lower wages than men.

The agreements concluded between 1799 and 1801 were not entirely novel, despite the special circumstances in which they were drawn up. In 1775, for example, the annual wages of Khoisan workers at the Company's post on the Riviersondereind comprised, in addition to food and tobacco, 'an ewe or two with lamb, or a heifer with calf, or else the value of them in money'.[127] Such payments were not confined to the Company: in 1763 the Hottentot Coridon, employed on a grazing farm belonging to Jacobus van

Reenen, told how during his ten years' service he had, 'through wages and those [sheep] brought with him', accumulated a flock of 100 sheep, and in 1776 Hendrik Swellengrebel reported from the Camdeboo that 'the Hottentots serve and are paid in cattle'.[128] Payments in cash were apparently not uncommon either: thus, for example, in 1781, it was recorded in the liquidation account of Johanna Maria Buys that 12 rix dollars were owed to the Hottentot Andries, 'in fulfilment of one year's wage' and in 1782 it was noted in the account of Frans Kruger *d'oude* that he owed the same amount to '*den Bastart Hottentot Willem*', also for one year's service.[129] More than twenty years later, in 1810, exactly the same amount – 12 rix dollars – was recorded as the annual wage of the 'Hottentots' in the employ of the *Weduwee* Gerrit Olivier.[130]

Perhaps, then, the wages agreed upon under Maynier's watchful eye represented not the best that could be achieved under competitive market conditions, but rather the best that could be achieved within a fundamentally coercive and custom-bound labour market. Maynier's contracts were drawn up in the midst of the servants' rebellion, it is true, but the outcome was far from decided and, though the coercive power of the Boers had been seriously challenged by the rebels and their Xhosa allies, it had not been destroyed. Perhaps a truer indication of the market value of unfettered labour power can be found, paradoxically, in the princely sums paid to those who hired out slave labour. The missionary Vanderkemp had noted in 1801 that 'many people live at the Cape entirely from their slaves, whom they let out to others, for 8 to 26 rix dollars per month'.[131] And it seems he did not exaggerate, for it was recorded in the liquidation account of Gerrit Coetzee that the hire of three slaves for the corn harvest had cost him 3 *schellingen* per man per day; that is, assuming a six-day week, approximately 9 rix dollars per month for each man.[132] As for the missionaries themselves, they paid 2 *schellingen* per day (6 rix dollars per month) to the men who worked in the mission grounds.[133]

Whatever the true market value of Khoisan labour power, it is sufficient for our purposes to observe that many farmers were reluctant to pay even the modest wages recommended by Maynier. We have already noted Maynier's instructions to Barend Grijling, issued in February 1800. Before that date, few servants complained to the authorities about inadequate wages – captives and *inboekselingen* were in any case not entitled to remuneration, and those who were were perhaps unwilling to risk their masters' wrath by laying a complaint. However, many individuals did complain that when they wished to leave, they were prevented from taking the livestock they had earned as wages[134] and some reported that after their departure their stock was appropriated by the master and his household.[135] And from time to time – during a court case, for example – it emerged that adults, as well as child apprentices, had been obliged to remain many years in service without remuneration. Thus, Sara, on trial for murder in 1792, testified that since the death of her former master Hans Jurgen de Beer in 1785, she had not received the food and clothing promised in return for her services.[136] The old man's sons, Andries Jacobus and Dawid de Beer, alleged that Sara had not asked for clothing, but merely for beads and copper arm rings, which she had received; but doubt was cast upon their integrity by the unanimous testimony of the other servants, all of whom said that since the widow and her sons had assumed control of the farm, they had received no food other than 'thin boiled corn soup, without meat, fat or salt'. The only time they ate meat, they said, was when the shepherds returned with game from the veld, 'and then only small quantities'.[137] The spare diet endured by the servants of the Widow de Beer was probably far from the norm. Indeed, the very phrasing of their protest suggests that they had been accustomed to more robust fare in the past. This would be consistent with the observations of contemporary visitors to the interior, many of whom made reference to the provision of ample meat rations to slaves and Khoisan servants. However, contrary to the impression created by Lichtenstein ('from the produce of the lands and flocks must the whole tribe be fed'),[138] the meat provided was unlikely to be mutton from the farmer's flocks, but rather buffalo or goat, both of which cost the farmer little in lost income.[139] In regions where game was scarce, the servants might be obliged, like Sara and her companions, to make do with bread or gruel, for, as Sparrman explained, '[the farmers] are very careful not to lavish their sheep on their slaves, these sheep being very frequently the only articles by which they can get a little ready cash and pay their taxes'.[140] If the farmer kept cattle, a diet of goats' meat and gruel might be supplemented with butter-milk and occasionally with the pluck of slaughtered oxen.[141] And under normal circumstances, it was customary to provide rations of *dagga* and tobacco.[142]

The significance of the De Beer case, however, is precisely that it shows how customary arrangements could break down in a household under pressure. At the time of Hans Jurgen de Beer's death in 1785, his household was among the most substantial in the Camdeboo (Fig. 23). His gross assets amounted to 18,365 rix dollars and he owned five farms, including De Vreede. However, he also owed the Orphan Chamber 11,000 rix dollars for two farms purchased at the *vendutie* of his late father-in-law, Dawid van der Merwe, in October 1784.[143] Consequently, when his estate was wound up, only 4,532 rix dollars remained for distribution to his heirs. The Widow de Beer received her *geregte helfte* and the eight surviving children got 285 rix dollars each. All the farms were sold at auction, with the exception of De Brakkefontijn (down on the dry flats near present-day

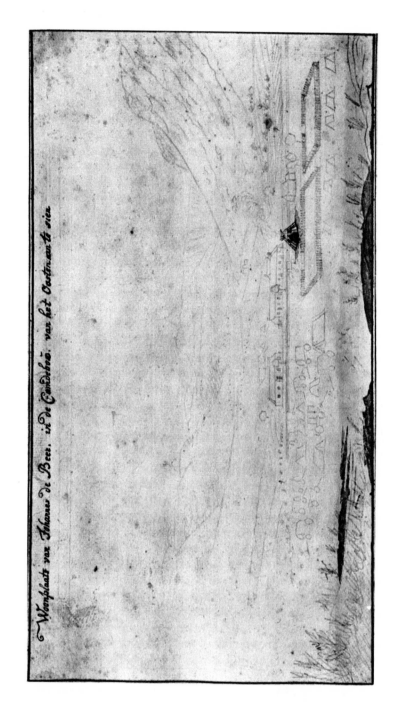

Figure 23   *Woonplaats van Johannes de Beer*, by Robert Jacob Gordon, Cape Archives, AG 7146.45.

Aberdeen), which was registered in the name of Hans Jurgen's eldest son, Dawid de Beer. De Vreede was bought by Adriaan van Jaarsveld, Dawid de Beer's father-in-law. If this latter transaction had been intended to serve as a means of keeping the home farm in the family, it failed, for Van Jaarsveld's estate was subsequently sequestrated and De Vreede changed hands again. When the Widow de Beer died in 1798, her estate was worth only 871 rix dollars and the sum total of her worldly goods comprised a chest, a lancet, a pair of spectacles, two bottles, a teapot and 'some rummage'.[144] Her son Dawid died the following year, landless and heavily indebted.[145] This, then, was the background against which Sara's tragedy unfolded. Knowledge of the circumstances should not be used to exonerate her tormentors, but it does shed further light on their behaviour. And it is important to understand that the De Beer case was not unique. Indeed, the family of Hans Jurgen de Beer was relatively fortunate: many less affluent households were catapulted into penury by the unexpected death of a spouse; others had never known anything else. For such households 12 rix dollars (equivalent to 9.6 sheep in 1782) represented a significant expense. The same – though this may arouse scepticism in the modern reader – can be said of wages paid in the form of clothing. In today's terms a dress, a jacket and trousers and even 'a complete suit of clothes' would be considered derisory compensation for a year's labour. But, given the adverse terms of trade in the eighteenth-century Cape, the same items held an altogether different value. Jackets and trousers, for example, were commonly made of blue or black broadcloth (*laken*). In 1781 one ell (27 inches) of broadcloth was twice the price of a sheep (see Fig. 24). By 1795, one ell was worth more than three sheep. Dirk Jacobus Pretorius was therefore not misrepresenting his costs when he made the following entry in his notebook:

> *Jan geheur*
> *den 9 juneij voor een jaar*
> *een hoet een broek een baatje*
> *twee bloou hemden 20 Rxders*
> *een tonteldoos een veuzlag 6 scheleng*
> *3 Pont toebak . . . 6 schelleng*
> *1 halsdoek . . . 1 Rxdaalder*[146]

In fact, one hat, one pair of trousers, two shirts and a jacket were a bargain at 20 rix dollars the lot, and a neckerchief did indeed cost 1 rix dollar – half the price of a sheep in the 1790s.

Women's clothing might cost less, especially if coarse Indian cottons were substituted for linen or broadcloth. The popular *voerchitzen*, for example, came in pieces large enough to make up a dress and several kerchiefs; even so, as can be seen from Fig. 25, they were relatively expensive. The head of the household, moreover, was expected to clothe his family as well as his servants and it is probable that the demands of the latter were deeply resented by the former, who no doubt felt they had a greater claim on his scant resources. It is here that questions of power and identity would have intersected with economic realities to undermine Maynier's attempts to liberalise the labour market. The Boers, as we have seen, had rejected the official view that the Khoisan were 'fellow human beings, having equal right with [themselves] to the protection of the law'. They might have failed to destroy the links which bound their servants to the natal community of the conquered, but they were none the less determined that servants should not be incorporated into their own community on equal terms. The Khoisan were heathen – not Christian – and as such, while they might live cheek by jowl with the master's household, they remained permanent outsiders, literally excommunicated from the colonial domain.[147] Thus, while they might have needs, they could not have rights, no matter what Maynier might pretend. Under conditions of plenty, when resources were abundant and productivity high, the implications of this belief system might, as it were, remain latent; the community of Christians might even lend an ear to Maynier's interpretation of its long-term interest. But under conditions of economic stress, the discourse of slavery would reassert itself and Maynier's defence of the rights of the heathen would appear (as it did in the 1790s) as a threat to civilisation itself. Such, at any rate, is the argument of this chapter.

But how many households could be justly described as suffering from 'economic stress'? How many could be classified as marginal producers, and how many were unable to survive without assistance? These questions return us to the project outlined at the beginning of this chapter: the attempt to assess the economic viability of frontier households at different levels of wealth.[148] It was suggested then that as many as 40 per cent of all households were struggling to make ends meet. The time has come to test that suggestion in the light of the data in our sample.

'We do not live like beasts'

The data for each sampled estate in the first five decimae (or 10 per cent 'slices') have been set out in tabular form in appendix 2, beginning with estates in the lowest 10 per cent 'slice' (named the first decima in the appendix).[149] Each table contains a breakdown of the decedent's productive assets, together with an estimate of the annual marketable yield thereof and the potential cash earnings therefrom, where applicable.[150] Before proceeding to a closer examination of the tables, it should perhaps be reiterated that the decedents have not been ranked according to the year

SCHELLINGEN

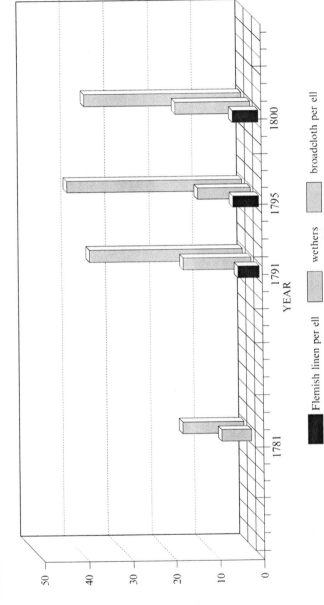

Figure 24 Terms of trade: linen, sheep and broadcloth. *Source:* MOOC series.

Figure 25   Terms of trade: sheep and *voerchitzen*. *Source:* MOOC series.

of their demise, but rather according to the level of their net wealth. Consequently, while the results obtained can be taken as representative with respect to variation in levels of wealth and profitability for the period as a whole, they cannot be said to reflect the situation in any particular year. That would have required a different ordering of the data.

It is also necessary to explain certain aspects of the procedures used to calculate marketable yield, particularly with respect to livestock, since the marketing of sheep, cattle and butter was the primary source of cash income for most households. The key figure in any such calculation is that of the *weaning percentage*, that is, with respect to sheep and cattle, the number of lambs and calves weaned for every 100 ewes put to the ram or every 100 cows put to the bull. Weaning percentages are in turn based upon lambing and calving percentages (the number of lambs or calves born per 100 females covered) after allowance has been made for mortality between birth and weaning. After weaning, there would be further deaths (in the region of 3 to 5 per cent in the case of sheep) before the lamb or calf crop reached maturity; but it is weaning percentages which form the basis for any assessment of marketable yield.

Unfortunately, Cape farmers did not record the births and deaths of their livestock in the eighteenth century (except where stock losses were the result of 'Bushman' raids); or rather, if they did, these records have not survived the passage of time. We are therefore obliged to make use of figures based on twentieth-century experience. In the case of sheep, contemporary figures can serve as a fairly reliable indicator, since the modern Ronderib Afrikaner is a direct descendant of the fat-tailed Cape sheep, which was in turn derived without hybridisation from the sheep kept by the Khoekhoe,[151] and it can therefore be assumed that the fertility of the Cape sheep was roughly the same as that of the modern Ronderib. However one must make due allowance for differences in farming methods and environmental conditions. Here I have simply deferred to the experts, all of whom agree that fertility would have been somewhat lower and mortality somewhat higher under eighteenth-century conditions than was the case in the 1950s and 1960s, when the Ronderib was still farmed commercially in the Central Karoo.[152] There are many factors which account for the difference, but the absence of fencing, the high level of predation, the lack of supplementary foods, the absence of antidotes to common viruses, and the practice (necessary in a country teeming with predators) of kraaling animals at night, were among the most important causes of lower birth rates and higher death rates in the eighteenth century. The animal scientists whom I consulted were reluctant to put a precise figure on the difference, but they suggested that an average lambing percentage of 70, a mortality rate of 15 to 20 per cent between birth and weaning, and a further 3 to 5 per cent loss prior to full maturity might not be too wide of the mark. This would give us a weaning percentage of between 59.5 and 56 per cent. I have chosen to work with the higher figure, so as to avoid being charged with having manipulated the figures to suit my argument.

In the case of cattle, which were important to farmers in the coastal forelands and the district of De Bruins Hoogte, the situation is a little more complicated, for the indigenous red Africander breed was hybridised to some extent following the introduction of a small number of Friesland cattle in the 1770s.[153] It seems, however, that the cross-breeds were not popular with the farmers of Graaff Reinet district, perhaps because, while they gave more milk than pure-bred Africanders, they were inferior as draught animals.[154] It would seem therefore that, as in the case of sheep, figures derived from modern studies of the breed can be used as a basis for the calculation of eighteenth-century calving and weaning percentages. Depending on the condition of the veld and the season of calving (there was no fixed breeding season for cattle), one could, according to Professor H. J. Heydenrich of the University of Stellenbosch, expect a calving percentage of between 50 and 55 per cent and a weaning percentage of between 47 and 52 per cent.[155]

Despite the fact that Africander cattle are not considered today to be a milking breed, eighteenth-century graziers derived a significant income from the production of butter, in addition to the sale of slaughter stock. Indeed the financial incentives for the production of butter were such that many families went without milk so as to maximise their output of butter[156] (see Fig. 26). It was well known even in the 1700s that Africanders were poor milkers (it was said that *vaderlandsche* cattle yielded five or six times more milk than indigenous cows[157]); nevertheless they could be counted on to produce an average of 1 gallon per day during the six months after calving.[158] Of this, not more than half a gallon could be used for human consumption without jeopardising the health of the calf crop.[159] Given a butterfat ratio of approximately 2.8 per cent, one could therefore expect to produce a maximum of 0.14 lb of butter per gallon.[160] This would amount to an annual butter output of 25.55 lb per cow in calf.

Besides sheep and cattle, many households also raised poultry, pigs, goats and horses. All four were raised mainly for domestic consumption; goats, as we have noted, were used to feed the servants and horses were used for transport, either as saddle-horses or cart-horses. However some of the more affluent colonists, particularly those who had access to pastures at high altitude, were able to supplement their income by breeding horses for sale. This could be lucrative – a good mount might fetch upwards of 40 rix dollars (see Fig. 27) and a cart-horse even more – but the frequent outbreaks of midge-borne horse sickness on the low-lying plains posed a grave risk to the breeder.[161] The horse sickness was known to have caused 95 per cent mortality in some areas.[162] In January 1789 the authorities in Graaff Reinet reported that 872 horses had died during the preceding eighteen months[163] and, as we have seen, the men of the district were wont to refuse commando duty on the grounds that all their horses were either dead or weakened by the sickness. Since horse sickness occurred at irregular intervals it is difficult to calculate weaning percentages with any confidence. One can estimate that for every 100 mares put to stud, between fifty and sixty foals would have been weaned. But these figures do not have the status of scientific findings.[164]

The calculation of weaning percentages allows one to estimate the annual (or triennial, in the case of horses) increase of a *veeboer*'s flock, herd or stud. But one cannot say how many animals he (or she, in the case of a widow) might place on the market until one has allowed for replacement of and additions to breeding stock. In the case of Cape sheep, one would need to replace at least 20 per cent of one's ewes and 33 per cent of one's rams each year. One would also have to retain one ram per every thirty additional female lambs kept for breeding purposes. In the case of cattle, one would replace at least 15 per cent of the cows and 20 per cent of the bulls each year, allowing for a ratio of one bull to every thirty cows. A farmer who owned one or more waggons would likewise be obliged to replace his trek oxen on a regular basis, perhaps at the rate of 25 per cent per annum.[165] In the case of horses, the replacement rate would be lower – perhaps 8 to 10 per cent of mares each year – but the risk of sickness would induce many breeders to keep their surplus mares. When all is said and done, then, a grazier who wished to increase his stock, or merely to maintain its present levels, would not be able to market more than a portion of his annual crop of lambs and calves. He would, however, be able to slaughter or sell the animals which had been replaced. In the case of sheep, I have assumed that 60 per cent of the animals replaced were slaughtered for home consumption, whereas in the case of cattle I have assumed that all animals replaced were sold to the butchers. I have also assumed that all female lambs, calves and foals were retained for breeding purposes, even where they were not required to replace aging stock. The figures given in appendix 2 next to the headings 'sheep, cattle or horses available for sale' reflect these calculations.

Finally, we must remember that that part of the new lamb or calf crop which was destined for the market could not be sold immediately after weaning. Wethers under one year old did not have sufficient strength or mass to survive the gruelling walk to Cape Town. As a rule, they were kept on the veld until the age of eighteen months or two years. Steers would be kept until they were four or five years old, Africander cattle being slow

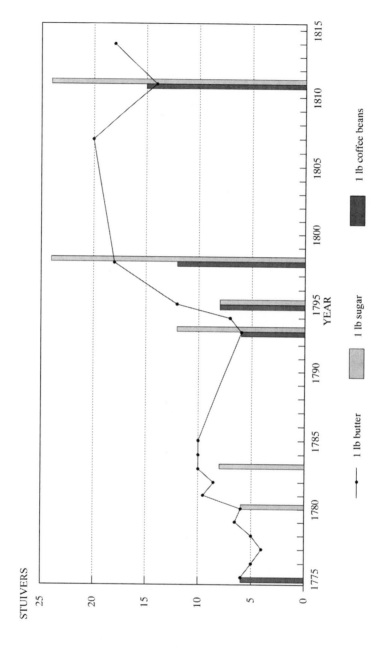

STUIVERS

1 lb butter

1 lb sugar

1 lb coffee beans

Figure 26   Terms of trade: butter, coffee and sugar. *Source: MOOC series.*

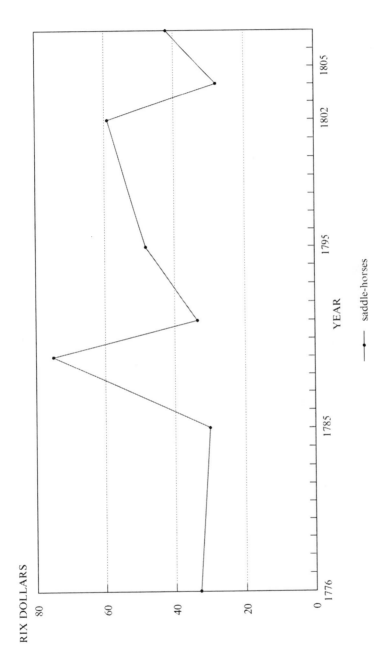

Figure 27 Horse prices. *Source:* MOOC series.

growing.[166] As for horses, they would normally not be sold before the age of three, for a prospective buyer would be unable to judge the conformation or tractability of a younger animal.[167] Strictly speaking, then, the figures given in appendix 2 as 'projected cash income' from the sale of livestock represent future rather than current earnings. In the case of cattle and horses, this has been indicated in the tables, whereas income from sheep sales has been entered as current income.

Livestock was the mainstay of the frontier economy, but those colonists who were favoured with good water were able to grow cereals as well and a select few produced a marketable brandy. Since I have eschewed the use of *opgaafrollen* on the grounds of unreliability, I have no means of assessing the total quantity of crops harvested or brandy distilled in the year of the decedent's demise. However, where wine-making or distilling equipment are listed in the *vendurollen*, this has been noted in appendix 2; and where grain, wine or brandy are listed, their value has been entered.[168] The same goes for miscellaneous items such as dried fruit, tobacco and clothes made up for sale. Finally, where it can be discerned from the documents that the deceased was an artisan of some sort, or that he or she was deriving income from money lent at interest, this has also been noted.

All marketable produce has been valued at prices prevailing in the year when the *vendutie* was held. Except where I have evidence to the contrary, I have assumed that the *vendutie* was held in the year of the decedent's demise.

We can now turn to appendix 2 to seek an answer to the question posed above: just how many households could accurately be described as 'suffering from economic stress'?

Let us begin with the twelve estates in the two poorest strata, that is, those with net assets worth less than 520 rds. Here there is little room for argument. Only two decedents – Volkert Schoenmaker (no. 28) and Sara Fourie (the *Weduwee* Adriaan van Wijk; no. 64) – could be said to have achieved a level of output consistent with financial security. Of the others, it could perhaps be argued that three (Marthinus Oosthuijzen, Louisa Erasmus and Catharina de Jong; nos. 34, 39 and 62) were able to eke out a living, though the first two had no land and the third no livestock. The remaining seven decedents (i.e. 58 per cent) were entirely unable to lead an independent existence: five were elderly people who were presumably supported by their children and two were bachelors without the means to farm on their own account.

Even Schoenmaker and Fourie could not be described as comfortably situated. Their earnings capacity is inflated (particularly in the case of Fourie) by the inclusion among their assets of a large number of mature wethers, which may have been kept on the veld for longer than usual, pending settlement of the estate. In a normal year, their marketable output would have been lower. Moreover Schoenmaker was very heavily indebted and lacked the most elementary domestic comforts. Born in Brewitz in eastern Germany, he had arrived at the Cape as a soldier in the service of the Company and worked for eighteen years as a stonemason and *knecht* before acquiring freeburgher status in 1789. When he died in 1797 he was still unmarried, and his domestic furnishings comprised little more than pots and pans, a bed, a blanket, a coffee grinder, two chests and some unnamed books. He had no crockery or cutlery and nothing which the vendumaster's clerk saw fit to describe as a chair or a table. He did, however, have five guns and a waggon in tolerable condition.[169]

Sara Fourie, by contrast, had allocated her resources so as to allow herself more domestic comforts – possibly she had made some judicious choices when the conjugal estate was auctioned at her husband's death. Whereas Schoenmaker had invested only 12 per cent of his assets in livestock, 58 per cent of Fourie's capital was in this form. Nineteen per cent of her capital was invested in land and the balance was fairly evenly distributed between producer and consumer goods, allowing her the relative luxury of a four-poster bed, two tables and eight chairs, three pairs of spectacles and a large quantity of porcelain plates. However, her waggon was described as 'old' and she owned no guns. She also owed the Company nearly eleven years' rent for the lease of her farm.[170]

As for Marthinus Oosthuijzen and his wife Johanna Calitz, our understanding of their earnings capacity is again distorted by the presence of 'accumulated' wethers in their deceased estate and it is doubtful that in life they could have supported eight children without outside aid. Indeed, Oosthuijzen owed 233 rix dollars to his father and his parents-in-law and he had yet to pay out the *kinderbewijs* due to his son by his first marriage. The family owned no beds or tables and had only three chairs. Still, there was an ox-waggon in working order and a plate, a spoon and a fork for each member of the household.[171]

Louisa Erasmus was equally unlikely to have been self-supporting. Once the accumulated wethers had been sold, she could (had she lived) have raised only twenty-three sheep for market in the ensuing year. This would scarcely cover the purchase of groceries, let alone the replacement of implements and the maintenance of a waggon. She also lacked the wherewithal to furnish a house, having no beds, chairs or tables.[172] In reality, she appears to have lived with her middle-aged daughter-in-law, Hendrina Johanna de Beer, and Willem Sterrenberg Marais, Hendrina de Beer's son by a previous marriage.[173]

Catharina de Jong and Gerrit Engelbrecht (no. 62) are something of a special case. They had no livestock but they did have a freehold plot at the foot of the Roodezand pass, on the main waggon route to the interior. Here Engelbrecht plied his trade as a carpenter.[174] He was poor, but there is no indication that he was unable to support his dependants before his wife's death in 1765. The family had few luxuries – some pictures, five chairs, a few porcelain plates – and only three beds between the ten of them, but Engelbrecht had been able to service his debt and he had taken no new loans since 1762.[175] When his wife died, however, he was unable to prevent the inventory and auction of their joint estate (since they had made no will) and the enforced settlement of his debt. After the sale he was left 'in a desolate state', as he himself attested, with neither home nor family to comfort him.[176] Each of his eight children was placed with a different individual – even the baby Martha Engelbrecht, who subsequently died.[177] Engelbrecht himself continued to work as a carpenter and cooper, though he had not been able to keep all his tools. He died in 1774, a single man owning only a bed, a set of cooper's tools and seventeen silver buttons.[178]

The other decedents in the first and second decimae lacked the where-withal to survive as independent producers. Most were old people living with their grown-up children. Some, like Maria Cloete and her surviving spouse Hendrik Mostert (no. 21), had kept all their remaining assets in the form of consumer goods. Cloete and Mostert's possessions included a four-poster bed, a red festoon blind, seven pictures, two mirrors and a Frisian clock – but then they lived in Cape Town, where standards of comfort and decorum were different from those in the interior, and they had no producer goods at all.[179] The people of the interior, by contrast, were more likely to reduce their possessions to a bare minimum (Elisabeth Nortje, no. 46, owned a bed, a casket of bottles and a lectern)[180] and invest their remaining assets in a small loan to a favoured child,[181] or, as with Erasmus Smit (no. 56), in cash which could be hoarded or lent at inter-est.[182]

Finally, there were the *eenlopende personen* (unmarried men) who made up a significant minority within the white frontier population. The two cases under consideration here – those of Jacobus Botha (no. 24) and Jan Nel (no. 52) – again illustrate the constraints placed on individuals of slender means. Botha's 181 rix dollars had secured him an ox-waggon, a musket, a chest and a bedding roll, but with only five oxen he was not well placed to seek employment as a waggoner or *smous*.[183] Perhaps, like so many other single men, he worked as a *knecht*, or lived with relatives as an unpaid helper. Jan Nel appears to have chosen the latter course. Thirty-eight years old and single, he lived with his widowed mother, Aletta van Deventer. His mother had not yet paid him the *erfportie* due to him upon his father's death, but in return, one assumes, she supported him from the common household fund. One trusts it was so, for Nel had neither chest, nor bed, nor waggon.[184]

Perhaps the most important finding to emerge from analysis of estates in the first two decimae concerns the need to revise Guelke's estimate of 'the low capital requirement of stock farming'. That the entry requirements of stock-farming were lower than those of the arable sector is not in dispute, but Guelke is clearly incorrect when he suggests that persons with a capital of 'about 1000 guilders' could earn a living as stock-farmers.[185] One thousand guilders was the equivalent of 333 rix dollars and, as we have seen, persons whose gross assets were at or below this level were unable to support themselves without assistance.[186] Even Jan Nel, who had invested 70 per cent of his gross capital of 390 rix dollars in livestock, was without a waggon, a horse or a gun – surely among the essentials of a grazier's existence? Indeed, the primary lesson to be drawn from examination of estates in the two lowest decimae is that an individual who wished to live in 'rough comfort' as an independent farmer required a gross capital of at least 900 rix dollars, and even at this level of operation he or she would be liable to sink into debt.

This conclusion is borne out by an analysis of sampled estates in the next stratum (those with a net value greater than 520 rix dollars and less than 890 rix dollars). Only two decedents in this stratum – Marthinus François Nel (no. 84) and Philip Snijman (no. 89) (both with gross assets in excess of 1,000 rix dollars) – could be said to have had 'a reasonable chance of earning a living while preserving their independence',[187] yet neither owned land and both had liabilities amounting to more than 40 per cent of their assets. Marthinus François Nel, like Jan Nel, who was his father's first cousin, had concentrated virtually all his resources in producer goods. But having a capital three times as large, he had been able to accumulate a viable flock of sheep as well as 'a half-worn waggon'. However his creature comforts were minimal: apart from a bed (well appointed, judging by the price it fetched at auction), a set of clothing and a few yards of cloth, he had only two pots, a meat fork, a soup ladle, three dishes, some pewter spoons and forks, an iron and a coffee jug.[188] Moreover, had he lived, he would have had little hope of acquiring land or slaves in the near future, for his 211 ewes would have yielded only 60 wethers for sale in the coming year. It is likely, then, that he was a trekboer in the true sense, or perhaps a *bijwoner*, sharing accommodation with his younger brother Daniel.[189]

Philip Snijman's household may likewise have been without a fixed address. He and his wife owned a waggon in a reasonable state of repair, some wooden storage vats, a few cooking pots, a Bible and some essential tools, but, besides their waggon-chest, they had no furniture whatsoever. They were poor even by the standards of travelling folk: according to the auctioneer's roll, they had but a single bedding roll and four sets of cutlery (spoons and forks, that is, for carving was performed with the aid of the men's pocket-knives)[190] for the use of themselves and their six unmarried children.[191] They may also have had skin blankets and wooden utensils, but these were not listed among their effects. Almost certainly they supplemented their diet by hunting and gathering, for their small flock could not have sustained them, except at the price of complete disengagement from the market economy. And this we know they could not achieve, since they owed a substantial sum to a *smous* 'for trade goods delivered'.[192] Indeed, Snijman's death might well have left the family destitute, had his widow not immediately entered into a new marriage with Gerrit Kruger, the widower of her late cousin, Susanna Lasya Buys.[193]

None of the other three decedents in this stratum could be described as an independent farmer. Aletta Dorothea Bester and her spouse Sybrand Gerhardus van Nieuwkerken (no. 78) were young newly weds, with little property besides their marriage bed, several sets of clothing and the few head of stock they had brought into the marriage.[194] The greater part of their assets were acquired posthumously, in the form of a *moedersbewijs* paid into the estate by Bester's father; indeed, the couple had been obliged to borrow 200 rix dollars in order to establish their home.[195] They did cultivate a little wheat, but since they owned no farm implements, they must have done so through the good offices of a landlord or a relative.[196]

Philippus du Plessis (no. 85), by contrast, was a bachelor of long standing. A man of few vanities, he seems to have lived a simple life among the burghers of Zwagershoek, but it is not clear how he supported himself. He may perhaps have been a pedlar, for he had an assortment of cloth among his scanty possessions, and several farmers in the area owed him money.[197]

Finally, Isabella Potgieter (no. 91) was clearly in retirement. She was the widow of the Oud Heemraad Philip du Preez of Grootvadersbosch in the Swellendam district; but if she had once been prosperous, she had since divested herself of her wealth. She was by no means destitute: the loan-farm Welbedagt was still registered in her name (though she had not paid rent for eighteen years) and she owned two male slaves, a valuable Bible and a fine four-poster bed. But besides the slaves, an old waggon and seven oxen, she had no producer goods at all.

It is only when one turns to examine decedents in the fourth stratum that one begins to find households which could be described as commercially viable. Two decedents – Carel Nicolaas van der Merwe (no. 104) and Anna Susanna Lombard (no. 115) – stand out as particularly well situated. Indeed, if one were to judge by the size of their projected income for the year ahead, one would describe them as positively prosperous. However a closer look reveals certain weaknesses in their position. First, both were heavily indebted, particularly Lombard. Second, Van der Merwe owned neither land nor slaves, though he did have an unregistered request-place. Third, as in the case of other decedents, the estimate of their annual income has been inflated by the presence of full-grown wethers and steers kept back from market until the holding of the *vendutie*. Had they not died, in other words, their receipts from livestock sales would probably have been spread over two years. Finally, neither household had much in the way of domestic comforts. Carel van der Merwe had just two old bedsteads and one set of bedding for the use of himself, his second wife Geesje Smit and their nine children, while Anna Lombard and her husband Pieter van der Westhuijzen apparently had no bed at all, and no kitchenware besides five tin plates, a tea-pot and a kettle.[198]

Of the two, in fact, Carel van der Merwe was probably the better off. He had no saleable land, but he was correspondingly free of the crushing debt borne by Lombard and Van der Westhuijzen. Apart from some minor trade debts, his sole liability was to his six children by his first marriage, to whom he owed *moederlijke erfenisse*, but he was not obliged to pay until they came of age and he might well have been able to defer payment even longer.[199] Lombard and Van der Westhuijzen, by contrast, had borrowed more than 3,000 rix dollars since their marriage in 1781, much of it in the form of interest-bearing loans from non-relatives.[200] After settlement of the joint estate, Pieter van der Westhuijzen was left with only 586 rix dollars, which he used judiciously to re-acquire a one-sixth share in the poorer of his two farms, along with a waggon, four untrained oxen, a horse, his three slaves, and the greater part of his flock.[201] He married again within the year, possibly with the intention of restoring his fortunes. His new bride was Susanna Cornelia Steyn, the 15-year-old daughter of the Heemraad Hermanus Steyn, and she bore him a further nine children.[202]

Of the other decedents in this stratum, there are two – Ockert Oosthuijzen (no. 105) and Gerrit Coetzee (no. 113) – who might be said to have been making a living, but their marginal position merely drives home the point that even at this level of wealth survival was not easy. Oosthuijzen, a middle-aged man with (in the year of his death) eleven children under the age of 25, owned a farm in a well-watered if remote location on the upper Olifants River, some five waggon-shifts from the Drostdy at Swellendam, in an easterly direction.[203] A brief examination of his *vendurol* reveals that here, at last, was a household living in the 'rough comfort' envisaged by Leonard Guelke.[204] The family had six beds, one a fully furnished *ledikant*, the others simple frames. They also had more seating than most households examined thus far and they had chests and cupboards for storage and pewter spoons for every member of the household and visitors besides.[205] However, they could not have achieved this level of comfort had they depended solely on Oosthuijzen's small flock, for, as appendix 2 shows, he would have been lucky to sell fifty-two wethers in the forthcoming year and a half. Since he was none the less 'free of large debts'[206] (apart from the *erfporties* still due to his seven minor children and 320 rix dollars owed to his brother-in-law), one must assume that he had another source of income. Perhaps this derived from the arable produce of his farm, though according to the figures he gave at *opgaaf*, this scarcely exceeded the family's own requirements.[207] However his *vendurol* provides a clue to the existence of an alternative source of income. It lists a full set of carpenter's tools, a pair of bellows, a load of ballast iron, some yellow-wood planks and an assortment of waggon wheel parts. As a wheelwright or waggoner, then, Oosthuijzen may have made a good living (as well as much of the family's furniture). But his death would have left his children destitute, like those of the carpenter Gerrit Engelbrecht, were it not that arrangements had been made for his 24-year-old son Jacobus Johannes to purchase the farm.[208] This left the newly wed youth deeply in debt, for his *erfportie* amounted to no more than 87 rix dollars, whereas the farm was valued at 1,000 rix dollars, but if, as seems likely, his father-in-law came to his aid by lending him the money with which to reimburse his father's estate, he may have been able to take up where the latter had left off, gradually improving the family's position.[209]

Coetzee, like Anna Lombard, was cut down in the prime of life. Had he lived longer he might have acquitted himself of the debt incurred for the purchase of his farm. But as it happened he died within two years of having set himself up as an independent farmer. In 1800 he and his wife had been *bijwoners* on a farm belonging to his sister's husband, Johannes Christoffel Grijling.[210] According to his *opgaaf*, he had reaped nothing at all in that year and he owned only twelve cattle and three horses. He was not without means, for he had lent 1,500 rix dollars (possibly an inherited sum) to distant relatives, but neither was he in a position to pay cash for the farm which he bought in November 1801.[211] With the purchase of this farm – Vrisgewagt on the Berg River – he became overnight a grain farmer of some substance, but he simultaneously acquired liabilities amounting to 3,137 rix dollars.[212] When additional expenditure for the hire of slaves and oxen had been accounted for, little remained for distribution to his widow and his baby daughter. His widow, who was only 20 years old when he died, bought little at the *vendutie*, apart from a young slave girl, a bed and an old chest and I do not know what became of her.

The remaining decedents in this category were either dependent parents (Gerbrecht Pretorius, Agatha Blom and Jacobus Louw; nos. 106, 111b and 117)[213] or bachelors like Hermanus Grijling (no. 123). At this level of wealth, a widowed or single person could live in some comfort, provided he or she was not required to be self-sufficient. Thus Agatha Blom occupied well-appointed rooms in her daughter's house in Cape Town: she had four tables and seventeen chairs, a copper tea-kettle, a feather bed and an array of porcelain crockery. When she went visiting, she was carried in her own sedan chair and when she was buried her estate was sufficient to provide cheese, olives and wine for the mourners in addition to the usual fare of coffee and gingerbread.[214] However, besides her slaves whom she may perhaps have hired out, she had no productive assets whatsoever, and one must assume that she was supported by her daughter and son-in-law.

Grijling too enjoyed the comfort of a feather bed, though he had little other furniture. His occupation at the time of his death is unknown, but he had previously served as *knecht* with a Cape Town merchant, earning 14 rix dollars per month and more when there was a special task to perform.[215] Over the years he had accumulated a tidy capital, much of which he had loaned out at interest. However, he had also permitted himself a number of indulgences, such as poorer single men (like his contemporary Philip du Plessis) were unable to afford. He could wear gold rings on his fingers, a brooch at his throat and silver buckles on his shoes, and his snuff box was made of silver and mother of pearl. He was also the first of the bachelors considered thus far to have a shaving kit and a pocket watch. These little luxuries set him apart from the common peasantry with their *velschoenen* and their blue cloth jackets and signalled his wish to be accepted by respectable society.[216]

The point, however, is that this modest display of respectability could only be achieved at the expense of economic independence.[217] At this level of wealth it was simply not possible to have it all. If, like Volkert Schoenmaker or Pieter van der Westhuijzen, one made a bid for independence and opted for the life of an upcountry *veeboer*, one had to do without the trappings of 'civilised' society. Conversely, if one set great store by the latter one was best advised to remain single, like Grijling, and attach oneself to a member of the urban merchant class. Even the rustic comfort achieved by Gerrit Engelbrecht or Marthinus Oosthuijzen was dependent, it seems, upon the exercise of artisanal skills.

Surprisingly, these conclusions hold good even for those decedents whose net wealth places them in the fifth decima, close to the median value of all estates examined in this study. Thus Johanna Maria Buys (no. 146), *Weduwee* Hendrik Venter, whose livestock holdings may have earned her more than 900 rix dollars in the last year of her life, was little better equipped than her poorer contemporaries. Her most valuable possessions, apart from her stock, were a Bible, a soap pot and a feather mattress: she had no beds and only one table.[218] She was a new arrival on the north-east frontier, having moved from the Roggeveld shortly before her death, probably in order to be near her daughters Hester and Alida Johanna, who were married to Hendrik and Johannes Petrus van der Walt, respectively.[219] It is possible that she and her younger children lived with one of the married daughters, sharing the costs of the joint household; if this were so it would merely serve to underline the point that, at this level of wealth, domestic prosperity was beyond the reach of the nuclear household, even one as well supplied with livestock as that of Maria Buys.[220]

Maria Erasmus (no. 138) may also have farmed *in maatschappij*, possibly with her brother-in-law Daniel van der Merwe,[221] though the loan-farm 'De Matjes Rivier' was registered in her name. She had more farm implements than Buys and she may have grown more grain, for she had a plough and a harrow in working order. She was also childless, which may account for her more plentiful furniture and kitchenware (she had three tables and six rustic chairs) and her relative freedom from debt. However, like Buys, she had no luxuries, unless one should so designate her four copper kettles, six porcelain plates and a copper tart pan, or the blankets and chintz cover on her simple feather bed.[222]

It would seem, then, that the frequent memorials and petitions by which the upcountry colonists attempted to represent their poverty to the authorities did not exaggerate its extent. Nearly half of them (at least 40 per cent and probably more) were living in 'very straitened circumstances'.[223] Many were too poor (or too old) to farm on their own account and of those who did, few had land of their own.[224] The living arrangements of landless farmers are not easily discerned from the sources I have used, but one assumes that they found a place as partners or tenants of wealthier inhabitants. Some, however, may have been truly nomadic, camping on unclaimed land and sleeping rough next to their outspanned waggons.

The surprise is that even those who did hold land *and* sufficient livestock holdings to ensure a regular income – however small – lived in the simplest manner, often lacking the most basic amenities taken for granted by townsmen. Shelves and cupboards were rare indeed, beds (if there were any) were shared by parents and children, fingers were substituted for spoons and forks and, as Sparrman observed, 'two people [were] frequently obliged to eat out of one dish, using it besides for every different article of food that comes upon the table'.[225]

One could of course argue that this want of domestic amenities was a matter of choice, rather than a sign of poverty. This was the interpretation favoured by Sparrman, who ascribed the 'slovenliness and penury' of domestic interiors in De Bruins Hoogte more to a love of idleness than to a lack of resources. Even wealthy men would go to any lengths, he believed, to avoid the trouble of improving their surroundings. By contrast, the

Boers took great pride in their livestock, vying with one another 'in the number and thriving condition of their cattle, and chiefly in the stoutness of their draught-oxen'.[226] These views were echoed by other Europeans, notably Lady Anne Barnard, who considered that even the much wealthier inhabitants of the Overberg paid little attention to the condition of their houses. 'How these people have everything', she wrote, 'but possess things so unneatly, so undiligently, that there is the appearance of misery where there might be all the charms of comfort!'[227]

There may be some truth in these explanations of the material poverty of *veeboer* households. If nothing else they remind us that standards of comfort are relative. However Sparrman's belief that there was no correspondence between the number of an individual's stock and the quality of his or her domestic environment is not borne out by the evidence. Even a cursory examination of the *vendurollen* of the wealthiest members of the frontier community (taken from sampled estates in the ninth and tenth decimae) reveals that greater wealth in livestock *did* go hand in hand with a higher degree of material comfort. Lifestyles remained very simple – there was still a want of 'all the little trifling things' valued by members of the urban middle class – but basic items such as beds, chairs, eating utensils, crockery and storage vessels were far more abundant in wealthier homes. Thus the *Weduwee* Dawid Schalk van der Merwe, whose livestock holdings included 2,418 ewes, 57 cows and 143 heifers, had six simple beds and two four-posters with cloth canopies, as well as four chests, nine chairs, four tables, twenty-three plates and a 'tea machine'.[228] Jurriaan Greeff, who produced brandy as well as mutton on his Camdeboo farm, was no more a slave to fashion than the Widow van der Merwe, but he did have enough crockery and cutlery for all the (white) members of his household and nine chairs on which to seat them at his solid table.[229]

In a sense, then, there is truth in Sparrman's observation that the *veeboeren* rated productive assets higher than the refinements of domestic life. Further examination of the sources would confirm that wealthy individuals tended to invest their surplus earnings in additional producer goods like ox-waggons, slaves and wine-making equipment rather than fancy furnishings. The Widow van der Merwe, for example, had eleven slaves, two ox-waggons, sixty-five trek oxen and a horse-drawn carriage. Few owned clocks or mirrors (though books and paintings were relatively common) and one hardly ever encounters the large heavy armoires so common in respectable Cape Town homes.[230] But this does not detract from the fact that a great many other frontier households lacked even the simple domestic amenities listed in the inventories of the wealthy. Moreover, as we have seen, a paucity of material possessions was often accompanied by a crushing burden of debt, and, most serious of all, by the looming spectre of destitution which haunted the heirs to a small estate.

For the affluent and educated Europeans who, in the cause of science or good government, occasionally journeyed to the outlying districts of the colony, the poverty of the inhabitants was cause for concern. They might differ in their understanding of its causes (indolence and isolation were the favoured culprits; only those well acquainted with the colony pointed to the destructive effects of the Company's monopolies), but on one thing they were agreed: the squalor and wretchedness of the *veeboer*'s lifestyle was eroding the difference between settler and native. Thus Swellengrebel, describing the 'tumble-down barns' of the Camdeboo settlers, which 'held, on some farms, two or even three families and their children', concluded that 'it may be prophesied that these people will wholly sink back into savagery'.[231] Of the Khoisan, by contrast, he wrote that observers had exaggerated their alleged commitment to preserving their own way of life:

It is universally reckoned that the Hottentots are so wedded to their way of life that they would rather dress in a sheepskin, consume their meat raw, and lie down in the open air than wear our clothes, eat our bread and cooked meat, and sleep in our homes. But, amongst all the tribes of Hottentots and Caffers that I have seen, I have found just the opposite. I could give no more highly valued present to the Hottentots who accompanied me on my journey than stockings, breeches, a jacket and a hat. They ate willingly bread and roast meat and drank a glass of wine, or more especially brandy, with pleasure . . . they would rather sleep under a roof than in their own huts; the fact that they run naked is due more to the poverty and barbarity of the farmers than to their own choice.[232]

Mentzel likewise observed that 'these shepherds live little better than the Hottentots' among whom they were raised, and asked rhetorically whether they would not 'with the passing of time, forget that there is a God who created them?'[233] And J. F. Kirsten, representing the plight of the Graaff Reinet colonists to General Craig in 1795, informed him that 'several families have been so completely ruined, particularly in the last war with the Caffres, that they are reduced to nudity, or at most to a Sheeps Skin, after the manner of the Hottentots'.[234]

European visitors also remarked upon the promiscuous intermingling of Boer and Khoisan, especially inside the houses of the former. Thus while shepherds and cowherds commonly built their own '*strooijhuijzen*' around the farmer's cottage, house-servants slept under the same roof as the master and his family, often in the same room, since many Karoo farm-houses lacked internal walls.[235] Even in one-room dwellings, however, distinctions of status were reflected in the sleeping arrangements: servants and slaves slept with the dogs on the floor of the hearth, whereas the householder and his family shared beds (if they had any) separated from the rest of the room by reed mats.[236] But visitors could seldom be accommodated with the same deference to status. Thus Sparrman records that he often chose to sleep in the open air, rather than share the hearth with the Hottentot servants of his host.[237] Swellengrebel too noted the ubiquitous presence of Khoisan servants, observing tersely that 'they make the houses not more attractive but more smelly'. However Swellengrebel's special concern was not with the cross-cultural influences at work within the typical Boer household, but rather with the 'various young men, [who] without means for settling down, have here or there a miserable hut where they live with a Hottentot woman'. This, he believed, could have 'no other consequence . . . than the bastardization of the nation, which could be as great a threat to the colony as the Bushman-Hottentots are at present'.[238]

Had the *veeboeren* been aware of these perceptions, they might have reacted with shock and indignation, especially the poor among them, to whom such comments specifically alluded. But it is more likely they would not have understood. The reason is not far to seek. Put simply, I have tried to show in this chapter that many *veeboeren* were too poor to employ free labour, even on the rather favourable terms proposed by the authorities. The payment of annual cash wages – even the modest sums imposed by custom on a subject population – was beyond the means of many households in the poorer strata of the white community and payment in breeding stock (though this did occur in some cases) would deplete the already subeconomic holdings of a struggling enterprise. By the same token, few farmers in the poorer strata were able to afford the large sums required for the purchase of slaves. Consequently they turned to coercion of the native population to get the labour they needed and tried, through informal means, to assimilate the Khoisan to the condition of *de jure* slaves. However, as Orlando Patterson reminds us, 'all power strives for authority',[239] and the *veeboeren*, like slaveholders everywhere, had armed themselves with a set of justificatory beliefs through which they had transformed their violent domination of the Khoisan from 'a power relationship' to a 'rights relationship'.[240] They may have failed to secure the acquiescence of the Khoisan in this, but their very failure served to strengthen their own conviction (though it lent it a hysterical edge). At the heart of this conviction was the representation of the Khoisan as fundamentally other – 'the product of a hostile, alien culture' – and therefore not entitled to the rights of citizens.[241] Consequently, however much master and servant might come to resemble one another in their dress and language (the Khoisan increasingly spoke 'a bastard form of Dutch' and many frontiersmen were fluent in both Khoe and San languages) and however close and even intimate the physical contact between the two parties, the Khoisan would remain forever outside the moral community.[242] Their origins in war were not forgotten – 'almost all of them were deserving of death' observed the authors of the *Klagtschrift* in 1795[243] – but above all, it was their lack of religion, their 'heathenness', which set them apart and conferred upon them a liminal identity on the fringes of the social order.[244] Conversely, it was membership (by birth) of a Christian community which established the settler's claims to belonging. In the face of such beliefs, the concern of educated townsmen with the apparent assimilation of Europeans to native ways would more probably have met with incomprehension than animosity.

By contrast, the wrath of frontiersmen could be instantly aroused by those who attempted to tamper with what they perceived to be the true basis of their collective identity: their privileged access to the institutions of civil society (symbolised by their possession of burgher rights) and their exclusive membership of the Dutch Reformed Church. Hence, as we have seen, their peculiar hatred of Landdrost Maynier, who sought to grant the Khoisan access to his court and, in the early 1800s, their violent reaction to the Reverend Johannes van der Kemp, who, with Maynier's permission, took the unprecedented step of admitting 'the heathen' to evening worship in the village church of Graaff Reinet.[245] The actions of these two men struck at the very foundations of the normative order and they were the more unsettling precisely because the colonists had looked to both men to uphold that order. Van der Kemp in particular represented all they loved and respected – indeed the elders of the church had initially offered him the position of *Dominee* – and despite their hostility to his actions they could never bring themselves to harm his person.[246]

As André du Toit and Hermann Giliomee have explained, equality before the law was understood by many frontiersmen to mean *gelykstelling* – the levelling of all social distinctions – and therefore the end of the social order as they knew it.[247] However, judging from the context in which the term *gelykstelling* was used in the memorials of disaffected colonists, it would seem that they took it to mean not so much a levelling as a complete inversion of the social order. Hence the anguished question: 'but why are we to be placed under the heathen?'

I suggested in the previous chapter that this terror of social inversion derived from the colonists' awareness of their precarious position: the uncertainty of their grip upon the frontier, in the face of resistance from both Xhosa and Khoisan, and their failure to achieve moral hegemony over their Khoisan servants. I would now add, at the risk of falling into the error of reductionism, that they also sensed the link between the fundamental 'otherness' of the Khoisan (inscribed somehow in the order of creation) and their own material survival, or at least their continued existence as independent farmers. To question the one was to destroy the basis of the other. Hence, I would suggest, the vivid images of economic ruin with which the rebel party embellished their protests against Maynier and his supporters in 1795: 'Is there a greater scourge than hunger ever threatened, even by God himself, against a land?', they asked. 'Are we too to be forced to wander about, and become banditti and highwaymen and draw our living from theft and robbery? Fathers no longer safe from their own children, nor one brother from another?'[248] They knew well, they added, that these evils had once befallen their ancestors – 'for we do not live like beasts, but like to search old histories' – and they would do all they could to preserve themselves from a similar fate. If this brought them into conflict with a new and more inclusive concept of humanity, so be it.

9   'A time of breathing'

In 1795 Maynier had lacked the power to impose his vision of order and even-handed justice upon the rebellious citizenry of Graaff Reinet. Having, as he later wrote, 'no Garrison to support my character and authority as Landdrost' he was obliged by the *volkstem* to quit his Drostdy and return to the western Cape, where he lived, according to his own account, in quiet retirement on his farm, De Burghers Post.[1] In August 1799, however, as the *veeboeren* fled westward to escape the rampageous progress of their rebellious servants, he returned to the eastern frontier at the urgent request of the Acting Governor, General Francis Dundas. By December he was back in the village of Graaff Reinet, where he was installed by Dundas as Resident Commissioner, with authority over the Landdrost and all other civil and military officials.[2] This time, his authority was buttressed by a small force of English dragoons and Khoisan infantry (members of the 'Hottentot Corps'), stationed in the village on the orders of the Dundas himself.[3] Maynier's instructions were to implement the conciliatory policies he had formulated during his previous tenure in Graaff Reinet: as far as possible to reconcile the disaffected 'Hottentots' with the 'Inhabitants' by ensuring that they were paid for their services and protected from arbitrary brutality and 'above all to entertain a friendly intercourse with the Caffres' and prevent the colonists from attacking their homes and villages.[4]

In the end, these goals proved impossible to achieve: the Boers could neither tolerate nor understand Maynier's attempts to treat the Khoisan as a free (albeit savage) people, entitled to choose their own masters and negotiate their terms of service. Nor could they accept his reasons for disallowing reprisal raids against the homesteads of suspected stock-thieves. In the medium term, however, Maynier had some success: for eighteen months he managed to prevent the resumption of the open warfare which had disrupted colonial social relations throughout the district and nearly emptied the coastal forelands of their white inhabitants in 1799. He persuaded many Boers to reoccupy their farms and induced upwards of 400 Khoisan to re-engage themselves as servants. Perhaps most significant in the long run, his system of written labour contracts, his refusal to surrender 'Hottentots' accused of murder to the summary justice of their masters and his collaboration with the missionaries Van der Kemp and Read opened new possibilities for the increasingly desperate Khoisan and sowed the seeds of a tentative faith in British (as opposed to colonial) justice which endured, despite many reverses, until it was at last rewarded with the passage of Ordinance 50 and the foundation of the Kat River Settlement in the late 1820s.

But what were the events which led to Maynier's reinstatement? How was it that the charged relations between the Boers and their Khoisan servants, which had hovered so long on the brink of implosion, finally *did* burst asunder, so that the servants felt for the first time their collective power, and the masters were quite undone? What was it that destabilised a relationship which, however fraught and violent (some might say abusive), seemed to have become stuck in a shaky equilibrium which might have endured for many years to come? What precipitated a *dénouement*, however temporary? The answer to these questions lies squarely in the domain of the contingent and the specific; the terrain of historical agency in all its marvellous unpredictability. It is necessary, then, to recount the sequence of events in all their contingent detail. I hope the reader will bear with me.

One could begin, I think, with the arrest of Adriaan van Jaarsveld on 17 January 1799, on a charge of fraud. At the trial of Van Jaarsveld and his fellow rebels in August 1800, the prosecution alleged that plans for a renewal 'of the former patriotism' had already been discussed in December 1798, as evidenced in a letter written by Jan *'Eenhand'* Botha at the behest of Marthinus Prinsloo.[5] But it was the arrest of Van Jaarsveld which precipitated a new outbreak of popular defiance against the local authorities. This event was the culmination of a long process of evasion and prevarication by which Van Jaarsveld had tried to keep his creditors, the Orphan Masters of Cape Town, at bay. It will be recalled that in 1785 Van Jaarsveld had bought the farm De Vreede from the deceased estate of Johannes Jurgen de Beer.[6] For four years he kept up the interest payments on the original capital of fl. 10,000; thereafter he fell into arrears. In April 1794, during a visit to Cape Town to attend his daughter's wedding, he paid the interest up to 31 December 1791, for which he received a 'regular receipt'.[7] He also promised to find two men to stand surety for the loan. By the end of the year he had still not come forward with their names and the Landdrost (Maynier) was obliged to warn him of the 'unpleasant proceedings' which would follow if he failed to make good his promise.[8] Nothing further happened (and no more interest was paid) until December 1797, when the Orphan Masters, apparently tiring of the situation, instituted a civil claim for repayment of the capital plus outstanding interest.[9] Van Jaarsveld ignored the summonses and the court passed sentence in his absence. On 30 March 1798 the district messenger, Gustav Erlang, was sent to inform him of the court's decision. Van Jaarsveld protested that he did not owe as much interest as the court alleged and in proof thereof he produced the receipt he had been given in 1794. The number 1 of the year 1791 had been altered to a 4, so that it now seemed he had paid the interest up to 31 December 1794.[10] On discovering this fraud, Maynier's successor, Landdrost Bresler, initiated criminal proceedings. Van Jaarsveld was given six months to present himself in Cape Town, 'allowing this term on account of his dwelling in so remote a part of the Colony'. When he failed to appear on the appointed day (29 November 1798), the court issued a warrant for his arrest.[11] There was to be no escape from the vengeance of bookkeepers!

Or so it may have seemed from the secure vantage point of the Castle in Cape Town, whence the warrant issued. It was, as J. S. Marais observed in his study of Maynier's administration, 'no light matter for a Landdrost, with only a few policemen at his disposal, to have a Boer arrested, especially if other Boers sympathised with him'.[12] Mindful of this, and of Van Jaarsveld's words when the warrant was read out to him ('Sir, I apprehend this will occasion a motion among the people'),[13] Bresler took precautions. On the night of his arrest, Van Jaarsveld was kept in a room in the Landdrost's house, 'with a sentry before the door'.[14] The next day (18 January 1799) he was despatched to the Cape in a waggon belonging to Secretary Oertel, escorted by a sergeant and two dragoons. The sergeant was ordered 'in his presence . . . to treat him in the most polite manner as far as such was compatible with the state of a prisoner, but in case of any of his Fellow Burghers endeavouring to rescue him, then the Sergeant to shoot him immediately and the Dragoons to defend themselves as much as possible'.[15] In the event, the sergeant (advised by the secretary) thought better of these instructions.[16] Hearing of a plot to rescue the prisoner, Bresler had sent an additional five dragoons to escort the waggon as far as the Poort (just east of present-day Prince Albert); soon after they turned back, on 21 January, the waggons with their diminished escort were ambushed by a band of some forty men, each armed (as Barrow later had it) 'with an enormous musquet used for killing elephants and other wild beasts' and led by Marthinus Prinsloo of De Bruins Hoogte.[17] Faced with the prospect of bloodshed, the sergeant reluctantly delivered up his prisoner and the secretary continued on his way to the Cape, where he informed the authorities of the rescue. Thus began the second burgher rebellion in the history of the troubled district of Graaff Reinet.

The rescue of Adriaan van Jaarsveld set in motion a train of events which was to lead, in the space of a few months, to the servants' rebellion which Maynier had foreseen. The British authorities in Cape Town were by now heartily fed up with the lawless behaviour of their upcountry subjects. In 1796 they had been disposed to deal leniently with the rebel colonists, partly from a reluctance to risk disruption of Cape Town's meat supplies and partly from a sense that the colonists' anger was directed more at their former rulers than at themselves.[18] This time it was different. The liberation of Van Jaarsveld was a direct challenge to lawful authority and the rebels' revolutionary rhetoric and their evident appetite for news of British defeats in the war against France invoked unhappy reminders of the Dutch Patriots who had welcomed the French to the Netherlands in 1795.[19] Dundas decided on firm action. 'I consider this violation as an overt act of Rebellion', he wrote, 'and shall proceed to punish it as such.'[20] On 16 February, when news of the rescue reached him, he immediately despatched troops to the eastern frontier with instructions to apprehend 'these outrageous disturbers of the peace' and co-operate with Bresler in clearing his district of 'all such as have shewn any disposition to renew the too frequent disturbances'.[21] Two detachments of infantry were sent by sea to Algoa Bay and a division comprising approximately a hundred dragoons and a hundred members of the 'Hottentot Corps' set off overland, via Swellendam and the Lange Kloof. The troops met up on 8 March and on the 13th began their march to Graaff Reinet to relieve the exhausted Landdrost who had been trapped in the village since 25 January, *'abandonné et comme une machine immobile'*.[22]

Besides besieging the Drostdy, and threatening to hang the Landdrost at his own door or deport him to the country of the Xhosa,[23] the rebel Boers accomplished little during this time. They appear to have had a genuine sympathy for Van Jaarsveld's plight, putting themselves forward collectively (though belatedly) as guarantors of the sum he owed and 'asserting that what had happened to Van Jaarsveld today might befal (*sic*) to another tomorrow, and that they were already sufficiently persecuted in Cape Town when they repaired thither to transact their domestic affairs'.[24] But the chief focus of their discontent seems to have been the increasing pressure exerted by Xhosa in the Zuurveld and De Bruins Hoogte. In 1799 Ndlambe was still in Ngqika's country between the Kat and Keiskamma Rivers,[25] but it is possible that more of his followers were crossing the Fish River to join Myaluza in the Zuurveld.[26] Certainly the Boers still in that region complained of 'numerous herds' of Xhosa cattle encroaching on their pastures.[27] There were also reports of an 'invasion' of Xhosa west of the Sundays River, probably amaGqunukhwebe 'driving their herds from their winter pastures' to their summer pastures as they did each year.[28] Behind De Bruins Hoogte the colonists were in conflict with the imiDange, who had become 'roving bandit-guerillas' nurturing an inveterate hatred of the Boers since the murder of their chiefs (by none other than Adriaan van Jaarsveld) in 1781.[29] Bresler himself noted the prominence of men from De Bruins Hoogte among the leaders of the *volkstem* in 1799 – indeed he referred to Van Jaarsveld's rescuers as '*un complot de Bruinshoogte &c*'.[30] Certainly the rebels demanded that government adopt a more aggressive policy towards the Xhosa. They forced Bresler to write to Dundas proposing that 'the Inhabitants residing on the banks of the Great Fish River . . . be allowed to send their cattle in the morning to graze on the other side', and that 'no Hottentot shall be sent to the Caffres with messages, much less with any presents'[31] and they complained that 'it was already long ago since the Caffers were to be expelled from this side, and they were still there'.[32]

Dundas chose to ignore these 'insolent' communications, which he correctly perceived to have been written under duress.[33] The British, embroiled in an epic struggle with post-revolutionary France, were no more willing to go to war against the Xhosa than their predecessors had been. In 1796 General Craig had issued a ringing denunciation of the *volkstem*'s request to be allowed to occupy 'a parcel of land in Caffraria':

with what face can you ask of me to allow you to occupy Lands which belong to other people, what right can I have to give you the property of others? . . . Would not the Caffers defend their right, and should I not in every view of morality and religion be responsible for every life that would be lost in such a contest as a Murder? Reflect one moment what would be your own sensation were you to hear that I was even debating on a proposal which might be made to me to turn you out of your Farms and to give them to others, and I am sure you will feel regret at having desired me to allow you to do that which you would consider as the highest act of cruelty and injustice if done to you. Cultivate the friendship and good will of the Caffers, receive them with kindness and hospitality, and if hereafter an extension of Limits be wanted, it may be in the power of Government to procure it by purchase or by agreement, on terms of mutual conveniency.[34]

Dundas had in any case already determined to send in the troops. He reiterated his intention to arrest the leaders of the *volkstem* and remove them 'to those countries of anarchy and confusion which have been the models of their conduct'.[35] And he made arrangements to block all communication between the western Cape and the district of Graaff Reinet, thereby depriving the rebels of fresh supplies of ammunition.[36]

The arrival of the soldiers at Algoa Bay spread alarm and confusion among the members of the *volkstem*. Jan *Eenhand* Botha and Gerrit Hendrik Rautenbach (who was known locally as 'Freedom's Child')[37] were deputed to form a camp at the Coega River to oppose the march of the troops. Letters were drafted, men were assembled and the rebel leaders reminded one another that they had sworn to 'be faithful to each other until the last drop of blood'.[38] Marthinus Prinsloo warned the Landdrost (in a letter transcribed by Adriaan van Jaarsveld) that 'should there appear the least report of the armed Hottentots, then Buys with the whole Caffer country will march against them'.[39] But in the end the troops were allowed to pass unmolested on their way inland to Graaff Reinet. The principal leaders of the insurrection were absent from the camp at Coega: Van Jaarsveld fell ill on the way from De Bruins Hoogte and Prinsloo turned back on the road.[40] As for Coenraad de Buys and Jan Botha, both had left the colony for Ngqika's country before the time came to attack the troops,[41] and neither returned with the promised Xhosa support.[42] Brigadier Vandeleur's 'little army' passed through the narrow defile at Zoutpan's Nek without incident, much to the disappointment of the soldiers, who had been expecting an ambush ('in my life I never saw ground more favourable for that purpose' wrote Major McNab),[43] and arrived at the Drostdy on March 19. There Vandeleur was informed that the rebels had deputed two neutral persons (one being Marthinus Prinsloo's brother Willem) to ask for a 'General Pardon'.[44] This Vandeleur refused, insisting instead on a public and collective act of submission. All those 'concerned in the late daring revolt' were to meet him at Willem Prinsloo's farm Boschberg in De Bruins Hoogte on 6 April (Fig. 28).

On the appointed day the majority of the rebels (some ninety-three in all), led by Marthinus Prinsloo, 'appeared in a body, and laid down their arms to His Majesty's Troops'.[45] According to John Barrow, then on his way to meet Vandeleur at Algoa Bay, the soldiers (including, it must be assumed, the men of the Hottentot Corps, who were with Vandeleur at De Bruins Hoogte)[46] found it hard to keep a straight face as the portly rebels dismounted and surrendered their arms: 'the awkward manner in which they dismounted, with the difficulty that some of them experienced on account of the protuberance of their bellies, in grounding their arms, were sufficient to throw the most serious off their guard'.[47] The ringleaders, including Prinsloo and Van Jaarsveld, were immediately arrested and conveyed under escort to His Majesty's ship *Rattlesnake*, then at anchor in Algoa Bay.[48] The remaining insurgents were pardoned on payment of a cash fine and the surrender of 'one or two horses' to the cavalry, 'in proportion to their means', and disarmed.[49] The next day, in Cape Town, Francis Dundas proclaimed martial law in the divisions of Graaff Reinet, De Bruins Hoogte, Zuurveld and Swartkops River and ordered that *all* the (white) inhabitants of these divisions be disarmed. One month later, having received Vandeleur's report on the events of 6 April, Dundas could write to his uncle, Henry Dundas, Secretary of State for War and the Colonies, that the disturbances in that part of the colony were finally at an end:

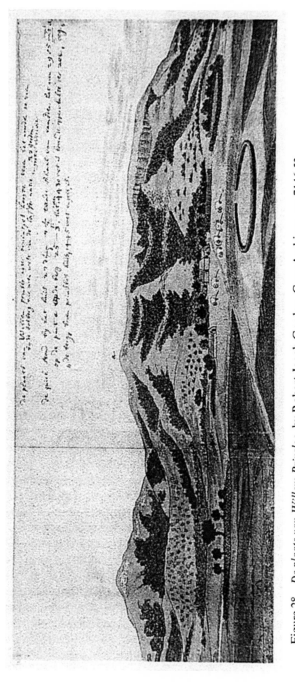

Figure 28 *De plaats van Willem Prinsloo*, by Robert Jacob Gordon, Cape Archives, AG 7146.53.

The steps which I have taken in the discharge of my public trust upon this occasion I may declare to you without arrogance have been attended with success, the prompt and effectual measures adopted in order to crush finally disorders which have so often prevailed in the District of Graaff Reinet and which the late Government of the Dutch East India Company could not at any time repress, have had the concurrence of the Inhabitants of the Colony at large ... and I have much pleasure in assuring you that there is no well-grounded expectation of further disquietude.[50]

How he must have lived to regret these words! The 'prompt and effectual measures' ordered by Francis Dundas led directly to the kind of undoing of the social order which Maynier had foreseen (and which the Boers' own paranoid fantasies had prefigured). Emboldened by the presence in the region of a force more powerful than any their masters could command (a force made up in part of 'Hottentots' like themselves) and buoyed up by news of the rebel Boers' humiliating surrender, Khoisan servants in the coastal forelands seized the day and began to desert their masters and mistresses, taking guns and clothing ('in lieu of wages') as they went. In the third week of April, Barrow and Vandeleur met up with 'a large party' of deserters not far from their base at the Swartkops River mouth. They were 'so disguised, and dressed out in such a whimsical and fantastical manner', Barrow later wrote, 'that we were totally at a loss . . . what to make of them. Some wore large three cornered hats, with green or blue breeches, the rest of the body naked; some had jackets of cloth over their sheepskin covering, and others had sheep-skins thrown over linen shirts. The women were laden with bundles and the men were all armed with musquets.' They made no secret of the fact that they had been plundering the Boers. Their leader, Klaas Stuurman,

stepped forwards, and, after humbly entreating us to hear him out without inter-ruption, began a long oration, which contained a history of their calamities and sufferings under the yoke of the boors; their injustice, in first depriving them of their country, and then forcing their offspring into a state of slavery; their cruel treatment on every slight occasion, which it became impossible for them to bear any longer; and the resolution they had therefore taken to apply for redress before the English troops should leave the country.[51]

In the published account of his journey, Barrow professed surprise and 'mortification' at this encounter. But archival evidence shows that he had become aware of the desertions some days before his meeting with Stuur-man's party. However he and Vandeleur were wholly preoccupied with the white rebels and, despite his frequent criticisms of the oppressive condi-tions of service in the Cape interior, he seems not to have understood just how brittle social relations in this part of the colony were. In a letter to Francis Dundas, dated 15 April 1799, Barrow mentioned in passing that parties of this nation [Xhosa] with vagabond Hottentots have taken the opportunity of the present disturbances to plunder several houses, but [he added dryly] they seem to have perfectly well understood the nature of the proclamation issued by General Vandeleur [to the effect that inhabitants who abandoned their farms would have their houses burnt and their cattle confiscated],[52] having confined their depredations to those farms alone that have been deserted by the tenants. I have no doubt that great pains will be taken to exaggerate the evil which the foolish people have brought upon themselves, and attribute it, as indeed they have already done, to the encouragement given to the Hottentots by the English troops, though they have been disarmed and dispersed wherever such parties have been fallen in with by the troops.[53]

With hindsight, however, Barrow acknowledged that the events of these few weeks in late April and early May were decisive: 'the connection that had long subsisted between the boors and the Hottentots, a connection that was kept up by violence and oppression on one side, and by want of energy and patient suffering on the other, seemed now to be entirely dissolved', he wrote. 'The farther we advanced, the more seriously alarming was the state of the country.'[54] Unsure what to do with Stuurman's party, Vandeleur allowed them to follow the troops into the Zuurveld, where he was going, as Barrow wrote in his *Travels*, 'to collect his scattered forces and to assemble them at head-quarters in Bruyntjes Hoogte'.[55] But, as Barrow's letter reveals, Vandeleur's journey eastward had an additional aim. Acting on instructions from Dundas, who had been informed (erroneously, as he later discovered) that the Xhosa west of the Fish River were all recent immigrants, 'Desertors from the Great Caffre Nation' east of the Fish River, Vandeleur intended to persuade the Zuurveld chiefs to leave the colony with their people.[56] To this end he met with the Gqunukhwebe chief Chungwa on the banks of the Sundays River. The meeting was friendly but inconclusive. Chungwa told him that 'the ground he then stood on was his own by inheritance', but when pressed he reluctantly agreed to move. However, as the English troops made their way back towards the Sundays River from De Bruins Hoogte they were ambushed 'in a narrow defile'. 'A Hottentot driver of one of the waggons was killed by a hassagai . . . Kaffers began to appear in great numbers on all the heights . . . and several were observed close upon us lurking in the bushes.' The soldiers extricated themselves by firing grape-shot into the surrounding bush and the column moved on. But some days later they were attacked again, this time at their camp near the Bushmans River. 'Rushing forward upon the open plain, with the iron part only of the Hassagai in their hands',[57] the Xhosa were again repulsed with heavy losses, but a third attack, against a patrol sent out towards the sea, evened the score: all but four of the twenty-one British soldiers were killed.[58] These skirmishes marked the beginning of the 'Third Frontier War', a war far 'more disas-trous for the farmers than the two preceding ones', as J. S. Marais has written, 'because so many Hottentot farm servants joined the Xhosa'.[59]

The British did what they could to prevent this alliance. After the first engagement with Chungwa's men, Vandeleur instructed Barrow to lead Stuurman's party back to the base at Algoa Bay.[60] There, to his dismay, Barrow found all the Boers who had been plundered by their runaway servants, 'with their cattle and waggons and the remains of their property'. They were waiting for Vandeleur's return, 'in order, as they said, to claim protection against the heathens'.[61] Of the latter there were now more than 500 assembled and Barrow found himself caught between the contending parties, 'each claiming protection, and each vowing vengeance against the other'.[62] He managed to keep them apart for some days, aided by a small force of dragoons and twenty armed sailors from the *Rattlesnake*, and a 'swivel gun . . . mounted on a post'. But this tense situation could not be sustained. Without authority from Dundas or Vandeleur and with the withdrawal of the troops imminent, Barrow could do little to allay the fears of the Khoisan. He could not grant Stuurman's demand for land[63] and he could not guarantee that, once the troops were withdrawn, the Boers would not 'in all probability murder' their runaway servants, as the latter believed.[64] One morning, before Vandeleur's return to base, Barrow awoke to find that 'a great number' of the Khoisan in his charge 'had stolen away in the night' and gone to join the Xhosa in the Sundays River bush.[65] Barrow attributed their sudden departure to a rumour spread by the Boers, to the effect that the English planned to put them aboard the *Rattlesnake* and send them to the Cape, but it seems more likely that, as Dundas believed, they decided to leave when they heard that the Xhosa had clashed with Vandeleur's troops and that a Boer commando was to be raised to assist the British.[66] They decided then, as Dundas later wrote, 'that a union with the Caffres would tend much to render them indepen-dent of the Boors'.[67]

The Boer commando, comprising '300 farmers' under the command of Hendrik Janse van Rensburg, took the field at the beginning of June 1799. Its instructions were 'first to clear the Sunday River region of Xhosa, from the Zwarte Ruggens to the mouth of the river, and then to drive them beyond the Fish'.[68] It failed entirely. Some time before 27 June it did battle with a party of '150 Caffres and Hottentots' and was roundly defeated, with the loss of three men ('two Christians and a Hottentot'), one hundred horses, fifty-two saddles and twenty-six great coats.[69] The Hottentots were said to have already 'in their possession upwards of 300 horses, indepen-dently of what they have afterwards taken from the farms along the Zondag River'.[70]

The plundering of Boer houses and the gathering of weapons, horses and livestock had begun, as we have seen, in mid-April, but by the end of June it was clear to all that the farmers' rebellious servants, united with the Gqunukhwebe of the Zuurveld and the imiDange of De Bruins Hoogte, had resolved to drive them out of the district altogether. Dr van der Kemp, who in mid-June was travelling eastwards across the Karoo to begin his mission to the Xhosa, was told as much by a group of 'Hottentots' from the Bushmans River who approached his camp on a frosty winter night and engaged his servant in conversation.[71] One of the group, a man named 'Courage [Couragie]', 'asked brother Vanderkemp, if it were not true that God had created them [the Hottentots] as well as the christians, and the beasts of the field; "for you know, (said he) that the Dutch farmers teach us, that he never created us, nor taketh any notice of us"'.[72] Van der Kemp 'then sat down, and explained to him man's equal misery, and the way to everlasting happiness through faith in Christ'. This encounter could be taken as the beginning of the Dutch missionary's egalitarian ministry to the Khoisan of the Cape interior and his words on this occasion as a shining example of the liberatory theology which would so outrage his fellow Europeans on his return to Graaff Reinet in 1801.[73] In the context of the times, when hundreds of Khoisan servants had embarked upon a campaign to reclaim their power and reverse their status as degraded outsiders, the elderly missionary's simple message was, as we have already noted, deeply subversive. Couragie, like so many Khoisan after him, was profoundly affected by it ('I'll always remember these words', he said, 'and I'll go in all my distress to Jesus') and declared his intention to follow the missionaries into Xhosa country once he had 'settled [his] affairs with his master'. They parted and Van der Kemp went on his way, still largely unaware of the fury his commitment to the conversion of the heathen would arouse.

By the end of July the 'heathen' were in control of much of the district. Vandeleur was trapped at his post near the Swartkops River mouth, unable to communicate with Bresler in Graaff Reinet or with his own subordinate, Captain Campbell, who had been instructed to join him from De Bruins Hoogte, after leaving reinforcements with Bresler for the defence of the Drostdy.[74] The direct route from the Drostdy to Algoa Bay had become impassable, 'on account of the number of rebellious Hottentots', and Campbell was obliged to make a long south-westerly detour, approaching Algoa Bay from the Lange Kloof.[75] Even this route was dangerous. Thrown into a panic by the desertion of their servants and despairing of the arrival of the seaborne reinforcements summoned by Vandeleur, the white inhabitants of the coastal forelands had fled into Swellendam district – 'they have stole away one after another' wrote

Vandeleur – allowing the enemy to occupy the ford at the Gamtoos River and cut off communication with the Lange Kloof. 'My situation here is rather critical', Vandeleur continued. 'At present all that can be done by the Troops is to keep our situation near the Bay and cover the building of the Block house.'[76] On 3 August he reported that 'there now remain on this side the Camtoos River (sic) only 2 families viz. Van Rooy's and Ferreira's, the former of which goes away this day'.[77] The news from the Camdeboo was equally grim: 'everybody flying before the Hottentots and Caffres'.[78] Zwagershoek and De Bruins Hoogte were said to be almost empty of [white] inhabitants ('the last man has this night removed from Zwagershoek' wrote Anna Elizabeth Olivier on 5 August[79]) and the Drostdy itself was now exposed to attack.[80] And Vandeleur was informed that the troubles had spread into Swellendam district: 'this contagion of the Hottentots has extended to the Long Kloof, where I understand they are also all running away from their masters and joining the Renegadoes in this country'.[81] The situation was indeed grave and the court which tried Van Jaarsveld and his comrades in August 1800 rightly described the forces unleashed by their ill-considered actions as 'in a thousand respects dangerous for this Colony'.[82]

All those in authority were agreed that the flight of the farmers aggravated the situation. Bresler's orders that beleaguered families in the Camdeboo and De Bruins Hoogte join together 'to be the better able to oppose the Banditti' were repeatedly ignored and, in the opinion of Vandeleur, the rampant progress of the Khoisan and their Xhosa allies in the coastal forelands was in no small part due to the 'dastardly conduct' of the inhabitants whose want of resistance had 'allowed the Country to be so completely overrun'.[83] 'If you trust to the Boers', Vandeleur wrote to Dundas in late August, 'upon the first shot being fired they will run away and leave you in the lurch.'[84]

In part, the flight of the farmers was due to a shortage of ammunition. The measures taken by Dundas in February, coupled with the disarmament of the Boer rebels and their sympathisers in April, had created an acute shortage of powder and lead in the interior districts. 'We are all of us entirely destitute of Powder and Lead', wrote Salomon Ferreira at the end of July. 'Should you have no ammunition at hand, then I think that the Burghers [of Swellendam] each of them might supply us with some of theirs, that we may not continue to be murdered without being able to make any defence.'[85] There was indeed a real risk of being murdered. The primary objective of the allies was to drive the 'Christians' away – 'beyond Attaquas Kloof' said some[86] – and to this end they set fire to houses, plundered livestock and seized arms and ammunition. But they were not above murdering those whom they managed to surprise: in late July, for

example, the families of Stephanus Scheepers and Hendrik Joseph Stry-
dom (both of the Winterhoek) were 'altogether murdered' and everything
burnt.[87] And on 18 July 'two Dutchmen and one Hottentot' who had gone
to fetch corn for Vandeleur's men were murdered within reach of the
British post, 'merely for the sake of the oxen in their waggons'. A number
of colonists were killed during battles between Boer refugees and the
imiDange at the Fish River, behind De Bruins Hoogte, and, while travelling with the refugees, Van der Kemp was told, again by 'a Hottentot from
the Boschemans River', that 'the Hottentots, united with the Caffrees (*sic*),
had resolved to destroy all the colonists'.[88]

However, besides the eminently practical desire to save their skins, there
were, I believe, deeper reasons for the panic-struck flight of the farmers of
Graaff Reinet. In the words of Brigadier Vandeleur: 'the desertion of their
Hottentots has completely unmanned them'. If, as Orlando Patterson has
so convincingly argued, 'in all slave societies' the master's sense of honour,
power and manhood grew in proportion to the degradation, powerlessness
and consequent dishonour of his slaves, then it follows that a sudden
reclamation of power by the slave (or one who was viewed as a slave)
would leave the master reeling, 'timid beyond all example', and as in this
case, 'terrified at even a single shot from a Hottentot'.[89] The *veeboeren*
were not 'by nature' cowardly, as Dundas believed. In 1781 and again in
1793, with their servants in their proper place, they had boldly done battle
with the Xhosa (though it must be said that there was much running away
during the war of 1793)[90] and Van der Kemp commended their courage
when attacked by the imiDange in 1799.[91] But the metamorphosis of
trusted servants, including 'chosen Hottentots bred up in the family', had
struck at the roots of their self-confidence and undermined their sense of
(masculine) identity. Hence, one might suggest, the fantasies of sexual
usurpation which had surfaced in 1795 and would do so again during
Maynier's second tenure in 1801.[92]

At the beginning of August General Dundas decided to assume personal
command of the British forces on the eastern frontier. Before leaving Cape
Town he made arrangements for the warship *Rattlesnake* to return to
Algoa Bay with ammunition and troop reinforcements and arranged that
the *Camel* should follow, carrying a 'prefab' block house, a party of
artisans to put it together and a garrison of fifty men.[93] He was accompanied on his overland journey by several hundred soldiers, drawn from
the garrison in Cape Town. These reinforcements would bring the total
number of troops on the eastern frontier to 800.[94]

None the less, before he reached Swellendam Dundas had concluded, on
the basis of information received from Vandeleur, that his best option
would be to sue for peace. Vandeleur had warned him that it would take at

Figure 29   *Gonah Hottentot*, by Samuel Daniell, *Sketches representing the native tribes, animals and scenery of southern Africa*, London: William Daniell and William Wood, 1820.

least 1,000 men to force 'the savages' into retreat: 'The country is so very extensive and woody', he wrote, 'that they can always avoid you if they are not attacked at several points at the same time.'[95] Dundas had been a soldier since the age of 16. He had fought in the American War of Independence and participated in the capture of Martinique and Guadeloupe in 1794.[96] It was the latter experience, perhaps, which led him to see similarities between the situation on the eastern frontier and 'the unfortunate events of St. Domingo [St Domingue]' and to seek a 'speedy' end to the servants' rebellion, lest the 'whole Colony' be exposed to ruin.[97] The number of the 'Combined Confederacy of Hottentots' (as Maynier called them) was daily increasing – in October Maynier estimated their number at 'upwards of 700 men' with more than 300 horses and 150 guns – and Dundas deemed it almost impossible to attack them 'in the nearly inaccessible woods and mountains'.[98] As for the Xhosa, Dundas thought it 'more than probable' that war with this nation 'would bring along with it disappointment and disgrace'.[99] By the time he reached the Gamtoos River in late August, he was confirmed in this opinion.[100] He thought it absolutely necessary to break the alliance between the rebellious Khoisan and the Zuurveld Xhosa and to this end he resolved to make separate peace agreements with the two parties. The Xhosa were to be allowed to remain where they were, on the banks of the Sundays and Bushmans Rivers, 'or in other words in the situation in which we found them';[101] the Khoisan, by contrast, who 'possess no property in the Country, having been deprived of their Cattle and lands by the European Settlers in Africa', were to be persuaded to return to service with the Boers, but under guarantee of protection against arbitrary abuse and breach of contract.[102] To help him achieve a negotiated peace, Dundas sought out a person who understood the savage mind; someone who 'had influence over the Hottentots, and on whom they would rely'.[103]

Such were the circumstances which led to the recall of ex-Landdrost Maynier to the district of Graaff Reinet. Maynier's views on the situation were very much in accord with those of Francis Dundas. During his time in exile from the district he had repeatedly told Bresler of his fears for its fate if the 'peasants' did not mend their ways and learn to treat their servants humanely, and he had advised him 'to bear himself with patience the complaints of the Hottentots, and in such cases as they were in the right, to administer justice to them'. On his return to Cape Town in 1795 he had warned the British authorities 'that the unhappy Natives of the country turning desperate by the bad treatment of the chief part of the Inhabitants, and by want of protection of their Rights, would one day commit the most horrid depredations'. Now he had been proved absolutely right.[104] His appointment was the obvious choice for a government seeking to restore order in the district through conciliation rather than (re)conquest.

The chief instrument of Dundas and Maynier's new Hottentot policy was the system of written labour contracts already discussed in chapter 8. The key to the success of this system was that – unlike Earl Caledon's notorious 'Hottentot Code' of 1809 – it was to be personally administered by the man who had designed it.[105] Maynier kept the register himself and dealt personally with disputes which arose. 'It was a difficult and demanding task', according to his deputy, William Somerville, 'because of the violent prejudices on both sides.'[106] But the Boers had been chastened by the events of the past six months – 'many who were prepossessed against me called me their deliverer', Maynier later wrote – and, according to Somerville, 'these prejudices were removed and the hostile parties were satisfied'.[107]

Maynier managed to persuade 402 Khoisan to re-enter service under the protection of written contracts. But it is not at all clear that most of these were, as he claimed, members of the 'Hottentot Confederacy'.[108] On the contrary, part of the reason for the temporary success of Dundas' peace policy was, paradoxically, that Maynier was not able to dislodge the 'Confederacy' from its base on the banks of the Sundays River. Dundas had envisaged that only 'a few of the Hottentot Captains' who 'had become particularly obnoxious' to the Boers, and whose lives would be endangered by returning to them, should be granted land. The remainder, with their followers, should find their sustenance 'at the Houses of the Country people'.[109] In practice, however, the principal leaders of the rebellion – the Stuurman brothers: Klaas, Andries and Dawid, Hans Trompetter, Ruiter Beesje, Boezak and Bovenland – remained entrenched in the Sundays River bush until the renewal of hostilities in November 1801.[110] Maynier was unable to retrieve any of the sheep and cattle captured during the war, though he later claimed that he had recovered 'some of the firearms, waggons etc. which were still in possession of the Hottentots'.[111] He was also unable to prevent a gradual drift of unattached Khoisan to the village of Graaff Reinet, where they came to live under his protection, in preference to returning to their former masters. By the time of Dr van der Kemp's return in May 1801, there were more than 200 such people in the village.[112] Thus, while Maynier may have been correct in his claim that hostilities ceased immediately after the peace negotiations of October 1799, and while he did indeed oversee the re-occupation of many abandoned farms, social relations in the district were by no means restored to the *status quo ante*.

In truth, the lull in hostilities secured by Dundas' policy was more a truce than a peace. From October 1799 until the resumption of war in 1802, there was a continual 'war of nerves' between the Boers and the

Khoisan.[113] In December 1799, while Dundas was still at the Drostdy in Graaff Reinet, Laurens Erasmus of De Bruins Hoogte apprehended a Khoisan 'meijt' who had allegedly been 'going about with all sorts of roguery and lies', telling the people who remained with the farmers that there was 'a commando of Hottentots and Bastards coming to catch us [the Boers] and to see what has become of our great hearts'. The commando was coming from Swartkops River she said, with the knowledge of the Governor.[114] And in November 1800 two Boers from the 'Onderveld' were accosted by Klaas Stuurman and Boezak and forced to surrender their oxen. Did they know, the captains asked, 'that *they* were English and that they had the power to bind them hand and foot, put them in a waggon and carry them to the Bay?'[115] The Boers, though initially on the defensive, increasingly retaliated in kind, threatening their servants with violence and chafing at the restrictions placed on military adventures. In June 1801 a large party of dissident Boers led by H. J. van Rensburg demanded permission 'to go on commandos against the Caffres and Hottentots' and said, allegedly, that they would burn Graaff Reinet to the ground and 'murder all the Hottentots'.[116]

By July 1801 it was clear that the centre could not hold. On 6 June Maynier heard that 'all the inhabitants of Bruins Hoogte and some from the Plat and Vogel Rivers had suddenly quitted their homes and assembled in Zwagershoek'. They had been alarmed by a rumour to the effect that government was planning to seize all the male inhabitants (excepting old men with grey heads) so as to make soldiers and sailors of them and that Maynier was charged with putting this plan into effect at the next *opgaaf*, which was to begin on 15 June. They were also, so it was said, so disturbed by the Xhosa that they could no longer remain at home.[117] They were dissatisfied with Maynier's contract system, wanting contracts to be administered by the *veldwagtmeesters* instead of the Landdrost. And they felt threatened by the large number of masterless Khoisan in the village of Graaff Reinet.[118] They believed, probably rightly, that among them were men who had attacked and plundered Boer homes. (Indeed Klaas Stuurman himself was seen in the village during the course of 1801 – apparently supervising labourers engaged in building the new barracks! – and Ruiter Platje was an occasional visitor.)[119] But above all, as we have already seen, they were incensed at the arrangements made by Maynier for the accommodation of the missionary Van der Kemp and his Hottentot congregation.

Van der Kemp returned to the village of Graaff Reinet on 14 May 1801. He refused the proffered ministry of the (white) church, passing this responsibility on to the Reverend van der Lingen, who had recently arrived in the village, along with James Read.[120] On 17 May, presumably with

Maynier's permission, Van der Lingen preached to 'a multitude of Hottentots' in the parish church. Shortly thereafter Maynier offered the missionaries the use of the church on a regular basis. Every evening at six o'clock
the Khoisan community 'was invited . . . to assemble' at the ringing of the
ell.[121] On 1 June, the villagers witnessed the extraordinary spectacle of a
joint evening service, attended by 'a great number of heathen' as well as
members of the established (white) congregation. The 'heathen' opened
the service by singing Psalm 134, an inoffensive three-verse psalm. The
'Christians' answered thus:

Thine enemies roar in the midst of thy congregations; they set up their ensigns for
signs. A man was famous according as he had lifted up axes upon the thick trees.
But now they break down the carved work thereof at once with axes and hammers.
They have cast fire into thy sanctuary, they have defiled by casting down the
dwelling place of thy name to the ground . . . We see not our signs: there is no more
any prophet: neither is there among us any that knoweth how long. O God, how
long shall the adversary reproach? Shall the enemy blaspheme thy name for ever?
(Psalm 74, vv. 4–10.)[122]

On 2 June, Van der Kemp and Read opened a 'reading and writing
school' for the heathen. Four days later, the burghers of the aforemen-
tioned districts gathered under arms at Zwagershoek, 'murmuring against
the instruction of the heathen . . . and their admission into the church'.[123]
In early July Maynier was informed that the dissidents, who had retreated
to the Tarka to muster their forces and now numbered some 300, were
approaching the village and planned to reduce it to ashes.[124] On 9 July
they appeared on the heights surrounding the village. Their emissaries
demanded that the five Khoisan who had allegedly murdered Klaas Prinsloo *d'oude*, and whom Maynier had released from custody, be delivered to
them or, at least, rearrested.[125] And they 'complained of the admission of
the Hottentots into the church, requesting that the seats should be washed,
the pavement broken up, the pulpit covered with black cloth, as a demonstration of mourning, on account of the absence of a regular clergyman,
the church-yard fenced by a stonewall, etc.'[126]

Maynier apparently failed to grasp the depths of the farmers' outrage at
the extension of Christian 'privileges' to the heathen. Displaying, perhaps,
the arrogance of which many historians have accused him, he dismissed
their complaints as 'idiocies' and continued to insist that the real reason for
their discontent was their gullibility (with respect to the alleged plan to
enlist them in the army and navy).[127] Van der Kemp, by contrast, understood very well. He was willing to withdraw from the church, he said, and
to meet with 'his' heathen in the missionaries' own house (which had been
rented from the church council), but he wished the colonists to understand
clearly that he 'never would preach in a church from which [his] heathen

congregation should be excluded'. Those who wished to join his congregation would always be welcome, but they would have to meet with him
outside the church.[128]

On 13 July, following a tense standoff at the edge of the village, the
dissident Boers retreated. Maynier hoped this would now be the end of it –
'que la chose a été terminée' – and that they would return to their homes. He
sent back all but thirteen of the troops who had come from Algoa Bay at
the insistence of the officer in command of the garrison. And he expressed
his hope that he would soon regain the confidence of 'the peasants'.[129] But
he underestimated the extent of their agitation. During the siege of the
village in mid-July the European inhabitants had refused to take arms
against their countrymen and Maynier had been obliged to rely largely on
Khoisan troops – nineteen members of the Hottentot Corps and eighty
irregulars recruited from among the Khoisan then in the village – in
addition to twenty-one dragoons.[130] He had always maintained that the
Khoisan bore the brunt of military operations on the frontier and thus
thought these arrangements quite appropriate.[131] But, for the veeboeren,
Maynier's use of Hottentot irregulars was proof (if proof were needed)
that he was conspiring with the heathen against them. In the aftermath of
the July demonstration, many more Khoisan left the farms, and came 'in
large bands' to the Drostdy, some bringing guns. By October there were
approximately 800 men, women and children in the village, grouped under
a number of captains: 'some bellicose, some frightened, all nursing grievances'.[132] Dominee Vos of Tulbagh, who visited the frontier in November
at the request of General Dundas, found the white inhabitants of the
village at their wits' end. The worst, they said, was that they had 'had to
endure all sorts of taunts and insults from the Hottentots and when they
went to complain to the Commissioner they got a second scolding'.[133] As
for the 'armed farmers', who were then gathered at the Bamboesberg, they
were 'desperate' and had lost faith in government, and they feared to go
home lest 'the armed Hottentots' broke out of Graaff Reinet and attacked
the nearby farms. A rumour was circulating among them, similar to one
which had done the rounds in 1795: that they would be 'captured and sent
away or killed by the heathen, and their wives would be given to the
heathen [and] that this year their wives still had white children on their
laps, but next year they would have black'.[134] They would rather die
beneath a hail of bullets than allow that to happen, they told Vos.

On the night of 22 October the rebel Boers again surrounded the village,
demanding that Maynier surrender the Khoisan accused of murdering
Klaas Prinsloo.[135] They attacked at dawn, showing more resolve than they
had in July. Throughout the day they battled it out with the garrison and
the Khoisan volunteers, but failed to capture either the barracks or the

Figure 30   *Een Hottentottin met haar kind by Christenen in dienst* (Sneeuberge, *c.* 1812), F. Steeb, William Fehr Collection, Cape Town, D 35.

fort. When night fell they remained at their posts, as the beleaguered townspeople could tell from the glow of the coals in their pipes. By morning they were gone. Remarkably, there were no casualties, though many buildings were reduced to ashes.[136] But the events of 23 October left Dundas' fragile peace in ruins. The Khoisan in the village of Graaff Reinet became increasingly militant, threatening to take pre-emptive action in order to protect themselves.[137] And in the coastal forelands the leaders of the 'Hottentot Confederacy', who had kept themselves informed of developments in the interior, resumed their attacks on Boer homes. On 22 November Veldwagtmeester Cornelis van Rooyen of Swartkops River was shot through the eye as he opened his front door at 2 a.m. to a band of Khoisan led by Klaas Stuurman, Hans Trompetter and Boezak.[138] By year's end the raiders had penetrated the Winterhoek mountains and the colonists had again begun to flee.[139] Maynier's middle road had reached a dead end.

From now on, in J. S. Marais' apt phrase, 'the commandos took over'.[140] Maynier's attempt to resolve the fundamental antagonisms of this frontier society through the application of the rule of law and the principles of common humanity had failed and it was to be left to military men to apply military solutions. Maynier deplored the resort to commandos. He knew that in the context of the times they could not bring lasting peace. And while the use of force might suppress the appearance of dissent among the Khoisan, it would in reality merely serve to drive it underground, and that only temporarily. 'It should not be imagined,' he wrote after his recall to the western Cape in November 1801, 'that the Hottentots who refrain from disturbances are quiet from Love and Attachment to the Boors. Such supposition will prove deceitful. Every circumstance shews that they think themselves to be the weaker party, and it is the fear of this ideal or imaginary superiority of the Boors which keeps them quiet.'[141] 'Tumults' and disobedience on the part of the Boers would do nothing to 'maintain this prepossession' and the activities of 'these inconsiderate and unnecessary' commandos would merely fan the flames of rebellion. The last state of the district would be worse than the first. As for himself, he added, 'wearied with a Life full of disquietudes and cares, nothing shall induce me again in any station whatever to visit these districts'.[142]

In the event, the violence of the commandos, coupled with new administrative controls introduced by the Batavians and the British of the 'second occupation', did eventually succeed in suppressing Khoisan claims to freedom for many years to come. And yet Maynier's achievements were more lasting than he himself realised. His role as official intermediary in 1799–1801 had given the Khoisan of the eastern Cape a breathing space, however brief. His insistence upon their free status, his attempts to protect them from arbitrary brutality and his collaboration with the missionaries Van der Kemp and Read helped lay the foundations of a vision of equal justice within an ethnically diverse society which their descendants – inhabitants of the mission stations and later, the Kat River Settlement – were to nurture and promote. In the words of Wensel Heemra of Bethelsdorp:

At the moment when the misery and sufferings of the Hottentots were at the highest, the King of England became master of the colony and took them, the Hottentots, under his protection, and saved them from utter ruin. Nearly at the same time it pleased God to send the missionaries to instruct them, after which they had a time of breathing.[143]

It is no accident that when 'Hottentot nationalism' re-emerged in the 1850s it was, as Robert Ross has written, not an atavistic movement of 'primary resistance', but a forward-looking Christian nationalism, with its sights firmly fixed on the incorporation of its adherents as equals in a colonial world.[144]

10   Postscript

It is just possible that the arguments advanced in this book could be read as a vindication of the influential 'frontier thesis' propounded by Eric Walker and I. D. MacCrone in the 1930s.[1] However that is not my intention. According to Walker and MacCrone, the special conditions of the frontier nurtured a highly developed sense of group identity and racial exclusivity among its white (Afrikaner) inhabitants. These segregationist attitudes were then carried over into the twentieth century, where they did battle with the egalitarian inheritance of the Enlightenment, first introduced to South Africa by British missionaries, settlers and officials. Now, while it should be obvious that my own work is not at all concerned with the twentieth century, and that I therefore have no quarrel with the underlying thrust of Martin Legassick's critique of the 'frontier tradition',[2] it is none the less true that I *have* emphasised the exclusivist and separatist elements in the *Weltanschauung* of Afrikaner frontiersmen. Perhaps I would even go so far as to say that, in general, and only as far as the Khoisan (not the Xhosa) are concerned, I reject Legassick's now famous statement that 'enemies and friends were not divided into rigid, static categories', and this despite an awareness of the mutual dependency that may have linked certain European masters and their Khoisan servants, and of the intimate personal relationships that sometimes developed between European men and Khoisan women. This said, however, there remain certain key differences between my own understanding of frontier exclusivism and that of Walker and MacCrone.

First, whereas they saw the heightened group consciousness of Europeans as a form of racism, I feel that the use of this term is an anachronism: to the best of my knowledge, the pseudoscientific thinking associated with racism and the related metaphors of blood, contamination and degeneration did not find their way into the language of South African frontiersmen until the coming of the British in the early nineteenth century. The issue is complicated, for there was indeed an awareness of colour at the Cape in the eighteenth century, and dark skin colour does seem to have been associated with savagery and heathenism. Thus Barrow records that colonists on the eastern frontier referred to the Khoisan as the '*Zwarte Natie*' and '*Zwarte Vee*', and there is also the heartbreaking testimony of Frans Mager of the Kat River Settlement, who recalled how, in his boyhood, he and his 'nation' were in 'such a miserable state, so much so that I even rubbed myself over with white clay to try to gain acceptance with my master'.[3] But, while colour may have been a marker of difference, there is no evidence that it was construed as part of a complex of physical traits which were inherently linked to mental or behavioural characteristics. The primary categories of difference, in other words, were not biological but cultural.

Second and perhaps more immediately important, there is a fundamental difference between the manner in which earlier commentators have explained frontier exclusivism and the approach that I have taken. Whereas exponents of the 'frontier tradition' have ascribed the frontiersman's strong sense of cultural identity and his adamant opposition to the extension of civil rights to native peoples to his *isolation* from the parent colony in the south-west, the line of argument followed above suggests that, on the contrary, his attitudes were a product of his *integration* into the parent society and particularly his subservience to its markets. True isolation, I suggest, would have led quite rapidly in the opposite direction, towards the very assimilation which townsmen like Swellengrebel so feared.

This said, I would also (perhaps vainly, in view of my own line of argument) wish to forestall the enlistment of my ideas in the cause of economic reductionism. It is true that I have explicitly suggested a link between the poverty of many *veeboeren* and their uncompromising commitment to the ideology of slavery, but perhaps the key word here is 'suggested' (as opposed to proven beyond reasonable doubt). Poverty, and the consequent inability to afford either free labour or *de jure* slaves, *might* have led in other directions had a particular set of attitudes towards the Khoisan not been ready to hand, available to shape action as much as to rationalise it after the event. One such direction was suggested by a group of Zuurveld Xhosa, who took a dim view of the new settlers' repeated attempts to recover their runaway servants. 'Why', they are alleged to have asked, 'do you not rear children to tend your cattle, and let the Hottentots return to their rocks and caves as before?'[4]

Why indeed? One might point to differences in social structure, noting that the *veeboeren* were not polygamous, or that they lacked the tradition of reciprocal obligations which enabled members of a Xhosa household to share the tasks of herding and hunting with their neighbours. And one might tie these differences to more fundamental differences in the relations of production – specifically to the presence or absence of private property in land. But one would still be hard put to it to explain why it was that people who complained constantly of their poverty and their difficulty in procuring labour could allow their own children (of whom they had many) to stand idly by while Khoisan children aged 7 or younger went out to tend their flocks. Lady Anne Barnard's description of the sons of her hosts near Swellendam as 'men who do hardly anything beside eating and smoking . . . certainly never digging, threshing, or holding the plough', might be ascribed to English prejudice, yet Sparrman made similar observations of his hosts at Agter Bruintjes Hoogte.[5] Moreover, when a dearth of non-European servants did oblige a man to send his children after his cattle, or go himself, he did so with a distinct sense of injury: 'I have no more than one Hottentot who can shoot', complained Cornelis du Plooij in 1789, 'and my son has to go out after the cattle himself.'[6] The general consensus appears to have been that herding was too dangerous a job for one's own children.[7]

Poverty, then, may go some way towards explaining the determination with which the good citizens of Graaff Reinet ignored the advice of their Landdrost and brought the district to the brink of ruin, but clearly there were other less material factors at work as well. Some of these have been explored in the preceding pages; the exploration of others must await a younger and more playful historian.

Appendix 1: Currency and measurements

Currency units

1 rijksdaalder (rix dollar)[1]	= 48 stuivers
1 schelling	= 6 stuivers
1 gulden[2] (Hollandse valuatie)	= 20 stuivers
1 gulden (Kaapse valuatie)	= 16 stuivers

Measures

1 muid	= 3.1 bushels
10 muids	= 1 waggon-load
1 leaguer	= 582 litres
1 morgen	= 2.12 acres

Notes

[1] At the time of the first British occupation of the Cape in 1795, 1 rix dollar was reckoned to be equal in value to 4 English shillings, but it rapidly depreciated thereafter.

[2] The gulden was initially money of account, but after 1680 it became an actual coin, minted by the Provinces of the Netherlands and (after 1786) by the VOC. The gulden is abbreviated as fl. or f.

Appendix 2: Earnings capacity of sampled estates

First decima

	No. 16	No. 21	No. 24	No. 28	No. 34	No. 39
	Anna Catharina Verkouteren	Maria Cloete and Hendrik Mostert	Jacobus Botha	Volkert Schoenmaker	Marthinus Oosthuijzen and Johanna Jacomina Calitz	Louisa Erasmus, *Weduwee* Dawid Fourie
date of death	1811	1804		1797	1799	1797
age at death	74 years	62 years	single	50–60 years	35 years	69 years
marital status	widow	married		single	married (3rd wife)	widow
surviving children	9 adults	9 adults		none	8 – all minors	8
gross assets	77 rds 14 sts	119 rds	181 rds 16sts	1956 rds 42 sts	737 rds 36 sts	461 rds 36 sts
net assets	26 rds 16 sts	42 rds 16 sts	103 rds 22 sts	118 rds 23 sts	205 rds 30 sts	228 rds 33 sts
liabilities as a percentage of assets	65%	65%	43%	94%	72%	51%
land ownership	none – possibly living with son	none	none	2 loan-farms	none	none
slaves	none	none	none	1 male slave uncertain.	none	none
size and composition of flock	none	none	none	Perhaps 39 ewes; 2 rams; 59 wethers	73 ewes; 2 rams; 111 wethers	63 ewes; 2 rams; 96 wethers

sheep available for sale	80 wethers; 6 old ewes	131 wethers; 1 old ram; 5 old ewes	69 wethers; 1 old ram; 3 old ewes	none	none
projected income from sale of sheep	215 rds	274 rds	182 rds 24 sts	none	none
composition of cattle herd	8 trek oxen; 7 cows; 11 heifers and young males	10 oxen	11 trek oxen; 1 bull; 38 cows	5 oxen	none
cattle available for sale	about 11 oxen; 1 old cow	none	6 young oxen; 3 old oxen; 6 old cows	none	none
projected income from cattle sales	120 rds (over 4 years)	none	143 rds	none	none
annual butter production	102.2 lb per annum	none	511 lb	none	none
income from butter production	32 rds	none	160 rds	none	none
composition of stud	none	2 mares	2 mares; 2 foals	none	none
projected income from horse sales	none	15 rds 24 sts	24 rds (over 3 years)	none	none
income from cereal production	none	none	none	none	none
other sources of income	soap manufacture – 20 rds or more	152 goats	100 goats; a little carpentry?	transport-riding? *knecht?*	none
total projected cash income	172 rds	289 rds 24 sts	509 rds 24 sts	unknown	zero

Second decima

	No. 46	No. 49	No. 52	No. 56	No. 62	No. 64
	Elisabeth Nortje	Jan Hendrik Oosthuijzen and Anna Botha	Jan Nel	Erasmus Smit *d'oude*	Catharina Elisabeth de Jong and Gerrit Engelbrecht	Sara Fourie
date of death age at death	1772 82 years	1785 71 years	1774 38 years	1771 approx. 70 years	1765 38 years	1771 66 years
marital status surviving children	widow 3 + children of 2 deceased	married 6 + children of 1 deceased	bachelor none	widower 9 and child of 1 deceased	married 8 (all minors)	widow 11 (2 minors)
gross assets	296 rds 8 sts	339 rds 30 sts	390 rds 44 sts	479 rds 12 sts	1,032 rds 8 sts	896 rds
net assets liabilities as a percentage of assets	284 rds 35 sts 4%	316 rds 14 sts 7%	345 rds 28 sts 12%	392 rds 41 sts 18%	454 rds 19 sts 56%	469 rds 17 sts 48%
land ownership	none	*vendurol* missing	none – lived with mother	none	smallholding on waggon road and loan-farm	1 loan-farm
slaves	none	n.a.	none	3 males *voetstoots*	none	1 male slave
size and composition of flock	none	n.a.	11 ewes; 1 ram; 2 young ewes; 13 wethers	none	none	209 ewes; 7 rams; 322 wethers

sheep available for sale	none	n.a.	16 wethers; 2 old ewes	none	none	377 wethers; 18 old ewes; 2 old rams
projected income from sale of sheep	none	n.a.	11 rds	none	none	262 rds
composition of cattle herd	none	n.a.	12 trek oxen; 44 cows; 25 calves	none	none	25 trek oxen; 24 cows; 8 calves; 1 bull; 5 heifers; 24 steers
cattle available for sale	none	n.a.	12 oxen; 7 old cows	none	none	20 steers; 9 trek oxen; 4 old cows
projected income from cattle sales	none	n.a.	85 rds 24 sts	none	none	166 rds 24 sts
annual butter production	none	n.a.	638.75 lb	none	none	204.4 lb
income from butter production	none	n.a.	80 rds	none	none	25 rds 24 sts
composition of stud	none	n.a.	none	none	none	1 saddle-horse; 8 mares
projected income from horse sales	none	n.a.	none	none	none	63 rds (over 3 years)
income from cereal production	none	n.a.	none	none	none listed	3 rds +
other sources of income	none	n.a.	none	74% of his assets in cash	carpentry; market gardening?	carpentry
total projected cash income	none	n.a.	176 rds 24 sts	unknown	unknown	490 rds

Third decima

	No. 78 Aletta Dorothea Bester and Sybrand Gerhardus van Nieuwkerken	No. 84 Marthinus François Nel	No. 85 Philippus Petrus du Plessis	No. 89 Philip Snijman Jacobuszoon	No. 91 Isabella Potgieter
date of death	1808	1800	1810	1808	1788
age at death	24 years	34 years	55 years	51 years	77 years
marital status	married	widower	bachelor	married	widow
surviving children	none	one (minor)	none	7 (6 minors)	8
gross assets	970 rds 43 sts	1,185 rds 24 sts	1,104 rds 36 sts	1,288 rds 6 sts	1,374 rds 6 sts
net assets	593 rds 47 sts	683 rds 8 sts	687 rds 46 sts	710 rds 20 sts	729 rds 19 sts
liabilities as a percentage of assets	39%	42%	38%	45%	47%
land ownership	none	none	none	none	loan-farm
slaves	none	none	none	none	2 male slaves
size and composition of flock	2 wethers	211 ewes; 7 rams; 324 wethers	none	212 ewes	none
sheep available for sale	2 wethers	383 wethers; 18 old ewes	none	57 wethers	none
projected income from sale of sheep	5 rds	852 rds	none	142 rds 24 sts	none

composition of cattle herd	11 oxen; 1 cow with calf	none	2 cows; 1 calf	8 oxen; 2 cows; 2 calves; 16 steers	7 trek oxen
cattle available for sale	7 oxen?	none	none	17 steers	none
projected income from cattle sales	84 rds	none	none	204 rds	none
annual butter production	25.55 lb	none	25.55 lb	51.1 lb	none
income from butter production	10 rds 24 sts	none	9 rds	21 rds	none
composition of stud	3 mares; 1 foal; 1 saddle-horse	3 mares	1 saddle-horse; 1 young horse	1 saddle-horse; 1 young gelding; 1 mare and 2 foals	none
projected income from horse sales	65 rds (over 3 years)	48 rds (over 3 years)	none	153 rds (over 3 years)	none
income from cereal production	40 rds	none	none	none	none
other sources of income	6 goats	190 nanny goats; 4 *kapaters*	possibly pedlar – has cloth in stock; interest on loans unknown	16 goats; soap	none
total projected cash income	139.5 rds now; 65 rds over 3 years	852 rds now; 48 rds over 3 years	unknown	367.5 rds now; 153 rds over 3 years	unknown

Fourth decima

	No. 104 Carel Nicolaas van der Merwe	No. 105 Ockert Oosthuijzen	No. 106 Gerbrecht Christina Pretorius	No. 111b Agatha Blom	No. 113 Gerrit Coetzee	No. 115 Anna Lombard	No. 116 Pieter van Wijk	No. 117 Jacobus Louw	No. 123 Hermanus Grijling
date of death	1811	1809	1804	1774	1803	1791	1809	1808	1811
age at death	40 years	54 years	52 years	79 years	?35 years	28 years	71 or 51 years	69 years	42 years
marital status	married	widower	widow	widow	married	married	unknown	widower	unmarried
surviving children	9 (all minors)	11 (7 minors)	4 (1 minor)	4 + children of 2 deceased	1 (minor)	3 (minors)	1 son aged 13	8 + child of 1 deceased	none
gross assets	2,033 rds 30 sts	2,497 rds 10 sts	2,092 rds 30 sts	1,249 rds 42 sts	5,915 rds 5 sts	4,739 rds 44 sts	1,425 rds	1,403 rds 30 sts	1,753 rds 28 sts
net assets	944 rds 1 st	953 rds 36 sts	958 rds 24 sts	1,031 rds 18 sts	1,107 rds 5 sts	1,173 rds 46 sts	1,205 rds 30 sts	1,254 rds 37 sts	1,409 rds 3 sts
liabilities as a percentage of assets	54% (mainly *erfportien* owed to the children of his first marriage)	62%	54%	17%	81%	75%	15%	11%	20%
land ownership	request place	loan-farm	none	none	loan-farm	1.5 loan-farms	n.a.	none	none
slaves	none	none	1 woman, 2 children	1 male, 1 female, 2 children	2 males, 1 woman with 2 children, 2 girls	1 male, two females	n.a.	none	none

size and composition of flock	475 ewes; 16 rams; 549 wethers and 190 lambs	203 ewes	42 ewes	none	n.a.	468 ewes; 16 rams; 631 wethers	none
sheep available for sale	768 wethers; 40 old ewes and rams	52 wethers; 25 old ewes	10 wethers; 8 old ewes	none	n.a.	762 wethers (over 2 years); 41 old ewes	none
projected income from sale of sheep	2,424 rds	192 rds 4 *schellingen*	34 rds	none	n.a.	1,556 rds	none
composition of cattle herd	16 young oxen; 24 cows	8 trek oxen; 2 cows; 3 calves	13 trek oxen; 1 bull; 12 cows; 2 calves	21 trek oxen; 1 bull; 7 cows; 5 heifers	16 trek oxen; 96 oxen; 1 bull; 8 young bulls; 23 heifers; 44 cows with 28 calves	12 trek oxen; 6 young oxen; 5 cows; 3 calves; 6 *beesten*	none
cattle available for sale	9 oxen (over 3 years); 4 old cows	2 oxen (over 3 years)	4 steers; 2 old cows (over 3 years)	1 old cow; 5 old trek oxen	30 oxen in 4–5 years time; 96 oxen now; 8 old cows; 4 old trek oxen	6 *beesten*; 3 young oxen (over 5 years); 4 old trek oxen; 1 old cow	none
projected income from cattle sales	130 rds (over 3 years)	20 rds	54 rds (over 3 years)	40 rds (over 3 years)	864 rds now; 270 rds in 4–5 years	110 rds now; 30 rds (over 5 years)	none
annual butter production	306.6 lb	25.55 lb	none	none	n.a.	none	none
income from butter production	89 rds	9 rds	48 rds	38 rds	149 rds	29 rds	none

Fourth decima (*cont.*)

	No. 104 Carel Nicolaas van der Merwe	No. 105 Ockert Oosthuijzen	No. 106 Gerbrecht Christina Pretorius	No. 111b Agatha Blom	No. 113 Gerrit Coetzee	No. 115 Anna Lombard	No. 116 Pieter van Wijk	No. 117 Jacobus Louw	No. 123 Hermanus Grijling
composition of stud	1 young stallion; 4 mares; 1 gelding	1 saddle-horse	2 stallions; 1 mare with foal; 1 saddle-horse	none	8 mares; 3 foals; 4 cart-horses	1 young stallion; 7 mares; 2 saddle-horses	n.a.	3 saddle-horses; 2 young geldings; 4 mares; 2 foals	none 1 saddle-horse
projected income from horse sales	124 rds (over 3 years)	none	44 rds (over 3 years)	none	104 rds (over 3 years)	60 rds (in 3 years time)	n.a.	146 rds (over 3 years)	none
income from cereal production	none	30 rds for grain; ?rds for 1 leaguer of wine	none	slave hire?	274 rds (46 muids + 2 waggon loads)	none	n.a.	about 8 rds	none
other sources of income	108 goats	40 goats; carpentry; waggon construc-tion?	40 goats	none	15 goats; pumpkins; 1,500 rds lent to distant relatives at 5%	fishing; 50 goats; vegetables; soap	n.a.	none	*knecht*'s wage; loan of rds 1,440 at 6% interest – should yield 86.4 rds per annum
total projected cash income	2,553 rds now; 254 rds over 3 years	231.5 rds now; 20 rds over 3 years	82 rds now; 98 rds over 3 years	none	312 rds now; 144 rds over 3 years	2,569 rds now; 330 rds over 3 years	unknown (see p. 158 above)	139 rds now; 176 rds over 5 years	unknown

Fifth decima

	No. 128 Anna van Wijk	No. 132 Johanna Kemp	No. 134 Sara Delport	No. 138 Maria Erasmus	No. 141 Cecilia du Preez	No. 146 Johanna Maria Buys	No. 150 Elisabeth Bronkhorst
date of death	1807	1778	1802 (murdered by Khoisan rebels)	1782	1781	1780	1805
age at death	73 years	82 years	73 years	56 years	68 years	55 years	83 years
marital status	widow	widow	widow (twice)	widow	widow	widow	widow
surviving children	6	5	4	none	5	9 (3 minors)	7
gross assets	1,875 rds 12 sts	2,395 rds 1 st	2,552 rds 20 sts	2,007 rds 6 sts	1,799 rds 25 sts	2,900 rds 36 sts	2,113 rds
net assets	1,486 rds 42 sts	1,520 rds	1,604 rds 34 sts	1,643 rds 25 sts	1,693 rds 18 sts	1,796 rds 19 sts	1,877 rds
liabilities as a percentage of assets	21%	37%	37%	18%	6%	38%	11%
land ownership	2 loan-farms in Camdeboo, bequeathed to eldest son	none – lived with her son in the Klijne Roggeveld	loan-farm in Winterhoek	loan-farm *agter de* Hex Rivier	loan-farm (Tulbagh)	loan-farm *agter de* Renosterberg	none

Fifth decima (*cont.*)

	No. 128 Anna van Wijk	No. 132 Johanna Kemp	No. 134 Sara Delport	No. 138 Maria Erasmus	No. 141 Cecilia du Preez	No. 146 Johanna Maria Buys	No. 150 Elisabeth Bronkhorst
slaves	1 male slave	none	none (killed or escaped)	1 woman with her 2 children	1 elderly man, 2 elderly women	none	1 woman with 2 children; 1 man; 2 women (all Cape born)
size and composition of flock	30 sheep	none	none (stolen)	235 ewes	none	474 wethers; 560 ewes; 12 lambs	none
sheep available for sale	20 wethers	none	none	60 wethers; 47 old ewes	none	628 wethers; 112 old ewes	none
projected income from sale of sheep	44 rds	none	none	134 rds	none	647.5 rds	none
composition of cattle herd	8 trek oxen; 4 cows; 3 heifers and 1 calf	none	none	47 cows; 6 calves; 28 oxen	6 cows; 1 bull; 5 calves	60 cows; 15 calves; 48 heifers; 1 bull; 18 young bulls; 26 trek oxen; 28 young oxen	13 cows; 6 heifers; 2 calves; 5 young bulls; 12 oxen
cattle available for sale	1 old cow	none	none	28 steers; 7 old cows; 3 old trek oxen	4 steers; 1 old cow	68 steers (over 5 years); 13 old cows; 7 old trek oxen	9 steers; 2 old cows

projected income from cattle sales	? 6 rds	none	none	39 rds now; 113 rds over 5 years	21.25 rds (over 5 years)	272 rds (over 5 years); 80 rds now	110 rds
annual butter production	76.65 lb	none	none	613.2 lb	76.65 lb	1,124.2 lb	204.4 lb
income from butter production	32 rds	none	none	109 rds	15 rds	222.5 rds	85 rds
composition of stud	1 gelding	none	none	5 mares; 4 foals; 2 stallions; 1 gelding	none	6 mares; 4 foals; 2 young stallions	none
projected income from horse sales	none	none	none	154 rds (over 3 years)	none	60 rds (over 3 years)	none
income from cereal production	none	none	none	12 muids wheat – 24 rds	none	2.5 muids wheat – 4 rds	none
other sources of income	4 goats	about 2,000 rds lent at 6%	about 993 rds lent at 6%	60 goats; 9 pigs; 1 sow with 7 piglets; 16 geese and 2 turkeys; 300 rds in cash	brandy-kettle; 733 rds lent at 6%	midwifery	slave hire?
total projected cash income	82 rds	120 rds p.a.	60 rds	306 rds now; 267 rds over 3–5 years; +18 rds interest if cash loaned	80 rds 12 sts	954 rds now; 332 rds over 5 years	195 rds

Notes

1 A NOTE ON THE NARRATION OF COLONIAL BEGINNINGS

1 Peter Hulme, *Colonial encounters: Europe and the native Caribbean, 1492–1797* (London and New York: Methuen, 1986), p. 159.
2 M. Harbsmeier, 'Elementary structures of otherness: an analysis of sixteenth century German travel accounts', in *Voyager à la Renaissance: actes du colloque de Tours, 1983* (Paris: Maisonneuve et Larose, 1987), pp. 337–55, cited in Peter Mason, *Deconstructing America: representations of the other* (London: Routledge, 1990), p.180.
3 Cf. Theophilus Hahn, *Tsuni-//Goam: the supreme being of the Khoi-Khoi* (London: Trübner and Co., 1881), p. 2; Jodocus Hondius, *Klare Besgryving van Cabo de Bona Esperança*, facsimile edition (Cape Town: Komitee vir Boekuitstalling, Van Riebeeck-fees, 1952), p. 26 and R. Raven-Hart, *Before van Riebeeck: callers at South Africa 1488 to 1652* (Cape Town: Struik, 1967), pp. 18, 19, 39. The Frenchman Jean Baptiste Tavernier compared the click sounds in Khoe speech to 'the breaking of wind backward' (J. B. Tavernier, *The six voyages of John Baptista Tavernier* (London, 1678). One should be aware, however, that an alternative etymology of the word 'Hottentot' traces its origin to a dance in which 'some such word as *hautitou'* was chanted. Cf. Isaac Schapera (ed.), *The early Cape Hottentots* (Cape Town: Van Riebeeck Society, 1933), p. 71, note 81. See also Richard Elphick, *Kraal and castle: Khoikhoi and the founding of white South Africa* (New Haven and London: Yale University Press, 1977), pp. xv, 180.
4 Hayden White, *Tropics of discourse: essays in cultural criticism* (Baltimore: Johns Hopkins University Press, 1978), chapters 3 and 4.
5 I do not wish to imply that all historians are male. They may be male or female, but it is better that they are not both in the same sentence.
6 *Ibid.*, p. 114. See also Raphael Samuel, *Past and present in contemporary culture*, London: Verso, 1994, pp. 429–47 for a more cautious statement of the same point.
7 J. M. Coetzee, 'The mind of apartheid: Geoffrey Cronje (1907–)', *Social Dynamics* 17 (1991), 30. In recent years a minority of talented historians have begun to rebel against this way of writing history. See, for example, Simon Schama, *Dead certainties (unwarranted speculations)* (New York: Alfred A. Knopf, 1991).

8 Dominick LaCapra, *Rethinking intellectual history: texts, contexts, language* (Ithaca: Cornell University Press, 1983), p. 64.

9 Present-day Cape Town was known simply as *De Kaap* in the eighteenth century.

10 See appendix 1 for an explanation of the currency in use at the Cape in the eighteenth century.

11 However in the case of slaves who had committed the crime of suicide or attempted suicide, the Landdrost might invoke the special powers granted him in terms of a resolution of the Court of Justice of July 1728, and pass sentence in his own court. See Hilton Fine, 'The administration of criminal justice at the Cape of Good Hope, 1795–1828', unpublished PhD thesis, University of Cape Town (1991), pp. 197–8.

12 If the Landdrost believed he had a *prima facie* case against the accused, he could apply for a warrant of arrest or for a summons (*ibid.*, pp. 195–6). For a full account of the judicial role of the Independent Fiscal, see *ibid.*, pp. 218–21, 226–46.

13 *Ibid.*, p. 215.

14 *Ibid.*

15 John Dugard, *Introduction to criminal procedure* (Cape Town: Juta, 1977), p. 8.

16 Fine, 'Administration of criminal justice', pp. 233–4. There seems to have been some confusion in the law itself as to the circumstances under which torture could be applied. See Marijke van der Vrugt, *De criminele ordonnantiën van 1570: enkele beschouwingen over de eerste strafrechtcodificatie in de Nederlanden* (Zutphen: De Walburg Pers, 1978), pp. 140–8. (I would like to thank Dr Heleen Gall of the University of Leiden for making this source available to me.)

17 See, for example, S. Newton-King, 'Hilletje Smits and the shadow of death', unpublished seminar paper, University of the Western Cape, October 1995.

18 Hilton Fine, personal communication, 15 July 1987, and Fine, 'Administration of criminal justice', p. 218.

19 Newton-King, 'Hilletje Smits and the shadow of death'.

20 P. J. Venter, 'Landdros en Heemrade (1682–1827)', *Archives Year Book for South African History* 2 (1940), 201–2.

21 Cf. O. F. Mentzel, *A complete and authentic geographical and topographical description of the famous and (all things considered) remarkable African Cape of Good Hope*, part III (Cape Town: Van Riebeeck Society, 1944), p. 119.

22 Robert Ross, *Beyond the pale: essays on the history of colonial South Africa* (Hanover: Wesleyan University Press, 1993), p. 184.

23 Jonathan Gerstner, *The thousand generation covenant: Dutch Reformed covenant theology and group identity in colonial South Africa, 1652–1814* (Leiden: E. J. Brill, 1991).

24 Cf. S. Newton-King and V. C. Malherbe, *The Khoikhoi rebellion in the eastern Cape, 1799–1803* (Cape Town: Centre for African Studies, University of Cape Town, 1981), pp. 36–8. See also Gerstner, *Thousand generation covenant*, pp. 199–200, for a description of the difficulties facing adult candidates for baptism.

25 Elphick, *Kraal and castle*. 'Khoekhoe' is the modern Nama variant of the name commonly used by the pastoralists of the southern and eastern Cape to refer to themselves. I have chosen to use the modern Nama orthography in preference

to the old orthography ('Khoikhoi'), since it more closely approximates the correct pronunciation of the name (see M. L. Wilson, 'Notes on the nomenclature of the Khoisan', *Annals of the South African Museum* 97 (1986), 253). With respect to the term 'Khoisan', however, there is no reason to modernise the spelling, since it is 'an artificial compound . . . which is a distinctly European and not a Khoisan word' (Alan Barnard, *Hunters and herders of southern Africa: a comparative ethnography of the Khoisan peoples* (Cambridge: Cambridge University Press, 1992), p. 7.

26 Nigel Penn, 'Pastoralists and pastoralism in the northern Cape frontier zone during the eighteenth century', in Martin Hall and Andrew Smith (eds.), *Prehistoric pastoralism in southern Africa*, The South African Archaeological Society Goodwin Series 5 (1986); 'Land, labour and livestock in the Western Cape during the eighteenth century', in W. G. James and M. Simons (eds.), *The angry divide: social and economic history of the Western Cape* (Cape Town: David Philip, 1989), pp. 2–19. See also Nigel Penn, 'The northern Cape frontier zone, 1700–c. 1815', unpublished PhD thesis, University of Cape Town (1995).

27 Shula Marks, 'Khoisan resistance to the Dutch in the seventeenth and eighteenth centuries', *Journal of African History* 13 (1972), 70.

28 The term was coined by the zoologist Leonhard Schultze in 1928 and adopted by Isaac Schapera as a generic name for the Khoekhoe and the San in 1930 (*The Khoisan peoples of South Africa: Bushmen and Hottentots,* London: Routledge, 1965), but its adoption by historians was a response to the arguments of Marks and Elphick in the 1970s.

29 See pp. 59–62, 80–1 and 90.

30 Martin Legassick, 'The frontier tradition in South African historiography', Institute of Commonwealth Studies, London, *Collected Seminar Papers on the Societies of Southern Africa* 12,2 (London: 1970). Subsequently published in S. Marks and A. Atmore (eds.), *Economy and society in pre-industrial South Africa* (London: Longman, 1980).

31 Hermann Giliomee, 'The eastern frontier, 1770–1812', in Richard Elphick and Hermann Giliomee (eds.), *The shaping of South African society, 1652–1840,* second edition (Cape Town: Maskew Miller Longman, 1989), pp. 421–71.

32 J. S. Marais, *Maynier and the first Boer Republic* (Cape Town: Maskew Miller, 1944).

33 Orlando Patterson, *Slavery and social death: a comparative study* (Cambridge, Mass.: Harvard University Press, 1982).

34 Nathan Wachtel, *The vision of the vanquished: the Spanish conquest of Peru through Indian eyes, 1530–1570* (New York: Harvester Press, 1977; French original, 1971).

2   INTRODUCING THE CHARACTERS

1 J. R. Bruijn, F. S. Gaastra and I. Schöffer, *Dutch-Asiatic shipping in the seventeenth and eighteenth centuries*, 3 vols. (The Hague: Martinus Nijhoff, 1987), vol. I, pp. 84, 112. Most outward bound ships spent an average of five weeks in Table Bay.

2 Freeburghers were private citizens who lived in territories controlled by the Dutch East India Company. Before being granted 'civil rights' (*burgerregten*) they were required to take an oath of loyalty both to the States-General of the

United Provinces and to the directors of the Company (the *Heren Zeventien*) and their servants abroad. Each generation was required to take the oath anew. Moreover, in the event of 'misbehaviour', *burgerregten* could be withdrawn and the miscreant brought back under Company discipline. He could then be banished to another of its possessions or made to serve on its ships at sea.

3 Henceforth referred to as the VOC or 'the Company'.

4 De Bruijn, Gaastra and Schöffer, *Dutch-Asiatic shipping*, vol. I, pp. 147–9; Leonard Guelke, 'Freehold farmers and frontier settlers, 1657–1780', in R. Elphick and H. Giliomee (eds.), *The shaping of South African society, 1652–1840*, second edition (Cape Town: Maskew Miller Longman, 1989), p. 67.

5 Virgin in the sense that it had not been cultivated before; though it had of course been grazed and managed for many centuries by the indigenous pastoralists whose territory it was.

6 Guelke, 'Freehold farmers and frontier settlers', pp. 69–71.

7 *Ibid*, p. 67.

8 *Ibid*, p. 79; Gerrit Schutte, 'Company and colonists at the Cape, 1652–1795', in Elphick and Giliomee (eds.), *Shaping*, p. 290.

9 S. D. Neumark, *Economic influences on the South African frontier, 1652–1836* (Stanford: Stanford University Press, 1957); Pieter van Duin and Robert Ross, 'The economy of the Cape Colony in the eighteenth century', *Intercontinenta* 7 (Leiden: Centre for the History of European Expansion, 1987), 58–80.

10 Robert Ross, 'The "white" population of South Africa in the eighteenth century', *Population Studies* 19 (1975), 221; reprint in Robert Ross, *Beyond the pale: essays on the history of colonial South Africa* (Hanover: Wesleyan University Press, 1993).

11 *Ibid*, pp. 223–30.

12 During the same period, only 360 European women immigrated to the Cape. See Ross, 'The "white" population', pp. 222–3 and J. A. Heese, *Die herkoms van die Afrikaner, 1657–1867* (Cape Town: Balkema, 1971).

13 J 107, *Opgaafrollen*, Graaff Reinet, 1787. See also J. Hoge,'Personalia of the Germans at the Cape 1652–1806', *Archives Year Book for South African History* 9 (1946). The area where German was spoken is difficult to define with precision, since there was a high degree of dialectical variation both within the German heartland and at its outer limits. Dr J. Hoge, the authority on German immigration to the Cape during the Company period, has designated as German all those who came from areas within the boundaries of Germany as it existed between 1870 and 1918 (Hoge, 'Personalia', preface).

14 Bruijn, Gaastra and Schöffer, *Dutch-Asiatic shipping*, vol. I, appendix 1. These wages remained the same throughout the seventeenth and eighteenth centuries. (Fl. was the abbreviation used for the Dutch guilder. See appendix 1 for an explanation of currency in use at the Cape during this period.)

15 Jan Lucassen, *Migrant labour in Europe, 1600–1900* (London: Croom Helm, 1987), pp. 54, 69, 75, 81.

16 Bruijn, Gaastra and Schöffer, *Dutch-Asiatic shipping*, vol. I, p. 150.

17 *Ibid.*, pp. 161, pp. 165–6.

18 *Ibid.*, pp. 123–4, 170.

19 *Ibid.*, pp. 75–6.

20 *Ibid.*, pp. 162–4, 171–2.

21 *Ibid.*, pp. 74, 89.

22 *Ibid.*, p. 162.
23 *Ibid.*, pp. 169–72.
24 Lucassen, *Migrant labour*, p 156.
25 Bruijn, Gaastra and Schöffer, *Dutch-Asiatic shipping*, vol. I, pp. 153–7.
26 Lucassen, *Migrant labour*, chapters 2 and 5.
27 *Ibid.*, p. 143.
28 Otto Mentzel, *Life at the Cape in the mid-eighteenth century, being the biography of Rudolph Siegfried Alleman* (Cape Town: Van Riebeeck Society, 1919), pp. 14–16; Carl Peter Thunberg, *Travels at the Cape of Good Hope, 1772–1775*, ed. V. S. Forbes (Cape Town: Van Riebeeck Society, 1986), p. 7.
29 Lucassen, *Migrant labour*, p. 48.
30 Bruijn, Gaastra and Schöffer, *Dutch-Asiatic shipping*, vol. I, p. 150.
31 On this see Thunberg, *Travels*, p. 7.
32 Bruijn, Gaastra and Schöffer, *Dutch-Asiatic shipping*, vol. I, pp. 156–7. According to Hoge, during the second half of the eighteenth century, 'nearly all' the members of the garrison in Cape Town were Germans (Hoge, 'Personalia', preface).
33 Thunberg, *Travels*, p. 9.
34 Work currently being done by James Armstrong and Kerry Ward on convicts and political exiles at the Cape in the Company period will help to fill this gap in our knowledge. See also Wayne Dooling, 'The Castle: its place in the history of Cape Town, *c.* 1666–1760', unpublished paper presented to the Cape Town History Project Workshop, University of Cape Town, November 1991. And for an excellent discussion of popular recreational pursuits in early nineteenth-century Cape Town, see Andrew Bank, 'Slavery in Cape Town, 1806–1834', MA thesis, University of Cape Town, 1991, published as *The decline of urban slavery at the Cape, 1806 to 1843*, Cape Town: Centre for African Studies, 1991.
35 Mentzel, *Geographical and topographical description*, part I, pp. 163–4; Thunberg, *Travels*, pp. 30–1.
36 Mentzel, *Geographical and topographical description*, part I, p. 164; Thunberg, *Travels*, p. 31.
37 The Dutch word *knecht* literally meant 'man-servant' or 'retainer', but, as Robert Shell has noted, this literal translation 'does not adequately encompass all the duties of this jack-of-all-trades' (Robert C.-H. Shell, *Children of bondage: a social history of the slave society at the Cape of Good Hope, 1652–1838* (Hanover: Wesleyan University Press, 1994), p. 11, note 30). Shell argues that the occupations available to *knechten* changed over time; in the 1600s they were mostly employed as manual labourers; during the early eighteenth century they were used as overseers and, as they were displaced from this role by the burghers' own sons, they became schoolteachers and livestock buyers (*ibid.*, p. 11, figs. 1–3.)
38 From the Dutch word *lichten*, meaning 'to raise or lift out'.
39 Thunberg, *Travels*, p. 51, note 161. Company servants could not marry without permission.
40 According to Governor General van Imhoff, who inspected the Cape settlement in 1743, artisans could earn from eight to nine *schellingen* per day (*The reports of De Chavonnes and his council, and of Van Imhoff, on the Cape* (Cape

Town: Van Riebeeck Society, no. 1, 1918), p. 137, cited in Guelke, 'Freehold farmers and frontier settlers', p. 80). Those who were paid monthly earned approximately 15 rix dollars (120 *schellingen*), whereas a soldier in Company employ earned 30 *schellingen* per month. See, for example, 1/swm 1/1, Minutes of Board of Landdrost and Heemraden, Swellendam, 15 November 1751; 1/GR 1/1, Minutes of Board of Landdrost and Heemraden, Graaff Reinet, 13 November 1786, 4 December 1786 and 11 May 1789. See also mooc 14/80, Annexures to liquidation account of Jacobus Botha *d'oude*, notebook entries for 1766 to 1771.

41 J 115, *Opgaafrol*, Graaff Reinet, 1798

42 Hoge, 'Personalia', pp. 265–7

43 Neumark, *Economic influences on the South African frontier*, p. 34; Guelke, 'Freehold farmers and frontier settlers', pp. 73–4 and 78.

44 For a description of the origins of the loan-farm system, see Guelke, 'Freehold farmers and frontier settlers', p. 78 and 'Land tenure and settlement at the Cape, 1652–1812', unpublished paper presented to a Symposium on the History of Surveying and Land Tenure in the Cape, 1652–1812, University of the Western Cape (July 1983), pp. 16–25. Until 1732 the annual rental (*recognitiegeld*) payable for a registered loan-farm was 12 rix dollars, and thereafter it was 24 rix dollars.

45 As a result, the arable farms of the south-west Cape were seldom subdivided in the eighteenth century and it became common practice for one of the younger sons to inherit the parental home (see S. Newton-King, 'In search of notability: the antecedents of Dawid van der Merwe of the Warm Bokkeveld', Institute of Commonwealth Studies, London, *Collected Seminar Papers on the Societies of Southern Africa* 20 (1994) and 'Hilletje Smits and the shadow of death').

46 Guelke, 'Freehold farmers and frontier settlers', p. 85.

47 See, for example, mooc 13/1/7, no 20, Liquidation account of Aletta Hendrina van der Heuvel; mooc 13/1/10, no. 25, Liquidation account of Elizabeth du Preez; mooc 13/1/11, no. 23, Liquidation account of Jasper Smit, Floriszoon; mooc 13/1/18, no. 42, Liquidation account of Douw Gerbrand Steijn.

48 See, for example, cj 2945, List of moneys owing to the burgher Andries van der Heyden; and G. J. Schutte (ed.), *Briefwisseling van Hendrik Swellengrebel JR oor Kaapse sake, 1778–1792* (Cape Town: Van Riebeeck Society, 1982), p. 302.

49 *Veeboer* was the contemporary Cape Dutch name for the European stockfarmer. My preference for this term as against the oft-used trekboer is explained on p. 23.

50 John Barrow, *An account of travels into the interior of southern Africa in the years 1797 and 1798*, 2 vols. (London: Cadell and Davies, 1801, 1804), vol. ii, pp. 409–10.

51 J. M. Coetzee, *White writing: on the culture of letters in South Africa* (New Haven: Yale University Press, 1988), p. 32.

52 Neumark, *Economic influences*, pp. 37–9.

53 S. Newton-King, 'Commerce and material culture on the eastern Cape frontier, 1764–1812', Institute of Commonwealth Studies, London, *Collected Seminar Papers on the Societies of Southern Africa* 14 (1988).

54 Guelke, 'Freehold farmers and frontier settlers', p. 88.

55 See p. 155.
56 Newton-King, 'Commerce and material culture'.
57 An auction was an important social occasion in the back country, 'a treat to which people flock for many miles round the country'. The relatives of the deceased were expected to provide food and drink for the assembled visitors, usually at the expense of the deceased's estate. (A 602, 'Auctions – their good and evil tendency', Hudson Collection, vol. 9.)
58 However, valuable items, such as jewellery and brass or silver buttons and buckles, were always sold, no matter how great their sentimental value (*ibid.*).
59 All information about the stock-farmers' possessions is taken from the *vendurollen* and other documents annexed to a stratified sample of seventy-four liquidation accounts drawn by a process of random selection from a statistical population of 303. A full discussion of the methods by which the data were collected and the sample selected can be found in chapter 8.
60 Newton-King, 'Commerce and material culture', p. 5.
61 C 994, Annexures to incoming letters, Woeke and Heemraden to Governor, 19 December 1791; MOOC 13/1/29, no 5, Liquidation account of Catharina Vermeulen and Mattheus Johannes van der Westhuijzen (1798); MOOC 13/1/26, Liquidation account of Dirk Jacobus Pretorius (1802).
62 See, for example, MOIC 2/340, no 17, Insolvent estate of Willem Bouwers (1807). For an explanation of the meat contract, see pp. 112–13.
63 According to extant documentation, the largest number of ewes lent to a single individual was 335 (MOOC 13/1/29, no. 5, Liquidation account of Catharina Vermeulen (1798)).
64 The calculation of weaning percentages is explained on pp. 191–2.
65 See p. 193.
66 See p. 193.
67 Even in the coastal forelands, where rainfall was higher, the river beds were often deeply incised and the banks consequently too steep for cattle or sheep to descend.
68 1/SWM 1/1, 5 January 1751. The Board explained that there was abundant water but that much of it was unusable owing to the steepness of the ravines through which the rivers ran.
69 A 447, Hendrik Swellengrebel, 'Journaal eener Landtogt gedaan in het noord oosten der Colonie tot in 't Kafferland en langs de Zuid Oostkust weder terug', 1 November 1776, p. 30.
70 See chapter 5, note 60.
71 Guelke, 'Land tenure and settlement', p. 25.
72 Henry Lichtenstein, *Travels in southern Africa in the years 1803, 1804, 1805 and 1806*, 2 vols. (London: Henry Colburn, 1812, 1815, reprinted Cape Town: Van Riebeeck Society, 1928, 1930), vol. II, p. 83. It should be understood, however, that many 'respectable' burghers, especially those whose home farms lay at high altitudes, practised a regular pattern of transhumance from summer to winter grazing grounds (see chapter 5, note 60).
73 1/SWM 1/1, 24 October 1755.
74 See MOOC 14/25-114, and MOOC 10/16, Vendue roll of Anna Susanna Lombard.
75 For a full discussion of the stock-farmers' consumption of imported clothing,

foodstuffs and narcotics, see Newton-King, 'Commerce and material culture', pp. 8–9

76 All prices are those paid by or to the *veeboeren*, i.e. prices ruling in the interior, as reflected in the annexures to liquidation accounts.

77 See pp. 146–7.

78 Under conditions of extensive farming in the Karoo (where lambs are carried on the veld for about one year) one would expect ewes to comprise approximately 39 per cent of the total flock (personal communication from Professor H. J. Heydenrich, Department of Animal Science, University of Stellenbosch, 10 December 1984).

79 Guelke, 'Freehold farmers and frontier settlers', pp. 87–9.

80 See pp. 199–200.

81 See, for example, J 115, List of Company servants in the district of Graaff Reinet, 1798.

82 Lichtenstein, *Travels*, vol. II, p. 96. Lichtenstein was a German who arrived at the Cape in 1802 as tutor to the young son of the Batavian Governor, J. W. Janssens.

83 See, for example, Nigel Worden, *Slavery in Dutch South Africa* (Cambridge: Cambridge University Press, 1985), pp. 108–9.

84 M. L. Wilson, 'Notes on the nomenclature of the Khoisan', *Annals of the South African Museum* 97 (1986). The term adopted by the Cape Khoekhoe seems to have been 'Khoena' (people) rather than 'Khoekhoena' and it is not clear whether it referred exclusively to themselves, or to all people; '-na' is the common-gender plural suffix and should rightly be included when the term 'Khoekhoe' is used to refer to a group of mixed or indeterminate gender. However, in order to avoid confusion, gender-number suffixes are generally omitted when Khoe words are used in English texts. A notable exception is the term 'San', which, if usage were consistent, should be written Sàà rather than San or Soaqua (*ibid.*, p. 255).

85 *Ibid*, pp. 254–6.

86 There are exceptions, even among Cape peoples; see, for example, Barnard, *Hunters and herders of southern Africa*, pp. 78–9, and this volume, chapter 4.

87 According to the linguist Anthony Traill, there were 'radical linguistic differences' between Khoekhoe and San languages. The latter were 'all members of the !Kwi group of Southern Bushman Languages', spoken throughout the area which came to be known as South Africa (Anthony Traill, '*!Khwa-ka Hhouiten*, 'The rush of the storm': the linguistic death of /Xam', in Pippa Skotnes (ed.), *Miscast: negotiating the presence of the Bushmen* (Cape Town: University of Cape Town Press, 1996).

88 See, for example, Barnard, *Hunters and herders of southern Africa*, chapters 1 and 2; Wilson, 'Notes on the nomenclature of the Khoisan'. The most pointed exchanges concern the historical experience of San groups in the Kalahari. The 'revisionists', led by Edwin Wilmsen and James Denbow, have portrayed the Kalahari San as members of an oppressed underclass within a single political economy dominated first by Tswana-speaking agro-pastoralists and later by European merchant capital. Richard Lee and Mathias Guenther, by contrast, have argued that contact between hunters (foragers) and herders could have

variable outcomes, depending on circumstance; contact did not lead inexorably to subordination and loss of cultural autonomy. In so far as the Kalahari debate has a bearing on the status of the pre-colonial San of the central and eastern Karoo, my own position is much closer to that of Lee and Guenther than to that of Wilmsen and Denbow. For a brief summary of the debate and bibliographical details of the main contributions, see Alan Barnard, 'Laurens van der Post and the Kalahari debate', in Skotnes (ed.), *Miscast*, pp. 239–47.

89 See especially Elphick, *Kraal and castle*, p. 33. It is generally agreed that Khoe-speaking pastoralists first entered the southern Cape nearly two thousand years ago, although, as Wilson observes, we cannot be sure to what extent the migration involved the movement of pastoralists or merely the spread of pastoralism (Wilson, 'Notes on the nomenclature of the Khoisan', pp. 262–3). However, given the major differences between Khoe languages and those of the Southern Bushman group, it seems likely that the southward spread of pastoralism did involve the migration of substantial groups of people as well as the diffusion of new methods of food production.

90 See, for example, J. S. Solway and Richard Lee, 'Foragers, genuine or spurious? Situating the Kalahari San in history', *Current Anthropology* 31 (1990) and Richard Lee and Mathias Guenther, 'Problems in Kalahari historical ethnography and the tolerance of error', *History in Africa* 20 (1993).

91 'Dagh-register, gehouden bij den Vaandrig Isaq Schrijver op sijn landtogt na de Inquahase Hottentots, beginnende den 4 January en eijndigende den 10 April 1689', in E. C. Godée Molsbergen (ed.), *Reizen in Zuid-Afrika in de Hollandse tijd*, 4 vols. (The Hague: Martinus Nijhoff, 1916, 1922, 1932), vol. III, pp. 107, 109, 112.

92 'Journaal gehouden door den Adsistend Carel Albregt Haupt op de togt door den Vaandrig August Frederik Beutler ter g'eerde ordre van den Wel Edelen Gestr. Heere Rijk Tulbagh . . .', in Godée Molsbergen (ed.), *Reizen*, vol. III, p. 292.

93 See chapter 4.

94 Elphick, *Kraal and castle*, p. 50.

95 J. B. Peires, *The house of Phalo: a history of the Xhosa people in the days of their independence* (Johannesburg: Ravan Press, 1981), p. 50; Gerrit Harinck, 'Interaction between Xhosa and Khoi: emphasis on the period 1620–1750', in Leonard Thompson (ed.), *African societies in southern Africa* (London: Heinemann, 1969), p. 159.

96 Peires, *House of Phalo*, p. 50.

97 Elphick, *Kraal and castle*, p. 148.

98 'Extracts from the Journal of Commander Van Riebeeck', in Donald Moodie (ed.), *The record: or a series of official papers relative to the condition and treatment of the native tribes of South Africa* (Cape Town: Balkema, 1960), p. 111. Gerrit Harinck has identified the Hancumqua/Hamcunqua with the Inqua. See Harinck, 'Interaction bteween Xhosa and Khoi', pp. 162–3.

99 'Extract from the Journal of Commander Van Riebeeck', in Moodie (ed.), *The record*, p. 215.

100 'Extracts of a despatch from Commander Simon van der Stell (*sic*) and Council to the Chamber XVII', in Moodie (ed.), *The record*, p. 432.

101 Schrijver had been recently promoted, perhaps in recognition of the importance of his forthcoming journey. In 1687 he had held the rank of sergeant. See
will of Isak Schrijver and Anna Hoeks, 1 January 1687, cj 2649.

102 Schrijver himself was illiterate (see will of Isak Schrijver and Anna Hoeks, 1
January 1687, cj 2649, and E. E. Mossop (ed.), *Journals of the expeditions of
the Honourable Ensign Olof Bergh (1682 and 1683) and the Ensign Isaq Schrijver (1689)* (Cape Town: Van Riebeeck Society, 1931), p. 196, note 8a.

103 'Dagh-register gehouden bij den Vaandrig Isaq Schrijver . . .', in Godée
Molsbergen (ed.), *Reizen*, vol. iii, p. 110. Moodie translated 'our people' (*ons
volk*) as 'our servants' (Moodie (ed.), *The record*, part ii, p. 436), but I prefer
my own translation, especially since Schrijver was not a freeburgher and may
not have been conversant with Cape parlance, in which '*ons volk*' did indeed
mean 'our servants' or 'our slaves'.

104 *Ibid.*, pp. 110, 111.

105 Elphick, *Kraal and castle*, chapter 3.

106 'Dagh-register gehouden bij den Vaandrig Isaq Schrijver . . .', in Godée
Molsbergen (ed.), *Reizen*, vol. iii, p. 111. See also Elphick, *Kraal and Castle*, p.
47, and Winifred Hoernlé, *The social organisation of the Nama and other
essays*, ed. Peter Carstens (Johannesburg: Witwatersrand University Press,
1985), p. 50.

107 Harinck, 'Interaction between Xhosa and Khoi', p. 163. See also Elphick,
Kraal and castle, p. 50.

108 'Dagh-register gehouden bij den Vaandrig Isaq Schrijver . . .', in Godée
Molsbergen (ed.), *Reizen*, vol. iii, p. 110.

109 *Ibid.*, p. 111.

110 *Ibid.*, pp. 282, 283, 292.

111 *Ibid.*, p. 111.

112 'Relaas van Adriaan Jansz kind van Maaslandsluys geweesen Bootsman op de
gestrande fluijt Stavenesse . . .', in Godée Molsbergen (ed.), *Reizen*, vol. iii, p.
61.

113 'Journaal gehouden door den Adsistend Carel Albregt Haupt . . .', in Godée
Molsbergen (ed.), *Reizen*, vol. iii, pp. 297, 295.

114 *Ibid.*, pp. 310–11.

115 Anders Sparrman, *A voyage to the Cape of Good Hope towards the Antarctic
Polar Circle round the world and to the country of the Hottentots and the Caffres
from the year 1772–1776*, ed. V. S. Forbes, 2 vols. (Cape Town: Van Riebeeck
Society, 1977), vol. ii, pp. 15–16.

116 François le Vaillant, *Travels from the Cape of Good Hope into the interior parts
of Africa in the years 1780–1785*, 2 vols. (London: G. G. and J. Robinson,
1790), vol. ii, p. 3.

117 *Ibid.*, vol. ii, p. 90. See also Elphick, *Kraal and castle*, p. 60.

118 Harinck, 'Interaction between Xhosa and Khoi', p. 158; vc 595, Diary of Col.
Robert Jacob Gordon, vol. iv, p. 85; Sparrman, *Voyage to the Cape of Good
Hope*, vol. ii, pp. 16–17.

119 Harinck, 'Interaction between Xhosa and Khoi', p. 158.

120 Le Vaillant, *Travels*, vol. ii, p. 2; Thunberg, *Travels*, p. 239.

121 Harinck, 'Interaction between Xhosa and Khoi', pp. 155–8.

122 Peires, *House of Phalo*, pp. 22–3 and chapter 2, note 51; pp. 45–6 and chapter 4, note 2.

123 *Ibid.*, pp. 23, 45–6.

124 Peires suggests that the Inqua were defeated and assimilated 'around 1700', but this cannot be so, for they were visited by expeditions from the colony in 1702 and again in 1719 (see p. 36).

125 Hermann Giliomee, 'The eastern frontier, 1770–1812', in Elphick and Giliomee (eds.), *Shaping*, p. 430.

126 'Journaal gehouden door den Adsistend Carel Albregt Haupt . . .', in Godée Molsbergen (ed.), *Reizen*, vol. III, p. 310.

127 'Relaas van Adriaan Jansz kind van Maaslandsluys . . .', in Godée Molsbergen (ed.), *Reizen*, vol. III, p. 61.

128 Harinck, 'Interaction between Xhosa and Khoi', pp. 164–5. See also Elphick, *Kraal and castle*, p. 65.

129 'Journaal gehouden door den Adsistend Carel Albregt Haupt . . .', in Godée Molsbergen (ed.), *Reizen*, vol. III, pp. 295, 297.

130 Moodie (ed.), *The record*, part V, pp. 9, 53. Tshatshu, heir to the Ntinde chief Bange, was said to have been of Gonaqua origin and he himself had 'Hottentot' wives.

131 Harinck, 'Interaction between Xhosa and Khoi', p. 159.

132 Le Vaillant, *Travels*, vol. II, pp. 14ff; Sparrman, *Voyage to the Cape of Good Hope*, vol. II, pp. 15–17; V.S. Forbes and John Rourke (eds.), *Paterson's Cape Travels, 1777 to 1779* (Johannesburg: Brenthurst Press, 1980), p. 127. For an account of the origins of the Gqunukhwebe, see Peires, *House of Phalo*, pp. 25–6.

133 'Journaal gehouden door den Adsistend Carel Albregt Haupt . . .', in Godée Molsbergen (ed.), *Reizen*, vol. III, p. 292.

134 Peires, *House of Phalo*, p. 23.

135 H. C. V. Leibbrandt, *The defense of Willem Adriaan van der Stel*, in the series *Précis of the archives of the Cape of Good Hope* (Cape Town: Government Printers, 1897), pp. 133–49. The party attacked at least three separate encampments on its journey home. The last of these was identified by some witnesses as belonging to 'the Hequon nation' and by others as belonging to the Gonaqua.

136 Anna Böeseken (ed.), *Suid-Afrikaanse argiefstukke: resolusies van die Politieke Raad*, 8 vols. (Cape Town: Cape Times, 1957), vol. V, 31 January 1719.

137 Sparrman, *Voyage to the Cape of Good Hope*, vol. II, p. 124; A 447, Hendrik Swellengrebel, 'Journaal eener Landtogt gedaan in het noord oosten der Colonie tot in 't Kafferland en langs de Zuid Oostkust weder terug', 8 November 1776.

3 INITIAL ENCOUNTERS OF AN UNCERTAIN KIND

1 C. W. de Kiewiet, *A history of South Africa: social and economic* (Oxford: Oxford University Press, 1941), p. 48; Richard Elphick, 'The Khoisan to c. 1770', in Elphick and Giliomee (eds.), *Shaping*, first edition, p. 24; Hermann

Giliomee, 'The eastern frontier, 1770–1812', in Elphick and Giliomee (eds.), *Shaping*, first edition, p. 291, and second edition, p. 421; Peires, *House of Phalo*, p. 53; Penn, 'Pastoralists and pastoralism'.

2 Elphick, 'Khoisan', p. 24; Giliomee, 'Eastern frontier', p. 430.

3 Shula Marks and Anthony Atmore, 'The imperial factor in South Africa in the nineteenth century: towards a reassessment', *Journal of Imperial and Commonwealth History* 3 (1974), 105.

4 Marks and Atmore (eds), *Economy and society*, p. 33.

5 *Ibid*, p. 34.

6 *Ibid*, p. 34. See also Martin Legassick, 'The frontier tradition in South African historiography', p. 66; Stanley Trapido, 'Reflections on land, office and wealth in the South African Republic, 1850–1900', in Marks and Atmore (eds.), *Economy and society*, pp. 350 and 355, and Roger Wagner, 'Zoutpansberg: the dynamics of a hunting frontier, 1848–67', in Marks and Atmore (eds.), *Economy and society*, pp. 319–20.

7 Legassick, 'Frontier tradition', pp. 60 and 68; Wagner, 'Zoutpansberg', p. 320; Trapido, 'Reflections on land, office and wealth', p. 350.

8 Wagner, 'Zoutpansberg', *passim*; Peter Delius, *The land belongs to us: the Pedi polity, the Boers and the British in the nineteenth-century Transvaal* (Johannesburg: Ravan Press, 1983), pp. 31–40; Peires, *House of Phalo*, pp. 53–4; Giliomee, 'Eastern frontier', *passim*; Marks and Atmore, 'Imperial Factor', p. 110, and *Economy and society*, p. 29.

9 Wagner, 'Zoutpansberg', p. 321.

10 See, for example, Giliomee, 'Eastern frontier'; Wagner, 'Zoutpansberg'; Delius, *The land belongs to us*; Philip Bonner, *Kings, commoners and concessionaires: the evolution and dissolution of the nineteenth-century Swazi state* (Johannesburg: Ravan Press, 1983), chapter 5. Recent research has demonstrated that the Ndebele were by no means the only instigators of disruption on the highveld. Slave-raids conducted by Voortrekker leaders and their Griqua, Koranna and Tswana partners caused equal or greater damage. See, for example, Julian Cobbing, 'The Mfecane as alibi: thoughts on Dithakong and Mbolompo', *Journal of African History* 29 (1988), 487–519 and Elizabeth Eldredge and Fred Morton (eds.), *Slavery in South Africa: captive labour on the Dutch frontier* (Pietermaritzburg: University of Natal Press, 1994).

11 Peires, *House of Phalo*, pp. 53–4.

12 Elphick and Giliomee (eds.), *Shaping*.

13 Giliomee, 'Eastern frontier', p. 430.

14 *Ibid.*, p. 431.

15 Elphick, p. 24.

16 Giliomee, 'Eastern frontier', p. 430.

17 *Ibid.*, p. 431.

18 *Ibid.*, p. 430.

19 *Ibid.*, *passim*.

20 *Ibid.*, p. 460.

21 *Ibid.*, p. 461.

22 *Ibid.*, p. 430.

23 *Ibid.*, pp. 426–7.

24 *Ibid.*, pp. 450–1.

25 *Ibid.*, pp. 450–1.

26 *Ibid.*, p. 451.

27 *Ibid.*, p. 459.

28 Legassick, 'Frontier tradition'.

29 *Ibid.*, p. 56.

30 *Ibid.*, p. 68.

31 Worden, *Slavery*.

32 *Ibid.*, especially chapter 10. For a contrary view, at least with respect to the role of violence within the Cape slave system, see Robert Shell, 'The family and slavery at the Cape, 1680–1808', in W. G. James and Mary Simons (eds.), *The angry divide: social and economic history of the Western Cape* (Cape Town: David Philip, 1989), pp. 20–30.

33 Worden, *Slavery*, p. 138.

34 *Ibid.*, p. 142.

35 See for example, Robert Ross, *Adam Kok's Griqua: a study in the development of stratification in South Africa* (Cambridge: Cambridge University Press, 1976); 'The "white" population of South Africa in the eighteenth century', *Population Studies* 19 (1975); 'The changing legal position of the Khoisan in the Cape Colony, 1652–1795', *African Perspectives* 5 (1982); 'Oppression, sexuality and slavery at the Cape of Good Hope', *Historical Reflections* 6 (1979); 'The rule of law at the Cape of Good Hope in the eighteenth century', *The Journal of Imperial and Commonwealth History* 9 (1980); 'Capitalism, expansion and incorporation on the southern African frontier', in H. Lamar and L. M. Thompson (eds.), *The frontier in history: North America and southern Africa compared* (New Haven: Yale University Press, 1981); 'The rise of the Cape gentry', *Journal of Southern African Studies* 9 (1983); D. van Arkel, G. C. Quispel and R. J. Ross, ' "De wijngaard des heeren?" Een onderzoek naar de wortels van "die blanke baasskap" in Zuid-Afrika', *Cahiers Sociale Geschiedenis* 4 (Leiden, 1983), published in translation in Robert Ross, *Beyond the pale: essays on the history of colonial South Africa* (Hanover: Wesleyan University Press, 1993); Robert Ross, *Cape of torments: slavery and resistance in South Africa* (London: Routledge and Kegan Paul, 1983) and Robert Ross and Pieter van Duin, *The economy of the Cape colony in the eighteenth century* (Leiden: Centre for the History of European Expansion, 1987).

36 Arkel, Quispel and Ross, ' "De wijngaard des heeren?" ', pp. 38–9.

37 *Ibid.*, pp. 35, 40.

38 *Ibid.*, p. 40.

39 *Ibid.*, p. 40. The quotation is taken from the instructions issued to Field-Commandant Godlieb Rudolph Opperman on 19 April 1774 and reprinted in Moodie (ed.), *The record*, part III, p. 29.

40 *Ibid.*, p. 40.

41 *Ibid.*

42 See J. Lockhart and S. B. Schwartz, *Early Latin America: a history of colonial Spanish America and Brazil* (Cambridge: Cambridge University Press, 1983), pp. 55–7.

43 See, for example, Richard Elphick and V. C. Malherbe, 'The Khoisan to 1828',

in Elphick and Giliomee (eds.), *Shaping*, second edition, p. 25, and Arkel, Quispel and Ross, 'De wijngaard des heeren?', p. 38.

44 Elphick, 'Khoisan', p. 26; Giliomee, 'Eastern frontier', p. 458, and Giliomee, 'The burgher rebellions on the eastern frontier, 1795–1815', in Elphick and Giliomee (eds.), *Shaping*, first edition, pp. 340, 342; Arkel, Quispel and Ross, 'De wijngaard des heeren?', pp. 39–40.

45 However, Arkel, Quispel and Ross are ambiguous on this point: on pp. 59–60 of 'De wijngaard des heeren?' they take essentially the position argued here. Nigel Penn has likewise commented upon the 'heightened fear and suspicion' generated by border conflict. See, for example, 'The frontier in the western Cape, 1700–1740', in John Parkington and Martin Hall (eds.), *Papers in the prehistory of the western Cape, South Africa* (Oxford: British Archaeological Reports International Series, 1987) and 'Pastoralists and pastoralism', p. 67.

46 P. J. van der Merwe, *Die noordwaartse beweging van die Boere voor die Groot Trek, 1770–1842* (The Hague: W. P. van Stockum and Zoon, 1937); *Die trekboer in die geskiedenis van die Kaapkolonie, 1657–1842* (Cape Town: Nasionale Pers, 1938); Neumark, *Economic influences on the South African frontier*; Leonard Guelke and R. Cole Harris, 'Land and society in early Canada and South Africa', *Canadian Journal of Historical Geography*, 1976; Leonard Guelke, 'Frontier settlement in early Dutch South Africa', *Annals of the American Association of Geographers* 66 (1976); 'Freehold farmers and frontier settlers, 1657–1780', in Elphick and Giliomee (eds.), *Shaping*, second edition.

47 Legassick, 'Frontier tradition', p. 68.

48 As in the case of legally instituted slavery in South Africa. See, for example, John Mason's fascinating study of the overlapping and conflicting world-views of master and slave in 'Paternalism under siege: slavery in theory and practice during the era of reform c1825 through emancipation', in Nigel Worden and Clifton Crais (eds.), *Breaking the chains: slavery and its legacy in the nineteenth-century Cape colony* (Johannesburg: Witwatersrand University Press, 1994) and Robert Shell's masterful *Children of bondage*.

49 See chapter 2.

50 See, for example, CJ 362, Documents in criminal cases, 1753; 1/STB 20/2, Landdrosts Faber and Mentz to Governor, 7 February 1770; Peires, *House of Phalo*, p. 98; Sparrman, *A voyage to the Cape of Good Hope*, vol. I, pp. 270–1, 281, 316; Moodie (ed.), *The record*, part III, pp. 23, 73, 76, note 1.

51 RLR 20/1

52 Extract of Resolution of Council, 13 February 1770, in Moodie (ed.), *The record*, part III, p. 5.

53 A 447, Hendrik Swellengrebel, 'Journal eener Landtogt gedaan in het noord oosten der Colonie tot in 't Kafferland en langs de Zuid Oostkust weder terug', 1 November 1776, p. 30. Swellengrebel was the son of Hendrik Swellengrebel who had been Governor of the Cape from 1739 to 1751. He was born in Cape Town but educated in the Netherlands where he lived until his death in 1803. He returned to the Cape in February 1776, on a visit to his 'fatherland', and remained there for a year, during which time he made three journeys inland. Thereafter he retained a keen interest in Cape affairs. (See G. J. Schutte (ed.),

Briefwisseling van Hendrik Swellengrebel Jr oor Kaapse sake, 1778–1792 (Cape Town: Van Riebeeck Society, 1982).)

54 RLR 20/1–23/2 It should be noted that many individuals registered two or more farms for their own use.

55 RLR 20/1–23/2 By 1774 fifteen loan-places situated east of the Gamtoos River had been formally registered.

56 RLR 20/1–23/2 See also Report on Boundaries by P. A. Myburgh, 1 May 1775, in Moodie (ed.), *The record*, part III, p. 48.

57 In terms of a resolution of the Council of Policy of 27 December 1775, the eastern boundary of Stellenbosch district was extended to the Fish River and that of Swellendam to the Bushmans River (Moodie (ed.), *The record*, part III, p. 50).

58 North of the Cape Fold Belt, the percentage of total annual rainfall which falls during the summer months increases in an easterly direction from about 66% in the vicinity of Beaufort West to about 75% just east of the Fish River. Total annual rainfall likewise increases in an easterly direction, rising from about 200 mm per annum north of the Swartberge to above 500 mm per annum in the Bamboesberg and Zuurberg. The southern edges of the Second Escarpment (the term refers to the south-east extension of the Sneeuberge range, from the Tandjesberg to the Winterberge) receive more rain owing to their high relief; thus Somerset East receives an average of 619.8 mm per annum and the Hogsback more than 1000 mm per annum. (See Map 2.)

59 J. J. Badenhorst, *A geographical study of the Cape Midlands and Karoo area, with special reference to the physiography and elements of land use*, 5 vols. (Grahamstown: Institute of Social and Economic Research, Rhodes University, 1970–5), vol. I, *Survey of the Cape Midlands and Karoo regions*, pp. 21, 45, Table 6. Rainfall in the Cape Fold Belt and coastal forelands ranges from about 300 to 700 mm per annum and is heavier in the spring (September–October) and autumn (March–April) than it is in mid-winter (June–July).

60 *Ibid.*, pp. 54–5.

61 J. P. A. Acocks, *Veld types of South Africa*, second edition, *Memoirs of the Botanical Survey of South Africa* 40 (1975), p. 52.

62 An indigenous macchia (heath), exceptionally rich in plant types, particularly 'ericoid, proteoid and restioid elements' (H. J. Deacon, *Where hunters gathered: a study of the Holocene Stone Age people in the eastern Cape* (Cape Town: South African Archaeological Society Monograph Series 1, 1976), pp. 18–19.)

63 *Ibid.*, p. 15.

64 Sparrman, *Voyage to the Cape of Good Hope*, vol. I, pp. 236–7. Sparrman's editor, Vernon Forbes, explains 'sourveld' as a term 'now used to describe vegetation zones where climate favours growth of types of grasses that are nutritious during the growing season and thereafter decline rapidly in food value'.

65 *Ibid.*, p. 238.

66 Barrow, *Travels*, vol. II, p. 85. According to Nigel Penn, Barrow was a self-made man, who 'remained suitably deferential towards his superiors all his life and had a strong sense of place and propriety within a strictly regulated social order'. The reference to 'a gentleman's park' should be seen in this context.

(Nigel Penn, 'Mapping the Cape: John Barrow and the first British occupation of the colony, 1795–1803', *Pretexts* 4 (1993).

67 A 447, Swellengrebel, 'Journal eener landtogt', 12 November 1776, p. 52.

68 I do not mean to underplay the ecological consequences of pre-colonial Khoe-khoe and even San settlement in the region (see, for example, A. B. Smith, 'Competition, conflict and clientship: Khoi and San relationships in the western Cape', in Hall and Smith (eds.), *Pastoralists and pastoralism*, and C. Garth Sampson, 'Veld damage in the Karoo caused by its pre-trekboer inhabitants: preliminary observations in the Seacow Valley', *The Naturalist* 30 (1986). But there is no doubt that the grazing practices of white pastoralists had far more drastic effects on the state of vegetation in the eastern Cape.

69 See above, pp. 45–6.

70 For a contemporary description of the country in the vicinity of present-day Humansdorp, see Sparrman, *Voyage to the Cape of Good Hope*, vol. I, p. 312 and V. S. Forbes, *Pioneer travellers in South Africa* (Cape Town: Balkema, 1965), p. 43. For the Kaggakamma, west of Port Elizabeth, see Sparrman, *Voyage to the Cape of Good Hope*, vol. II, p. 238.

71 Forbes, *Pioneer travellers*, pp. 14, 88.

72 Godée Molsbergen (ed.), *Reizen*, vol. III, p. 286; Forbes, *Pioneer travellers*, p. 14; Lichtenstein, *Travels*, vol. I, p. 417; A 447, Swellengrebel, 'Journal eener Landtogt', pp. 49–53.

73 Forbes, *Pioneer travellers*, pp. 14, 88.

74 Report from the Landdrost and Heemraden of Swellendam to Governor van Plettenberg and Council, 17 March 1775, in Moodie (ed.), *The record*, part III, p. 48.

75 Acocks, *Veld types*, p. 60.

76 The farm of Zacharias de Beer on the site of present-day Prince Albert (Forbes, *Pioneer travellers*, p. 64).

77 A 447, Swellengrebel, 'Journal eener Landtogt', 29 September–7 October 1776. According to Garth Sampson, Swellengrebel would have formed a better impression of the available water supply had he had guides who were more familiar with the terrain. (Personal communication, 14 January 1989.)

78 Forbes, *Pioneer travellers*, p. 65.

79 A 447, Swellengrebel, 'Journal eener Landtogt', 9–17 October 1776.

80 *Ibid.*, 16 October 1776. Cited in translation in Forbes, *Pioneer travellers*, p. 68. The Camdeboo extends along the foot of the mountains from present-day Aberdeen to Groot Bruintjes Hoogte. Swellengrebel exaggerated the difference in altitude between the Camdeboo and the plains to the south – it is scarcely more than 100–200 m.

81 Then the home farm of Johannes Jurgen de Beer (Forbes, *Pioneer travellers*, p. 67).

82 VC 592, Diary of Col. R. J. Gordon, vol. I, p. 56, November 1777.

83 Eve Palmer, *The plains of Camdeboo*, revised edition (Johannesburg: Lowry Publishers, 1986), p. 45. Deacon, *Where hunters gathered*, p. 18; Barrow, *Travels*, vol. II, pp. 373–4.

84 A 447, Swellengrebel, 'Journal eener Landtogt', 9–17 October 1776; VC 592, vol. I, 13 November 1777, p. 58.

85 Barrow, *Travels*, vol. II, p. 373.
86 A 447, Swellengrebel, 'Journal eener Landtogt', 22 October 1776, p. 27.
87 Family Podocarpaceae.
88 Barrow, *Travels*, vol. II, p. 373.
89 *Ibid.*, p. 123.
90 VC 592, vol. I, p. 65. See also Deacon, *Where hunters gathered*, p. 17, and Acocks, *Veld types*, p. 79.
91 VC 592, vol. I, p. 62.
92 Garth Sampson, personal communication, 14 January 1989. Professor Sampson, of Southern Methodist University, Dallas, Texas, is Director of the Zeekoe Valley Archaeological Project.
93 Badenhorst, *Geographical study*, Map 15
94 *Ibid.*, pp. 56–7; Acocks, *Veld types*, p. 9.
95 A 447, 'Journal eener Landtogt', 16 October 1776, pp. 23–4. Swellengrebel refers to an A. van den Berg whom he met on the Swart River. According to the *wildschutteboeken*, Abraham van den Berg, Jacobuszoon, registered the farm 'De Plattedrift' on the Swart River on 26 March 1771 (RLR 21/2).
96 Barrow, *Travels*, vol. II, p. 374.
97 John Campbell, *Travels in South Africa* (Cape Town: Struik, 1974), p. 124. Campbell visited the Camdeboo in April 1813, at the end of the rainy season, when the grasses would normally be at their best.
98 See p. 30.
99 S. L. Hall has suggested such a pattern for the Coastal Plateau south of the Winterberge, arguing that Khoekhoe pastoralists may have moved seasonally between the sourveld of the Winterberge and the mixed veld of the low-lying areas to the south, but he notes that this movement 'appears not to have been absolutely essential' (S. L. Hall, 'Pastoral adaptations and forager reactions in the eastern Cape', in Hall and Smith (eds.), *Pastoralists and pastoralism*, p. 44).
100 See, for example, Deacon, *Where hunters gathered.*
101 The contracted butchers were under licence to supply meat to the VOC at fixed prices. In return, they were granted a monopoly on sales to foreign ships. Jacobus van Reenen (born at the Cape in 1727) was a major figure in the colony's meat trade and in other aspects of its commercial life. See the valuable thesis by Gerard Wagenaar, 'Johannes Gysbertus van Reenen – sy aandeel in die Kaapse Geskiedenis tot 1806', unpublished MA thesis, University of Pretoria (1976), chapter 1.
102 W. Blommaert and J. A. Wiid (eds.), *Die joernaal van Dirk Gysbert van Reenen, 1803* (Cape Town: Van Riebeeck Society, 1937), p. 83. Gamtoos-riviermond had been granted to Jacobus van Reenen in 1766 and Kabeljouws-rivier in 1765 (RLR 18, p. 467).
103 Blommaert and Wiid (eds.), *Joernaal*, p. 84. See also Mentz to Governor van Plettenberg, 24 August 1774, in Moodie (ed.), *The record*, part III, pp. 33–4.
104 Sparrman met Rundganger on 10 September 1775 near the farm of the Widow Louis Fourie, on the Duivenhoks River (Sparrman, *Voyage to the Cape of Good Hope*, vol. I, pp. 226–31).
105 *Ibid.*, vol. I, pp. 229–31 and vol. II, p. 12. Rundganger's staff had been given

him by Ensign August Beutler in 1752, in recognition for his services to the expedition of that year.

106 Moodie (ed.), *The record*, part III, pp. 11–13.

107 1/STB 3/10, Landdrost of Swellendam to Governor, 15 November 1788. See also S. Newton-King, 'Khoisan resistance to colonial expansion, 1700–1828', in T. Cameron and S. B. Spies (eds.), *A new illustrated history of South Africa* (Cape Town: Human and Rousseau, 1986), p. 108, and Russell Viljoen, 'Revelation of a revolution: the prophecies of Jan Parel, alias *Onse Liewe Heer*', *Cronos* 21 (1994).

108 Sparrman, *Voyage to the Cape of Good Hope*, vol. II, p. 234.

109 *Ibid.*, pp. 232 and 234, note 12.

110 A 447, 'Journal eener Landtogt', 15 November 1776, p. 56. In March 1776 Gerrit Scheepers had registered the farm Chougaswagendrift 'geleegen op 't eijnd van de Winterhoeksberg over de Swartkops Rivier' (RLR 24, p. 209, cited in Forbes, *Pioneer travellers*, p. 74).

111 Stephanus Ferreira registered Coegaswagendrift in April 1776 (RLR 24, p. 225, cited in Forbes, *Pioneer travellers*, p. 73). Presumably this farm was across the river from Scheepers' place.

112 A 447, 'Journal eener Landtogt', 15 November 1776, p. 56. Possibly Lucas Meyer, then living between the Sundays and Bushmans Rivers. Meyer later settled on a farm named 'de Rietfontein', situated where Grahamstown is today.

113 Forbes, *Pioneer travellers*, p. 73.

114 A 447, 'Journal eener Landtogt', 14 November 1776, p. 54; C. C. de Villiers and C. Pama, *Geslagregisters van die ou Kaapse families*, 3 vols. (Cape Town: Balkema, 1966), vol. I, pp. 219–20.

115 A 447, 'Journal eener Landtogt', 6 November and 13–14 November 1776, pp. 45, 53–4. See also Sparrman, *Voyage to the Cape of Good Hope*, vol. II, pp. 32–8.

116 Forbes, *Pioneer travellers*, p. 73.

117 A 447, 'Journal eener Landtogt', 8 November 1776, p. 47.

118 *Ibid.*, pp. 45–52. Sparrman writes that Ruiter had three sons; however, unlike Swellengrebel, Sparrman did not visit Ruiter, but heard about him from his Christian hosts (Sparrman, *Voyage to the Cape of Good Hope*, vol. II, p. 125).

119 Patrick Cullinan (trans. and ed.), 'The travel journals of Robert Jacob Gordon', First Journey, 9 January 1778, p. 98. I am very grateful to Mr Cullinan for allowing me to consult his unpublished manuscript.

120 *Ibid.*, 9 January, p. 124.

121 *Ibid.*, 9–13 January 1778, pp. 97–103. Two years earlier, Swellengrebel had noted a clear distinction between the 'Hottentots' and 'basterd Kaffers' among Ruiter's following (A 447, 'Journal eener landtogt', pp. 46, 48–9).

122 He had come to the Cape in 1742 with his brother Jan Janse Nieuwenhuys. Both worked as shepherds and *bouknegte*. Jan became a burgher in 1754, the year after his marriage to Susanna Maria Brits, but Heinrich died unmarried 'in 't nieuweveld' in May 1781, three years after Paterson's visit. (De Villiers and Pama, *Geslagsregisters*, vol. II, p. 651.)

123 A Scots 'plant collector' who arrived at the Cape in May 1777 under the

patronage of the Countess of Sutherland (Forbes, *Pioneer travellers*, p. 81).

124 William Paterson, *A narrative of four journeys into the country of the Hottentots and Caffraria*, second edition (London: J. Johnson, 1787, 1790), p. 29.

125 Cullinan, 'Travel journals of Robert Jacob Gordon', 8 November 1777, p. 27. Gordon has Nieuwenhuys wearing 'a hide overcoat'.

126 For a brief and incisive discussion of the concept of clientship, see V. Tellis-Nayak, 'Power and solidarity: clientage in domestic service', *Current Anthropology* 24 (1983), p. 67.

127 Sparrman, *Voyage to the Cape of Good Hope*, vol. II, p. 124.

128 A 447, 'Journal eener Landtogt', p. 49. For Ruiter's role in trade between the Europeans and the Xhosa, see *ibid.*, p. 47.

129 Sparrman, *Voyage to the Cape of Good Hope*, vol. II, p. 125. Sparrman's view, as noted above, may well have been coloured by the prejudices of his informants.

130 V. S. Forbes and J. Rourke (eds.), *Paterson's Cape travels, 1777 to 1779* (Johannesburg: Brenthurst Press, 1980), p. 127. Paterson does not identify 'the old German', but it may have been Jacob Kok, of Sachsenhausen in Waldeck, who had registered the farm Zandvlakte on the Coerney River in 1778.

131 Report of the Landdrosts and Commissioned Heemraden of Stellenbosch and Swellendam to Governor Rijk Tulbagh, 7 February 1770, in Moodie (ed.), *The record*, part III, p. 3.

132 Blommaert and Wiid, *Joernaal*, pp. 83–7. Gamtoosriviermond was renamed 'De Vlakte' and registered under Muller's name in 1780 (V. C. Malherbe, personal communication).

133 Blommaert and Wiid, *Joernaal*, pp. 83–7.

134 See chapter 5.

135 Sparrman, *Voyage to the Cape of Good Hope*, vol. I, p. 281. Petrus Hendrik Ferreira was the elder brother of Stephanus Ferreira, mentioned above. He had two farms in the Lange Kloof, one near the Aapjes River (now the Louterwater River) and the other at Misgunst on the Diep River (*ibid.*, p. 281, note 47).

136 *Ibid.*, p. 282.

137 Many valuable documents belonging to the Drostdy of Swellendam were destroyed in a fire in 1865. However the records of the Court of Justice in Cape Town provide vivid glimpses of commando activities in this district. See, for example, the record of the trial of Jacobus Botha (CJ 362) for a graphic account of a mid-century commando against 'Bushmen' in the Swartberge.

138 Sparrman, *Voyage to the Cape of Good Hope*, vol. I, pp. 317–20.

139 *Ibid.*, vol. II, pp. 27–8.

140 *Ibid.*, vol. II, pp. 34–5.

141 Jalamba was the son of the imiDange chief, Mahote (Peires, *House of Phalo*, p. 50). His village was situated at the time on the Kroomie River, a tributary of the Koonap (Forbes, *Pioneer travellers*, p. 71).

142 A 447, 'Journal eener Landtogt', pp. 34–7. According to Peires, Phalo had died in 1775 and Gcaleka was now king (*House of Phalo*, p. 48).

143 Elphick, *Kraal and castle*, p. 32.

144 Carmel Schrire, 'An inquiry into the evolutionary status and apparent identity of San hunter-gatherers', *Human Ecology* 8 (1980), 9–32; 'Wild surmises on

savage thoughts', in Schrire (ed), *Past and present in hunter-gatherer studies* (New York: Academic Press, 1984).

145 John Parkington, 'Soaqua and Bushmen: hunters and robbers', in Schrire (ed.), *Past and present*; A. H. Manhire, J. Parkington and T. S. Robey, 'Stone tools and Sandveld settlement', in M. Hall, G. Avery, D. M. Avery, M. L. Wilson and A. J. B. Humphreys (eds.), *Frontiers: southern African archaeology today* (Oxford: British Archaeological Reports International Series 207, 1984); J. Parkington, R. Yates, A. Manhire and D. Halkett, 'The social impact of pastoralism in the southwestern Cape', *Journal of Anthropological Archaeology* 5 (1986), 316-18; R. Yates, A. Manhire and J. Parkington, 'Rock painting and history in the south-western Cape', in T. A. Dowson and D. Lewis-Wiliams (eds.), *Contested images: diversity in southern African rock art research* (Johannesburg: Witwatersrand University Press, 1994).

146 Parkington, 'Soaqua and Bushmen', pp. 165-9. Parkington's most recent work also points to significant changes in the cultural practices of hunter-gatherers as a result of exposure to pastoralism. These changes, reflected primarily in changes in painting styles and an eventual cessation of the tradition of finely detailed painting, appear later among the mountain people than among the hunters of the coastal plain (see Yates, Manhire and Parkington, 'Rock painting and history').

147 'Soaqua' is merely the masculine plural form of the Khoe word 'sa-' (Barnard, *Hunters and herders of southern Africa*, p. 8).

148 Smith, 'Competition, conflict and clientship'. See also A. B. Smith, 'Khoi/San relationships: marginal differences or ethnicity?', in Skotnes (ed.), *Miscast*, and Parkington, 'The social impact of pastoralism', pp. 316-18.

149 Parkington, 'Soaqua and Bushmen', p. 164.

150 *Ibid.*, p. 165.

151 C 1266, *Memorials and reports*, Landdrost and Krijgsraad of Stellenbosch to Governor, 7 May 1776.

152 CJ 362, 'Eijsch ende Conclusie' of Landdrost J. A. Horak.

153 *Ibid.*, Testimony of the Oud Heemraad Esaias Engelbrecht Meyer, 17 October 1750.

154 *Ibid.*, Interrogation of Dirk Marx by the accused, Jacobus Botha.

155 See pp. 131-2 and CJ 362, 'Duplicq' of Jacobus Botha, 28 October 1751, p. 149.

156 For accounts of commando attacks on 'Robber-Bushmen' in the coastal forelands, see the reports of Tjaart van der Walt, 6-12 April 1782 and Daniel Willem Kuhne, Commandant at Zwartkops River, 6 August 1784, both in 1/STB 13/13. Van der Walt reported that his commando had killed 'een groote hondert' of the robbers and captured seventeen.

157 Marks, 'Khoisan resistance to the Dutch'.

158 See chapters 4 and 5.

4 'A MULTITUDE OF LAWLESS BANDITTI'

1 See p. 60.

2 Marks, 'Khoisan resistance to the Dutch', p. 64.

3 Elphick, *Kraal and castle*, p. 56.
4 *Ibid.*, p. 34.
5 *Ibid.*, p. 225. For a more detailed account of these raids, see Penn, 'The frontier in the western Cape'.
6 *Dag Register*, 13 March 1701, p. 125, cited in Elphick, *Kraal and castle,* p. 225.
7 Elphick, *Kraal and castle*, pp. 225–6.
8 The identity of the Guriqua is something of a puzzle. They may once have been a powerful group, but at the time of their first contacts with the Dutch they appeared relatively poor and politically fragmented. It has been suggested that 'the original Guriqua may have been a Strandloper group which acquired livestock', which would explain why other Khoekhoe sometimes called them 'Bushmen', but Nigel Penn plausibly concludes that the Guriqua, like their more powerful allies, the Namaqua, 'were Khoikhoi who had San clients'. (Penn, 'The northern Cape frontier zone'. See also Elphick, *Kraal and castle*, pp. 134–5.)
9 'Journal of Landdrost Johannes Starrenburgh kept on his journey to the Gonnemas, Grigriquas, Namaqua Hottentots etc,' in Leibbrandt (ed.), *Précis of the archives of the Cape of Good Hope*, p. 161.
10 See Elphick, *Kraal and castle*, p. 229 and Penn, 'Northern Cape frontier zone', pp. 60–1.
11 *Ibid.*, p. 226.
12 For a detailed account of this expansion, see Penn, 'Northern Cape frontier zone', chapter 2.
13 See Marks, 'Khoisan resistance', p. 70.
14 For a discussion of the impact of this epidemic upon the Khoekhoe of the northern borderlands, see Elphick, *Kraal and castle*, pp. 231–4 and Penn, 'Northern Cape frontier zone', chapter 2.
15 Penn, 'Northern Cape frontier zone', pp. 82–3.
16 c 10, Resolutions, 20 November 1715, cited in Van der Merwe, *Die noordwaartse beweging*, p. 7.
17 Penn, 'The frontier in the western Cape', p. 5.
18 *Ibid.*, p. 9.
19 Immediately prior to the mobilisation of the General Commando of 1774, *veldcorporaals* were promoted to the rank of *veldwagtmeester* (sergeant).
20 For a defence of this practice, see 'Letter from Commandant Opperman to the Landdrost of Stellenbosch', 17 May 1776 in Moodie (ed.), *The record,* part iii, p. 57.
21 Penn, 'The frontier in the western Cape', p. 9. See also Van der Merwe, *Noortdwaartse beweging*, pp. 26–7.
22 Van der Merwe, *Noordwaartse beweging*, pp. 26–7.
23 Penn, 'The frontier in the western Cape', p. 11. See also Elphick, *Kraal and castle*, p. 234.
24 Cited in Van der Merwe, *Noordwaartse beweging*, p. 8. It is possible that there were herders among this group, for the commando took sixty-two cattle from them, over and above those originally stolen from the Boers (Penn, 'The frontier in the western Cape', p. 12, and 'Northern Cape frontier zone', p. 94).
25 Penn, 'The frontier in the western Cape', p. 14.

26 Penn, 'Northern Cape frontier zone', pp. 96–7. This group was armed only with bows and arrows, whereas the first group had assegais too – a further indication that there may have been Khoekhoe among them (*ibid.*, p. 94; see also Parkington, 'Soaqua and Bushmen', p. 159).

27 The first was in 1715, when the commando led by Potgieter and Van der Merwe seized eight 'Bushman women and nine children'. (A. J. Böeseken, 'Die Nederlandse kommissarisse en die 18de eeuse samelewing aan die Kaap', *Archives Year Book for South African History* (1944), 81.)

28 Cited in Marks, 'Khoisan resistance', p. 71.

29 c 453, Incoming letters, Louwrensz to Governor, 22 October 1738.

30 See Penn, 'The frontier in the Western Cape', p. 14.

31 Mentzel, *Geographical and topographical description*, vol. III, pp. 217–18; Sparrman, *A voyage to the Cape of Good Hope*, vol. II, p. 112.

32 For an account of this war (against the Cochoqua of Gonnema) see Elphick, *Kraal and castle*, pp. 130–4.

33 Penn, 'The frontier in the western Cape'.

34 The ban on freeman involvement in livestock barter with the Khoekhoe had been reimposed in 1725.

35 The origins of the latter are unclear, but it seems likely that they were San clients or allies of the Little Namaqua (see Penn, 'Northern Cape frontier zone', pp. 100, 131).

36 Penn, 'The frontier in the western Cape', p. 15.

37 Penn, 'Northern Cape frontier zone', pp. 99–100, 118.

38 Penn, 'The frontier in the western Cape', pp. 17–18.

39 *Ibid.*, p. 18.

40 *Ibid.*, p. 19.

41 Penn, 'Northern Cape frontier zone', p. 118.

42 Penn, 'The frontier in the western Cape', p. 20.

43 *Ibid.*, p. 21.

44 *Ibid.*, pp. 24–7, 29.

45 *Ibid.*, p. 30.

46 Guelke, 'Frontier settlement in early Dutch South Africa', p. 66 (1976), 26, Figure 1. For a chronology of white settlement in the Onder Bokkeveld, the Hantam and the Roggeveld, see Penn, 'Northern Cape frontier zone', pp. 171–8.

47 Nigel Penn, 'Labour, land and livestock', p. 9. See also Penn, 'Northern Cape frontier zone', chapter 5.

48 Guelke, 'Frontier settlement in early Dutch South Africa', pp. 34–5.

49 Penn, 'Labour, land and livestock', pp. 9–10.

50 Acocks, *Veld types*, p. 64.

51 Penn himself implies this. See 'Northern Cape frontier zone', pp. 174–5.

52 CJ 403, Documents in criminal cases, Confession of Jantje Links, 29 July 1772, p. 447. The 'dry mountain' may refer to a specific chain of mountains in the Onder Roggeveld, called the Dröeberge.

53 Penn, 'Land, labour and livestock', pp. 11–13; 'Northern Cape frontier zone', p. 187.

54 1/STB 3/10, Testimony of the Hottentots Ontong, Jantje and Maurits, the

burgher Johannes Swanepoel and the Corporaal Fredrik Sigmond Modeman, 21 February 1750. See also 1/STB 3/10, Testimony of the Hottentot Captain Oubaas, 21 February 1750. On 14 August 1756 Johannes Jurgen de Beer signed a service contract with Jan Baltzer Martens of Rostock (c 1145). In 1749, however, De Beer was only 20 years old and not yet married. It is possible that the witnesses confused him with his older brother, Zacharias.

55 c 490, Incoming letters, Landdrost van Schoor to Governor, 20 November 1754.

56 Penn interprets 'Duijkerpens' to be the name of a band rather than an individual ('Northern Cape frontier zone', p. 188). However, while one source is ambiguous on this point, a second makes it clear that Duijkerpens was a person (see c 491, Incoming letters, Van Schoor to Governor, 3 April 1755).

57 c 491, Landdrost van Schoor to Governor, 3 April 1755.

58 See 1/STB 3/10, Statement of the Hottentot Danser, 2 November 1763; Statement of Jacob of Mallebar, slave of Jacobus van Reenen, 20 November 1763; Statement of the Hottentot Coridon, 20 November 1763. See also Penn, 'Land, labour and livestock', pp. 11–13.

59 See for example CJ 403, Case 13: confession of the Hottentot Jas, 27 July 1772; confession of the Bastard Hottentot Thys, 31 July 1772. See also c 1266, Landdrost and Krijgsraad of Stellenbosch to Governor, 7 May 1776.

60 See p. 45.

61 Penn, 'Land, labour and livestock', p. 11.

62 Colonel Richard Collins, 'Report on the Bosjesmen' (1809), in Moodie (ed.), The record, part v, p. 34. Other details concerning this incident were obtained from a footnote in Moodie (ed.), The record, part III, pp. 64–5. See also George Thompson, Travels and adventures in southern Africa, 2 vols., ed. V. S. Forbes (Cape Town, Van Riebeeck Society, 1967, 1968), vol. II, p. 9, who alleges that 'hundreds of innocent people were massacred to avenge this ruffian'.

63 Thompson, Travels and adventures, vol. II, p. 9.

64 A 447, 'Journaal eener Landtogt', 11 October 1776. See also Sparrman, Voyage to the Cape of Good Hope, vol. II, p. 113; François le Vaillant, New travels into the interior parts of Africa by way of the Cape of Good Hope in the years 1783, 1784 and 1785, 3 vols. (London: Robinson, 1796), vol. III, pp. 174, 178, and Collins, 'Report on the Bosjesmen', p. 34.

65 Landdrost of Stellenbosch to Governor Tulbagh, 4 July 1770, in Moodie (ed.), The record, part III, pp. 7–8. In August 1770 Van Jaarsveld had registered the farm de Klaverfontijn 'op de Sneeuwberg over de Buffels [Kariega] rivier' (RLR 21/1).

66 c 565, Landdrost Faber to Governor, 3 May 1771.

67 Ibid.

68 Landdrost of Stellenbosch to Acting Governor van Plettenberg, 10 April 1772, in Moodie (ed.), The record, part III, p. 11.

69 Landdrost of Stellenbosch to Acting Governor van Plettenberg, 23 May 1772, in Moodie (ed.), The record, part III, p. 11; Landdrost of Stellenbosch to Cape Government, 22 June 1772, in Moodie (ed.), The record, part III, p. 13; Landdrost of Stellenbosch to Cape Government, 20 October 1772, in Moodie (ed.), The record, part III, p. 17. For a full account of the events surrounding the Tuytman murder, see Penn, 'The northern Cape frontier zone', pp. 197–210.

70 Landdrost of Stellenbosch to Cape Government, 20 October 1772, in Moodie (ed.), *The record*, part III, p. 17.

71 Minutes of a meeting of the combined Boards of Landdrost and Heemraden and Landdrost and Militia Officers of Stellenbosch, 28 December 1773, in Moodie (ed.), *The record*, part III, p. 19.

72 See Sparrman, *Voyage to the Cape of Good Hope*, vol. I, p. 215, note 28: 'Horse sickness (Pestis Equorum) is a virus disease transmitted by blood-sucking midges that occur in low-lying areas during the summer rains. Hence horses were removed to elevated areas in December to remain there till the first frosts of winter. Severe outbreaks occurred at intervals of 20 to 30 years.' See also Blommaert and Wiid (eds.) *Die Joernaal van Dirk Gysbert van Reenen*, p. 29. Horse sickness was at its worst in autumn (March and April), the months of heaviest rainfall on the Escarpment.

73 Adriaan van Jaarsveld to Landdrost and Militia Officers, Stellenbosch, 30 April 1773, in Moodie (ed.), *The record*, part III, p. 65.

74 *Ibid.*

75 *Ibid.*

76 A. van Jaarsveld to G. R. Opperman, Sneeuwberg, 20 June 1774, in Moodie (ed.), *The record*, part III, p. 66, and 1/STB 10/162, Letters received from ward masters, A. van Jaarsveld to Landdrost of Stellenbosch, 26 June 1774.

77 Combined Boards of Landdrost and Heemraden and Landdrost and Krijgsraad to Van Plettenberg, 19 April 1774, in Moodie (ed.), *The record*, part III, p. 25.

78 Opperman's father, Gotlieb Christiaan Opperman of Krossen on the Oder, came to the Cape as a mercenary soldier in 1725. Godlieb Rudolph was christened on 19 June 1729. (Hoge, 'Personalia').

79 'Instructions according to which the newly appointed Field Commandant Godlieb Rudolph Opperman shall have to regulate his conduct upon the expedition about to attack the Bosjesmans Hottentots, who still continue to commit murder and robbery', 19 April 1774, in Moodie (ed.), *The record*, part III, p. 28.

80 Combined Boards of Landdrost and Heemraden and Landdrost and Militia Officers of Stellenbosch to Governor van Plettenberg and Council, 19 April 1774, in Moodie (ed.), *The record*, part III, p. 25. 'Bastard Hottentots' here refers to the offspring of slaves and Khoekhoe, not to people of mixed European and Khoekhoe ancestry.

81 Records of a meeting of the combined Boards of Landdrost and Heemraden and Landdrost and Militia Officers of Stellenbosch, 28 December 1773, in Moodie (ed.), *The record*, part III, p. 28.

82 *Ibid.*, 28 March 1774, in Moodie (ed.), *The record*, part III, p. 23.

83 The decision to attack in the spring seems to have been the result of a compromise based on the different conditions prevailing in the winter-rainfall region of the Bokkeveld and Onder Bokkeveld on the one hand and the summer-rainfall region of the Escarpment on the other. In winter the rivers of the Bokkeveld were swollen and impassable, whereas in summer, as Van Jaarsveld had observed, the robbers could more easily conceal themselves and the horses were weakened by sickness.

84 Report of Field-Commandant Nicolaas van der Merwe, 7 November 1774, in

Moodie (ed.), *The record*, part III, pp. 35–7. In October 1988 Dr Janette Deacon and I attempted to trace the route of this commando in the field. I am most grateful for her patient and expert guidance on this occasion!

85 The Graaff Reinet *Opgaafrollen* for the years 1787, 1791, 1793 and 1798 record the presence of a family of 'Gedoopte Basters' named Miemie or Mienie. See also De Villiers and Pama, *Geslagsregisters*, vol. I, p. 581.

86 Journal of the commando under the orders of Gerrit van Wyk, 2–28 September 1774, in Moodie (ed.), *The record*, part III, pp. 37–8.

87 VC 32, Journals of Cape Governors, 13 January 1775.

88 *Ibid.*, note in margins of report of Field-Commandant Nicolaas van der Merwe, 16 August 1774.

89 Journal of the commando under Gerrit van Wyk, 2 September 1774, in Moodie (ed.), *The record*, part III, p. 38.

90 *Ibid.*, note 1.

91 Report of Commandant Opperman, 1 May 1775, in Moodie (ed.), *The record*, part III, supplementary papers, p. 67.

92 *Ibid.*

93 Report of Corporal W. Steenkamp, Onder Roggeveld, 29 April 1776, in Moodie (ed.), *The record*, part III, supplementary papers, p. 69.

94 *Ibid.*

95 Report of Gerrit Putter, 9 February 1776, in Moodie (ed.), *The record*, part III, supplementary papers, p. 68.

96 Enclosure in report of Field-Corporal A. van Zyl, Hantam, 16 May 1776, in Moodie (ed.), *The record*, part III, supplementary papers, p. 70.

97 Sparrman, *Voyage to the Cape of Good Hope*, vol. II, p. 111.

98 Penn, 'Land, labour and livestock', p. 9. See also Penn, 'Northern Cape frontier zone', pp. 195–6.

99 'Land, labour and livestock', pp. 9–10 and 13; 'Northern Cape frontier zone', pp. 195–6. For Penn's views on the importance of the all-season rainfall corridor, see 'Northern Cape frontier zone', pp. 173–9.

100 'Northern Cape frontier zone', p. 222.

101 *Ibid.*, pp. 179–80.

102 Van der Merwe, *Noordwaartse beweging*, p. 10.

103 H. C. Bredekamp and S. Newton-King, 'The subjugation of the Khoisan during the 17th and 18th centuries', unpublished paper presented to the Conference on Economic Development and Racial Domination, University of the Western Cape, October 1984, pp. 23–4.

104 C. Garth Sampson, 'Atlas of Stone Age settlement in the Central and Upper Seacow Valley', *Memoirs van die Nasionale Museum Bloemfontein* 20 (1985), 12–13.

105 *Ibid.*

106 C. G. Sampson, personal communication, 14 January 1989.

107 Sampson, 'Atlas of Stone Age settlement', pp. 93, 108–9.

108 C. Garth Sampson 'Site clusters in the Smithfield settlement pattern', *South African Archaeological Bulletin* 39 (1984), 5, and 'Model of a prehistoric herder-hunter contact zone: a first approximation', in M. Hall and A. B. Smith

(eds.), *Prehistoric pastoralism in southern Africa*, The South African Archaeological Society Goodwin Series 5, 1986, p. 50.

109 Sampson, 'Atlas of Stone Age settlement', pp. 87, 93.

110 *Ibid.*, pp. 93, 109. The apparent population increase in the valley around this time may be partly explained by the arrival of herders from the south (see p. 80).

111 *Ibid.*, p. 87.

112 C. Garth Sampson, Grant Proposal to the National Science Foundation, [USA] 1986, pp. 3–5.

113 Sampson, Grant Proposal, 1986, pp. 4–5 and Grant Proposal to the National Science Foundation, 1987, pp. 3–4 and Figure 5.

114 The ZVAP has mapped a total of 221 permanent springs in their survey area (Sampson, 'Atlas of Stone Age settlement', p. 17).

115 C. Garth Sampson, 'A prehistoric pastoralist frontier in the Upper Zeekoe Valley, South Africa', in M. Hall, G. Avery, D. M. Avery, M. L. Wilson and A. J. B. Humphreys (eds.), *Frontiers: Southern African archaeology today* (Oxford: British Archaeological Reports International Series 207, 1984), p. 98 and 'Atlas of Stone Age settlement', p. 17.

116 Patrick Cullinan (editor and translator), 'The travel journals of Robert Jacob Gordon', unpublished manuscript, pp. 43 and 45 (17 and 19 November 1777) and Deacon, *Where hunters gathered*, p. 135.

117 See chapter 3, p. 5. See also Sampson, 'Atlas of Stone Age settlement', p. 17 and Cullinan, 'Travel journals of Robert Jacob Gordon', pp. 41–3 (16 and 17 November 1777).

118 Sampson, 'Atlas of Stone Age settlement', p. 17. See also Deacon, *Where hunters gathered*, p. 147.

119 Sampson, 'Model of a prehistoric hunter-herder contact zone', p. 50.

120 See pp. 74–5.

121 c 1266, G. R. Opperman to Governor, March 1776.

122 Collins, 'Report on the Bosjesmen', in Moodie (ed.), *The record*, part v, p. 34.

123 *Ibid.*, p. 35.

124 *Ibid.*, p. 35.

125 In May 1804 Lichtenstein crossed the Sak River just above its junction with the Sout River (north of present-day Fraserburg) and found it 'entirely dry'. According to the colonists, he added, 'it had never been otherwise for the last six years'. However at the site of the Reverend Kicherer's mission, a quarter of a mile west of the crossing place, there was 'a spring of very fine clear water, which never dries up'. And Lichtenstein describes several other such water sources in the course of his journey north to the Karreeberge. (Lichtenstein, *Travels*, vol. II, pp. 229, 255.)

126 J. P. A. Acocks, *Veld types*, p. 65. I am indebted to Dr Janette Deacon for information about underground springs in the Kareeberge.

127 See Janette Deacon, ' "My Place is the Bitterpits": the home territory of Bleek and Lloyd's /Xam San informants', *African Studies* 45 (1986).

128 See chapter 2, pp. 30–2.

129 Sampson, Proposal, 1986, pp. 6–7; Proposal, 1987, p. 4; personal communica-

tion, 14 January 1989. There is evidence that ceramics of the type usually associated with herder communities were introduced into the upper valley some 1100 –1200 years ago. However, while these ceramics were found in association with stone kraals, there is at present no hard evidence that livestock were present in the valley before the fifteenth century AD. (See I. Plug, C. A. Bollong, T. J. G. Hart and C. G. Sampson, 'Context and direct dating of pre-European livestock in the upper Seacow River Valley', *Annals of the South African Museum* 104 (1994).)

130 Sampson, 'Model of a prehistoric herder-hunter contact zone', pp. 50–5; 'Atlas of Stone Age settlement', pp. 87, 103.
131 Sampson, 'A prehistoric pastoralist frontier', p. 100.
132 *Ibid.*, p. 100.
133 Sampson stresses that this is 'a label of convenience and does not necessarily imply that the Zeekoe valley herders spoke a Khoi dialect' ('A prehistoric pastoralist frontier', p. 103). See also 'Model of a prehistoric herder-hunter contact zone', p. 53.
134 Sampson, 'A prehistoric pastoralist frontier', p. 103.
135 *Ibid.*, p. 105; 'Model of a prehistoric herder-hunter contact zone', p. 50.
136 Sampson, 'Model of a prehistoric herder-hunter contact zone', *passim.*
137 See chapter 3, pp. 59–60 and Elphick, *Kraal and castle*, p. 30.
138 Sampson, 'A prehistoric pastoralist frontier', p. 108. See also Parkington, 'Soaqua and Bushmen'.
139 Sampson, 'Model of a prehistoric herder-hunter contact zone', p. 50; Grant proposal, 1986, pp. 5–7; personal communication, 14 January 1989. Recent attempts to date bone fragments from pre-European livestock in the Haaskraal rock shelter on the upper Zeekoe River have lent support to this view (Plug *et al.*, 'Context and direct dating of pre-European livestock', p. 47).
140 Sampson, 'Model of a prehistoric herder-hunter contact zone', p. 50.
141 See Elphick, *Kraal and castle*, p. 30.
142 Sampson has recently gone so far as to suggest (as one of several options) that the eighteenth-century 'Bushmen' of the upper Zeekoe valley may have been the direct descendants of dispossessed herders (C. G. Sampson, 'Bushman (Oesjwana) survival and acculturation on the colonial frontier of South Africa, 1770–1890', *Historical Archaeology* (1993); see also Plug *et al.*, 'Context and direct dating of pre-European livestock', p. 34). However, he offers no explanation as to how the the herders might have been dispossessed.
143 There is scant documentary evidence of this refugee influx, but Sampson believes that its impact can be demonstrated in the archaeological record (see Proposal, 1987).
144 Godée Molsbergen (ed.), *Reizen*, vol. III, p. 324. Elphick suggests that the term 'd'gau' may be a corrupted form of the Khoe word '/=ou', which in Nama means 'tame' (*Kraal and castle*, p. 28, note 19).
145 Godée Molsbergen (ed.) *Reizen*, vol. III, pp. 326, 328.
146 *Ibid.*, pp. 325, 327.
147 *Ibid.*, p. 327.
148 *Ibid.*, p. 324.
149 *Ibid.*, pp. 326–7.

150 Sparrman, *Voyage to the Cape of Good Hope*, vol. II, p. 116.
151 Cullinan, 'Travel journals of Robert Jacob Gordon', First Journey, 16 November 1777, p. 41. The paintings referred to here were found in a rock shelter at De Schanse Kraal, on the headwaters of the Elandskloof River, but Gordon observed such paintings 'everywhere on the rocks, even in the Camdeboo on Opperman's farm' (*ibid.*, 14 November 1777, p. 40).
152 *Ibid.*, 14 November 1777, p. 40. The term 'Oeswana' or 'Oesjwana' recurs in le Vaillant as 'Housouana' (le Vaillant, *New travels*, vol. III, pp. 174, 178–9). Elphick has suggested that this may have the same derivation as 'd'Gauas', being /=ou + sa + na, i.e. 'tame San' (*Kraal and castle*, p. 28, note 19).
153 Sparrman, *Voyage to the Cape of Good Hope*, vol. II, p. 113; Cullinan, 'Travel journals of Robert Jacob Gordon', First Journey, 12 November 1777–1 January 1778, pp. 36–92.
154 Report of Landdrosts and Commissioned Heemraden of Stellenbosch and Swellendam, 7 February 1770, in Moodie (ed.), *The record*, part III, p. 3.
155 Cullinan, 'Travel journals of Robert Jacob Gordon', First Journey, 13 November 1777, p. 36. There is still a large pile of stones on the farm Vreede, roughly in the location described by Gordon.
156 Sampson, 'Model of a prehistoric herder-hunter contact zone', pp. 53–4.
157 Cullinan, 'Travel journals of Robert Jacob Gordon', First Journey, 16 December 1777, p. 72.
158 Le Vaillant, *New travels*, vol. II, p. 333, January 1783. Le Vaillant's journals are widely regarded as less accurate than those of his contemporaries, such as Sparrman and Gordon (Forbes, *Pioneer travellers*, pp. 117–18).
159 Le Vaillant, *New travels*, vol. II, p. 358 (February 1783).
160 This was due as much to the intense cold in winter as to the 'sourveld' vegetation (see chapter 3, p. 46).
161 Journal of Governor van Plettenberg, in Godée Molsbergen, *Reizen*, vol. IV, pp. 75–6. See also pp. 67, 111.
162 *Ibid.* See also Adriaan van Jaarsveld to ?, Sneeuwberg, 1773; W. S. van Ryneveld to Lord Macartney, 24 May 1797, Macartney Papers, no. 73; 'Collins' report on the Bosjesmen', in Moodie (ed.), *The record*, part V, p. 33.
163 1/GR 12/2, Letters and reports, Anonymous and otherwise undated, but *c.* 1786.
164 1/GR 12/2, Anonymous *veldwagtmeester* to Landdrost, undated, but *c.* 1786.
165 1/GR 12/2, Report of *Oud-Commandant* Dawid de Villiers, 10 July 1786.
166 1/GR 12/2, Tjaart van der Walt to Landdrost, 24 August 1786. The Agter Renosterberg was known as the Rodeberg in the 1770s. For later references to the herding skills of the Zeekoe valley Bushmen, see Plug *et al.*, 'Context and direct dating of pre-European livestock', p. 33.
167 1/STB 10/162, G. R. Opperman to Landdrost of Stellenbosch, 27 March 1776.
168 Opperman to Landdrost, Stellenbosch, 17 May 1776, in Moodie (ed.), *The record*, part III, p. 57.
169 General report of Field-Sergeant D. S. van der Merwe, 13 March 1777, in Moodie (ed.), *The record*, part III, pp. 62–3. Carel van der Merwe was then 21 years old and had just married Anna Magdelena van der Merwe. He lived at Doornbos near the sources of the Buffels and Drooge Rivers. (De Villiers and

Pama, *Geslagsregisters*, vol. II, p. 560; Cullinan, 'Travel journals of Robert Jacob Gordon', First Journey, 13 November 1777, p. 38.)

170 There is a mountain with this name 20 km south-east of Murraysberg, overlooking the Buffels River

171 General report of Field-Sergeant D. S. van der Merwe, 13 March 1777, in Moodie (ed.), *The record*, part III, pp. 62–3.

172 Report of Commandant G. R. Opperman, 10 April 1777, in Moodie (ed.), *The record*, part III, p. 68. Van den Berg had registered the farm 'de Rietfontein agter de Sneeuwberg' in 1774 (RLR 23/1). His farm was mapped by Gordon east-south-east of the Compassberg (Forbes, *Pioneer travellers*, p. 97) hence it is reasonable to assume that the kraal referred to was in the Agter Sneeuberg.

173 See above, note 151.

174 The kraal was attacked on 30 June 1786 (1/GR 12/2, Report of Commandant Dawid de Villiers, 10 July 1786). See also 1/GR 12/2, Alewijn Jacobus Forster to Landdrost, 2 February 1787; C 213, Resolutions, 12 February 1793 and CO 6, Letters received, Andries Stockenstrom to Fiscal, 27 February 1807.

175 T. M. O'C. Maggs, 'Some observations on the size of human groups during the Late Stone Age', in M. Schoonraad (ed.), *Rock paintings of southern Africa*, supplement to the *South African Journal of Science*, special issue, 2 (1971), 49–53.

176 J. D. Lewis-Williams, 'The economic and social context of southern San rock art', *Current Anthropology* 23 (1982), 431. Lewis-Williams prefers to refer to San residential groups as 'camps' rather than 'bands', for reasons explained on pp. 431–2 of the above article.

177 J. D. Lewis-Williams, *The rock art of southern Africa* (Cambridge: Cambridge University Press, 1983), p. 15.

178 *Ibid.*, p. 16.

179 C. Garth Sampson, 'Veld damage in the Karoo caused by its pre-trekboer inhabitants', p. 39.

180 Lewis-Williams, 'The economic and social context of southern San rock art', p. 436.

181 Anthropologist Elizabeth Cashdan has demonstrated that among the Kalahari San the permeability of territorial boundaries varies with the nature of the resource base. See E. Cashdan, 'Territoriality among human foragers: ecological models and an application to four Bushman groups', *Current Anthropology* 24 (1983).

182 Lewis-Williams, *Rock art of Southern Africa*, p. 16.

183 Godée Molsbergen (ed.), *Reizen*, vol. III, p. 327.

184 Report of Field-Corporal Adriaan van Jaarsveld, Sneeuwberg, 4 September 1775, in Moodie (ed.), *The record*, part III, p. 45. See also 1/STB 10/162, Hendrik Meintjies van den Berg to Landdrost, 11 April 1776.

185 Cullinan, 'Travel journals of Robert Jacob Gordon', First Journey, 13 November 1777, p. 38. Dawid Schalk van der Merwe was the elder brother of Carel and lived at De Kust on a tributary of the upper Sundays River, not far from J. J. de Beer's farm De Vreede.

186 Cullinan, 'Travel Journals of Robert Jacob Gordon', First Journey, 13 November 1777, p. 38. Many of the families recently settled in the Camdeboo had

indeed come from further west, in the Roggeveld or Nuweveld.

187 *Ibid.*, p. 39.
188 Marks, 'Khoisan resistance', pp. 57–8.

5   STRONG THINGS

1 W. H. I. Bleek, 'Remarks on Orpen's "Mythology of the Maluti Bushmen"', *Cape Monthly Magazine* 9 (1874), 10–13 (cited in J. D. Lewis-Williams, *Believing and seeing: symbolic meanings in southern San rock paintings* (London: Academic Press, 1981) p. 7).

2 Lewis-Williams, *Believing and seeing*, pp. 4–5; T. Manhire, J. Parkington and Royden Yates, *Pictures from the past: a history of the interpretation of rock paintings and engravings from southern Africa* (Pietermaritzburg: Centaur Publications, 1990), p. 21.

3 Patricia Vinnicombe, *People of the eland: rock paintings of the Drakensberg Bushmen as a reflection of their life and thought* (Pietermaritzburg: University of Natal Press, 1976), p. 349.

4 *Ibid.*, pp. 347–9.

5 *Ibid.*, pp. 353.

6 *Ibid.*, pp. 350–3.

7 See above, p. 89.

8 See, for example, *Rock art*; *Discovering southern African rock art* (Cape Town: David Philip, 1990) and, with T. Dowson, *Images of power: understanding Bushman rock art* (Johannesburg: Southern Book Publishers, 1989).

9 Lewis-Williams, *Rock art*, p. 12.

10 Lewis-Williams, 'The economic and social context of southern San rock art', p. 431; 'Reply', *Current Anthropology* 23 (1982), 446–7; *Believing and seeing*, pp. 75, 100; 'Ideological continuities in prehistoric southern Africa', in C. Schrire (ed.), *Past and present in hunter-gatherer studies* (New York: Academic Press, 1984), pp. 225–52.

11 See, for example, R Yates, J. Golson and M. Hall, 'Trance performance: the rock art of Boontjeskloof and Sevilla', *South African Archaeological Bulletin* 40 (1985), 70–80, and T. N. Huffman, 'The trance hypothesis and the rock art of Zimbabwe', in *New approaches to southern African rock art*, The South African Archaeological Society Goodwin Series 4, 1983, pp. 49–53.

12 Lewis-Williams, *Rock art*, pp. 12, 14, 54; 'Economic and social context', pp. 431, 436 and 'Reply', *Current Anthropology* 24 (1983), 541–2.

13 Royden Yates, Anthony Manhire and John Parkington, 'Rock painting and history in the south-western Cape', in T. A. Dowson and D. Lewis-Williams (eds.), *Contested images: diversity in Southern African rock art research* (Johannesburg: Witwatersrand University Press, 1994), pp. 29–60.

14 Pieter Jolly, 'Melikane and Upper Mangolong revisited: the possible effects on San art of symbiotic contact between south-eastern San and Southern Sotho and Nguni communities', *South African Archaeological Bulletin* 50 (1995), 68–80.

15 See, for example, Mathias Guenther, 'The relationship of Bushman art to ritual and folklore', in Dowson and Lewis-Williams, *Contested images*, pp. 257–69

and Megan Biesele, *Women like meat: the folklore and foraging ideology of the Kalahari Ju/'hoan* (Johannesburg: Witwatersrand University Press, 1993), chapter 4.

16 David Lewis-Williams and Thomas Dowson, 'Aspects of rock art research: a critical perspective', in Dowson and Lewis-Williams (eds.), *Contested images*, pp. 201–21.

17 Richard Katz, *Boiling energy: community healing among the Kalahari Kung* (Cambridge, Mass.: Harvard University Press, 1982), p. 28.

18 *Ibid.*, p. 35.

19 For further explanation of the expression 'strong things', see Lewis-Williams, *Believing and seeing*, p. 77.

20 *Ibid.*, pp. 84, 123.

21 *Ibid.*, pp. 89–100.

22 *Ibid.*, p. 104.

23 Katz, *Boiling energy*, p. 31.

24 Compare A. R. Radcliffe-Brown, *Structure and function in primitive society: essays and addresses* (London: Cohen and West, 1952), cited in Vinnicombe, *People of the eland*, p. 349.

25 Sparrman, *A voyage to the Cape of Good Hope*, vol. II, p. 202.

26 Patricia Vinnicombe, 'Rock art, territory and land rights', in M Biesele, R. Gordon and R. Lee (eds.), *The past and future of !Kung ethnography: critical reflections and symbolic perspectives: essays in honour of Lorna Marshall* (Hamburg: Helmut Buske Verlag, 1986), p. 285.

27 *Ibid.*, p. 287.

28 Lewis-Williams, *Believing and seeing*, p. 88.

29 Mathias Guenther, *The Nharo Bushmen of Botswana: tradition and change* (Hamburg: Helmut Buske Verlag, 1986), pp. 227, 238.

30 See Lewis-Williams, *Believing and seeing*, pp. 95–7.

31 *Ibid.*, p. 238.

32 Lewis-Williams, 'Reply', *Current Anthropology* 23 (1982), 447.

33 Vinnicombe, 'Rock art, territory and land rights', p. 283.

34 T. Arbousset, *Narrative of an exploratory tour of the North-East of the Cape of Good Hope* (Cape Town: Robertson, 1846), p. 253, cited in Lewis-Williams, *Believing and seeing*, p. 124.

35 Lewis-Williams, *Believing and seeing*, pp. 124–6.

36 W. H. I. Bleek and L. C. Lloyd, *Specimens of Bushman folklore* (London: George Allen, 1911), pp. 365–71; Katz, *Boiling energy*, pp. 29, 40–1.

37 See Peter Carstens (ed.), *The social organisation of the Nama and other essays by Winifred Hoernlé* (Johannesburg: Witwatersrand University Press, 1985), p. 80.

38 Janette Deacon, 'The power of a place in understanding southern San rock engravings', *World Archaeology* 20 (1988), 129–40.

39 Janette Deacon, 'Rock engravings and the folklore of Bleek and Lloyd's /Xam San informants', in Dowson and Lewis-Williams (eds.), *Contested images*, pp. 253, 256.

40 Guenther, *The Nharo Bushmen of Botswana*, pp. 228–9 and Deacon, 'The power of place', p. 138.

41 Northern Lands Council Appeal to Govt of Australia, 22 February 1985, cited

in Vinnicombe, 'Rock art, territory and land rights', p. 290.
42 See above, chapter 3.
43 Cullinan, 'The travel journals of Robert Jacob Gordon', First Journey, 15 November 1777, p. 39. It is difficult to determine Gordon's route through the mountains with certainty (compare Forbes, *Pioneer travellers*, pp. 100–1), but from his description of the topography, it would seem that he chose the passage east of the Meiringsberg, following the Elandskloof River northwards. If so, the Willem Burgers to whom he refers (and whose farm is marked on his map as belonging to Barend Burgers) was probably Barend Jacobus Burgers, Schalkzoon, who had registered the loan-farm 'Verregelegen, leggende op de Sneeuwberg' in 1771. (See RLR 21/2 and South Africa 1 : 250,000 Topographical Sheet no. 3124.) Stephanus Christiaan Smit had been granted 'De Driefonteijnen gelegen aan de Kraanvogels Valleij op de Sneeuwberg' in 1772 (RLR 22/1).
44 Cullinan, 'Travel journals of Robert Jacob Gordon', First Journey, 14 November 1777, p. 39.
45 See Barrow, *Travels*, vol. II, p. 122 and Lichtenstein, *Travels*, vol. II, p. 6, where it is noted that few farmers in the Sneeuberge had fewer than 3,000 sheep.
46 J 210, *Opgaafrollen*, 1777. Tjaard van der Walt and Barend Jacobus Burgers, Schalkzoon each held two registered loan-farms in 1777 (RLR 21/2 and 22/1).
47 Cf. Worden, *Slavery*, p. 24 and Van Duin and Ross, 'The economy of the Cape Colony in the eighteenth century', pp. 21, 59.
48 Parkington, Yates, Manhire and Halkett, 'The social impact of pastoralism', p. 325.
49 Janette Deacon, personal communication, 23 February 1989. Garth Sampson, however, has found that the herder incursion into the Zeekoe Valley between 850 and 900 AD 'seems to coincide with a grass-drop episode registered in the dassie-pollen record' (personal communication, 14 January 1989).
50 Sparrman, *Voyage to the Cape of Good Hope*, vol. I, p. 238.
51 *Ibid.*, p. 238.
52 1/SWM 1/1, Memorandum dated 26 October 1757, presented to a combined meeting of Landdrost, Heemraden and Krijgsraad, 25 January 1758.
53 C 1266, Landdrost, Heemraden and Krijgsraad of Stellenbosch to Governor, 7 May 1776. See also Blommaert and Wiid (eds.), *Die Joernaal van Dirk Gysbert van Reenen, 1803*, p. 71, and this volume, p. 52.
54 See, for example, William Cronon's perceptive examination of European attitudes to Indian lifestyles in *Changes in the land: Indians, colonists, and the ecology of New England* (New York: Hill and Wang, 1983).
55 Sparrman, *A voyage to the Cape of Good Hope*, vol. I, p. 239.
56 Cronon, *Changes in the land*, p. 80.
57 Schapera, *The Khoisan peoples of South Africa*.
58 Loan-farms could not be subdivided, however, nor leased to third parties. See Guelke, 'Land tenure and settlement at the Cape'.
59 The reader will find a full discussion of the role of market forces in the frontier economy in chapter 8.
60 Among the more common arrangements were the *bijwoner* system, which allowed landless burghers to live on land owned by wealthier people, in return for assistance with a wide range of tasks, including defence, and the *aanteelt*

system, in terms of which one man would pasture another's livestock, in exchange for half the increase. Quite often, a simple cash payment was made for the hire of grazing land. (See MOOC 13/1/2, no. 13 (1782), Estate of Frans Kruger d'oude; MOOC 13/1/21, no. 40, Estate of Laurens Erasmus, Laurenszoon; MOOC 13/1/19, no. 4 (1792), Estate of Sara Johanna Wiese and Adriaan van Zijl; MOOC 13/1/31, no. 56 (1807), Estate of Hendrik Johannes Louw, Jacobuszoon; C 994, Landdrost and Heemraden to Governor, 19 December 1791; MOOC 13/1/29, no. 5, Estate of Catharina Vermeulen and Mattheus Johannes van der Westhuizen; MOOC 13/1/25, no. 24 (1800), Estate of Willem van Wijk, Willemzoon; A 447, 'Journal eener landtogt', 1 November 1776; J 115, Opgaafrollen, 1798 and J 118, Opgaafrollen, 1800.) Sharing of pasture without payment of rent took place in the trekvelden, the winter grazing lands used by the inhabitants of the Roggeveld and Sneeuberge. Even here, however, each farmer or group of farmers would have a designated legplaats, to which they returned each year. (CO 2580, Letters received from Swellendam and Graaff Reinet, Stockenstrom to Colonial Secretary, 10 July 1811. See also Penn, 'Northern Cape frontier zone', p. 172.)

61 Lichtenstein, Travels, vol. I, p. 26 and vol. II, p. 83; CO 2580, Andries Stockenstrom to Colonial Secretary, 20 September 1810; 1/SWM 1/1, 24 October 1755.

62 Penn, 'Northern Cape frontier zone', p. 175.

63 Guelke, 'Land tenure', p. 25.

64 See, for example, Lichtenstein, Travels, vol. I, p. 116; 1/SWM 3/10, Criminal interrogatories, Statement of Julij van Balij, 16 February 1753; CJ 361, Documents in criminal cases, no. 9 (1753); 1/GR 3/16 Criminal interrogatories, Testimony of Nicolaas Moras, 30 October 1790; 1/GR 1/1, 2 May 1787; 1/GR 16/1, Letters despatched, Landdrost to Dawid de Beer, Zwarteberg, 2 June 1774 and 1/GR 13/2, Letters received, Abraham Paulus van den Berg to Landdrost, 11 December 1799.

65 For references to overstocking, see Blommaert and Wiid (eds.), Joernaal, p. 71 and 1/GR 1/4, 5 August 1805.

66 Guelke, 'Land tenure', pp. 12–13, 25.

67 Vinnicombe, 'Rock art, territory and land rights', p. 287.

68 Cullinan, 'Travel journals of Robert Jacob Gordon', First Journey, 9 November 1977, p. 30 (see also ibid., p. 25); CO 2559, Letters received from Uitenhage, Cuyler to Colonial Secretary, 16 May 1806; Mentzel, Geographical and topographical description, part III, p. 114.

69 Thunberg, Travels, p. 94.

70 Ibid.

71 Ibid., Sparrman, Voyage to the Cape of Good Hope, vol. II, p. 58. Velschoenen were soft shoes made of treated animal skin. See P. Lubbe, The story of the velskoen (Grahamstown: Leather Industries Research Institute, 1971).

72 Yates, Parkington and Manhire, Pictures from the past, p. 43.

73 V. C. Malherbe, 'Diversification and mobility of Khoikhoi labour in the eastern districts of the Cape Colony prior to the labour law of 1 November 1809', unpublished MA thesis, University of Cape Town (1978), p. 54.

74 Thunberg, Travels, p. 217; VC 592, p. 49; Lichtenstein, Travels, vol. I, p. 122; Mentzel, Geographical and topographical description, part III, p. 202.

75 See chapter 8.

76 Mentzel, *Geographical and topographical description*, part III, pp. 127–8. Neumark believes that the official price of 16 stuivers per pound for first-grade ivory and 8 stuivers per pound for the smaller tusks allowed elephant hunters a fair margin of profit (Neumark, *Economic influences on the South African frontier*, pp. 65–6).

77 Thunberg, *Travels*, p. 141.

78 *Ibid.*, p. 228; Sparrman, *Voyage to the Cape of Good Hope*, vol. I, pp. 270–1, 296, 317; VC 595, p. 87.

79 Mentzel, *Geographical and topographical description*, part III, p. 128.

80 *Ibid.*, p. 127; 1/SWM 1/1, 1 May 1753.

81 Sparrman, *Voyage to the Cape of Good Hope*, vol. I, p. 316; 1/SWM 1/1, 1 May 1753; CJ 362, *Eijsch ende Conclusie*, 11 February 1751; 1/SWM 3/10, p. 75, Statement of the Hottentots Diederik and Pieter.

82 A 447, 'Journal eener landtogt', October 1776; 1/SWM 3/14, Criminal interrogatories, Statement of the Hottentot Piet, 17 January 1778; Sparrman, *Voyage to the Cape of Good Hope*, vol. I, p. 303, vol. II, pp. 113–14, 123. One of the earliest colonial elephant hunting expeditions to venture into Xhosa territory was that led by Hermanus Hubner, who was killed by Xhosa in 1736, somewhere near present-day Butterworth (see Peires, *House of Phalo*, chapter 4, note 4).

83 Thunberg, *Travels*, p. 207.

84 Sparrman, *Voyage to the Cape of Good Hope*, vol. I, pp. 253, 289; Thunberg, *Travels*, pp. 278, 303.

85 Mentzel, *Description*, part III, p. 126.

86 Thunberg, *Travels*, p. 197. See also Sparrman, *Voyage to the Cape of Good Hope*, vol. II, p. 60 and 1/SWM 1/1, 1 May 1753.

87 Lichtenstein, *Travels*, vol. I, p. 120. Lewis-Williams notes that 'a full-grown eland can weigh up to 1200 lbs' (*Rock art*, p. 44).

88 Cullinan, 'Travels of Robert Jacob Gordon', First Journey, November 1777, pp. 41–55.

89 Nicolas Denys, *The description and natural history of the coasts of North America*, ed. William F. Ganong (Toronto: Champlain Society Publications, 1908), p. 426, cited in Cronon, *Changes in the land*, p. 98.

90 See Mentzel, *Geographical and topographical description*, part III, pp. 338–40, for a description of Khoekhoe methods of elephant hunting.

91 Lichtenstein, *Travels*, vol. I, pp. 121–2.

92 Sparrman, *Voyage to the Cape of Good Hope*, vol. I, pp. 287–8.

93 See p. 90. Also see p. 72 and Sparrman, *Voyage to the Cape of Good Hope*, vol. II, p. 113, for further evidence of co-operation between colonists and San on the Escarpment.

94 Report of Field-Corporal Adriaan van Jaarsveld, Sneeuwberg, 4 September 1775, in Moodie (ed.), *The record*, part III, p. 44.

6   'THE FRENZY OF THE HEATHEN'

1 A. P. Burgers to D. S. van der Merwe, 30 December 1776, in Moodie (ed.), *The record*, part III, p. 62.

2 1/GR 1/1, Heemraden to Governor, 12 July 1791; Landdrost and Heemraden to Governor, 21 December 1791.

3 VC 871, Donald Moodie's manuscript notes, vol. VIII, Proposals of J. G. van Reenen with respect to the Bushmen, 25 August 1791.

4 See, for example, the letters in the series 1/STB 13/13 and 1/GR 12/2, Reports of *veldwagtmeesters.*

5 C 1300, Memorials and reports, The burghers of Camdeboo to Landdrost Woeke, 1 February 1788.

6 Journal of Governor van Plettenberg, 30 September 1778, in Godée Molsbergen (ed.), *Reizen,* vol. II, pp. 75–6.

7 Report of Field-Sergeant C. Kruger, 12 March 1778, in Moodie (ed.), *The record,* part III, p. 74.

8 General Report of Field-Sergeant D. S. van der Merwe, 13 March 1777, in Moodie (ed.), *The record,* part III, p. 62.

9 1/GR 1/1, March 1791, p. 158.

10 1/GR 1/1, A. van Jaarsveld to Governor, 12 July 1791, enclosed with minutes of Board of Landdrost and Heemraden.

11 1/GR 12/2, Alewijn Jacobus Forster to Landdrost, 2 February 1787.

12 1/GR 12/2, A. C. Grijling to Veldwagtmeester Nicolaas Smit, 14 April 1786.

13 Journal of Van Plettenberg, in Godée Molsbergen (ed.), *Reizen,* vol. II, p. 76.

14 C 1300, Enclosure in Woeke to Governor, 5 January 1789.

15 1/STB 13/13.

16 1/GR 1/1. Adriaan van Jaarsveld and Heemraden to Governor, 12 July 1791.

17 C 492, Incoming letters, Landdrost Horak of Swellendam to Governor, 20 May 1755.

18 CJ 403, Case no 13: testimony of the Hottentot Jas, 27 July 1772; testimony of Nicolaas Claassen; confession of the Bastaard Hottentot Thys, 31 July 1772.

19 Extract of the Journal, Colonial Office, 31 December 1772, in Moodie (ed.), *The record,* part III, p. 17. For a full account of these events, see Penn, 'Northern Cape frontier zone', pp. 197–210.

20 1/STB 10/162, Veldwagtmeester Gerrit Maritz of Middelste Roggeveld and 30 landholders to Landdrost, 3 March 1787.

21 C 1266, A. van Jaarsveld to G. R. Opperman, Sneeuwberg, 17 March 1776.

22 Letter from Commandant Opperman to the Landdrost of Stellenbosch, 17 May 1776, in Moodie (ed.), *The record,* part III, p. 58.

23 See 'Report of Field-Sergeant Carel van der Merwe to the Landdrost of Stellenbosch', 3 September 1779, in Moodie (ed.), *The record,* part III, p. 82.

24 Collins, 'Report on the Bosjesmen', in Moodie (ed.), *The record,* part V, p. 33.

25 1/GR 16/1, Woeke to Governor, 5 January 1789.

26 C 1300, Enclosure in Woeke to Governor, 2 February 1789.

27 1/GR 12/1, p. 30. (Document damaged, date and signature missing.)

28 1/GR 12/1, unsigned and undated.

29 See Newton-King and Malherbe, *The Khoikhoi rebellion,* pp. 19, 25, 26.

30 See CO 2564, Letters received from Graaff Reinet, Andries Stockenstrom to Caledon, 5 August 1808.

31 See p. 60 and A. B. Smith, 'The Ju/wasi of Namibia in transition', in *Newsletter of the Centre for African Studies, University of Cape Town* 4 (1988).

32 c 1266, G. R. Opperman to Governor, 17 March 1776. Opperman was among many who referred to the colonists as '*de duijtse*' – one wonders whether this is just a colloquialism, or whether it refers specifically to the German origin of so many Graaff Reinet settlers. (See chapter 2.)

33 See for example 1/stb 13/13, 6 June 1783; 1/gr 12/1, January 1790; 1/gr 1/1, Minutes, p. 158, 12 July 1791.

34 1/stb 13/43, Commando papers, Andries Petrus Burgers to Landdrost, 4 September 1785.

35 c 1300, M. H. O. Woeke to Governor, 5 January 1789.

36 See mooc 13/1/13, no. 2 (1785); 1/gr 1/1, 4 December 1786; mooc 10/15, *Vendurol* of Jacoba van der Merwe (1787); mooc 13/1/15, no. 24 (1787).

37 Report of Field-Sergeant Carel van der Merwe to the Landdrost of Stellenbosch, 3 September 1779, in Moodie (ed.), *The record*, part iii, p. 82.

38 1/gr 12/2, D. S. van der Merwe to Nicolaas Smit, 16 May 1786. (Grijling had requested an armed man to help him guard his place.)

39 '. . . we have to pay 180 rix dollars for a waggon these days', complained the burghers of De Bruins Hoogte in 1781. (1/stb 13/13, Memorial addressed to 'Adriaan van Jaarsveld, Lieutenant Commandant van het Oostleggende velt', by the burghers of De Bruins Hoogte, 28 September 1781.

40 1/gr 12/2, J. H. Bakemeyer to Field-Corporal Cornelius Botma, 2 April 1786.

41 General report of Field-Sergeant D. S. van der Merwe, 13 March 1777, in Moodie (ed.), *The record*, part iii, p. 63.

42 1/gr 16/1, Petition from the inhabitants of Graaff Reinet to Landdrost Woeke, 1 February 1788.

43 c 1300, M. H. O. Woeke to Governor, 5 January 1789.

44 Report of Field-Sergeant Carel van der Merwe to the Landdrost of Stellenbosch, 3 September 1779, in Moodie (ed.), *The record*, part iii, p. 82.

45 Report of Field-Sergeant D. S. van der Merwe, 5 January 1780, in Moodie (ed.), *The record*, part iii, p. 102.

46 Letter from Field-Corporal Albertus van Jaarsveld to the Landdrost of Stellenbosch, 15 November 1779, in Moodie (ed.), *The record*, part iii, p. 86; see also p. 86, note 1.

47 Adriaan van Jaarsveld to G. R. Opperman, 20 June 1774, in Moodie (ed.), *The record*, part iii, pp. 65–6, supplementary papers.

48 c 1266, G. R. Opperman to Governor, 17 March 1776; Report of Field-Sergeant Joshua Joubert to the Landdrost and Militia Court, Stellenbosch, 29 September 1779, in Moodie (ed.), *The record*, part iii, p. 86.

49 c 1266, G. R. Opperman to Governor, 13 April 1776 and 17 March 1776; G. R. Opperman to Landdrost of Stellenbosch, 17 May 1776, in Moodie (ed.), *The record*, part iii, p. 57; c 565, Incoming letters, Woeke to Governor, 9 May 1787.

50 vc 871, vol. viii, Proposals of J. G. van Reenen with respect to the Bushmen, 25 August 1791.

51 1/gr 12/2, Johannes Ludovicus Pretorius to Landdrost, 28 June 1786.

52 Letter from Adriaan van Jaarsveld to the Landdrost and Militia Officers, Stellenbosch, in Moodie (ed.), *The record*, part iii, p. 65. See also Collins, 'Report on the Bosjesmen', in Moodie (ed.), *The record*, part v, p. 33 and Godée Molsbergen (ed.), *Reizen*, vol. ii, pp. 75–6.

53 A 447, 'Journal eener landtogt', 11 October 1776.
54 Godée Molsbergen (ed.), *Reizen*, vol. II, p. 76.
55 *Ibid.*, vol. IV, pp. 39–40.
56 Report of Field-Sergeant Carel van der Merwe to the Landdrost of Stellenbosch, 3 September 1779; Godée Molsbergen (ed.), *Reizen*, vol. IV, pp. 39–40.
57 K. Wyndham-Smith, *From frontier to Midlands: a history of the Graaff Reinet district, 1786–1910* (Grahamstown: Institute of Social and Economic Research, Rhodes University, 1976), p. 17.
58 H. J. Deacon, *Where hunters gathered*, p. 171.
59 See, for example, C 563, Woeke to Governor, 4 November 1786; C 473, Woeke to Governor, 10 November 1790; 1/GR 1/1, 1 November 1790; 1/GR 1/1, Adriaan van Jaarsveld and Heemraden to Governor, 12 July 1791; Wagenaar, 'Johannes Gysbertus van Reenen', p. 113.
60 Public Record Office, London, WO 1/324, Craig to Dundas, 18 December 1795, enclosure no 4.
61 See C 565, Woeke to Governor, 9 May 1787; C 1300, Woeke to Governor, 5 January 1789; 1/GR 1/1, Adriaan van Jaarsveld and Heemraden to Governor, 12 July 1791.
62 WO 1/324, Craig to Dundas, 18 December 1795, enclosure no 9.
63 See C 157, Resolutions, 1 February 1779, pp. 82–3, cited in Wagenaar, 'Johannes Gysbertus van Reenen', p. 42. For a full discussion of the components of the Company's demand for meat, see *ibid.*, pp. 43–4.
64 *Ibid.*, pp. 37–42. In the two-year period May 1779–April 1781 the Company consumed 900,000 lb of fresh meat and 2,500 live sheep each year. By 1790 the quantity of fresh meat consumed by the Company had risen to 1,100,000 lb per annum (*ibid.*, pp. 44, 81).
65 *Ibid.*, pp. 49–54.
66 *Ibid.*, pp. 54–5.
67 *Ibid.*, pp. 51–2, 84. Wagenaar estimates that by the 1790s more than 1,000 Company employees bought their meat from the private butchers, instead of receiving Company rations.
68 *Ibid.*, p. 93. Wagenaar's thesis contains a full account of the business dealings of Jacobus van Reenen and his sons.
69 VC 871, vol. VIII, Proposals of J. G. van Reenen with respect to the Bushmen, 25 August 1791.
70 *Ibid.*
71 *Ibid.* See also Wagenaar, 'Johannes Gysbertus van Reenen', pp. 78–9, 98.
72 VC 871, Proposals of J. G. van Reenen, 25 August 1791.
73 C 213, 12 February 1793, p. 785. The Veldwagtmeester Diederik Hatting reported that 11,000 sheep and 253 cattle had been taken, but Van Reenen's *knechten* gave the figures cited here (see Wagenaar, 'Johannes Gysbertus van Reenen', p. 107, note 72).
74 C 213, 12 February 1793; C 1017, Annexures to incoming letters, Nicolaas Smit to Maynier, 31 August 1792.
75 C 1017, J. P. van der Walt to Rhenius, 23 November 1792.
76 C 1017, Nicolaas Smit to Maynier, 31 August 1792; J. P. van der Walt to Rhenius, 23 November 1792.

77 Wagenaar, 'Johannes Gysbertus van Reenen', pp. 107, 113–14.
78 Böeseken, 'Die Nederlandse kommissarisse', pp. 84–7.
79 vc 871, vol. viii, proposals of J. G. van Reenen with respect to the Bushmen, 25 August 1791.
80 Fernand Braudel, *Civilisation and capitalism, 15th–18th century*, 3 vols. (London: Collins, 1984; Fontana, 1985), vol. iii, *The perspective of the world*, pp. 227–32.
81 Van Reenen's scheme would have cost the Company an estimated 23,900 rix dollars. In 1776 a similar scheme had been proposed by the retired Lieutenant of the Cape District, N. Laubscher, but it had likewise foundered for lack of funds (Moodie (ed.), *The record*, part iii, p. 59).
82 Böeseken, 'Nederlandse kommissarisse', p. 84.
83 c 697, Report with annexures, Nederburgh en Frijkenius, *Verslag van Commissarissen-Generaal*, part 3, p. 120, 24 July 1793.
84 Böeseken, 'Nederlandse kommissarisse', p. 87. The premiums were fixed at 15 rix dollars for full-grown Bushmen and 10 rix dollars for children under 7 years.
85 See pp. 39–40.

7   THE ENEMY WITHIN

1 The new district was named for Governor Cornelis Jacobus van de Graaff (Governor of the Cape from 1784 to 1791) and his wife Reinet.
2 Nigel Penn's doctoral thesis was not available to me when this chapter was written. His findings with respect to the nature of master–servant relations on the north-west frontier largely accord with mine, though we might disagree about the approximation of these relations to slavery. See Penn, 'Northern Cape frontier zone', chapter 7.
3 According to the instructions issued to Godlieb Rudolph Opperman in 1774 and again to Adriaan van Jaarsveld, Commandant of the Eastern Country in 1780, the prisoners were to be divided among the members of the commando 'to serve for their subsistence for a fair term of years, according to the prisoner's age'; or, failing this, they were to be divided among the other inhabitants, 'always preferring those who are the poorest' (Moodie (ed.), *The record*, part iii, pp. 29, 101). In practice, however, prisoners were nearly always allocated among the members of a commando before it disbanded.
4 Best translated as 'apprentices' or 'indentured servants'.
5 See 1/GR 15/43, Lijst van de Ingeboekte Hottentotten beginnende met de maand December 1786; Aantekening der Ingeboekten Hottentotten, beginnende van Primo September 1795 tot 1799; Register van zodanige Hottentotten die als huisboorlingen gehouden zijn, hunne hieronder gespecifeerde meesters den tijd van 25 jaaren te dienen.
6 *Ibid.*
7 This figure is based upon data culled from the reports of Veldcommandant Opperman and the *veldwagtmeesters* within his jurisdiction, as published in Moodie (ed.), *The record*, part iii and preserved in the archival series 1/STB

10/163, 13/13 and 13/43. Whereas reports compiled in the 1770s regularly list the number of 'Bushmen' killed and captured, those compiled in the early 1780s seldom do so.

8 Wyndham-Smith, *From frontier to Midlands*, p. 17.

9 See note 5 above.

10 See, for example, CJ 362, pp. 148–9; 1/GR 3/16, 1786–92: Statement of the female Hottentot Hester, 25 November 1791; Statement of the Hottentot Captain Ruijter Platje, November 1791; Statement of Theunis Botha Jacobzoon, 7 November 1792; Statement of Christiaan Kok, 29 December 1792. See also Sparrman, *Voyage to the Cape of Good Hope*, vol. I, pp. 198–9.

11 The figures for 1798 can be found in J 115 and those for 1800 in J 118.

12 In 1787 there were 470 slaves in the district of Graaff Reinet; by 1791 there were 672 and in 1796 there were 579. See Graaff Reinet *Opgaafrollen*: J 107 (1787), J 108 (1788) and J 113 (1796).

13 1/GR 15/43, Lijst van de Ingeboekte Hottentotten.

14 Martin Klein, 'The Atlantic slave trade and the development of slavery within West Africa', unpublished paper presented to the South African and contemporary history seminar, University of the Western Cape, July 1996, p. 8.

15 I could find no record of such rules in the *Kaapse Plakaatboeke, 1652–1795*, edited by K. A. Jeffreys and S. D. Naudé, 6 vols. (Cape Town: Government Printer, 1944, 1948, 1949, 1950 and 1951).

16 John Philip, *Researches in South Africa: illustrating the civil, moral, and religious condition of the native tribes*, 2 vols. (London: James Duncan, 1828, reprinted New York: Negro Universities Press, 1969), vol. I, p. 180.

17 1/STB 10/162, January 1775.

18 See for example 1/GR 12/1, Statement of D du Toit.

19 Report of Commandant Opperman, 1 May 1775, in Moodie (ed.), *The record*, part III, p 67, supplementary papers.

20 See Trapido, 'Reflections on land, office and wealth', pp. 351–2. Legassick does not specifically refer to slave-raiding, but stresses the general economic functions of the commando (Martin Legassick, 'The northern frontier to c. 1840: the rise and decline of the Griqua people', in R. Elphick and H. Giliomee (eds.), *The shaping of South African society, 1652–1840*, second edition (Cape Town: Maskew Miller Longman, 1989), p. 361). More recently, several contributors to *Slavery in South Africa: captive labour on the Dutch frontier* (Pietermaritzburg: University of Natal Press, 1994), a collection of essays edited by Elizabeth Eldredge and Fred Morton, have reinforced the idea of the commando as a slave-raiding machine (see especially pp. 114–21 and 261). This may well have been true for the period of which they write (the nineteenth century).

21 See, for example, CJ 362, *Duplicq* of Jacobus Botha Jacobuszoon, 28 October 1751, pp. 148–9.

22 That is, hired Hottentots.

23 Sparrman, *Voyage to the Cape of Good Hope*, vol. I, pp. 198–9.

24 CJ 362, Trial of Jacobus Botha Jacobuszoon, Statement of the Hottentot Ruijter, 30 December 1750.

25 See p. 104.

26 See, for example, Instructions . . . to . . . the newly appointed Field-Comman-

dant Godlieb Rudolph Opperman . . . 19 April 1774; Extract of records of the Landdrost and Militia Officers, Stellenbosch, 5 March 1776; Extract from resolution of Council, 5 June 1777; Instructions for the Commandant of the Eastern Country, 5 December 1780, in Moodie (ed.), *The record*, part III, pp. 29, 52–3, 71, 101.

27 Instructions . . . to . . . the newly appointed Field-Commandant Godlieb Rudolph Opperman, 19 April 1774; Instructions for the Commandant of the Eastern Country, 5 December 1780, in Moodie (ed.), *The record*, part III, pp. 29, 101; Böeseken, 'Die Nederlandse kommissarisse', pp. 84–5.

28 Ross, 'Changing legal position'. Similar considerations had induced the Carolina Proprietors to restrict the enslavement of Native Americans in the seventeenth century (see Peter Wood, *Black majority: negroes in colonial South Carolina from 1670 through the Stono rebellion* (New York: Norton Library, 1975), pp. 38–9).

29 Ross, 'Changing legal position', and Elphick, *Kraal and castle*, p. 102.

30 See p. 115.

31 c 221, *Resolutions*, 11 January 1794.

32 vc 68, Extract from minutes of Krijgsraad, 2 June 1795, pp. 132–7. See also 1/GR 1/1, 16 March 1795, pp. 300–5.

33 vc 68, Extract from minutes of Krijgsraad, 2 June 1795, pp. 132–7.

34 Instructions . . . to . . . the newly appointed Field-Commandant Godlieb Rudolph Opperman, 19 April 1774, in Moodie (ed.), *The record*, part III, p. 29.

35 Böeseken, 'Nederlandse kommissarisse', pp. 84–5.

36 1/GR 15/43, Register van zodanige Hottentotten die als huisboorlingen gehouden zijn, hunne hieronder gespecifeerde meesters den tijd van 25 jaaren te dienen.

37 GH 28/1, Landdrost of Graaff Reinet to Governor, 17 July 1807, enclosed in despatch no 11, Caledon to Colonial Secretary, 1807.

38 Stockenstrom to Mr Smit, 20 October 1815, cited in W. M. Macmillan, *The Cape colour question: a historical survey* (Cape Town: Balkema, 1968), p. 129.

39 1/STB 10/152, Letters received, 1798–9, Johannes Schalk Hugo to Landdrost van der Riet, 13 November 1798 For the relationship between Hugo and Jooste, see De Villiers and Pama, *Geslagsregisters*, vol. I, pp. 339, 368.

40 Patterson, *Slavery and social death*, p. 5.

41 *Ibid.*, p. 9.

42 Many eminent students of slavery would agree. Moses Finley, for example, is uncompromising on this point (see M. I. Finley, *Ancient slavery and modern ideology* (London: Chatto and Windus, 1980), pp. 73–5). Patterson, however, regards chattel status as a by-product of the more fundamental characteristic of slavery – natal alienation.

43 vc 882, Donald Moodie's manuscript notes, vol. XIX, 'Extracts from the records of the Military Court, Graaff Reinet, 2nd June 1795'.

44 Honoratus Christiaan David Maynier, christened at the Cape on 20 July 1760, son of Horatius Conrad Maynier of Leipzig; appointed to the secretaryship of Graaff Reinet in 1789 and to the magistracy in 1792. For a full account of the Graaff Reinet burgher rebellion see Marais, *Maynier*, chapter 7.

45 vc 871, vol. vIII. Complaints of 276 Boers of Graaff Reinet against Maynier, 16 April 1795.
46 *Ibid.*
47 vc 887, Donald Moodie's manuscript notes, vol. xxIv, p. 676.
48 Cited in Philip, *Researches*, vol. II, pp. 265–6.
49 Robin Blackburn, 'Slavery – its special features and social role', in Leonie Archer (ed.), *Slavery and other forms of unfree labour* (London: Routledge, 1988), p. 268.
50 Patterson, *Slavery and social death*, pp. 110 and 112.
51 *Ibid.*, p. 111.
52 *Ibid.*, pp. 36–46.
53 I am not arguing here that slaves who were true outsiders had no sense of dignity, merely that they had to fight against greater odds to achieve it. I think this is Patterson's meaning too. Indeed, he argues that the greater the sense of alienation, the greater the striving to overcome it.
54 Guenther, *Nharo Bushmen*, pp. 232–2.
55 'Libros de los coloquios de los doce', in Walter Lehmann, *Sterbende Gotter und Christliche Heilsbotschaft* (Stuttgart: 1949), p. 102, cited in Wachtel, *The vision of the vanquished*, p. 27. In the late 1960s, the farm Bushmen of Ghanzi in Botswana called themselves *k'amka kweni*, which means 'voiceless people' or 'rubbish people', and some of those attending services at the mission church had come to believe that indigenous myths and tales were just 'the lies of the old people' (Mathias Guenther, 'From "lords of the desert" to "rubbish people": the colonial and contemporary state of the Nharo of Botswana', in Pippa Skotnes (ed.), *Miscast: negotiating the presence of the Bushmen* (Cape Town: University of Cape Town Press, 1996), p. 236).
56 Le Vaillant, *New travels*, vol. II, p. 347.
57 Barrow, *Travels*, vol. II, pp. 110–11.
58 Blackburn, 'Slavery', p. 268.
59 The role of the free population, including those who did not own slaves, in maintaining a slave system is strongly emphasised by Patterson (*Slavery and social death*, pp. 36, 81–97, 99–100).
60 Unconquered natives living beyond the borders of foreign colonies might also be willing to harbour fugitives.
61 Richard Price (ed.), *Maroon societies: rebel slave communities in the Americas*, second edition (Baltimore: Johns Hopkins University Press, 1979), pp. 2–3.
62 See, for example, Godée Molsbergen (ed.), *Reizen*, vol. IV, p. 76.
63 See pp. 108 and 109.
64 Extract of the Journal, Colonial Office, 25 March 1773, in Moodie (ed.), *The record*, part III, p 17.
65 Report of Commandant R. G. Opperman, 10 April 1777, in Moodie (ed.), *The record*, part III, p. 68.
66 Report of Field-Sergeants H. M. van den Berg and Adriaan van Jaarsveld to the Landdrost and Militia Court, 11 September 1779, in Moodie (ed.), *The record*, part III, p. 85.
67 Report of Corporal Albertus van Jaarsveld to Sergeant D. S. van der Merwe, 24 November 1779, in Moodie (ed.), *The record*, part III, p. 87, note 1.

68 Robben Island.
69 Commandant A. van Jaarsveld's report of the expulsion of the Kafirs, 20 July 1781, in Moodie (ed.), *The record*, part III, p. 112.
70 Patterson, *Slavery and social death*, p. 111.
71 The phrase is borrowed from Robin Lane Fox, *Pagans and Christians in the Mediterranean world from the second century AD to the conversion of Constantine* (London: Penguin Books, 1986).
72 Sparrman, *Voyage to the Cape of Good Hope*, vol. I, p. 201.
73 1/GR 3/16, Statement of the Hottentot Piet, living with Johannes van der Wald; Statement of the Hottentot Jan Bries, 30 December 1788; Statement of the Hottentot Willem, 30 December 1788; Statement of the Hottentot Ruijter, 6 January 1789.
74 1/GR 3/16, Statement of the Hottentot Jan Bries, 30 December 1788.
75 1/GR 3/16, Order to whip wandering Hottentots, *c.* 1784.
76 1/GR 3/16, Statement of the Hottentot Jager, in service with the Heemraad Hendrik van der Walt Schalkzoon.
77 Sparrman, *Voyage to the Cape of Good Hope*, vol. I, p. 199.
78 The farm was called Jakkalsfontein and was situated '*agter de Groot Tafelberg*' (M3i Proceedings of the Circuit Court of Graaff Reinet, 1817).
79 *Ibid.* Report of the Field-Cornet Michiel Adriaan Oberholster, 3 February 1817.
80 *Ibid.* Statement of the Bastaard Hottentot Klaas, 19 April 1817.
81 See, for example, in connection with the whipping of Bushman servants: CJ 362, Statement of the soldier Jan Hendrik Klem *van 't Graafschap Lippe*, 10 December 1750, and 1/STB 10/150, Letter unsigned and undated, but *c.* 1800.
82 See, for example, CJ 3387, Circuit Court, Uitenhage, 1812, Testimony of the Bastaard Hottentot Jan Mager, 10 November 1812; Testimony of the slave September, 10 November 1812.
83 There is no mention of a Trina or Catharina de Klerk in the genealogical tables compiled by De Villiers and Pama; however it may be worth noting that the wife of Jacob de Klerk Jacobzoon (christened in April 1757) was a woman named Johanna Steenkamp, born in 1764, who in 1790 was accused of having brutally maltreated her female servants (see De Villiers and Pama, *Geslagsregisters*, vol. I, p. 397 and 1/GR 3/16).
84 University of Cape Town Manuscripts Collection, BC 151, LVIII-19, pp. 7657–70. I am indebted to Dr Janette Deacon for drawing my attention to this reference.
85 See pp. 60–1, 98.
86 Extract from Resolution of Council, 5 June 1777, in Moodie (ed.), *The record*, part III, p 71.
87 See p. 55.
88 CJ 362, Trial of Jacobus Botha Jacobuszoon, *Duplicq* of Jacobus Botha Jacobuszoon, 28 October 1751.
89 Unsigned paper appended to the journal of the commando under the orders of Gerrit van Wyk, 2 September 1774, in Moodie (ed.), *The record*, part III, p. 38, note 1.
90 Sparrman, *Voyage to the Cape of Good Hope*, vol. II, p. 34.

91 1/GR 3/16, Statement of the Hottentot Jacob, 10 January 1791.
92 1/GR 3/16, Statement of the Hottentot Truij, 30 November 1791; Statement of the burgher Jacobus Schalkwijk Gertzoon, 30 November 1791.
93 See pp. 106–7.
94 For evidence of the authorities' efforts to restrict Khoisan access to guns, see, for example, c 492, Landdrost Horak to Governor, 20 May 1755; Sparrman, *Voyage to the Cape of Good Hope*, vol. I, p. 228, note 20; 1/STB 10/162, Gerrit Maritz and 30 landholders to Landdrost, 3 March 1787.
95 c 1266, G. R. Opperman to Governor, 13 April 1776.
96 See p. 42. See also Van Arkel, Quispel and Ross, 'De wijngaard des heeren?' p. 40.
97 See pp. 121–2.
98 See pp. 117–18.
99 Worden, *Slavery*, pp. 54–5 and Table 5.3. Worden notes that in 1787, 37% of the slave population of Graaff Reinet was female.
100 1/GR 15/43.
101 Sparrman, *Voyage to the Cape of Good Hope*, vol. I, pp. 200–1; Barrow, *Travels*, vol. II, pp. 406–7; Philip, *Researches*, vol. I, chapter IX.
102 Philip, *Researches*, vol. I, pp. 185–8.
103 CJ 446, Statement of the Hottentot Sara, 12 June 1792, pp. 311–15.
104 CJ 446, *Ibid.* The other witnesses all denied that there had been a carnal connection between Feitje and Andries Jacobus de Beer.
105 CJ 446, Document in criminal cases, Statement of the Hottentot Leentje, 5 November 1792; 1/GR 3/16, Statement of the Hottentot Flink, 3 February 1789.
106 CJ 446, Statement of A. J. de Beer, 5 November 1792; Statement of the Hottentot Leentje, 5 November 1792. David de Beer, incidentally, was the son-in-law of Adriaan van Jaarsveld (De Villiers and Pama, *Geslagsregisters*, vol. I, pp. 32, 352). The De Beer family had moved after Johannes (Hans) Jurgen de Beer's death and now lived at the farm 'De Brakkefontijn', near present-day Aberdeen.
107 1/GR 3/16, Statement of the burgher Matthys Booyens, 26 January 1789. Orlando Patterson's comments on self-inflicted violence among slaves are pertinent here. See *Slavery and social death*, p. 12. There is also the magnificent novel *Beloved*, by American author Toni Morrison, which deals with a similar theme.
108 Marais, *Maynier*, pp. 76–7.
109 J. H. Fischer was Landdrost of Graaff Reinet from 1812 to 1815.
110 ACC 50 (3), Letters from James Read, Report of a meeting held at Philipston on 4 August 1834.
111 1/GR 3/16, Statement of Christiaan Rudolph Opperman, 18 July 1792. Christiaan Rudolph was the son of Godlieb Rudolph, who had led the General Commando of 1774.
112 1/GR 3/16, Statement of Godlieb Rudolph Opperman, 18 July 1792. For similar cases, see 1/GR 3/17, Statement of Johannes de Wit and Johan Hendrik Vos, 1 August 1788; 1/GR 1/2, 1 June 1795, and vc 887, vol. XVIII.
113 1/STB 20/30, Letters despatched, Landdrost to Veld-Cornet Jan Hugo, 29

March 1800. See also CJ 362, Trial of Jacobus Botha, *Eisch ende Conclusie* of Landdrost Horak (prosecuting); Ross, 'Changing legal position of the Khoisan', pp. 80–1.

114 1/GR 3/16, Statement of Johannes Nel Willemzoon, 15 December 1790.

115 *Ibid.*

116 1/GR 3/16, Statement of the Hottentot Willem Bruintjes, 20 January 1789.

117 See Ross, 'Changing legal position of the Khoisan', pp. 86 and Newton-King and Malherbe, *Khoikhoi rebellion*, pp. 30 and 32.

118 CJ 446, Statement of the Hottentot Leentje, 5 November 1792.

119 CJ 361, Case no. 5, Statement of the Hottentot Kieviet, 30 November 1752.

120 *Ibid.*, Statement of the burgher Hans Jurgen Gilbert, 28 October 1752; Statement of Francina Vosloo, 28 October 1752.

121 *Ibid.*, 'Eisch ende Conclusie' of Landdrost Horak, prosecutor; emphasis added.

122 Ross, 'Changing legal position of the Khoisan,' pp. 82–5; CJ 362, 'Eisch ende Conclusie' of Landdrost Horak, 11 February 1751.

123 Robert Ross, 'Changing legal position of the Khoisan', pp 84–5; 'The rule of law at the Cape of Good Hope in the eighteenth century', *The Journal of Imperial and Commonwealth History* 9 (1980), 6–9.

124 CJ 362, 'Eisch ende Conclusie' of Landdrost Horak, 11 February 1751.

125 1/GR 3/16, Statement of the Hottentot Jacob, 10 January 1791.

126 1/GR 3/18, no. 69, Statement of the Hottentot Draabok, 7 October 1794.

127 1/GR 3/18, Statement of Okkert Goosen, 7 October 1794.

128 1/GR 3/18, Statement of the Hottentot Draabok, 7 October 1794. Draabok's efforts were not entirely in vain, however: in June 1795 Goosen was summoned to appear before the Court of Justice in Cape Town, but his case was postponed to a later date and, as far as I can establish, was never tried. (CJ 77–80, Original rolls and minutes, 1795–8.)

129 Ross, 'Rule of law', p. 7 and Fiscal Denyssen to Sir John Cradock, 16 March 1813, 'Statement of the laws of the Colony of the Cape of Good Hope regarding slavery', in G. M. Theal (ed.), *Records of the Cape Colony from February 1793 to April 1831*, 36 vols. (London: Government Printers, 1897–1905), vol. IX, pp. 143–61.

130 Theal (ed.), *Records*, vol. IX, Article 9, p. 147.

131 *Ibid.*, Article 15, p. 148.

132 *Ibid.*, Articles 13 and 14, pp. 147–8.

133 *Ibid.*, Article 33, p. 152.

134 *Ibid.*, Article 30, p. 151.

135 See, for example, CJ 28, Original rolls and minutes, 3 November 1746.

136 CJ 28, 3 November 1746.

137 1/SWM 3/10, Statement of the soldier Hendrik Tessenaar, 10 September 1746.

138 1/SWM 3/10, Statement of Coert Cnoetse, 16 November 1746.

139 CJ 28, 3 November 1746.

140 CJ 483, 'Eisch ende Conclusie' of F. R. Bresler, Landdrost of Graaff Reinet, 28 May 1801.

141 Ross, 'Changing legal position of the Khoisan', pp. 80–1.

142 CJ 47, Original notes and minutes, 1765.

143 Nigel Penn, 'Anarchy and authority in the Koue Bokkeveld, 1739–1779: the banishing of Carel Buijtendag', *Kleio* 17 (1985).

144 For a discussion of the relationship between slavery, power and honour, see Patterson, *Slavery and social death*, chapter 3. One may note, *à propos* this issue, that when Hendrik Tessenaar had asked the burgher Coert Cnoetse to help him beat the Hottentot Stuurman, Cnoetse had replied: 'Hendrik, ik sal wel wijser weesen – jij weet wel dat ik een ander mans volk niet mag slaan' (1/swm 3/10, Statement of Coert Cnoetse, 16 November 1746).

145 1/stb 3/11, Statement of the Hottentot Coridon, 30 November 1763. Brits was also banished, though only for five years. His crime was committed at a time when the authorities in Graaff Reinet were endeavouring to pacify the rebellious Khoisan, and they may have wished to make an example of him, so as to convince the Khoisan of their good intentions.

146 See p. 137.

147 1/gr 3/16, Statement of the burgher Johannes Nel, Willemzoon, 15 December 1790, emphasis added. See also the statement of the burgher Andreas Hendrik Krugel, 5 January 1791, for a longer version of Kiewiet's declaration.

148 Denyssen to Cradock, 16 March 1813, in Theal (ed), *Records*, vol. ix, p. 150. Compare Patterson, *Slavery and social death*, p. 112.

149 Ruiter Platje was also known as Ruiter Beesje and as Benedictus (Newton-King and Malherbe, *Khoikhoi rebellion*, pp. 38, 62 (note 102), 70, 71, 73 (notes 26 and 27). He was a grandson of the Hoengeyqua Captain Ruiter, but by the end of the century he was usually referred to in the records as Gonaqua. Until 1791, when he moved onto the farm of Coenraad de Buys, he had lived 'on a certain stretch of veld next to the Bushman River', that is, close to his grandfather's former territory. (1/gr 3/16, Statement of the Hottentot Captain Ruiter Platje, November 1791.)

150 1/gr 3/16, Statement of the Hottentot Captain Ruiter Platje, November 1791. Ruiter's wife Hester and her child were kidnapped by Christiaan Kok, while Hester's cousin/niece Mietje and a young boy named Jantje Kaffer were carried off by Alewijn Rautenbag. Both burghers alleged in court that Hester and Mietje were runaways who had worked for them before (1/gr 3/16, Statement of the female Hottentot Hester, 25 November 1791; Statement of the burgher Theunis Botha Jacobuszoon, 7 November 1792; Statement of the burgher Christiaan Kok, 7 November 1792).

151 Böeseken, 'Nederlandse kommissarisse', p. 86.

152 See pp. 114–15.

153 c 219, Resolutions, 8 November 1793, pp. 258ff.; c 601, Incoming letters, Secretary of Swellendam to Sluyksen, 12 October 1793.

154 During the war of 1793 C. F. Bezuidenhout had been singled out by the Zuurveld Xhosa as one of the chief provocateurs. He had allegedly 'taken their women and used them as . . . concubines' and had locked the Gqunukhwebe chief Chungwa in a flour mill 'and under severe threats ordered him to turn it in person' (Marais, *Maynier*, pp. 28–9).

155 1/gr 16/1, part i, Secretary of Graaff Reinet to C. F. Bezuidenhout, 20 June 1794.

156 See p. 129.

157 Penn, 'Labour, land and livestock', p. 18, note 87.

158 Report of Field-Sergeant Willem Steenkamp, 3 February 1778, in Moodie (ed.), *The record*, part III, p 74. See also p. 108.

159 See, for example, the case of the runaway servants of Pieter and Stephanus Venter, in CJ 69, Original notes and minutes, 22 March 1787, and 1/GR 3/17, Statement of Petrus Pienaar, 7 December 1786; Statement of Albertus Viljoen, 7 December 1786; Statement of Pieter Venter, 9 December 1786, and C 563, Incoming letters, Woeke to Governor, 10 December 1786. See also 1/GR 15/71, Contracts of service, Wynant Brijtenbach to Landdrost, 12 November 1797; CJ 450, Documents in criminal cases, Case of the Bastard Hottentot Toontje; ZL 1/3/2, London Missionary Society, Letters received, Alberti to Vanderkemp, 7 January 1804.

160 See p. 128. See also the case of the runaway servants of Adriaan Louw in Moodie (ed.), *The record*, vol. III, pp. 11, 13, 14, 17, and CJ 403, and, for a later example, V. C. Malherbe, 'Hermanus and his sons: Khoi bandits and conspirators in the post-rebellion period (1803–1818)', *African Studies* 41 (1982).

161 Marais, *Maynier*, p 26. The two major Xhosa chiefdoms in the Zuurveld at this time were the Gqunukhwebe under Tshaka and the Mbalu under Langa (Peires, *House of Phalo*, pp. 48–51).

162 *Ibid.*, pp. 48, 62.

163 CJ 3387, no. 5: Statement of the Hottentot Candace, wife of Jan Blaauw, 24 September 1810 and pp. 497ff. For further examples of hostile reactions to servants who complained, see 1/GR 3/16, Statement of Johannes Nel Willemzoon, 15 December 1790, and 1/GR 3/32, Statement of the Hottentot Piet Stamper, 1800–1.

164 See p. 123.

165 Marais, *Maynier*, pp. 71, 73; VC 68, 29 January 1795, p. 185.

166 VC 68, 29 January 1795, p. 186.

167 VC 871, vol. VIII, *Klagtschrift*, 16 April 1795, emphasis in original.

168 VC 65, Letter books, Sluyksen to Commissioners, 25 October 1793. See also C 219, 8 November 1793, p. 258. For earlier references to Captain Kees, see this volume, pp. 53–4 and 57.

169 C 219, 8 November 1793, pp. 258ff. By November 1793 the identity of the assailants was still unknown. The daughter of one of the victims said she had seen them from afar and counted 'fourteen or so' (1/SWM 3/17, Statement of the burgher Johannes Jacobus Oosthuizen, 25 November 1793).

170 1/STB 10/7, Letters received, Council of Policy to Landdrost, 1 April 1793: 'The Hottentot Captain Kees complains bitterly of several injuries', wrote the Colonial Secretary, 'amongst other things, that they are refusing to give his children back to him.'

171 VC 66, part 1, Statement of P. A. Meyburg, 2 October 1793, pp. 191–2. For an account of the Hangklip maroons, see Ross, *Cape of torments*, chapter 5.

172 VC 66, Statement of P. A. Meyburg, 2 October 1793. A *klipspringer* is a species of mountain antelope. The reader may recall that Kees had been sent on a similar mission in 1772 (see p. 53).

173 C 601, Landdrost of Stellenbosch to Council of Policy, 28 August 1793 and 10 September 1793.

174 VC 66, part 1, J. H. Wagener to Sluyksen, 24 and 28 September 1793, pp. 168–9, 173–4, 176.

175 C 601, W. L. van Hardenbergh to Governor, 29 September 1793.

176 Böeseken, 'Nederlandse kommissarisse', p. 87. See also VC 66, Statement of P. A. Meyburg, 2 October 1793, pp. 191–2; Statement of Hermanus Engelbrecht d'oude, 20 October 1793, pp. 193–4.

177 Böeseken, 'Nederlandse kommissarisse', p. 87.

178 Wagenaar, 'Johannes Gysbertus van Reenen', p. 117; VC 68, Adriaan van Jaarsveld to Maynier, 24 September 1794. The Groote Tafelberg lies about 25 km south-east of present-day Middelburg, on the Middelburg–Cradock road (see Map 3).

179 Marais, Maynier, p. 65.

180 Ibid., pp. 48–51, 58–9; 1/GR 1/2, 7 May 1795; Peires, House of Phalo, p. 51. Ndlambe was the second son of Rharhabe, ruler of the most powerful Xhosa chiefdom west of the Kei River. When Rharhabe and his Great Son Mlawu were killed in battle in 1782, Ndlambe became ruler of the chiefdom in the name of Mlawu's baby son Nqgika. In 1795 Ngqika, then 17 years old, rebelled against his uncle's authority and held him prisoner at his Great Place. Some of Ndlambe's followers, led by his brother Myaluza, crossed into the colony west of the upper Fish River. (Peires, House of Phalo, pp. 48–51.)

181 Marais, Maynier, p. 62.

182 Ibid, pp. 62–3.

183 Wagenaar, 'Johannes Gysbertus van Reenen', p 118. The depression had been precipitated by a fall in the number of foreign ships, especially British ships, calling at the Cape. See also Kirsten to Craig, October 1795, in Theal (ed.), Records, vol. I, p. 170.

184 Wagenaar, 'Johannes Gysbertus van Reenen', pp. 112, 123–4.

185 Ibid., pp. 96 and 116. The shortage of specie was at least partly due to the decline in the number of foreign ships calling at the Cape. British ships in particular had been a major source of hard cash.

186 Wagenaar, 'Johannes Gysbertus van Reenen', p. 116. See also ibid., pp. 120–2.

187 Ibid., pp. 109–13; VC 68, Statement of the burgher Christoffel Aucamp, 25 October 1793, enclosed in Wagener to Sluyksen, 30 December 1793, pp. 636–7.

188 This is apparent from the liquidation accounts in the series MOOC 13/1/5–36, 1760–1813.

189 Wagenaar, 'Johannes Gysbertus van Reenen', p. 110; PRO, WO 1/324, Enclosure in Craig to Dundas, 18 December 1795.

190 Wagenaar, 'Johannes Gysbertus van Reenen', p 113.

191 Ibid., p. 119.

192 Ibid., p. 128.

193 Marais, Maynier, pp. 83–4.

194 VC 887, vol. XXIV, p. 687. See also 1/GR 1/2, 11 July 1795, and CJ 2492, O. G. de Wet to Bletterman, 24 August 1795. Gordon had allegedly despatched several Hottentot captains into the interior to raise recruits for his new corps.

195 The volkstem, meaning 'voice of the people', was the name adopted by the insurgents who expelled Maynier from the Drostdy in February 1795. For a

full account of of the burgher rebellion of 1795, see Marais, *Maynier*, chapter 7. See also Herman Giliomee, 'The burgher rebellions'.

196 For a graphic description of the expulsion of O. G. de Wet, see vc 68, pp. 138–51.

197 vc 887, vol. xxiv, p. 700. After the expulsion of O. G. de Wet from Graaff Reinet in June 1795, a number of 'people's representatives' attended combined meetings of the Heemraden and Krijgsraad. It is not clear how these 'representatives' were chosen. (See Marais, *Maynier*, p. 83.) C. D. Gerotz had succeeded J. Booysen as Provisional Landdrost some time in July 1795. Both were freeburghers.

198 Possibly the same Louis who in 1793 had been one of Kees' accusers, though he was then described as 'a slave of the burgher Coenraad de Buijs' (c 219, 8 November 1793).

199 See p. 146.

200 1/gr 1/2, Saturday, 11 July 1795.

201 *Ibid.*

202 *Ibid.* The Cogmans Kloof is situated in the south-west Cape between present-day Ashton and Montagu, i.e. several hundred kilometres from the Rodeberg.

203 *Ibid.*

204 Rautenbach to Prinsloo, Bester and other representatives of the people, cited in vc 887, vol. xxiv, pp. 699–700. I have not been able to find the original of this letter, despite a thorough search.

205 vc 887, vol. xxiv, pp. 701–2.

206 'Maynier's provisional justification', April 1802, in Theal (ed.), *Records*, vol. iv, pp. 320–1.

207 Maynier to Jan Booysen, 1801, cited as an epigraph to Marais, *Maynier*.

208 See Newton-King and Malherbe, *Khoikhoi rebellion*, pp. 18–22.

8 'WE DO NOT LIVE LIKE BEASTS'

1 See p. 141. See also the article by John Mason, in which he examines the relationship between slavery and honour in the context of the British amelioration policies of the 1820s ('Hendrik Albertus and his ex-slave Mey: a drama in three acts', *Journal of African History* 31 (1990)).

2 S. D. Neumark, *Economic influences on the South African frontier*; Leonard Guelke, 'Freehold farmers and frontier settlers'; 'Frontier settlement in early Dutch South Africa', Guelke and Cole Harris, 'Land and society in early Canada and South Africa'.

3 See, for example, Giliomee, 'The eastern frontier', p. 424; Penn, 'Pastoralists and pastoralism', p. 63; Ross, 'Capitalism, expansion and incorporation', pp. 212–17.

4 *The economy of the Cape Colony'*, pp. 4–5 and chapter 5 *passim*.

5 For an explanation of this term in relation to the definition of a household, see Richard Wall (ed), *Family forms in historic Europe* (Cambridge: Cambridge University Press, 1983), pp. 5, 7–8, 99–100.

6 Neumark, *Economic influences, passim*, especially pp. 17, 39, 51, 79; Ross and Van Duin, *Economy of the Cape Colony, passim*, especially pp. 3, 88–9.

7 Ross and Van Duin, *Economy of the Cape Colony*, pp. 3, 59.
8 Ross and Van Duin have calculated that the number of sheep in the colony increased six times between 1704 and 1793 (from an estimated 230,000 in 1704 to 14 million in 1793, assuming a constant level of evasion in the tax returns), and the number of cattle more than six and a half times (*Economy of the Cape Colony*, pp. 61–4). It is more difficult to assess the rate of increase in the number of people involved in stock-farming, since the census was taken by district, and the districts of Stellenbosch, Drakenstein and Swellendam always included arable farmers as well as ranchers, though the latter were in the majority. The district of Graaff Reinet was almost entirely pastoral, however, and its white population increased from 2,391 in 1787 to 3,079 in 1795, a 28% increase in eight years.
9 Ross and Van Duin, *Economy of the Cape Colony*, pp. 7, 59, 88.
10 Neumark, *Economic influences*, pp. 17, 39, 133.
11 Ross and Van Duin, *Economy of the Cape Colony*, p. 88.
12 Guelke, 'The white settlers', p. 67.
13 It should be noted here that Guelke, together with Robert Shell, has published a very valuable study of wealth differentials within the colonial population as a whole, between the years 1682 and 1731. However, pastoralists figure in this study only as members of the lowest two quintiles; moreover, the analysis is largely based on title deeds and *opgaafrollen*, which do not give a full and accurate statement of an individual's assets and liabilities. Finally, it is not clear how the authors arrived at their computation of the rate of return or 'interest' on livestock. (L. Guelke and R. C.-H. Shell, 'An early colonial landed gentry: land and wealth in the Cape Colony, 1682–1731', *Journal of Historical Geography* 9 (1983).)
14 These accounts are to be found in the series MOOC 13/1/5–35. Annexures to the accounts are in the series MOOC 14/25–114, and the *Vendurollen* are in the series MOOC 10/8–25.
15 The population was stratified using the deciles of the variable 'net wealth', where the latter was greater than zero. The eleven cases in which liabilities were greater than assets (i.e. estates with a net wealth of minus zero) were retained in a separate category, and numbered 1–11. In other words, the 292 solvent estates were divided into ten strata, each comprising 10% of the total, and all except the tenth stratum containing twenty-nine estates. The tenth stratum contained thirty-one estates.
16 The tax roll for 1787 (J 107) listed 637 tax-payers, all but twenty-three of them male. All male burghers over the age of 16 were assessed for tax purposes, whereas women were not, unless they headed households as widows or divorcées. The 1787 returns listed twenty widows and three married women as tax-payers, the latter being regarded as heads of household for tax purposes because they were married to Company servants who had not yet acquired burgher status. For the purposes of lineage reconstruction, I have grouped widows with their late husbands' male kin. The reconstruction of kin groups would have been impossible without the heroic efforts of C. C. de Villiers and C. Pama, the authors of *Geslagsregisters van die ou Kaapse families*.
17 Exceptions were made in the case of large families which were poorly represen-

ted in the pastoral districts (often with only one member on the Graaff Reinet tax roll) and whose members I knew to be essentially residents of the south-west Cape: the Morkels, Mosterts, Malans and Myburghs, for example. Estates belonging to members of these families were not included in the study unless the household concerned had a direct connection with the frontier. This might be considered an unsound procedure, given that a handful of non-pastoral estates belonging to members of other lineages well represented in the pastoral districts were included in the study; however to have included all the Malans, Myburghs, etc., would have been to alter the nature and scope of the study, and might well have rendered it unmanageable.

18 That is not to say that I believe Afrikaner society to have been structured along strictly patrilineal lines. Affinal relations played a very important role in the accumulation of wealth and its transmission from one generation to the next. Affinal relations might also influence choice of residence.

19 A process of random selection was adopted in order to obviate the possibility of any bias of selection on my part, whether conscious or unconscious. The generation of random numbers was performed by Dr Tim Dunne of the University of Cape Town's Department of Mathematical Statistics. I am deeply grateful to him for his help with all the statistical procedures used in this chapter.

20 The *vendurollen* are auction rolls, which list all moveable and immoveable assets sold by public auction on the instructions of the Orphan Chamber, together with the identities of the purchasers and the prices fetched by each item. They are to be found in the series MOOC 10/1–48, Vendue rolls, 1691–1834.

21 That is, *Transporten en Scheepenkennissen*, some of which are available on microfilm in the Cape Archives (ZK 8/1/1–9).

22 In Fréderick le Play's sense of 'the patriarchal three-generational family' (see Wall (ed.), *Family forms*, pp. 18–19 and p. 318, note 14).

23 Neither Guelke nor Shell has yet published figures illustrating the distribution of net wealth among arable farmers during this period. However, it is possible to deduce from the figures given in Table 2.3 in Guelke's article 'The white settlers', p. 56, that, during the decade 1770–80, the average net value of arable estates in the highest third of his sample was 16,266 rix dollars.

24 Men and women from the interior districts were almost always married in community of property; ante-nuptial contracts were extremely rare.

25 That is, as a group of people who share a distinct living space and eat at least one main meal together. See Wall (ed.), *Family forms*, pp. 6–13.

26 Decimae are one tenth parts of the ordered array of (positive) population values defined by the corresponding deciles. (For an explanation of the term decile, see p.158.)

27 That is, the ages of the deceased in each case.

28 For examples of wills made by the inhabitants of the district of Graaff Reinet, see 1/GR 15/1. The value of the sums set aside for the children was seldom specified in the will, but one may assume that each child received an equal amount, approximating to what he or she would have received had the estate been liquidated at the time of the parent's death. According to law, each child was entitled to *at least* one third of the amount he or she would have received

had there been no will. This was known as the *'legitime portie'* (legitimate portion).

29 See, for example, 1/GR 15/1, Last will and testament of Daniel Willem Kuhne and Anna Pretorius, *Weduwee* Johannes Jurgen van Staden, 22 December 1787.

30 In many of the cases where an estate was liquidated despite the existence of a surviving spouse, one finds that the deceased spouse already had children by a previous marriage or marriages. That is, the parties to the present marriage had not seen fit to make a will.

31 The problems of step-families have not yet been explored by historians of Dutch South Africa. Yet this is a subject with tremendous potential, given that there were so many households headed by adults who had made second, third and even fourth marriages.

32 By which time it would no longer be a joint estate from a legal point of view.

33 One notices, for example, that where the deceased was an aged person, the composition of wealth is often markedly different from that found where the decedent was young or middle-aged. Among the rich, for example, one notices a tendency for wealth to be concentrated in the form of slaves or loan capital, rather than productive assets such as land, livestock or waggons.

34 See, for example, David Gaunt, 'The property and kin relationships of retired farmers in northern and central Europe' and Reinhard Sieder and Michael Mitterauer, 'The reconstruction of the family life course: theoretical problems and empirical results,' in Wall (ed.), *Family forms.*

35 Gaunt, 'Property and kin relationships'.

36 *Ibid.*

37 See, for example, MOOC 13/1/10, no 25; MOOC 14/55, no. 43; MOOC 14/95, no. 7; MOOC 13/1/32, no. 21.

38 MOOC 14/95, no. 7, Annexures to the liquidation account of Sijbrand van Dijck *d'oude.*

39 In most cases, age at death cannot be exactly calculated: births were not recorded by the VOC and De Villiers and Pama therefore give the date of an individual's baptism rather than his or her birth. Deaths were occasionally recorded by the church. The liquidation accounts seldom mention an exact date of death but they do give the date on which the property of the deceased was auctioned and this was normally within a year of his or her demise. The ages given in the table are therefore estimates, with a margin of error of one or two years.

40 This imbalance could be a function of the impoverishment which often accompanied widowhood, as a result of the liquidation and break-up of the conjugal estate.

41 The minimal majority with respect to any given good is 'the smallest number of individuals who between them account for more than 50% of [that] good' (Guelke and Shell, 'Early colonial landed gentry', footnote 17). The concept should be used with caution in the present context, however, since not all those households whose estates comprise the statistical population were co-existent in time.

42 Or 55 per cent, if we include the eleven insolvent estates.

43 As noted above, the households and individuals whose average wealth is reflected in Table 2 were not all co-existent in time. However I think that if the figures were to be reorganised on chronological lines, the results would be essentially the same.

44 Braudel, *Civilisation and capitalism*, vol. I, chapters 3 and 4, especially pp. 183, 199, 311, 333.

45 See Neumark, *Economic influences*, chapter 7.

46 Ross and Van Duin, *The economy of the Cape Colony*, p. 6.

47 The exclusive right granted to contracted butchers to supply foreign ships was probably of key importance in this regard. In 1793, for example, at a time when foreign demand was at its lowest level for many years, the butchers were still able to make a 145 per cent profit on each sheep sold to foreign vessels.

48 Craftsmen such as carpenters, coopers, waggon-makers, tailors, blacksmiths, coppersmiths and silversmiths were allowed to practise their trades freely, but manufacture on a larger scale, with the exception of wine-making, brandy-distilling, brewing and milling, was entirely prohibited.

49 Böeseken, 'Nederlandse kommissarisse', p. 177.

50 Mentzel, *Geographical and topographical description*, vol. II, pp. 38–9.

51 Mentzel, *Geographical and topographical description*, vol. II, p. 38.

52 Ross and Van Duin, *Economy of the Cape Colony*, Appendix 11.

53 Mentzel, *Geographical and topographical description*, vol. II, p. 38; Wagenaar, 'Johannes Gysbertus van Reenen', pp. 138–9.

54 Mentzel, *Geographical and topographical description*, vol. II, p. 38.

55 *Ibid.*

56 Thunberg, *Travels*, p. 4.

57 *Ibid.*, p. 141.

58 Böeseken, 'Nederlandse kommissarisse', p. 18.

59 Mentzel, *Geographical and topographical description*, vol. II, p. 55.

60 Böeseken, 'Nederlandse kommissarisse', pp. 179, note 41 and 205, note 154; Thunberg, *Travels*, p. 35.

61 Böeseken, 'Nederlandse kommissarisse', pp. 179, note 41 and 205, note 154.

62 Thunberg, *Travels*, p. 141.

63 Resolutions of the Commissioners-General, vol. I, p. 233 (6 September 1792), cited in Böeseken, 'Nederlandse kommissarisse', p. 19.

64 See, for example, the arrangements made by Jacobus van Reenen for the despatch of merchandise from Amsterdam to his son Johannes Gysbert in Cape Town, between 1779 and 1781 (Wagenaar, 'Johannes Gysbertus van Reenen', pp. 131–3 and Appendix A).

65 *Ibid.*, pp. 132–3.

66 Ross and Van Duin, *Economy of the Cape Colony*, pp. 84–7.

67 Ross and Van Duin, *Economy of the Cape Colony*, pp. 86–7 and Appendix 12; Wagenaar, 'Johannes Gysbertus van Reenen', chapter 5; MOOC 14/73, Estate of Andries Brink *d'oude*.

68 This would appear to be the position taken by Robert Ross in 'The Cape of Good Hope and the world economy, 1652–1835', in the second edition of *The shaping of South African society* (Cape Town: Maskew Miller Longman, 1989), p. 246.

69 Mentzel, *Geographical and topographical description*, vol. I, p. 99.

70 *Ibid.*, p. 76.

71 *Ibid.*

72 C. de Jong, *Reizen naar de Kaap de Goede Hoop, Ierland en Noorwegen in de jaren 1791 tot 1797...*, 3 vols. (Harlem: F. Bohn, 1802, 1803), vol. II, pp. 56–7. De Jong was writing in the context of the Revolutionary Wars which disrupted shipping on the route around the Cape.

73 Thunberg, *Travels*, p. 35. See also Böeseken, 'Nederlandse kommissarisse', p. 182, note 62 and V. M. Golovnin, *Detained in Simon's Bay: the story of the detention of the imperial Russian sloop Diana, April 1808–May 1809* (Cape Town: Friends of the South African Library, 1964), p. 64, footnote.

74 In 1794 the Company made a profit of 286 per cent on the sale of its Indian imports (Böeseken, 'Nederlandse kommissarisse', p. 182, note 62).

75 The attorney J. J. F. Wagener reported that the interior farmers spent 'only one or two days' at *De Kaap* before setting out on their homeward journey. They could not stay longer because of the great scarcity of grazing at the outspan-places near the town. (vc 68, Report of J. J. F. Wagener to Commissioner Sluyksen, 30 December 1793; Malherbe, 'Diversification and mobility of Khoikhoi labour', p. 102.)

76 J. B. Peires, 'The British and the Cape, 1814–1834', in Elphick and Giliomee (eds.), *Shaping*, second edition, p. 492; Robert Shell, 'Auctions – their good and evil tendency', part I, *Quarterly Bulletin of the South African Library* 39 (1985), 147.

77 Shell, 'Auctions', 147. To the best of my knowledge, women never stood surety for the liabilities of others.

78 BO 104, Miscellaneous documents, The inhabitants of Hantam, Bokkeveld, to Governor Macartney, November 1798, pp. 126–34.

79 De Jong, *Reizen naar de Kaap*, vol. I, p. 156, cited in Böeseken, 'Nederlandse kommissarisse', p. 189; Golovnin, *Detained in Simon's Bay*, pp. 57–8. See also, C. S. Woodward, 'From multi-purpose parlour to drawing room: the development of the principal *voorkamer* in the fashionable Cape house, 1670–1820', in *Bulletin of the South African Cultural History Museum* 4 (1983), 10.

80 Mentzel, 'A geographical and topographical description', vol. II, p. 79.

81 Guelke, 'Freehold farmers and frontier settlers', pp. 89–91; GR 1/1, 1 November 1790; A 124, Extracts from Fitzgerald's journal of excursions to Graaff Reinet and the east coast, 1797–8.

82 For evidence of these men's involvement in the frontier economy, see the series MOOC 13/1/5–35 (Liquidation accounts) and MOOC 14/73, Annexures to the liquidation account of Andries Brink *d'oude*.

83 Barrow, *Travels*, vol. II, p. 387.

84 'A boor in the Cape can do nothing for himself', he wrote. 'Unaccustomed to any society but that of his family and his Hottentots, he is the most awkward and helpless being on earth, when he gets into Cape Town, and neither buys nor sells but through his agent.'

85 J. Hoets to D. J. Pretorius, 15 February 1797, in MOOC 14/96, Annexures to the liquidation acount of Dirk Jacobus Pretorius.

86 *Ibid.*

87 See pp. 146–7.

88 See p. 146 and vc 68, J. J. F. Wagener to Sluyksen, 30 December 1793.
89 mooc 13/1/5–35, mooc 14/233, J. M. Hertzog to Johannes Slabbert, 18 December 1799, in annexures to liquidation account of the Widow Johannes Slabbert d'oude; mooc 14/82, Annexures to liquidation account of Jurgen Smit, note dated 30 November 1786.
90 See for example, mooc 14/233, J. M. Hertzog to the Widow Johannes Slabbert, 18 December 1799.
91 Resolution of Governor and Council, 5 April 1774, in Moodie (ed.), The record, part iii, p. 24.
92 Extract of Council resolution, 7 June 1774, in Moodie (ed.), The record, part iii, p. 35. Their transgressions had been aggravated, in the Council's view, by their involvement in cattle barter with the Xhosa beyond De Bruins Hoogte.
93 mooc 14/73, Annexures to liquidation account of Andries Brink d'oude. Account books dated 1780–1.
94 zk 1/159, Magistrate of Swellendam to Governor, 12 October 1789.
95 See mooc 13/1/13, no. 36, Liquidation account of Dawid van der Merwe d'oude (1785); mooc 14/96, Annexures to liquidation account of Dirk Jacobus Pretorius; mooc 13/1/29, no. 22, Liquidation account of Hermanus Lambertus Potgieter. See also the extract from Pretorius' notebook, reproduced overleaf.
96 co 2567, Letters received from Graaff Reinet, Stockenstrom to Bird, 24 October 1809.
97 1/gr 3/16, no. 204, 4 June 1792; see also nós. 195 and 196, 24 March 1792 and mooc 14/69, Annexures to liquidation account of Fredrik Potgieter.
98 Ross, 'The Cape and the world economy', pp. 245–8.
99 1/swm 1/1, Memorandum signed by 'some burghers and inhabitants' of Swellendam Colonie, 26 October 1757 in Minutes of Landdrost and Heemraden, 25 January 1758.
100 Cape guilders, i.e. two rix dollars.
101 The reference is to waggon-shifts. Each shift was approximately eight hours long, and the waggons moved at an average speed of 2 to 3 miles per hour, so that fifteen shifts represented between 240 and 360 miles. (Forbes, Pioneer travellers, p. 48; William Burchell, Travels in the interior of southern Africa, 2 vols. (London: 1822, reprinted Cape Town: Struik, 1967), vol. i, p. 28).
102 1/stb 13/13, Memorandum addressed to Adriaan van Jaarsveld by forty-eight burghers of De Bruins Hoogte, 28 September 1781.
103 W. F. Freund, 'The Cape under the transitional governments, 1795–1814', in Elphick and Giliomee (eds.), Shaping, second edition, pp. 328–9; Ross, 'The Cape and the world economy', pp. 264–8. It is possible that textile prices began to fall after 1810. If so, this would have meant a considerable saving to frontiersmen, since textiles made up a large portion of their annual expenditure; on the other hand, though, the prices of land and slaves had begun a steady rise.
104 PRO, wo 1/327, Craig to Dundas, 5 October 1796; Macartney to Dundas, 20 February 1798.
105 bo 104, pp. 126–34, Inhabitants of the Hantam, Bokkeveld, to Governor, November 1798.
106 mooc 14/25–114 (1760–1812).

107 E.g. Memorials and requests, resolutions of the Council of Policy, diverse papers of the Court of Justice and the incoming and outgoing letters of district magistrates. All livestock prices reflected in the graphs are prices paid to producers.

108 Data for the 1760s and 1770s were too thin to permit the construction of credible averages.

109 MOOC 14/65, *Vendurol* of Johannes Jurgen de Beer, 23 October 1785. The reader will recall that, in theory, it was only the farm buildings and other improvements, collectively known as the *opstal*, that could be sold; however, the price of the *opstal* reflected the value of the land as well.

110 MOOC 10/15, *Vendurol* of Fredrik Potgieter, 16 March 1786; MOOC 10/17, *Vendurol* of Laurens Erasmus and Abigail Geertruy Pienaar, 28 March 1796.

111 The Swart River flowed right through De Beer's land. The old *leiwater* channels are still visible on the farm. (I was able to see them in 1995, thanks to the generosity of Andrew McNaughton, then resident at De Vreede.)

112 These prices have been included for the reasons explained on p. 153.

113 According to Leonard Guelke, the average cost of an *opstal* between 1731 and 1780 varied from 300 to 500 guilders (100 to 167 rix dollars) ('Freehold farmers and frontier settlers', p. 86).

114 When land was bought at auction, the purchase price was normally paid in three instalments, sometimes over a period of nine months and sometimes over three years.

115 I have no sheep prices for 1805–6.

116 Given a weaning percentage of 59.5 and a post-weaning mortality of 3 per cent, one can estimate that for every 100 ewes in his flock, a farmer could produce twenty-seven wethers per annum. (See pp. 191–2 for an explanation of weaning percentages.)

117 These figures include the four insolvent estates in the sample.

118 That is, in return for half the increase of the livestock pastured thereon. (See above, p. 21.)

119 Slave prices could vary as widely as land prices. In 1784, for example, a number of Mozambiquan and Cape-born slaves fetched prices in excess of 1,000 rix dollars, whereas others were sold *voetstoots* for less than 200 rix dollars. For a discussion of the domestic market in slaves, see Shell, *Children of bondage*, chapter 4.

120 The net present value of a male slave would be calculated by discounting the net income stream from the slave over his working life at the prevailing market rate of interest. The latter is known – it varied between 5 and 6 per cent in the eighteenth century – but net income stream and even life expectancy cannot be readily assessed.

121 VC 882, vol. XIX, Extract from the records of Landdrost and Heemraden, 2 June 1795. (See this volume, p. 123.)

122 See pp. 120–1, and Marais, *Maynier*, pp. 118–19.

123 See Marais, *Maynier*, pp. 117–19 and Newton-King and Malherbe, *Khoikhoi rebellion*, p. 32.

124 Marais, *Maynier*, p. 71.

125 1/GR 16/1, Maynier to Grijling, 24 February 1800. Cited in Marais, *Maynier*, p. 119.

126 1/GR 15/43, Contracts of service, Hottentots or free persons of colour, 1786–1882.

127 Sparrman, *Voyage to the Cape of Good Hope*, vol. I, p. 181. See also C 492, Horak to Governor, 20 May 1755.

128 1/STB 3/11, 'Relaas van den Hottentot Coridon', 2 November 1763; A 447, 'Journal eener landtogt', 16 October 1776.

129 MOOC 13/1/11, no. 31, Estate of late Johanna Maria Buys, *Weduwee* Jan Hendrik Venter (July 1781); MOOC 13/1/12, Estate of the late Frans Kruger *d'oude* (1782).

130 MOOC 14/115, Estate of Hester Myburgh, *Weduwee* Gerrit Olivier, Hendrik-zoon (1813).

131 LMS, Box 1, Folder 4D, Vanderkemp to the Directors, 14 October 1801.

132 MOOC 14/98, no. 2, Annexures to the liquidation account of Gerrit Coetzee Dirkzoon (1804).

133 LMS, Box 2, Folder 1A, Vanderkemp to Directors, 1 February 1802.

134 See, for example, Fiscal to Landdrost of Swellendam, 5 February 1771; 1/GR 3/16, Statement of Jacob Johannes Kruger, Franszoon, 20 June 1787; Statement of Willem Bruintjes *de jonge*, 20 January 1789; 1/STB 10/7, Council of Policy to Landdrost of Swellendam, 16 April 1793.

135 Penn, 'Anarchy and authority', pp. 35–7; 1/STB, 3/11, Statement of the Hottentot Danser, 2 November 1763; 1/GR 3/16, Statements of the Hottentots Mijse, Jas, Mietje and Magerman, 6 May 1790; CJ 3387 (Black Circuit), Case no. 5, statement of Jacobus Scheepers *de jonge*, 24 September 1810; ZI 1/25, Documents in the Public Record Office Northern Ireland, Belfast, Case P.

136 CJ 446, Statement of the Hottentot Sara, 12 June 1792. For an account of the trial, see this volume, pp. 134–5.

137 CJ 446, Statement of Andries Jacobus de Beer, 5 November 1792; Statements of the Hottentots Kaalkop, Leentje, Slinger, Agnita and Antje. See also 1/GR 3/16, Statement of the Hottentot Barend, deserter from the service of Christiaan Lessing, 1791.

138 Lichtenstein, *Travels*, vol. I, pp. 57, 446.

139 Thunberg, *Travels*, p 94; Barrow, *Travels*, vol. I, pp. 67–8. See also this volume, p. 100.

140 Sparrman, *Voyage to the Cape of Good Hope*, vol. I, p. 176.

141 *Ibid.*, vol. I, p. 233; vol. II, p. 176; Mentzel, *Geographical and topographical Description*, part III, p. 202.

142 CJ 361, Case against the Hottentot Valentijn, *Eijsch* of Landdrost Horak, 25 January 1753; MOOC 14/96, Annexures to liquidation account of Dirk Jacobus Pretorius. Dagga was the local name for *cannabis indica*.

143 MOOC 13/1/14, no. 7, Liquidation account of Johannes Jurgen de Beer and Christina van der Merwe (April 1786).

144 MOOC 10/18, *Vendurol* of de *Weduwee* Hans Jurgen de Beer, 20 November 1798.

145 MOOC 13/1/23, no. 23 and MOOC 10/18, Liquidation account and *vendurol* of Dawid de Beer, Hans Jurgenzoon.

146 'Hired Jan on 9 June for one year, a hat, a pair of trousers, a jacket, two blue shirts 20 rix dollars, a tinderbox and flint 6 *schellingen*, 3 pounds tobacco . . . 6 *schellingen*, 1 neckerchief . . . 1 rix dollar (MOOC 14/96, Annexures to liquidation account of Dirk Jacobus Pretorius, undated but *c.* 1790).

147 Historians of Dutch South Africa have yet to explore the full meaning of the term 'heathen' in the discourse of the time. Gerstner has emphasised its theological significance: Christians (in the eyes of the colonists) were either already redeemed or set apart for redemption in adulthood; heathen were destined only for damnation (Gerstner, *The thousand generation Covenant*, chapter 11). But the term may have carried other meanings handed down from medieval times. Like wild men and witches, perhaps, the heathen stood as a symbol of all that was anti-self. On this, see, for example, Mason, *Deconstructing America*.

148 See pp. 154 and 160–1.

149 The reader may like to refer back to Table 1, where the deciles and the number of sampled estates in each decima are clearly shown.

150 Since the tables in appendix 2 are intended to serve as a basis for the assessment of profitability, consumer goods have not been included in the breakdown of the decedent's assets (though their value is reflected in the statement of gross assets).

151 There is some dispute about the part played by selective breeding in the evolution of the Ronderib Afrikaner. It differs in certain ways from the Namaqua Afrikaner which was kept by the Khoekhoe of the north-west Cape, but since we do not know enough about the differences between the Namaqua Afrikaner and the sheep raised by the Khoekhoe of the southern Cape, we cannot say how closely the Ronderib resembled the latter. There is no doubt, however, that the Ronderib is an indigenous breed. For further information, see H. Epstein (ed.), *The origin of the domestic animals of Africa*, 2 vols. (New York: Africana Publishing Corporation, 1971), vol. II, pp. 142–59.

152 My thanks are due in particular to Professors H. J. Heydenrich and P. J. de Wet from the Department of Animal Science at the University of Stellenbosch, Dr P. J. Posthumus, Regional Director of Veterinary Services in Pietermaritzburg and the staff of the Carnarvon Experimental Farm, all of whom were unstintingly generous in their efforts to explain the mysteries of stock-breeding to a complete novice.

153 H. B. Thom (ed.), *Willem Stephanus van Ryneveld se aanmerkingen over de verbetering van het vee aan de Kaap de Goede Hoop, 1804* (Cape Town: Van Riebeeck Society, 1942), pp. 104–81.

154 *Ibid.*, p. 117.

155 Professor H. J. Heydenrich, personal communication, 10 February 1984 and 5 February 1991. It must be stressed that these figures are merely an estimate. However, in those cases where the number of cows and calves are listed separately in eighteenth-century *vendurollen*, the weaning percentage would indeed appear to be exactly within the range predicted by Professor Heydenrich.

156 Malherbe, 'Diversification and mobility', p. 51.

157 Thom (ed.), *Aanmerkingen*, pp. 107, 163–5, 177–81; Thunberg, *Travels*, p. 134.

158 Professor H. J. Heydenrich, verbal communication, 8 February 1991; H. Heyns, 'The growth of the Afrikaner calf in relation to the production and

composition of the milk of its dam', *Afrikanerbees Joernaal* 5 (1960).

159 H. J. Heydenrich, verbal communication, 15 February 1991.

160 One gallon of Africander milk weighs 10 lb.

161 See p. 74, note 72.

162 Thompson, *Travels*, vol. II, p. 12, note 2.

163 C 1300, Enclosure in Woeke to Governor, 5 January 1789.

164 I would like to thank Professor C. H. van Niekerk, formerly of the Faculty of Agriculture, University of Stellenbosch, for explaining to me the basic principles of equine reproduction (personal communication, 15 February 1991).

165 I would like to thank Professor Heydenrich for explaining to me the principles of stock replacement.

166 Professor H. J. Heydenrich, personal communication, 10 December 1984.

167 Professor C. H. van Niekerk, personal communication, 15 February 1991.

168 I have used *opgaafrollen* in exceptional cases, such as that of Okkert Oosthuijzen (see pp. 201–2).

169 MOOC 10/19, *Vendurol* of Volkert Schoenmaker, 9 February 1797. Schoenmaker died at the farm of Nicolaas Orban on the Kafferkuils River in Swellendam district, but his two loan-farms were situated in the district of Graaff Reinet.

170 MOOC 10/10, *Vendurol* of Sara Fourie, *Weduwee* Adriaan van Wyk; MOOC 13/1/8, no. 6, Liquidation account of Sara Fourie.

171 MOOC 13/1/24, no. 3, Liquidation account of Marthinus Oosthuijzen and Johanna Jacomina Calitz; MOOC 10/19, *Vendurol* of Marthinus Oosthuijzen and Johanna Jacomina Calitz.

172 MOOC 10/18, *Vendurol* of the *Weduwee* Dawid Fourie, 25 May 1797.

173 European frontier families were linked through intermarriage in endlessly complex ways. Willem Sterrenberg Marais was married to Maria Fourie, daughter of Louisa Erasmus. He was thus both Erasmus' step-grandson and her son-in-law. Helena Johanna de Beer had married again after the death of her second husband, Louis Fourie, and now lived with a man thirteen years her junior, by whom she had four children. (De Villiers and Pama, *Geslagsregisters*, vol. I, pp. 31, 209, 231.)

174 MOOC 10/9, *Vendurol* of Catharina de Jong and Gerrit Engelbrecht, 15 July 1765; Hoge, 'Personalia', p. 89.

175 He owed 340 rix dollars to the trader Frans Lens (MOOC 13/1/7, no. 33, Liquidation account of Gerrit Engelbrecht, 7 June 1769).

176 MOOC 14/31, Annexures to liquidation accounts, Gerrit Engelbrecht to an anonymous 'uncle', 19 June 1769.

177 MOOC 13/1/7, no 33, Liquidation account of Catharina de Jong and Gerrit Engelbrecht, 7 June 1769. On the role of the Diaconie of the Dutch Reformed Church in the placement of 'orphans' with foster-parents, see M. M. Marais, 'Armesorg aan die Kaap onder die Kompanjie, 1652–1795', *Archives Yearbook for South African History* (1943), chapter 5. In 1795 the British authorities were informed by J. F. Kirsten that several frontiersmen had 'been forced to put their children to sale, merely because they had no means to give them bread'. ('Mynheer F. Kerstein's Letter on the state of the Colony', in C. F. J. Muller, *Johannes Frederik Kirsten oor die toestand van die Kaapkolonie in 1795* (Pretoria: J. L. van Schaik, 1960), p. 56).

178 MOOC 10/11, *Vendurol* of Gerrit Engelbrecht *de oude*, 7 November 1774.

179 MOOC 10/20, *Vendurol* of Maria Cloete and Hendrik Mostert, Ernstzoon, 18 April 1804.

180 MOOC 10/10, *Vendurol* of Elisabeth Nortje, *Weduwee* Matthijs Strijdom, 12 October 1772.

181 MOOC 10/10 and MOOC 13/1/8, no. 24, *Vendurol* and liquidation account of Elisabeth Nortje, *Weduwee* Matthijs Strijdom.

182 MOOC 13/1/7, Liquidation account of Erasmus Smit *d'oude*.

183 MOOC 10/11, *Vendurol* of Jacobus Botha, Christoffelszoon, 31 July 1776.

184 MOOC 13/1/9, no. 11 and MOOC 10/11, Liquidation account and *vendurol* of Jan Nel, 13 January 1775.

185 Guelke, 'Freehold farmers and frontier settlers', pp. 87, 89.

186 One should note that Guelke's conclusions are based on a study of estates administered by the Orphan Chamber between 1731 and 1780, whereas mine are based on a study of estates administered between 1765 and 1812. If it could be shown that the cost of living had risen substantially between the second and third quarters of the eighteenth century, then the difference between Guelke's and my findings could be partly ascribed to the effects of inflation. As yet, no attempt has been made to construct a cost of living index for the eighteenth century. Given the rapid price fluctuations which characterised the Cape market, this would not be an easy task.

187 Guelke, 'White settlers', p 89.

188 MOOC 10/19, *Vendurol* of Marthinus François Nel, 28 July 1800.

189 The latter possibility is suggested by Daniel's prominence among the purchasers at the *vendutie*.

190 'The boor carries in the pocket of his leather breeches a large knife, with which he carves for the rest of the family, and which stands him in as many services as the little dagger of Hundebras' (Barrow, *Travels*, vol. II, p. 401). See also Sparrman, *Voyage to the Cape of Good Hope*, vol. II, p. 132.

191 MOOC 10/23, *Vendurol* of Philip Snijman, 21 May 1808.

192 MOOC 13/1/32, no. 53, Liquidation account of Philip Snijman and Anna Sophia Venter, 20 October 1809.

193 MOOC, 14/108, Annexures to liquidation account of Philip Snijman: extract of a letter from the Landdrost of Graaff Reinet to the Secretary of the Orphan Chamber, 17 September 1808. See also De Villiers and Pama, *Geslagsregisters*, vol. I, pp. 125, 437.

194 On gifts of livestock to newborn children and newly weds see Mentzel, *Geographical and topographical Description*, part III, p. 112.

195 MOOC 13/1/32, no. 70, Liquidation account of Aletta Dorothea Bester and Sybrand Gerhardus van Nieuwkerken, 22 December 1809.

196 MOOC 10/23, *Vendurol* of Aletta Dorothea Bester, 3 October 1808.

197 MOOC 13/1/36, no. 2, *Vendurol* and liquidation account of Philippus Petrus du Plessis, 3 May 1810 and 16 March 1813.

198 MOOC 10/26, *Vendurol* of Carel Nicolaas van der Merwe, 28 June 1811; MOOC 10/16, *Vendurol* of Anna Susanna Lombard, 16 September 1791.

199 MOOC 13/1/36, Liquidation account of Carel Nicolaas van der Merwe, 23 November 1813.

200 MOOC 13/1/19, no. 12, Liquidation account of Anna Susanna Lombard and

Pieter van der Westhuijzen, Pieterzoon, 2 December 1793.

201 MOOC 10/16, *Vendurol* of Anna Susanna Lombard, 16 September 1791.

202 De Villiers and Pama, *Geslagsregisters*, vol. III, pp. 928, 1119–20.

203 MOOC 13/1/35, no. 23, Liquidation account of Okkert Oosthuijzen, 28 November 1812; J 319, *Opgaafrollen*, Swellendam, 1806. Five waggon-shifts equalled a journey of some forty-three hours.

204 As noted above, 'comfort' is a relative concept. My use of the term here is determined by a sense of the range of material possibilities open to eighteenth-century Cape colonists. I suspect this is also what Guelke had in mind when he used the phrase 'rough comfort'.

205 MOOC 10/25, *Vendurol* of Okkert Oosthuijzen, 24 April 1809.

206 Compare Guelke, 'White settlers', p. 93.

207 J 319. I have assumed that Oosthuijzen's harvest in 1809 was similar in volume to that of 1806 (i.e. 10 muids of wheat, 5 muids of barley, 2 leaguers of wine) and that half was kept for domestic consumption.

208 MOOC 13/1/35, no. 23, Liquidation account of Okkert Oosthuijzen, 28 November 1812.

209 The role of his father-in-law, Daniel Jacobus Strijdom, is inferred from the latter's active participation as a buyer at the *vendutie*. There is no direct evidence to prove that he put up the money which enabled Jacobus Johannes Oosthuijzen to buy the family farm. However I know of many cases in which in-laws played a critical role in the transfer of landed property from one generation to the next.

210 J 226, *Opgaafrollen*, Drakenstein (1800). J. C. Grijling was at one and the same time brother-in-law to Gerrit Coetzee and maternal uncle to Coetzee's wife, the latter being some fifteen years younger than himself (De Villiers and Pama, *Geslagsregisters*, vol. I, pp. 145, 205, 263).

211 MOOC 13/1/27, no. 2, Liquidation account of Gerrit Coetzee, Dirkzoon, 18 April 1804.

212 *Ibid.*

213 There is some doubt about the mode of life of Gerbrecht Pretorius. Her livestock holdings were too small to support her, but she may have grown some grain. The inventory of her property includes a waggon, a plough and a number of tools.

214 MOOC 10/11 and 14/37, *Vendurol* and annexures to liquidation account of Agatha Blom, *Weduwee* Lucas Meyer.

215 MOOC 14/114, Annexures to the liquidation account of Hermanus Grijling, 2 March 1812.

216 See A. M. Lewin Robinson (ed.), *The letters of Lady Anne Barnard* (Cape Town: Balkema, 1973), pp. 135, 143, 158.

217 It will be understood, in the light of what has been written above about the relations between the *veeboeren* and the Cape Town mercantile community, that 'independence' is used here in a relative sense.

218 MOOC 10/13, *Vendurollen* of Johanna Maria Buys, 24 July and 16 November 1791.

219 MOOC 13/1/11, no. 31, Liquidation account of Johanna Maria Buys, 22 May 1782; De Villiers and Pama, *Geslagsregisters*, vol. III, pp. 1007, 1097–99.

220 During his journey through the Sneeuberge and De Bruins Hoogte, Swellen-grebel had explicitly noted that it was common for two or three households to combine in order to share expenses (A 447, 'Journal eener landtogt', 1 November 1776).

221 Daniel van der Merwe, Jacobuszoon, younger brother of Maria Erasmus' late husband, Schalk Jacobus van der Merwe, was married to Erasmus' sister Hester. He was the beneficiary of a private deed executed by Maria Erasmus on 13 May 1782, in terms of which he would acquire the *opstal* of her loan-farm upon her death, together with the slave woman Stijn and her two children, in exchange for the payment of 250 rix dollars to Erasmus' estate. He also organised her funeral and the subsequent auction of her assets. (MOOC 13/1/12, no. 8, Liquidation account of Maria Elisabeth Erasmus, *Weduwee* Schalk Jacobus van der Merwe, Jacobuszoon.)

222 MOOC 10/12 or 10/13, *Vendurol* of Maria Elisabeth Erasmus, 18 October 1782. According to the *vendurol*, 'De Matjes Rivier' (also known as 'De Rietvallij') was 'in the Caro . . . behind the Hex River'. There was a Matjes Rivier in Swellendam district, north of the Outeniqua Mountains, but it is more likely that Erasmus lived in the Ceres Karoo, on the farm still known as 'Rietvallei'. This farm was close to the Warm Bokkeveld, where Daniel van der Merwe lived. (South Africa: 1 : 250,000 topographical sheet no. 3319. See also MOOC 10/10, *Vendurol* of Schalk Jacobus van der Merwe, 12 October 1772.)

223 The phrase is Swellengrebel's ('Journal eener landtogt', 16 September 1776).

224 Few whose net assets placed them in the first five decimae, that is.

225 Sparrman, *Voyage to the Cape of Good Hope*, vol. II, p. 132.

226 *Ibid.*

227 Lewin Robinson (ed.), *The letters of Lady Anne Barnard*, p. 135. See also Mentzel, *Geographical and topographical description*, part III, p. 115 and Barrow, vol. II, pp. 401–2.

228 MOOC 10/18, *Vendurol* of the *Weduwee* Dawid Schalk van der Merwe, 29 November 1798. Dawid Schalk van der Merwe farmed in the Camdeboo until his death in the 1790s.

229 MOOC 10/18, *Vendurol* of Jurriaan Hendrik Greeff, 25 October 1798. The estates of Greeff and Van der Merwe belong in the ninth decima.

230 The scarcity of clocks and mirrors may, as Robert Ross observes, have 'something to do with transport problems' (Robert Ross, personal communication, 1993). The bumping and jolting of ox-waggons has been graphically described by many Cape travellers. See for example, Burchell, *Travels*, vol. I, p. 192.

231 A 447, 'Journal eener landtogt', pp. 21–4, cited in Forbes, *Pioneer travellers*, p. 68.

232 Draft of a personal letter from Swellengrebel to a member of the Dutch government in Dordrecht, C. de Gijselaar, 26 June 1783, appendix A, in Schutte (ed.), *Briefwisseling van Hendrik Swellengrebel Jr*, pp. 360–1.

233 Mentzel, *Geographical and topographical description*, part III, pp. 115–16.

234 J. F. Kirsten to Craig, 'Memorandum on the condition of the Colony, 1795', in Theal (ed.), *Records*, vol. I, p. 169.

235 Barrow, *Travels*, vol. I, p. 401.

236 *Ibid.*; A 447, 'Journal eener landtogt', pp. 21–4.

237 Sparrman, *Voyage to the Cape of Good Hope*, vol. I, p. 137.

238 Schutte (ed.), *Briefwisseling van Hendrik Swellengrebel Jr*, p. 358.

239 Patterson, *Slavery and social death*, p. 35.

240 Siegfried Lauffer, '*Die Sklaverei in der griechisch-römischen Welt*', in *Rapports* II, Eleventh International Congress of Historical Sciences, Stockholm, August 21–28, 1960 (Uppsala: Almquist and Wiksell, 1960), cited in Patterson, *Slavery and social death*, p. 36, note 3.

241 The quotation is from Patterson, *Slavery and social death*, p. 39.

242 For references to stock-farmers who could speak Khoe and/or San languages, see, for example: CJ 362; VC 592, vol. I, p. 149; Sparrman, *Voyage to the Cape of Good Hope*, vol. I, p. 202; CO 2564, Stockenstrom to Caledon, 4 April 1808.

243 VC 871, vol. VIII, *Klagtschrift*, Bruins Hoogte, 16 April 1795.

244 As noted above (note 147), the full meaning of 'heathenness' in the context of the eighteenth-century Cape has yet to be explored, but one might add here that it seems to have been equated with a lack of moral faculties and an inability to discipline oneself or submit voluntarily to a higher authority, which put one 'almost on a par with the animals'. These notions are well expressed in the oft-quoted extract from a letter written by Landdrost Alberti of Uitenhage in 1805: 'According to the unfortunate notion prevalent here, a heathen is not actually a human, but at the same time he cannot really be classed among the animals. He is, therefore, a sort of creature not known elsewhere. His word can in no wise be believed, and only by violent measures can he be brought to do good and shun evil' (BR 68, Annexures to the resolutions of the Council of Policy, pp. 280–1: Alberti to Janssens, 12 June 1805).

245 *Transactions of the London Missionary Society* 1 (1804), 479–95.

246 'Transactions of Dr Vanderkemp in the year 1801', *Transactions of the London Missionary Society* 1 (1804), 479, 485. On 23 October 1801, during a battle for control of Graaff Reinet village, a group of rebel colonists shot at Dr van der Kemp; but they missed, and one wonders whether they had not done so on purpose (*ibid.*, pp. 493–4).

247 André du Toit and Hermann Giliomee, *Afrikaner political thought: analysis and documents 1780–1850*, vol. I (Cape Town: David Philip, 1983), pp. 84–6.

248 VC 871, vol. VIII, p. 12, *Klagtschrift*, Bruins Hoogte, 16 April 1795. See also the *Tesamenstemming* in *ibid.*, p. 186.

9   'A TIME OF BREATHING'

1 'Provisional justification of Honoratus Christiaan David Maynier, in his quality as Commissary of the District of Graaff Reinet . . .', in Theal (ed.), *Records*, vol. IV, pp. 287, 290.

2 *Ibid.*, p. 293; Marais, *Maynier*, p. 116.

3 Marais, *Maynier*, p. 116. For a brief account of the formation of the Hottentot Corps, as it was then called, see Elphick and Malherbe, 'The Khoisan to 1828', pp. 35–6.

4 'Provisional justification of H. C. D. Maynier', in Theal (ed.), *Records*, vol. IV, pp. 294, 286–7, 298.

5 'Criminal claim and conclusion made and demanded by the Fiscal versus Marthinus Prinsloo and his accomplices', in Theal (ed.), *Records*, vol. III, pp. 234–5. The would-be rebels were allegedly emboldened by the receipt of a letter from the Cape-based schoolmaster Cornelis Edema (formerly employed by Alewijn Jacobus Kruger of Graaff Reinet), which told of the defeat of an English expeditionary force at Ostend, the conquest of 'the whole West Indies' by the French and the Dutch and the departure of three British regiments from the Cape to India. 'All foreign nations are pressed', the writer concluded. (CJ 840, Trial of Cornelis Edeman (*sic*).)

6 See p. 187.

7 'Criminal claim and conclusion', in Theal (ed.), *Records*, vol. IV, p. 214; CJ 731, Examination of Adriaan van Jaarsveld *de oude*.

8 1/GR 16/1, Secretary of Graaff Reinet to Adriaan van Jaarsveld, 3 December 1794.

9 CJ 900, 14 December 1797.

10 'Criminal claim and conclusion', in Theal (ed.), *Records*, vol. IV, p. 215; CJ 80, 31 May 1798.

11 'Criminal claim and conclusion', in Theal (ed.), *Records*, vol. IV, pp. 215–16. Van Jaarsveld later gave illness, 'first of my wife, and then myself', as the reason for his failure to appear. (CJ 731, Examination of Adriaan van Jaarsveld *de oude*.)

12 Marais, *Maynier*, p. 31.

13 'Journal kept by Landdrost Bresler', in Theal (ed.), *Records*, vol. II, p. 389. Bresler had personal experience of the rebellious tendencies of the local citizenry. In March 1796, like Maynier before him, he had been driven from the drostdy by the *volkstem*. On both occasions, Adriaan van Jaarsveld had been among the chief spokesmen of the 'people's will'. (Marais, *Maynier*, pp. 86–7.)

14 'Journal kept by Landdrost Bresler', in Theal (ed.), *Records*, vol. II, p. 389.

15 *Ibid.*

16 'Deposition of Hendrik Oertel', in Theal, *Records*, vol. II, pp. 355–6.

17 *Ibid.*, pp. 355 and 390; Barrow, vol. II, p. 34.

18 PRO WO 1/324, Commodore Blankett to Henry Dundas, 23 December 1795; WO 1/325, Craig to Henry Dundas, 8 March 1796.

19 On the Dutch Patriots, see Jonathan Israel, *The Dutch Republic: its rise, greatness and fall, 1477–1806* (Oxford: Clarendon Press, 1995), pp. 1120–1. South African historians have tended to discount the influence of European revolutionary thought on the burgher rebels of 1795–1801. However there is some evidence to suggest that the colonists of the Cape interior were more aware of overseas developments than has been thought. (See above, note 5 and compare Marais, *Maynier*, pp. 88–90 and Giliomee, 'The burgher rebellions on the eastern frontier'.)

20 Dundas to Faure, 16 February 1799, in Theal (ed.), *Records*, vol. II, p. 356.

21 Dundas to Bresler, 17 February 1799, in Theal (ed.), *Records*, vol. II, pp. 358–60.

22 Dundas to Bresler, 23 February 1799, in Theal (ed.), *Records*, vol. II, pp. 366–7

and McNab to Dundas, 12 March 1799, in *ibid.*, pp. 383–5. For estimates of the number of Khoisan soldiers, see 'Criminal claim and conclusion', in *ibid.*, vol. III, pp. 252–3. The quotation is from Bresler to Dundas, 24 January 1799, in *ibid.*, vol. II, pp. 351–2. Bresler wrote in French in case his letter should fall into rebel hands.

23 Theal (ed.), *Records*, vol. II, pp. 368, 370, 380, 392.

24 'Journal kept by Landdrost Bresler', in Theal (ed.), *Records*, vol. II, p. 391. Andries Petrus Burger, Marthinus Prinsloo, Johannes Petrus van der Wald and Barend Jacobus Bester offered 'in the name of the assembled burghers' to stand surety for the sum owed by Van Jaarsveld (Landdrost and Heemraden of Graaff Reinet to Dundas, 25 January 1799, in *ibid.*, vol. II, p. 349). Burger may have lived to regret this undertaking, for when Van Jaarsveld died (in prison) some years later, he was apparently obliged to pay up. A sum of 1,817 rix dollars owed to Andries Petrus Burger 'for a surety paid to the Orphan Chamber' was listed among the outstanding debts of the Widow van Jaarsveld's insolvent estate in 1809 (MOIC 2/4, no. 351, Insolvent estate of the late Anna Elizabeth de Beer, *weduwee* Adriaan van Jaarsveld).

25 'Second attempt [of Dr Van der Kemp] to enter Caffraria in the year 1800 [should read 1799]', *Transactions of the London Missionary Society* 1 (1804), 397–409.

26 See chapter 7, p. 146 note 180.

27 Marais, *Maynier*, pp. 96–7.

28 *Ibid.*, p. 97. For references to the transhumant movements of the amaGqunu-khwebe, see Peires, *House of Phalo*, pp. 9, 57.

29 Newton-King and Malherbe, *Khoikhoi rebellion*, p. 22; 'Commandant A. van Jaarsveld's report of the expulsion of the Kafirs', in Moodie (ed.), *The record*, part III, p. 110. For references to the presence of the imiDange behind De Bruins Hoogte in 1799, see 'First attempt [of Dr Van der Kemp] to enter Caffraria', *Transactions of the London Missionary Society*, 1 (1804), 382, 384.

30 Bresler to Dundas, 24 January 1799, in Theal (ed.), *Records*, vol. II, p. 351. See also McNab to Dundas, 12 March 1799, in *ibid.*, p. 384; Marais, *Maynier*, p. 101 and Giliomee, 'The burgher rebellions', p. 343.

31 Landdrost and Heemraden of Graaff Reinet to Dundas, 25 January 1799 and 19 February 1799, in Theal (ed.), *Records*, vol. II, pp. 349–50, 365.

32 Journal kept by Landdrost Bresler, in *ibid.*, p. 393.

33 *Ibid.*, p. 381.

34 'Criminal claim and conclusion', in *ibid.*, vol. III, pp. 264–5.

35 Dundas to Bresler, 23 February 1799, in *ibid.*, vol. II, p. 367.

36 Dundas to Faure, 16 February 1799, in *ibid.*, vol. II, pp. 356–7.

37 Vandeleur to Dundas, 'Widow Scheepers, 20 miles north of Swartkops Bay', in *Ibid.*, p. 387.

38 'Criminal claim and conclusion', in *ibid.*, vol. III, pp. 224–8. Literacy played an important role in these events. Letters from one rebel leader to another were usually carried by Khoisan servants.

39 'Journal of Landdrost Bresler', in *ibid.*, vol. II, p. 395. Much has been written about the extraordinary life of Coenraad de Buys and his role in the civil unrest of 1795–1803. See, for example, Marais, *Maynier*, pp. 29–32, 99–103; Peires,

House of Phalo, pp. 52–4, 58, 97 and Legassick, 'The frontier tradition in South African historiography', pp. 65–6.

40 'Criminal claim and conclusion', in Theal (ed.), *Records*, vol. III, pp. 226, 244.

41 *Ibid.*, pp. 224, 227, 244.

42 In my view, Nggika's involvement in the burgher rebellion was never a real possibility. De Buys was certainly close to Ngqika (though he was not living with his mother as Peires alleges), but their relations were showing signs of strain in 1799 and it is unlikely that Ngqika would have wished to jeopardise his good relations with the colony by collaborating with De Buys. (See 'Second attempt [of Dr Van der Kemp] to enter Caffraria' and 'Transactions of Dr. Vanderkemp in the year 1800' in *Transactions of the London Missionary Society* 1 (1804). Compare Peires, *House of Phalo*, pp. 52–4, 58.)

43 McNab to Dundas, 21 March 1799, in Theal (ed.), *Records*, vol. II, p. 398. For the planned attack on the troops at Zoutpan's Nek, see Vandeleur to Dundas, Swartkops Bay, in *ibid.*, p. 388; McNab to Dundas, 21 March 1799, in *ibid.*, p. 398 and 'Criminal claim and conclusion' in *ibid.*, vol. III, pp. 227, 253.

44 'Journal of Landdrost Bresler', in *ibid.*, vol. II, p. 395; 'Criminal claim and conclusion', in *ibid.*, vol. III, p. 229.

45 'Criminal claim and conclusion', in *ibid.*, vol. II, p. 229.

46 Only thirty men had remained behind in the village to guard the Drostdy (Vandeleur to Barrow, 27 March 1799, in *ibid.*, vol. II, p. 404). Barrow had been stationed at the foot of Attaquas Kloof with twelve dragoons, so as to intercept travellers moving between Swellendam and the eastern frontier and monitor the activities of suspected rebel sympathisers. ('Memorandum for John Barrow, Esqre.', 8 March 1799, in *ibid.*, vol. II, pp. 381–2.)

47 Barrow, *Travels*, vol. II, p. 38.

48 'Criminal claim and conclusion', in Theal (ed.), *Records*, vol. III, p. 230. Twenty prisoners were transported to Cape Town, where they were held until August 1800, when eighteen were charged with High Treason.

49 The fines must have been quite substantial, for 9,000 rix dollars were collected from between 93 and 150 insurgents (Dundas to Yonge, 20 February 1800, in Theal (ed.), *Records*, vol. III, p. 55).

50 Francis Dundas to Henry Dundas, 14 May 1799, in *ibid.*, vol. II, p. 425.

51 Barrow, *Travels*, vol. II, pp. 94–5.

52 'Proclamation by Major General Francis Dundas', 17 February 1799, in Theal (ed.), *Records*, vol. II, p. 359.

53 BO 68, Barrow to Dundas, Zwartkops Bay, 15 April 1799.

54 Barrow, *Travels*, vol. II, pp. 95–6.

55 *Ibid.*, p. 93.

56 Dundas to Yonge, in Theal (ed.), *Records*, vol. III, pp. 50–2; BO 68, Barrow to Dundas, 15 April 1799.

57 Barrow, *Travels*, vol. II, p. 129.

58 *Ibid.*, p. 130.

59 Marais, *Maynier*, p. 108. Barrow believed that the Xhosa had been instigated by fugitive Boer rebels, but there is nothing to support this opinion.

60 It is not clear that Stuurman was still with the group.

61 Barrow, *Travels*, vol. II, p. 128.

62 *Ibid.*, p. 128.
63 See chapter 7, p. 126.
64 Dundas to Yonge, 20 February 1800, in Theal (ed.), *Records*, vol. III, p. 59.
65 Barrow, *Travels*, vol. II, p. 130.
66 Dundas to Yonge, 20 February 1800, in Theal (ed.), *Records*, vol. III, p. 59.
67 Dundas to Yonge, 20 February 1800, in *ibid.*, vol. III, p. 59.
68 Marais, *Maynier*, p. 108.
69 'Journey [of Dr van der Kemp] to Caffraria from the Cape of Good Hope in the year 1799', p. 378. Other sources name 'the Rebellious Hottentots' as the main protagonists on the enemy side and say five Boers were killed. (P. H. van Rooyen to Landdrost of Swellendam, 31 July 1799, in Theal (ed.), *Records*, vol. II, p. 453; Barnard to Henry Dundas, 13 September 1799, in *ibid.*, p. 481.)
70 Van Rooyen to Landdrost of Swellendam, 31 July 1799, in *ibid.*, vol. II, p. 453.
71 LMS, Africa: incoming letters, Box 1, Folder 2, Journal of Dr Vanderkemp, 19 June 1799.
72 'Journey [of Dr van der Kemp] from the Cape of Good Hope . . . in the year 1799', 376. Punctuation as in the original.
73 I do not mean to suggest that Dr van der Kemp's beliefs had anything in common with the liberation theology of the late twentieth century, but only that his conviction that the rewards of faith were available to all human beings, regardless of race or ethnicity, was liberatory in the context in which he preached.
74 Vandeleur to Francis Dundas, 31 July 1799, in Theal (ed.), *Records*, vol. II, p. 453.
75 P. H. van Rooyen to Landdrost of Swellendam, 31 July 1799, in *ibid.*, p. 452.
76 Vandeleur to Francis Dundas, 31 July 1799, in *ibid.*, p. 454.
77 Vandeleur to Dundas, 3 August 1799, in *ibid.*, p. 456.
78 *Ibid.*, p. 456.
79 Anna Elizabeth Olivier to her husband, Stephanus Naudé, 5 August 1799, in *ibid.*, p. 461.
80 Bresler to Francis Dundas, 6 August 1799, in *ibid.*, pp. 461–2.
81 Vandeleur to Dundas, 31 July 1799 and 3 August 1799, in *ibid.*, pp. 453 and 457.
82 'Criminal claim and conclusion', in *ibid.*, vol. III, p. 231.
83 Vandeleur to Dundas, 31 July 1799, in *ibid.*, vol. II, pp. 453–5; Bresler to Dundas, 29 July 1799, in *ibid.*, p. 446.
84 Vandeleur to Dundas, 22 August 1799, in *ibid.*, p. 474.
85 Salomon Ferreira to Landdrost of Swellendam, 31 July 1799, in *ibid.*, p. 450. See also *ibid.*, pp. 446, 452, 459.
86 Vandeleur to Dundas, 3 August 1799, in *ibid.*, p. 457.
87 Okkert Oosthuijzen to P. H. van Rooyen, undated, in *ibid.*, p. 449; P. H. van Rooyen to L. Fourie, J. Meyer and G. Meyer, 31 July 1799, in *ibid.*, pp. 450–1.
88 'First attempt [of Dr van der Kemp] to enter Caffraria', pp. 383–4.
89 Patterson, *Slavery and social death*, pp. 10–13 and chapter 3; Dundas to Deputy Secretary Ross, Attaqua's Kloof, 20 August 1799, in Theal (ed.), *Records*, vol. II, p. 473; Dundas to Ross, Piet van Rooy's, 23 August 1799, in *ibid.*, pp. 475–6.
90 Marais, *Maynier*, chapter 4.
91 'First attempt [of Dr van der Kemp] to enter Caffraria', p. 386.

92 See chapter 7, page 148.
93 Vandeleur to Francis Dundas, 13 August 1799, and Barnard to Henry Dundas, 14 September 1799, in Theal (ed.), *Records*, vol. II, pp. 467, 483.
94 Barnard to Henry Dundas, 14 September 1799, in *ibid.*, p. 482.
95 Vandeleur to Dundas, 3 August 1799, in *ibid.*, p. 458.
96 D. W. Kruger and C. J. Beyers (eds.), *Dictionary of South African biography*, 4 vols. (Johannesburg: Nasionale Boekhandel, 1968; Cape Town: Tafelberg, 1972, 1977; Durban: Butterworth, 1981), vol. III, pp. 245–6.
97 'Provisional justification of H. C. D. Maynier', in Theal (ed.), *Records*, vol. IV, p. 292.
98 *Ibid.*, pp. 91–2.
99 Dundas to Yonge, 20 February 1800, in *ibid.*, vol. III, p. 56.
100 Dundas to Ross, Long Kloof, 24 August 1799, in *ibid.*, vol. II, p. 476.
101 Dundas to Yonge, 20 February 1800, in *ibid.*, p. 54.
102 *Ibid.*, pp. 52–4; 'Provisional justification of H. C. D. Maynier', in *ibid.*, vol. IV, p. 292.
103 Dundas to Yonge, 20 February 1800, in *ibid.*, vol. III, p. 53; 'Provisional justification of H. C. D. Maynier', in *ibid.*, vol. IV, p. 290.
104 'Provisional justification of H. C. D. Maynier', in *ibid.*, p. 289.
105 The implementation of Caledon's Code was largely given over to the field-cornets (*veldwagtmeesters*), who were themselves farmers and usually shared the prejudices of the latter regarding the proper place of Khoisan servants in the moral and social order. (See Philip, *Researches in South Africa*, vol. I, chapter 8. See also S. Newton-King, 'The labour market of the Cape Colony, 1807–1828', in S. Marks and A. Atmore (eds.), *Economy and society in pre-industrial South Africa* (London: Longman, 1980), pp. 176–7.)
106 CJ 653, Commission of inquiry into Maynier's conduct; questions put to William Somerville, 5 May 1802.
107 *Ibid.*
108 'Provisional justification of H. C. D. Maynier', in Theal (ed.), *Records*, vol. IV, p. 294.
109 Dundas to Yonge, 20 February 1800, in *ibid.*, vol. III, pp. 53–4.
110 Newton-King and Malherbe, *Khoikhoi rebellion*, p. 31. For a sensitive and detailed inquiry into the identity of these captains and their status within Khoekhoe communities, see V. C. Malherbe, 'Khoi captains and the third frontier war', in *ibid.*, part II.
111 'Provisional justification of H. C. D. Maynier', in Theal (ed.), *Records*, vol. IV. See also Dundas to Yonge, 20 February 1800, in *ibid.*, vol. III, p. 55.
112 'Transactions of Dr Vanderkemp in the year 1801', *Transactions of the London Missionary Society* 1 (1804), 480.
113 Newton-King and Malherbe, *Khoikhoi rebellion*, p. 88.
114 L. J. Erasmus to Roets, 1 December 1799, in VC 888, Donald Moodie's manuscript notes, vol. XXV, cited in Malherbe, 'The Khoi captains and the third frontier war', p. 89.
115 BO 69, H. J. van Rensburg to J. van Reenen, 2 February 1801, p. 578.
116 Maynier to Dundas, July 1801, in Theal (ed.), *Records*, vol. IV, p. 32; 'Provisional justification of H. C. D. Maynier', in *ibid.*, pp. 297–8; 'Transactions of

Dr Vanderkemp in the year 1801', p. 480.
117 Maynier to Dundas, July 1801, in Theal (ed.), *Records*, vol. IV, pp. 26–7.
118 Marais, *Maynier*, pp. 128–9.
119 Malherbe, 'Khoi captains and the third frontier war', in Newton-King and Malherbe, *Khoikhoi rebellion*, p. 90; 'Journey [of Dr van der Kemp] to Caffraland', pp. 493 and 501.
120 See chapter 8, p. 208. The Reverend Ballot had presumably left the district by this time. In February 1799 he had told his friend, Fiscal van Ryneveld, of his fervent desire to get away (Ballot to Van Ryneveld, 24 February 1799, in Theal (ed.), *Records*, vol. II, p. 370).
121 'Transactions of Dr Vanderkemp in the year 1801', p. 480.
122 *Ibid.*
123 *Ibid.*, pp. 480–1.
124 Maynier to Dundas, July 1801, in *ibid.*, vol. IV, p. 27.
125 'Provisional justification of H. C. D. Maynier', in *ibid.*, pp. 324–5; Maynier to Dundas, July 1801, in *ibid.*, pp. 30–1.
126 'Transactions of Dr Vanderkemp in the year 1801', p. 483.
127 Maynier to Dundas, July 1801, in Theal (ed.), *Records*, vol. IV, pp. 31, 33. On Maynier's 'highhandedness' in his dealings with the colonists, see Giliomee, 'Burgher rebellions on the eastern frontier'.
128 'Transactions of Dr Vanderkemp in the year 1801', p. 483.
129 Maynier to Dundas, July 1801, in Theal (ed.), *Records*, vol. IV, pp. 34–5.
130 'Transactions of Dr Vanderkemp in the year 1801', pp. 483–4.
131 'Provisonal justification of H. C. D. Maynier', in Theal (ed.), *Records*, vol. IV, p. 306.
132 Newton-King and Malherbe, *Khoikhoi rebellion*, pp. 89–90.
133 BO 69, Vos to Dundas, Graaff Reinet, 8 December 1801.
134 *Ibid.*
135 'Transactions of Dr Vanderkemp in the year 1801', p. 493.
136 *Ibid.*, pp. 493–4. For an account of Dr van der Kemp's narrow escape on 23 October, see chapter 8, note 246.
137 LMS, Box 1, Folder 4C, Journal of Dr van der Kemp, 25 December 1801. See also Sherlock to Dundas, Graaff Reinet, 30 November 1801, in Theal (ed.), *Records*, vol. IV, pp. 98–9.
138 BO 69, J. S. van Nieuwkerk to Dundas, undated.
139 Newton-King and Malherbe, *Khoikhoi rebellion*, pp. 39–41, 96–8.
140 Marais, *Maynier*, p. 136.
141 'Provisional justification of H. C. D. Maynier', in Theal (ed.), *Records*, vol. IV, p. 328.
142 *Ibid.*, pp. 326–8.
143 'Public dinner given by the Hottentots of Bethelsdorp to the Reverend Dr Philip and Mr Fairburn', *South African Commercial Advertiser*, 13 March 1830.
144 Robert Ross, 'The Kat River rebellion and Khoikhoi nationalism: the fate of an ethnic identification', unpublished paper presented to the conference on Khoisan identities and cultural heritage, University of the Western Cape, Cape Town, July 1997.

10 POSTSCRIPT

1 Christopher Saunders has given a detailed account of the intellectual genesis of the frontier thesis, tracing it from the work of Leo Fouche in 1909 through W. M. Macmillan, C. W. de Kiewiet and Eric Walker, to its fullest exposition in I. D. MacCrone's *Race Attitudes in South Africa*, published in 1937 (Christopher Saunders, *The making of the South African past: major historians on race and class* (Cape Town: David Philip, 1988), pp. 70, 92, 114–15, 120).

2 See pp. 40–1.

3 Barrow, *Travels*, vol. II, p. 98; *South African Commercial Advertiser*, 3 September 1834, 'Report of a meeting held at Philipton on 5 August 1834'.

4 VC 888, undated manuscript.

5 Lewin Robinson (ed.), *The letters of Lady Anne Barnard*, p. 143; Sparrman, *A voyage to the Cape of Good Hope*, vol. II, pp. 130–2. See also Barrow, *Travels*, vol. I, pp. 28–9 and 31–2.

6 1/GR 12/1, Cornelis du Plooij to Pieter Ernst Kruger, 16 May 1789. See also 1/GR 1/2, 30 April 1795 and 1/GR 13/10, 1 August 1803.

7 Reply of the Colesberg memorialists to Lieutenant-Governor Stockenstrom, July 1837, in Du Toit and Giliomee (eds.), *Afrikaner political thought*, vol. I, p. 117.

Select bibliography

1 PRIMARY SOURCES

A   CAPE ARCHIVES DEPOT, CAPE TOWN

A   Accessions
A 50   W. R. Morrison Collection
A 50(4)   Statutes of India, 1642
A 124   Extracts from Fitzgerald's journal of excursions to Graaff
             Reinet and the east coast
A 447   Swellengrebel papers
A 602   S. E. Hudson Collection

ACC 50(3)   Letters from J. Philip, C. L. Stretch, J. Read and others

BO   First British occupation
BO 26   Letters received from military, 1798–9
BO 68   Disturbances in the interior of the colony, 1795–9
BO 69   Disturbances in the interior of the colony, 1799–1802
BO 104   Miscellaneous documents, 1797–8

BR   Batavian Republic
BR 68   Annexures to the resolutions of the Council of Policy, July
             1805

C   Council of Policy
C 10   Resolutions, 1676–7
C 157   Resolutions, 1799
C 213   Resolutions, February 1793
C 219   Resolutions, October–November 1793
C 221   Resolutions, 11 January 1794
C 453   Incoming letters, 1738–9
C 473   Incoming letters, January–July 1748
C 490   Incoming letters, 1754
C 491   Incoming letters, January–April 1755

c 492	Incoming letters, April–December 1755
c 563	Incoming letters, 1786–7
c 565	Incoming letters, 1786–7
c 601	Incoming letters, 1793
c 697	Report with annexures, Nederburgh *en* Frijkenius, Part 1, 24 July 1793
c 994	Annexures to incoming letters, March 1792
c 1017	Annexures to incoming letters, February 1793
c 1145	Requests and nominations, 1766
c 1266	Memorials and reports, 1776
c 1300	Memorials and reports, 1789
CJ	Court of Justice
CJ 28	Original rolls and minutes, 1746
CJ 47	Original rolls and minutes, 1765
CJ 69	Original rolls and minutes, 1787
CJ 77–80	Original rolls and minutes, 1795–8
CJ 361	Documents in criminal cases, 1753
CJ 362	Documents in criminal cases, 1753
CJ 403	Documents in criminal cases, 1772
CJ 446	Documents in criminal cases, 1793
CJ 450	Documents in criminal cases, 1794
CJ 483	Documents in criminal cases, 1801
CJ 653	Judicial papers, Maynier's defence and charges, 1802
CJ 731	Documents in criminal cases, 1800
CJ 840	Original rolls and minutes, civil section, 1746
CJ 900	Rolls and minutes in civil cases, 1797
CJ 2492	Letters received, 1793–5
CJ 2649	Wills and codicils, 1686–1708
CJ 2945	*Vendurollen*, 1789
CJ 3387	Minutes, rolls and records of proceedings, Circuit Court, Uitenhage, 1812
CO	Colonial Office
CO 6	Letters received, 1807
CO 2559	Letters received from Uitenhage, 1806
CO 2564	Letters received from Graaff Reinet, 1808
CO 2567	Letters received from Graaff Reinet, 1809
CO 2580	Letters received from Swellendam and Graaff Reinet, 1812
GH	Government House
GH 28/1	Enclosures to despatches, June 1807–January 1809
1/GR	District of Graaff Reinet
1/GR 1/1–4	Minutes of Board of Landdrost and Heemraden, 1786–1806
1/GR 3/16–18	Judicial declarations, interrogatories and *insinuatien* in criminal cases, 1786–1802

1/GR 3/32	Judicial declarations, interrogatories and *insinuatien* in criminal cases, 1795–1834
GR 12/1–2	Letters and reports from field-cornets, *veldwagtmeesters*, *veldkommandants* and private individuals, Graaff Reinet, 1781–1809, 1782–94
1/GR 13/2	Letters received from private individuals, 1781–1800
1/GR 13/10	Letters received from private individuals, 1804
GR 15/1	Notarial deeds, 1786
1/GR 15/43	Contracts of service, Hottentots and free persons of colour, 1786–1882
1/GR 15/71	Contracts of service, Hottentots, Bushmen and free persons of colour, 1792–1848
1/GR 16/1	Letters despatched, 1786–1813
J	*Opgaafrollen*
J 107	*Opgaafrollen*, Graaff Reinet, 1787
J 108	*Opgaafrollen*, Graaff Reinet, 1788
J 113	*Opgaafrollen*, Graaff Reinet, 1796
J 115	*Opgaafrollen*, Graaff Reinet, 1798
J 118	*Opgaafrollen*, Graaff Reinet, 1800
J 210	*Opgaafrollen*, Stellenbosch, 1777
J 226	*Opgaafrollen*, Stellenbosch and Drakenstein, 1800–2
J 319	*Opgaafrollen*, Swellendam, 1806
M	Miscellaneous documents
M3i	Criminal cases in District of Graaff Reinet
MOIC 2/340	Master of the Supreme Court, insolvency branch
MOIC 2/4	Insolvent liquidation and distribution accounts, 1803
MOOC	Master of the Supreme Court
MOOC 10/8–25	Vendue rolls, 1760–1812
MOOC 13/1/5–36	Liquidation accounts, 1760–1813
MOOC 14/25–115	Annexures to liquidation accounts, 1760–1813
MOOC 14/233	Account book, 1791–1801
RLR	Receiver of Land Revenue
RLR 16/1–27/1	Receiver of Land Revenue, 1760–80
1/STB	District of Stellenbosch
1/STB 3/10–15	Sworn statements in preparatory examinations, 1749–1804
1/STB 10/7	Letters received from the Governor and Council of Policy
1/STB 10/150	Letters received from fieldcornets and private individuals, 1787–1801
1/STB 10/152	Letters received from fieldcornets and private individuals 1798–9
1/STB 10/162	Letters received from ward masters, 1773–93
1/STB 10/163	Letters received from ward masters, 1773–95

1/STB 13/13	Letters received by the *krijgsraad*, 1780–97
1/STB 13/43	Commando papers, 1776–1846
1/STB 20/2	Letters despatched, 1749–1780
1/STB 20/30	Letters despatched, 1795–1801

1/SWM	District of Swellendam
1/SWM 1/1	Minutes of Board of Landdrost and Heemraden, 1747, 1750–8
1/SWM 3/10	Criminal interrogatories, 1746–58
1/SWM 3/14	Criminal interrogatories, 1777–83
1/SWM 3/17	Criminal interrogatories, 1793–5

VC	Verbatim Copies
VC 32	Journals of Cape Governors, 1775–9
VC 45	General Muster Rolls, 1760–71
VC 65–6	Letter books of Commissioner General A. J. Sluyksen, 1793–4
VC 68	Letter book of Commissioner A. J. Sluyksen, 1796
VC 592	Diary of Col. R. J. Gordon
VC 595	Diary of Col. R. J. Gordon, vol. IV
VC 871	Donald Moodie's manuscript notes, 1789–1803
VC 882	Donald Moodie's manuscript notes, 1786–95
VC 887	Donald Moodie's manuscript notes, nd
VC 888	Donald Moodie's manuscript notes, 1780–96

Z	Microfilms
ZI 1/25	Microfilm of documents in the Public Record Office of Northern Ireland, Belfast; papers relative to the prosecution of Mr Maynier, late Commissioner at Graaff Reinet, 1802
ZK 8/1/1–9	Deeds Office, title deeds, 1652–1736
ZK 1/159	Council of Policy, incoming letters, 1789–92
ZL 1/3/2	London Missionary Society, letters received (South Africa), 1802–4

B   SCHOOL OF ORIENTAL AND AFRICAN STUDIES, LONDON UNIVERSITY

| LMS | London Missionary Society, incoming letters and reports, Africa (South), 1799–1812 |

C   PRIVATE COLLECTIONS

Cullinan, P. (translator and editor), 'The travel journals of Robert Jacob Gordon'.

D   PUBLISHED PRIMARY SOURCES

Barrow, J., *An account of travels into the interior of southern Africa in the years 1797 and 1798*, 2 vols., London: Cadell and Davies, 1801, 1804.

Blommaert, W. and Wiid, J. A. (eds.), *Die joernaal van Dirk Gysbert van Reenen, 1803*, Cape Town: Van Riebeeck Society, 1937.

Böeseken, A. (ed.), *Suid-Afrikaanse argiefstukke: resolusies van die Politieke Raad*, 8 vols., Cape Town: Cape Times, 1957–75.

Burchell, W., *Travels in the interior of Africa*, 2 vols., London, 1822, reprinted, Cape Town: Struik, 1967.

Campbell, J., *Travels in South Africa*, Cape Town: Struik, 1974.

De Jong, C., *Reizen naar de Kaap de Goede Hoop, Ierland en Noorwegen in de jaren 1791 tot 1797. . .*, 3 vols., Harlem: F. Bohn, 1802, 1803.

Du Toit, A. and Giliomee, H. (eds.), *Afrikaner political thought: analysis and documents*, vol. I, *1780–1850*, Cape Town: David Philip, 1983.

Forbes, V. S. and Rourke, J. (eds.), *Paterson's Cape travels, 1777 to 1779*, Johannesburg: Brenthurst Press, 1980.

Godée Molsbergen, E. C. (ed.), *Reizen in Zuid-Afrika in de Hollandse tijd*, vol. III, The Hague: Martinus Nijhoff, 1922.

Golovnin, V. M., *Detained in Simon's Bay: the story of the detention of the imperial Russian sloop Diana, April 1808–May 1809*, Cape Town: Friends of the South African Library, 1964.

Hondius, J., *Klare Besgryving van Cabo de Bona Esperança*, facsimile edition, Cape Town: Komitee vir Boekuitstalling, Van Riebeeck-fees, 1952.

Jeffreys, K. A. and Naudé, S. D. (eds.), *Kaapse Plakaatboeke, 1652–1795*, 6 vols., Cape Town: Government Printer, 1944, 1948, 1950 and 1951.

Le Vaillant, F., *Travels from the Cape of Good Hope into the interior parts of Africa in the years 1780–1785*, 2 vols., London: G. G. and J. Robinson, 1790.
    New travels into the interior parts of Africa by way of the Cape of Good Hope in the years 1783, 1784 and 1785, 3 vols., London: Robinson, 1796.

Leibbrandt, H. C. V., *Précis of the archives of the Cape of Good Hope: the defence of Willem Adriaan van der Stel*, Cape Town: Government Printers, 1897.

Lewin Robinson, A. M., (ed.), *The letters of Lady Anne Barnard*, Cape Town: Balkema, 1973.

Lichtenstein, H., *Travels in southern Africa in the years 1803, 1804, 1805 and 1806*, 2 vols., London: Henry Colburn, 1812, 1815, reprinted Cape Town: Van Riebeeck Society in 1928, 1930.

Mentzel, O. F., *Life at the Cape in the mid-eighteenth century; being the biography of Rudolph Siegfried Alleman, Captain of the military forces at the Cape of Good Hope*, Cape Town: Van Riebeeck Society, 1919.
    A complete and authentic geographical and topographical description of the famous and (all things considered) remarkable African Cape of Good Hope, 3 parts, Cape Town: Van Riebeeck Society, 1921–44.

Moodie, D. (ed.), *The record: or a series of official papers relative to the condition and treatment of the native tribes of South Africa*, Cape Town: Balkema, 1960.

Mossop, E. E. (ed.), *Journals of the expeditions of the Honourable Ensign Olof Bergh (1682 and 1683) and the Ensign Isaq Schrijver (1689)*, Cape Town: Van Riebeeck Society, 1931.

Paterson, W., *A narrative of four journeys into the country of the Hottentots and Caffraria*, second edition, London: J. Johnson, 1787, 1790.

Philip, J., *Researches in South Africa: illustrating the civil, moral, and religious condition of the native tribes*, 2 vols., London: James Duncan, 1828, reprinted in 1969 by Negro Universities Press, New York.

Raven-Hart, R., *Before Van Riebeeck: callers at South Africa 1488 to 1652*, Cape Town: Struik, 1967.

Schapera, I. (ed.), *The early Cape Hottentots*, Cape Town: Van Riebeeck Society, 1933.

Schutte, G. J., (ed.), *Briefwisseling van Hendrik Swellengrebel Jr oor Kaapse sake, 1778–1792*, Cape Town: Van Riebeeck Society, 1982.

Sparrman, A., *A voyage to the Cape of Good Hope towards the Antarctic Polar Circle round the world and to the country of the Hottentots and the Caffres from the year 1772–1776*, ed. V. S. Forbes, 2 vols., Cape Town: Van Riebeeck Society, 1977.

Tavernier, J. B., *The six voyages of John Baptista Tavernier*, London, 1678.

Theal, G. M., *Records of the Cape Colony from February 1793 to April 1831*, 36 vols., London: Government Printers, 1897–1905.

Thom, H. B. (ed.), *Willem Stephanus van Ryneveld se aanmerkingen over de verbetering van het vee aan de Kaap de Goede Hoop, 1804*, Cape Town: Van Riebeeck Society, 1942.

Thompson, G., *Travels and adventures in southern Africa*, 2 vols., ed. V. S. Forbes, Cape Town: Van Riebeeck Society, 1967, 1968.

Thunberg, C. P., *Travels at the Cape of Good Hope, 1772–1775*, ed. V. S. Forbes, Cape Town: Van Riebeeck Society, 1986.

Transactions of the London Missionary Society, vol. I (1795–1801), London, 1804.

Wet, G. C. de (ed.), *Suid Afrikaanse Argiefstukken. Kaap*, vol. V, *Resolusies van die Politieke Raad, 1716–1719*, Cape Town: Government Printer, 1964.

2   SECONDARY SOURCES

Acocks, J. P. A., *Veld types of South Africa*, second edition, *Memoirs of the Botanical Survey of South Africa* 40 (1975).

Arkel, D. van, Quispel G. C. and Ross, R. J., '"De wijngaard des heeren?" Een onderzoek naar de wortels van "de blanke baasskap" in Zuid-Afrika', *Cahiers sociale geschiedenis* 4 (Leiden, 1983). Published in translation in R. Ross, *Beyond the pale: essays on the history of colonial South Africa* (Hanover: Wesleyan University Press, 1993).

Badenhorst, J. J., *A geographical study of the Cape Midlands and Karoo area, with special reference to the physiography and elements of land use*, 5 vols. Grahamstown: Institute of Social and Economic Research, Rhodes University, 1970–5. Vol. I, *Survey of the Cape Midlands and Karoo regions*.

Bank, A., 'Slavery in Cape Town, 1806–1834', MA thesis, University of Cape Town, 1991, published as *The decline of urban slavery at the Cape, 1806 to 1843*, Cape Town: Centre for African Studies, University of Cape Town, 1991.

Barnard, A., *Hunters and herders of southern Africa: a comparative ethnography of the Khoisan peoples*, Cambridge: Cambridge University Press, 1992.

Beyers, C. J. and Kruger, D. W. (eds.), *Dictionary of South African biography*, 4 vols., Johannesburg: Nasionale Boekhandel, 1968; Cape Town: Tafelberg, 1972 and 1977; Durban: Butterworth and Co., 1981.

Biesele, M., *Women like meat: the folklore and foraging ideology of the Kalahari Ju/'hoan*, Johannesburg: Witwatersrand University Press, 1993.

Blackburn, R., 'Slavery – its special features and social role', in Leonie Archer (ed.), *Slavery and other forms of unfree labour*, London: Routledge, 1988.

Bleek, W. H. I. and Lloyd, L. C., *Specimens of Bushman folklore*, London: George Allen, 1911.

Böeseken, A. J., 'Die Nederlandse kommissarisse en die 18de eeuse samelewing aan die Kaap', *Archives Year Book for South African History* 7 (1944).

Bonner, P., *Kings, commoners and concessionaires: the evolution and dissolution of the nineteenth-century Swazi state*, Johannesburg: Ravan Press, 1983.

Braudel, F., *Afterthoughts on material civilisation and capitalism*, Baltimore: Johns Hopkins University Press, 1977.

Civilisation and capitalism, 15th–18th century, 3 vols.: vol. I, *The structures of everyday life*, London: Fontana Paperbacks, 1985; vol. III, *The perspective of the world*, London: Collins, 1984.

Bredekamp, H. and Newton-King, S., 'The subjugation of the Khoisan during the 17th and 18th centuries', unpublished paper presented to the Conference on Economic Development and Racial Domination, University of the Western Cape, 1984.

Bruijn, J. R. de, Gaastra, F. S. and Schöffer, I., *Dutch-Asiatic shipping in the seventeenth and eighteenth centuries*, 3 vols., The Hague: Martinus Nijhoff, 1987.

Carstens, P. (ed.), *The social organisation of the Nama and other essays by Winifred Hoernlé*, Johannesburg: Witwatersrand University Press, 1985.

Cashdan, E., 'Territoriality among human foragers: ecological models and an application to four Bushman groups', *Current Anthropology* 24 (1983).

Coetzee, J. M., 'The mind of apartheid: Geoffrey Cronje (1907–)', *Social Dynamics* 17 (1991).

White writing: on the culture of letters in South Africa, New Haven: Yale University Press, 1988.

Cronon, W., *Changes in the land: Indians, colonists, and the ecology of New England*, New York: Hill and Wang, 1983.

Deacon, H. J., *Where hunters gathered: a study of the Holocene Stone Age people in the eastern Cape*, Cape Town: South African Archaeological Society Monograph Series 1, 1976.

Deacon, J., ' "My place is the Bitterpits": the home territory of Bleek and Lloyd's /Xam San informants', *African Studies* 45 (1986).

'The power of a place in understanding southern San rock engravings', *World Archaeology* 20 (1988).

'Rock engravings and the folklore of Bleek and Lloyd's /Xam San informants', in T. Dowson and D. Lewis-Williams (eds.), *Contested images: diversity in southern African rock art research*, Johannesburg: Witwatersrand University Press, 1994.

Delius, P., *The land belongs to us: the Pedi polity, the Boers and the British in the nineteenth-century Transvaal*, Johannesburg: Ravan Press, 1983.

Dooling, W., 'The Castle: its place in the history of Cape Town, c. 1666–1760', unpublished paper presented to the Cape Town History Project Workshop, University of Cape Town, November 1991.

Dugard, J., *Introduction to criminal procedure*, Cape Town: Juta, 1977.

Eldridge, E. and Morton, F. (eds.), *Slavery in South Africa: captive labour on the Dutch frontier*, Pietermaritzburg: University of Natal Press, 1994.

Elphick, R., *Kraal and castle: Khoikhoi and the founding of white South Africa*, New Haven: Yale University Press, 1977.

Elphick, R. and Giliomee, H. (eds.), *The shaping of South African society, 1652–1820*, first edition, Cape Town: Longman, 1979; second edition (*1652–1840*), Cape Town: Maskew Miller Longman, 1989.

'The Khoisan to c. 1770', in R. Elphick and H. Giliomee (eds.), *The shaping of South African society, 1652–1820*, first edition, Cape Town: Longman 1979.

Elphick, R. and Malherbe, V. C., 'The Khoisan to 1828', in R. Elphick and H. Giliomee (eds.), *The shaping of South African society, 1652–1840*, second edition, Cape Town: Maskew Miller Longman, 1989.

Epstein, H. (ed.), *The origin of the domestic animals of Africa*, 2 vols., New York: Africana Publishing Corporation, 1971.

Fine, H., 'The administration of criminal justice at the Cape of Good Hope, 1795–1828', unpublished PhD thesis, University of Cape Town, 1991.

Finley, M. I., *Ancient Slavery and modern ideology*, London: Chatto and Windus, 1980.

Forbes, V. S., *Pioneer travellers in South Africa*, Cape Town: Balkema, 1965.

Freund, W. F., 'The Cape under the transitional governments, 1795–1814', in R. Elphick and H. Giliomee (eds.), *The shaping of South African society, 1652–1840*, second edition, Cape Town: Maskew Miller Longman, 1989.

Genovese, E., *Roll, Jordan, roll: the world the slaves made*, London: André Deutsch, 1975.

Gerstner, J. N., *The thousand generation covenant: Dutch Reformed covenant theology and group identity in colonial South Africa, 1652–1814*, Leiden: E. J. Brill, 1991.

Giliomee, H., 'The eastern frontier, 1770–1812', in R. Elphick and H. Giliomee (eds.), *The shaping of South African society, 1652–1840*, second edition, Cape Town: Maskew Miller Longman, 1989.

'The burgher rebellions on the eastern frontier, 1795–1815', in R. Elphick and H. Giliomee (eds.), *The shaping of South African society, 1652–1820*, first edition, Cape Town: Longman, 1979.

Guelke, L., 'Frontier settlement in early Dutch South Africa', *Annals of the American Association of Geographers* 66 (1976).

'The white settlers, 1652–1780', in R. Elphick and H. Giliomee (eds.), *The shaping of South African society, 1652–1820*, first edition, London: Longman, 1979.

'Land tenure and settlement at the Cape, 1652–1812', unpublished paper presented to the Symposium on the History of Surveying and Land Tenure in the Cape, 1652–1812, University of the Western Cape, July 1983.

'Freehold farmers and frontier settlers, 1657–1780', in R. Elphick and H. Giliomee (eds.), *The shaping of South African society, 1652–1840*, second edition, Cape Town: Maskew Miller Longman, 1989.

Guelke, L. and Cole Harris, R., 'Land and society in early Canada and South Africa', *Journal of Historical Geography* 3 (1977).

Guelke, L. and Shell, R. C.-H., 'An early colonial landed gentry: land and wealth in the Cape Colony, 1682–1731', *Journal of Historical Geography* 9 (1983).

Guenther, M., *The Nharo Bushmen of Botswana: tradition and change*, Hamburg: Helmut Buske Verlag, 1986.

'The relationship of Bushman art to ritual and folklore', in T. Dowson and D. Lewis-Williams (eds.), *Contested images: diversity in southern African rock art research*, Johannesburg: Witswatersrand University Press, 1994.

'From "lords of the desert" to "rubbish people": the colonial and contemporary state of the Nharo of Botswana', in Pippa Skotnes (ed.), *Miscast: negotiating the presence of the Bushmen*, Cape Town: University of Cape Town Press, 1996.

Hahn, T., *Tsuni-//Goam: the supreme being of the Khoi-Khoi*, London: Trübner and Co., 1881.

Hall, S. L. 'Pastoral adaptations and forager reactions in the eastern Cape', in M. Hall and A. B. Smith (eds.), *Prehistoric pastoralism in southern Africa*, The South African Archaeological Society Goodwin Series 5, 1986.

Harbsmeier, M., 'Elementary structures of otherness: an analysis of sixteenth century German travel accounts', in *Voyager à la Renaissance: actes du colloque de Tours, 1983*, Paris: Maisonneuve et Larose, 1987.

Harinck, G., 'Interaction between Xhosa and Khoi: emphasis on the period 1620–1750', in Leonard Thompson (ed.), *African societies in southern Africa*, London: Heinemann, 1969.

Heese, J. A., *Die herkoms van die Afrikaner, 1657–1867*, Cape Town: Balkema, 1971.

Heyns, H., 'The growth of the Afrikaner calf in relation to the production and composition of the milk of its dam', *Afrikanerbees Joernaal* 5 (1960).

Hoernlé, W., *The social organisation of the Nama and other essays*, ed. Peter Carstens, Johannesburg: Witwatersrand University Press, 1985.

Hoge, J., 'Personalia of the Germans at the Cape, 1652–1806', *Archives Year Book for South African History* 9 (1946).

Huffman, T. N., 'The trance hypothesis and the rock art of Zimbabwe', in *New approaches to southern African rock art*, The South African Archaeological Society Goodwin Series 4 (1983).

Hulme, P., *Colonial encounters: Europe and the native Caribbean, 1492–1797*, London and New York: Methuen, 1986.

Hunt, L. (ed.), *The new cultural history*, Berkeley and Los Angeles: University of California Press, 1989.

Israel, J., *The Dutch Republic: its rise, greatness and fall, 1477–1806*, Oxford: Clarendon Press, 1995.

Jolly, P., 'Melikane and Upper Mangolong revisited: the possible effects on San art of symbiotic contact between south-eastern San and Southern Sotho and Nguni communities', *South African Archaeological Bulletin* 50 (1995).

Katz, R., *Boiling energy: community healing among the Kalahari Kung*, Cambridge, Mass.: Harvard University Press, 1982.

Kiewiet, C. W. de, *A History of South Africa: social and economic*, Oxford: Oxford University Press, 1941.

Klein, M. A., 'The Atlantic slave trade and the development of slavery within West Africa', unpublished paper presented to the South African and contemporary history seminar, University of the Western Cape, July 1996.

Kruger, D. W. and Beyers, C. J. (eds.), *Dictionary of South African biography*, 4 vols., Johannesburg: Nasionale Boekhandel, 1968; Cape Town: Tafelberg, 1972, 1977; Durban: Butterworth, 1981.

LaCapra, D., *Rethinking intellectual history: texts, contexts, language*, Ithaca: Cornell University Press, 1983.

Lane Fox, R., *Pagans and Christians in the Mediterranean world from the second century AD to the conversion of Constantine*, London: Penguin Books, 1986.

Lee, R. and Guenther, M., 'Problems in Kalahari historical ethnoography and the tolerance of error, *History in Africa* 20 (1993).

Legassick, M., 'The frontier tradition in South African historiography', Institute of Commonwealth Studies, London, *Collected Seminar Papers on the Societies of Southern Africa* 12, 2 (1970–1). Subsequently published in S. Marks and A. Atmore (eds.), *Economy and society in pre-industrial South Africa*, London: Longman, 1980.

'The northern frontier to c. 1840: the rise and decline of the Griqua people', in R. Elphick and H. Giliomee (eds.), *The shaping of South African society, 1652–1840*, second edition, Cape Town: Maskew Miller Longman, 1989.

Lewis-Williams, J. D., *Believing and seeing: symbolic meanings in southern San rock paintings*, London: Academic Press, 1981.

'The economic and social context of southern San rock art', *Current Anthropology* 23 (1982).

The rock art of southern Africa, Cambridge: Cambridge University Press, 1983.

'Ideological continuities in prehistoric southern Africa', in C. Shrire (ed.), *Past and present in hunter-gatherer studies*, New York: Academic Press, 1984.

Discovering southern African rock art, Cape Town: David Philip, 1990.

Lewis-Williams, J. D. and Dowson, T., *Images of power: understanding Bushman rock art*, Johannesburg: Southern Book Publishers, 1989.

'Aspects of rock art research: a critical perspective', in T. Dowson and D. Lewis-Williams (eds.), *Contested images: diversity in southern African rock art research*, Johannesburg: Witwatersrand University Press, 1994.

Lockhart, J. and Schwartz, S. B., *Early Latin America: a history of colonial Spanish America and Brazil*, Cambridge: Cambridge University Press, 1983.

Lubbe, P., *The story of the velskoen*, Grahamstown: Leather Industries Research Institute, 1971.

Lucassen, J., *Migrant labour in Europe, 1600–1900*, London: Croom Helm, 1987.

Macmillan, W. M., *The Cape colour question: a historical survey*, Cape Town: Balkema, 1968.

Maggs, T. M. O'C., 'Some observations on the size of human groups during the Late Stone Age', in M. Schoonraad (ed.), *Rock paintings of Southern Africa*, supplement to the *South African Journal of Science*, special issue, 2 (1971).

Malherbe, V. C., 'Diversification and mobility of Khoikhoi labour in the eastern districts of the Cape Colony prior to the labour law of 1 November, 1809', unpublished MA thesis, University of Cape Town, 1978.

'Hermanus and his sons: Khoi bandits and conspirators in the post-rebellion period (1803–1818)', *African Studies* 41 (1982).

Manhire, A. H., Parkington, J. and Robey, T. S., 'Stone tools and Sandveld settlement', in M. Hall, G. Avery, D. M. Avery, M. L. Wilson and A. J. B. Humphreys (eds.), *Frontiers: southern African archaeology today*, Oxford: British Archaeological Reports International Series 207, 1984.

Manhire, A. H., Parkington J. and Yates, R., *Pictures from the past: a history of the interpretation of rock paintings and engravings of southern Africa*, Pietermaritzburg: Centaur Publications, 1990.

Marais, M. M., 'Armesorg aan die Kaap onder die Kompanjie, 1652–1795', *Archives Yearbook for South African History* (1943).

Maynier and the first Boer Republic, Cape Town: Maskew Miller, 1944.

Marks, S., 'Khoisan resistance to the Dutch in the seventeenth and eighteenth centuries', *Journal of African History* 13 (1972).

Marks, S. and Atmore, A., 'The imperial factor in South Africa in the nineteenth century: towards a reassessment', *Journal of Imperial and Commonwealth History* 3 (1974).

Marks, S. and Atmore, A. (eds.), *Economy and society in pre-industrial South Africa*, London: Longman, 1980.

Mason, J., 'Hendrik Albertus and his ex-slave Mey: a drama in three acts', paper presented to the Conference on Cape Slavery and After, University of Cape Town, August 1989, subsequently published in *Journal of African History* 31 (1990).

Mason, P., *Deconstructing America: representations of the other*, London: Routledge, 1990.

Merwe, P. J. van der, *Die noordwaartse beweging van die Boere voor die Groot Trek, 1770–1842*, The Hague: W. P. van Stockum and Zoon, 1937.

Die trekboer in die geskiedenis van die Kaapkolonie, 1657–1842, Cape Town: Nasionale Pers, 1938.

Muller, C. F. J., *Johannes Frederik Kirsten oor die toestand van die Kaapkolonie in 1795*, Pretoria: J. L. van Schaik, 1960.

Neumark, S. D., *Economic influences on the South African frontier, 1652–1836*, Stanford: Stanford University Press, 1957.

Newton-King, S., 'The labour market of the Cape Colony, 1807–1828', in S. Marks and A. Atmore (eds.), *Economy and society in pre-industrial South Africa*, London: Longman, 1980.

'Commerce and material culture on the eastern Cape frontier, 1764–1812', Institute of Commonwealth Studies, London, *Collected Seminar Papers on the Societies of Southern Africa* 14 (1988).

'Khoisan resistance to colonial expansion, 1700–1828', in T. Cameron and S. B. Spies (eds.), *A new illustrated history of South Africa*, Cape Town: Human and Rousseau, 1986.

'In search of notability: the antecedents of Dawid van der Merwe of the Warm

Bokkeveld', Institute of Commonwealth Studies, London, *Collected Seminar Papers on the Societies of Southern Africa* 20 (1994).

'Hilletje Smits and the shadow of death', unpublished seminar paper, University of the Western Cape, October 1995.

Newton-King, S. and Malherbe, V. C., *The Khoikhoi rebellion in the eastern Cape, 1799–1803*, Cape Town: Centre for African Studies, University of Cape Town, 1981.

Palmer, E., *The plains of Camdeboo*, revised edition, Johannesburg: Lowry Publishers, 1986.

Parkington, J., 'Soaqua and Bushmen: hunters and robbers', in C. Schrire (ed.), *Past and present in hunter-gatherer studies*, New York: Academic Press, 1984.

Parkington, J., Yates, R., Manhire, A. and Halkett, D., 'The social impact of pastoralism in the southwestern Cape', *Journal of Anthropological Archaeology* 5 (1986).

Patterson, O., *Slavery and social death: a comparative study*, Cambridge, Mass.: Harvard University Press, 1982.

Peires, J. B., *The house of Phalo: a history of the Xhosa people in the days of their independence*, Johannesburg: Ravan Press, 1981.

'The British and the Cape, 1814–1834', in R. Elphick and H. Giliomee (eds.), *The shaping of South African society, 1652–1840*, second edition, Cape Town: Maskew Miller Longman, 1989.

Penn, N., 'Anarchy and authority in the Koue Bokkeveld, 1739–1779: the banishing of Carel Buijtendag', seminar paper, History Department, University of Cape Town, May 1984, subsequently published in *Kleio* 17 (1985).

'Pastoralists and pastoralism in the northern Cape frontier zone during the eighteenth century', in Martin Hall and Andrew Smith (eds.), *Prehistoric pastoralism in southern Africa*, The South African Archaeological Society Goodwin Series 5, 1986.

'The frontier in the western Cape, 1700–1740', paper presented to a workshop organised by the Spatial Archaeology Research Unit, University of Cape Town, October 1984, subsequently published in J. Parkington and M. Hall (eds.), *Papers in the prehistory of the western Cape, South Africa*, Oxford: British Archaeological Reports International Series, 1987.

'Land, labour and livestock in the western Cape during the eighteenth century', in W. G. James and M. Simons (eds.), *The angry divide: social and economic history of the western Cape*, Cape Town: David Philip, 1989.

'Mapping the Cape: John Barrow and the first British occupation of the colony, 1795–1803', *Pretexts* 4 (1993).

'The northern Cape frontier zone, 1700–c. 1815', unpublished PhD thesis, University of Cape Town, 1995.

Plug, I., Bollong, C. A., Hart, T. J. G. and Sampson, C. G., 'Context and direct dating of pre-European livestock in the upper Seacow River Valley', *Annals of the South African Museum* 104 (1994).

Price, R. (ed.), *Maroon societies: rebel slave communities in the Americas*, second edition, Baltimore: Johns Hopkins University Press, 1979.

Ross, R., 'The "white" population of South Africa in the eighteenth century', *Population Studies* 19 (1975). Reprinted in Ross, *Beyond the pale: essays on the history of colonial South Africa*, Hanover: Wesleyan University Press, 1993.

Adam Kok's Griqua: a study in the development of stratification in South Africa, Cambridge: Cambridge University Press, 1976.

'Oppression, sexuality and slavery at the Cape of Good Hope', *Historical Reflections* 6 (1979).

'The rule of law at the Cape of Good Hope in the eighteenth century', *The Journal of Imperial and Commonwealth History* 9 (1980).

'Capitalism, expansion and incorporation on the southern African frontier', in H. Lamar and L. M. Thompson (eds.), *The frontier in history: North America and southern Africa compared*, New Haven: Yale University Press, 1981.

'The changing legal position of the Khoisan in the Cape Colony, 1652–1795', *African Perspectives* 5 (1982)

Cape of torments: slavery and resistance in South Africa, London: Routledge and Kegan Paul, 1983.

'The rise of the Cape gentry', *Journal of Southern African Studies* 9 (1983).

'The Cape of Good Hope and the world economy, 1652–1835', in R. Elphick and H. Giliomee (eds.), *The shaping of South African society, 1652–1840*, second edition, Cape Town: Maskew Miller Longman, 1989.

Beyond the pale: essays on the history of colonial South Africa, Hanover: Wesleyan University Press, 1993.

'The developmental spiral of the white family and the expansion of the frontier', in Robert Ross, *Beyond the pale: essays on the history of colonial South Africa*, Hanover: Wesleyan University Press, 1993.

'The Kat River rebellion and Khoikhoi nationalism: the fate of an ethnic identification', unpublished paper presented to the conference on Khoisan identities and cultural heritage, University of the Western Cape, Cape Town, July 1997.

Ross, R. and P. van Duin, *The economy of the Cape colony in the eighteenth century*, Leiden: Centre for the History of European Expansion, 1987.

Sampson, C. G., 'Site clusters in the Smithfield settlement pattern', *South African Archaeological Bulletin* 39 (1984).

'A prehistoric pastoralist frontier in the Upper Zeekoe Valley, South Africa', in M. Hall, G. Avery, D. M. Avery, M. L. Wilson and A. J. B. Humphreys (eds.), *Frontiers: southern African archaeology today*, Oxford: British Archaeological Reports International Series 207, 1984.

'Atlas of Stone Age settlement in the Central and Upper Seacow Valley', *Memoirs of the National Museum, Bloemfontein* 20 (1985).

'Veld damage in the Karoo caused by its pre-trekboer inhabitants: preliminary observations in the Seacow Valley', *The Naturalist* 30 (1986).

'Model of a prehistoric herder-hunter contact zone: a first approximation', in M. Hall and A. B. Smith (eds.), *Prehistoric pastoralism in southern Africa*, The South African Archaeological Society Goodwin Series 5, 1986.

'Bushman (Oesjwana) survival and acculturation in the colonial frontier of South Africa, 1770–1890', *Historical Archaeology* (1993).

Samuel, R., *Past and present in contemporary culture*, London: Verso, 1994.

Saunders, C., *The making of the South African past: major historians on race and class*, Cape Town: David Philip, 1988.

Schama, S., *Dead certainties (unwarranted speculations)*, New York: Alfred A. Knopf, 1991.

Schapera, I., *The Khoisan peoples of South Africa*, London: Routledge, 1930.

Schrire, C., 'An inquiry into the evolutionary status and apparent identity of San hunter-gatherers', *Human Ecology* 8, (1980).

'Wild surmises on savage thoughts', in C. Schrire (ed.), *Past and present in hunter-gatherer studies*, New York: Academic Press, 1984.

Schutte, G., 'Company and colonists at the Cape, 1652–1795', in R. Elphick and H. Giliomee (eds.), *The shaping of South African society, 1652–1840*, second edition, Cape Town: Maskew Miller Longman, 1989.

Shell, R. C.-H., 'Auctions – their good and evil tendency' [Part I], *Quarterly Bulletin of the South African Library* 39 (1985).

'The family and slavery at the Cape, 1680–1808', in W. G. James and Mary Simons (eds.), *The angry divide: social and economic history of the western Cape*, Cape Town: David Philip, 1989.

Children of bondage: a social history of the slave society at the Cape of Good Hope, 1652-1838, Hanover: Wesleyan University Press, 1994.

Skotnes, P. (ed.), *Miscast: negotiating the presence of the Bushmen*, Cape Town: University of Cape Town Press, 1996.

Smith, A. B., 'Competition, conflict and clientship: Khoi and San relationships in the western Cape', in M. Hall and A. Smith (eds.), *Prehistoric pastoralism in southern Africa*, South African Archaeological Society Goodwin Series 5, 1986.

'The Ju/wasi of Namibia in transition', *Newsletter of the Centre for African Studies, University of Cape Town* 4 (1988).

Solway J. S. and Lee, R. B., 'Foragers, genuine or spurious? Situating the Kalahari San in history', *Current Anthropology* 31 (1990).

Tellis-Nayak, V., 'Power and solidarity: clientage in domestic service', *Current Anthropology* 24 (1983).

Trapido, S., 'Reflections on land, office and wealth in the South African Republic, 1850–1900', in S. Marks and A. Atmore (eds.), *Economy and society in pre-industrial South Africa*, London: Longman, 1980.

Venter, P. J., 'Landdros en Heemrade (1682–1827)', *Archives Year Book for South African History* 2 (1940).

Viljoen, R., 'Revelation of a revolution: the prophecies of Jan Parel, alias *Onse Liewe Heer*', *Cronos* 21 (1994).

Villiers, C. C. de and Pama, C., *Geslagsregisters van die ou Kaapse families*, 3 vols., Cape Town: Balkema, 1966.

Vinnicombe, P., *People of the eland: rock paintings of the Drakensberg Bushmen as a reflection of their life and thought*, Pietermaritzburg: University of Natal Press, 1976.

'Rock art, territory and land rights', in M. Biesele, R. Gordon and R. Lee (eds.), *The past and future of !Kung ethnography: critical reflections and symbolic perspectives: essays in honour of Lorna Marshall*, Hamburg: Helmut Buske Verlag, 1986.

Vrugt, Marijke van der, *De criminele ordonnantiën van 1570: enkele beschouwingen over de eerste strafrechtcodificatie in de Nederlanden*, Zutphen: De Walburg Pers, 1978.

Wachtel, N., *The vision of the vanquished: the Spanish conquest of Peru through Indian eyes, 1530-1570*, New York: Harvester Press, 1977; French original, 1971.

Wagenaar, G., 'Johannes Gysbertus van Reenen – sy aandeel in die Kaapse geskiedenis tot 1806', unpublished MA thesis, University of Pretoria, 1976.

Wagner, R., 'Zoutpansberg: the dynamics of a hunting frontier, 1848–67', in S. Marks and A. Atmore (eds.), *Economy and society in pre-industrial South Africa*, London: Longman, 1980.

Wall, R. (ed.), *Family forms in historic Europe*, Cambridge: Cambridge University Press, 1983.

White, H., *Tropics of discourse: essays in cultural criticism*, Baltimore: Johns Hopkins University Press, 1978.

Wilson, M. L., 'Notes on the nomenclature of the Khoisan', *Annals of the South African Museum* 97 (1986).

Wood, P., *Black majority: negroes in colonial South Carolina from 1670 through the Stono rebellion*, New York: Norton Library, 1975.

Woodward, C. S., 'From multi-purpose parlour to drawing room: the development of the principal *voorkamer* in the fashionable Cape house, 1670–1820,' in *Bulletin of the South African Cultural History Museum* 4 (1983).

Worden, N., *Slavery in Dutch South Africa*, Cambridge: Cambridge University Press, 1985.

Worden, N. and Crais, C. (eds.), *Breaking the chains: slavery and its legacy in the nineteenth-century Cape colony*, Johannesburg: Witwatersrand University Press, 1994.

Wyndham-Smith, K., *From frontier to Midlands: a history of the Graaff Reinet district, 1786–1910*, Grahamstown: Institute of Social and Economic Research, Rhodes University, 1976.

Yates, R., Golson, J. and Hall, M., 'Trance performance: the rock art of Boontjeskloof and Sevilla', *South African Archaeological Bulletin* 40 (1985).

Yates, R., Manhire, A. and Parkington, J., 'Rock painting and history in the south-western Cape', in T. A. Dowson and D. Lewis-Williams (eds.), *Contested images: diversity in southern African rock art research*, Johannesburg: Witwatersrand University Press, 1994.

Index

98, 119–20, 129, 134, 205, 207, 234
stock-farming, *see* livestock farming
Stuurman, Dawid, 225
Stuurman, Klaas, 57–8, 126, 217, 218, 219,
   225, 226, 230
Swart River, 50, 52, 83, 86
Swellengrebel, Hendrik, 45n.53, 49, 50, 59,
   111, 206, 207

trade
   and frontier households, 19–24, 151, 162,
     168–71
   credit, 169–70
   private imports, 164–5, Fig. 14
   public auctions, 168, 174
   see also Dutch East India Company;
     livestock; prices
transportbrief, 15
Trompetter, Hans, 225, 230

Vandeleur, Brigadier T. P., 215, 217, 218,
   219, 220–1, 222
vegetation, 49—52, 49n.68, 97–8

VOC, *see* Dutch East India Company
volkhouders, 15
volks representanten, 147, 148
volkstem 147n.195, 148
Vos, *Dominee* M. C., 228

water, 70
weaning percentages, *see* livestock farming
Wet, O. G. de, 120–1, 124, 147, 148
Worden, Nigel, 41

/Xam, 93, 96, 125
Xhosa, 29, 32, 49, 59, 144, 213–14, 218
   and Khoisan rebels, 218, 219–20, 221,
     224
   war with colony, 144, 146, 149, 210, 214,
     218–20, 222, 224

Zeekoe River, 51, 74, 77, 79, 80, 97, 122
Zeekoe Valley Archaeological Project,
   78–81
zielverkopers, 15
Zuurveld, 29, 49n.64, 146, 213, 218

Other books in the series

CPSIA information can be obtained at www.ICGtesting.com
Printed in the USA
BVOW040546210613

323954BV00001B/66/P